Economic and Financial Market Behaviour

Emil Dinga • Camelia Oprean-Stan
Cristina Roxana Tănăsescu
Vasile Brătian • Gabriela-Mariana Ionescu

Economic and Financial Market Behaviour

The Autopoietic Market Hypothesis

palgrave
macmillan

Emil Dinga
Romanian Academy
Bucharest, Romania

Camelia Oprean-Stan
Lucian Blaga University of Sibiu
Sibiu, Romania

Cristina Roxana Tănăsescu
Lucian Blaga University of Sibiu
Sibiu, Romania

Vasile Brătian
Lucian Blaga University of Sibiu
Sibiu, Romania

Gabriela-Mariana Ionescu
Romanian Academy
Bucharest, Romania

ISBN 978-3-031-31701-9 ISBN 978-3-031-31702-6 (eBook)
https://doi.org/10.1007/978-3-031-31702-6

This Palgrave Macmillan imprint is published by the registered company Springer Nature Switzerland AG.
The registered company address is: Gewerbestrasse 11, 6330 Cham, Switzerland

Acknowledgement

This work has been supported by a Hasso Plattner Excellence Research Grant (LBUS-HPI-ERG-2020-XX), financed by the Knowledge Transfer Center of the Lucian Blaga University of Sibiu.

Contents

List of Figures

List of Tables

CHAPTER 1

Social Selection in the Financial Market: Preliminary Issues

Elements of Social Selection in the Financial Market

The General Concept of Social Selection

Preamble

Selection is one of the components of evolution. In fact, evolution includes two inter-dependent components: (a) genotype mutation and (b) phenotype selection. The mutation can be both random[1] and deliberate, as well as (most often, in the social field, which is the subject of this study) mixed—by combining random with deliberative character. Instead, the selection is not random, it is directed/directional. For example, in the case of biological (i.e., natural living[2]) this directionality (or evolutionary arrow) is represented by the fitness checking of the phenotype (adult individual) concerned. Therefore, in this field, although we have directionality of selection, we do not have a purpose—the environment of the natural biological individual[3] selects without awareness of the selection action, so although there is an evolutionary arrow in this type of selection, there is no axiological arrow or hermeneutic or programmatic[4] one. In the social field—as will be shown further—there is a combination of directional selection and programmatic selection. The general scheme of the two components of the evolution of life (note that, for the moment, we are

E. Dinga et al., *Economic and Financial Market Behaviour*,
https://doi.org/10.1007/978-3-031-31702-6_1

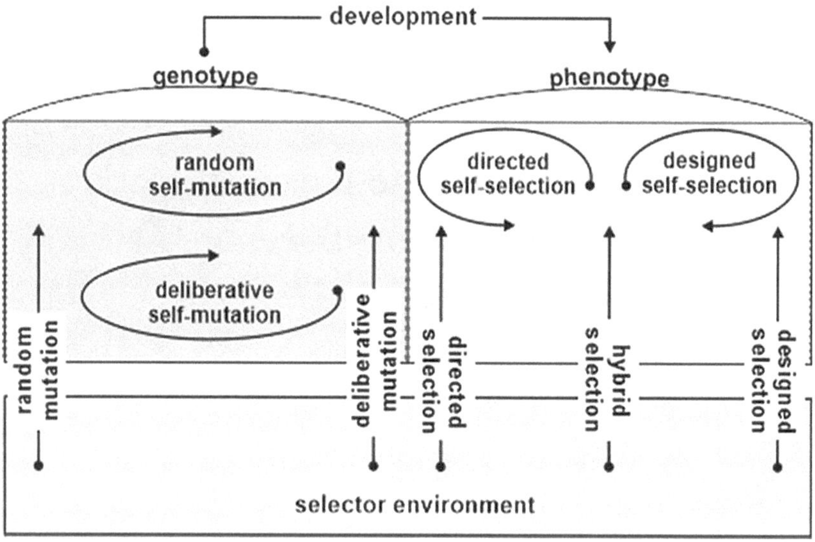

Fig. 1.1 Typology of mutation and selection in the living world (biological, respectively logical). (*Source*: Authors)

only talking about proper individuals and species, not symbolic) is represented by Fig. 1.1.

Social Selection Versus Natural Selection
We have seen, in general terms, what natural selection is in the world of biology. We also saw the content of the selection (within co-evolution) of symbolic species preference, price and information. In this paragraph we aim to establish the relationship (similarities and differences) between natural selection and what we might call social selection (or, as we prefer to say, cultural selection).

How the Current Hypothesis in the Financial Field Call the Concept of Social Selection?

We discussed many times and in many places[5] the incompleteness, unrealism and lack of 'roundness' of the main hypotheses (theories, models) proposed in the matter of financial market. All the same, before examining the concept of social selection, we will synthesize the most relevant features of those proposals:

- the dominance of the *neoclassical basis* on which the theories in the case were built up—the striking example is, of course, Efficient Market Hypothesis (EMH). The problem with the neoclassical approach is that the humans are thought either as (mechanical) balls on a table or as (unconscious) molecules in a gas;
- the ubiquitous *'axiom' of the randomness*[6] (*Nota bene*: correctly, it is about stochasticity) of information generating, although some kind of information is deliberatively created (e.g., public information, norms, etc.), and other kind of information is latent in the (non-random) behaviour of the agents in the financial market;[7]
- either if the agents are considered capable of hyper-rationality or just of bounded rationality, the deliberation and decision-making are almost always associated with a kind of *rationality*;
- even the *heresies* are maintained more or less close to a rational calculus, although based on other postulates (Peters, 1994—the fractally distribution of returns related to time horizon of economic game is more postulated than demonstrated, since exactly based on these fractal structure, the stability and efficiency of the financial market are proved; Dowling, 2005—the deriving of the memes, themes, sentiments and strategies is close enough to the same neoclassical ground, based on molecular replication paradigm, although the author claims an evolutionary approach of the financial phenomenon; Lo, 2019—whose intention to move away from the neoclassical school seems to be the most determined, generally fails to provide a solid evolutionary theory, that is, with all of its conceptual and mechanistical ingredients);
- any case, the current approaches of the financial market functioning, has too less to do with a structural (or structuralist) examination of this crucial market of the contemporary economies. However, in the society (although in rather a Lamarckian way than in a Darwinist one), so including the financial market is clearly working a selection, namely, a social selection, that is, exactly what we will provide in this chapter. Because the evolutionism necessarily implies the structuralism and vice versa.

What Social Selection Is It?

Social selection is a selection that has, as its selector environment, the human society as a whole. Of course, the phenotypes on which social selection is exerted belong to symbolic species, as they have been previously defined and described. As we will show, social selection is not pure, but it is a hybrid that combines different types of selection—including natural selection. The relevance of the examination of social selection applied to symbolic species derives directly from the previously introduced assumption that the environment of symbolic species in society is the cultural geodesic (CG), as a 'device' for objectifying the situational context that characterizes the society in question.

Predicates of Sufficiency of Social Selection

For a rigorous and unambiguous definition of the concept of social selection, we will use, as usual, the defining tool called the predication of sufficiency, that is, the establishment of the minimum list of predicates of sufficiency.[8] We consider that the following predicates of sufficiency define social selection:

- ($\boldsymbol{PS_{SS}^1}$) the phenotype subject to selection belongs to a symbolic[9] (not biological) species;
- ($\boldsymbol{PS_{SS}^2}$) the selector (or selector medium) is the cultural geodesic;
- ($\boldsymbol{PS_{SS}^3}$) the selection criterion is the social fitness;
- ($\boldsymbol{PS_{SS}^4}$) the phenomenology of selection is bi-polar: directed and projected.[10]

Therefore, from a logical point of view, social selection takes place at the conjunction of the four predicates of sufficiency (we note with SS the social selection):[11]

$$SS \leftarrow \left(PS_{SS}^1\right) \wedge \left(PS_{SS}^2\right) \wedge \left(PS_{SS}^3\right) \wedge \left(PS_{SS}^4\right)$$

Social Fitness

The criterion of social selection is the social fitness. This concept is an extension, on the one hand, and a particularization, on the other hand, of biological fitness. Therefore, in the most general sense, social fitness means the property of a symbolic individual (and, consequently, of a symbolic species) to be in a relationship of adequacy with the environment in which both the individual and the species are contained and are functioning.[12]

The literature does not treat the concept of social fitness from an abstract and generalizing perspective but rather in an applicative manner, most often associated with the concept of wellbeing. To this end, a number of welfare objectives or purposes are listed and checked whether and to what extent they are met in the society concerned. Also, most of the time, the very concept of wellbeing is limited to socio-professional categories and examined as such (McGene, 2013).

For the abstract and generalized treatment of the concept of social fitness, the term *adequacy*—which is the hallmark or essence of fitness—requires some clarification. We will say that an individual/species is suitable for his/her environment if the following predicates of sufficiency are verified (note with SF social fitness):

- (PS_{SF}^{1}) *mutual* verification of individual/species expectations[13] and cultural geodesic. Through this predicate of sufficiency, the fitness sphere is extended from the subject to the subject-environment pair.[14]
- (PS_{SF}^{2}) the expectations, both of the individual/species and of the cultural geodesic, must be *generic*. The predicate *generic* used here is intended to ensure that we are referring to the common aspects of these expectations, from both 'sides'—for example, the common character of these expectations is provided by the character of the norm in cultural geodesic: a norm must have in view social categories or even, as the case may be, the whole society, not a group or, at the limit, an individual.[15]
- (PS_{SF}^{3}) the measurable expression of social fitness (more precisely, its commensurable[16] component, both in time and space) is represented by the *way of life*,[17] so it refers to the communitarian/social aspect (trans-individual and even trans-special—*Nota bene*: the trans-special actually turns into inter-special, at the level of society) of these expectations.[18]

So, logically, social fitness takes place at the conjunction of the three predicates of sufficiency:[19]

$$FS \leftarrow \left(PS_{FS}^{1}\right) \wedge \left(PS_{FS}^{2}\right) \wedge \left(PS_{FS}^{3}\right)$$

Some additional details on our position on the matter of adequacy (and, implicitly, social fitness) are useful here:

(1) adequacy/fitness are not a-contextual, but are 'dated'—both temporally and spatially. We say that fitness is dependent on the context or is contextual. Thus, whenever we want to talk about the social fitness of

an individual (or, rather, of a species), the correct notation must be the following:

$$SF_t^{i/s} = \{A_t^{i/s}, CG_t \mid SC_t^L\}$$

notation that must be read as follows: the *social fitness* of individual *i* or species *s* ($SF_t^{i/s}$) is given by the *adequacy* (or degree of adequacy) of individual '*i*' or of the species '*s*' ($A_t^{i/s}$) to the cultural geodesic (CG_t) necessarily generated by the *situational context* of the locality '*L*' (SC_t^L)—the lower index '*t*' means the moment (or sometimes, the time interval) for which the social fitness assessment is made—*Nota bene*: the logical constant '|' will be read 'conditioned by…';

(2) adequacy/social fitness does not only refer to the state (vector of state) of the individual (or species) in question—as is generally done in the literature on this subject—but addresses both directions of interaction between individual/species and cultural geodesic. As already shown in previous discussions, there is a co-evolution of the symbolic species and the environment in which the first is 'submerged', so that phenomena of mutual adaptation (co-adaptation) occur with the co-evolutionary process, and therefore the environment (in our case the cultural geodesic and, further, the situational context) changes under the pressure of the species it selects—somewhat, through language abuse, it can be said that the species (through the component individuals, makes a selection of the environment,[20] otherwise, the concept of co-evolution would be devoid of content[21]); for example, one of the components that must characterize social fitness is social justice or, more precisely, the degree of achievement of social justice in the society in question.[22]

A synoptic scheme to integrate the above proposals on the concept of social fitness is presented in Fig. 1.2.

Short Discussion

- There is a causal correspondence between expectations (or, as some authors call them, affections or even emotions, of course, in a general sense) and the predicates of sufficiency of social fitness—and this both with regard to the symbolic individual/species and regarding cultural geodesic.

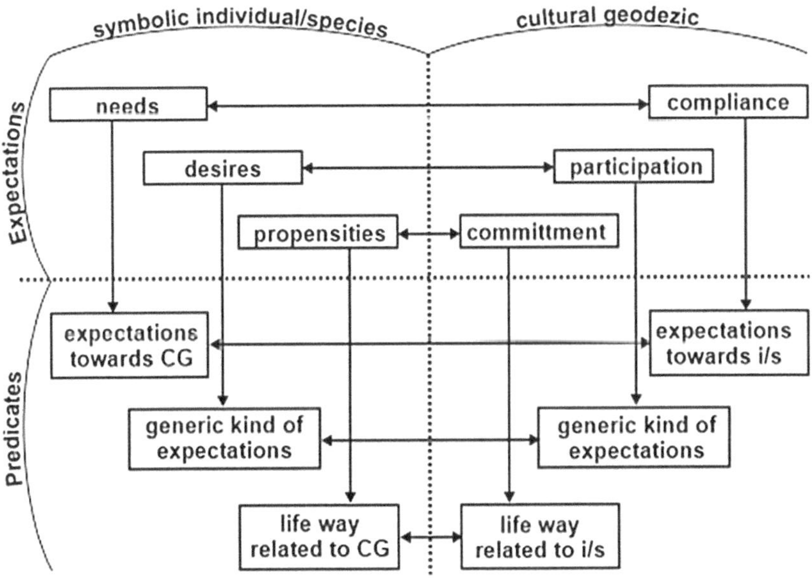

Fig. 1.2 Social fitness functioning. (*Source*: Authors)

- Both inside the expectations and inside the predicates of sufficiency, there is an inter-conditioning between the symbolic individual/species, on the one hand, and the cultural geodesic, on the other hand.

Nota bene: only the predominant aspects/degrees were retained, both for the causal relations and for the inter-conditioning ones (thus, e.g., in the case of the causal relations, we can have determinations of the way of life from the needs or desires, too, respectively from compliance or participation; likewise, in the case of inter-conditionings, we can have inter-conditionings also between expectations addressed to CG and way of life towards *i/s*, etc.).

Similarities and Differences Between Social Selection and Natural Selection

The examination of the similarities and differences between social selection (i.e., selection operating on symbolic or logical species) and natural selection (i.e., selection operating on biological or natural species) is, in our view, of the greatest importance and relevance for highlighting the mechanism of social selection. We will continue to point out the most important similarities, respectively differences, between the two types of selection (we note with NS: natural selection, respectively with SS: social selection; we also note with NF: natural fitness, respectively with SF: social fitness).

- Similarities
  - direct selection is exercised on the phenotype (adult individual);
  - the application of the fitness criterion is made on the instantiation/manifestation of the phenotype (if the phenotype does not manifest or, equivalently, does not acquire an instantiation of space and time, i.e., a locality, the fitness criterion cannot be applied);
  - the 'observable' evolution occurs from a population perspective—the species transits,[23] from an evolutionary point of view, depending on the share that the selected individuals acquire at the level of the population of individuals;[24]
  - the evolutionary process is complete: genetic mutation, epigenetic impact, transcription, translation, directed/directional selection;
  - the selector environment is a hybrid/mixed environment (an-anthropic and anthropic);[25]
  - behaviour is based on two types of causation: (a) genetical and (b) memetical.
- Differences
  - the natural phenotype is a result of its development (the criterion for completing the development is, in general, the acquisition of reproductive capacity)—the social phenotype is 'born' directly adult (we no longer have a developmental process);
  - in the NS, the instantiation of the phenotype, as an object of selection, directly targets the phenotype as such, while in the case of SS, the instantiation of the phenotype does not directly target the phenotype as such, but a derivative of it (e.g., as we saw earlier in the case of the species called financial market, the phenotype is the trading strategy, but the SS is exercised over the individual transaction);[26]
  - the evolutionary process has notable differences in the two cases: (a) regarding the genetic mutation: in the case of NS it is random, while in the case of SS it is hybrid (both random and deliberative—

see also Fig. 1.1); (b) regarding the cumulative selection: in the case of NS the selection is predominantly cumulative/gradual, while in the case of SS it is predominantly saltationist;
in the case of SS, in addition to genetic and memetic causality, there is also semetic causality. In this context, there is also a difference in the weight of the three types of causalities of behaviour: (a) in the case of NS: genetically caused behaviour predominates; (b) in the case of SS: semetically caused behaviour predominates (on the '2nd place', as a share in the total causality, the memetic causality is located).

As the examination of social selection becomes more in-depth, other correlations between the two types of selection will be highlighted, the fundamental reason for this possibility being, of course, that the human individual (natural biological phenotype) is also the sole generator of the symbolic/logical species that work or can work in society—for example, the trading strategy, that is, the financial individual of the symbolic species called financial market, is imagined, designed and implemented by the biological individual (*Nota bene*: remember that all symbolic species are initiated/created by the biological individual, thus they being a species of artefacts).

The Relationship Between Social Selection and Natural Selection
The question is: what is the relationship between natural selection and social selection, in systems where biological species and symbolic/logical species co-exist and where, in particular, biological individuals are also components (in one way or another) of symbolic species? We will examine this issue in the particular case of interest in this study, namely, the symbolic species called financial market.

- The human individual has certain actional/praxiological predispositions that are allowed by (or derived from) his biological configuration: for example, one of his primary affections/emotions is the need (see Fig. 1.2) to feed.[27] Satisfaction of this need is achieved within society (usually in the form of an economic action/activity), so there is an impact of the biologic on the social or, equivalently, there is a direct causality from natural selection to social selection. If, for example, a genetic mutation in the biological individual would cause the need for low entropy for the survival of the organism to be provided by photosynthesis, then, of course, the economic behaviour of the biological individual would generate completely different social individuals (i.e., other symbolic individuals and species), completely different from the commonly known ones. Such causality acts either from the natural genotype on the social genotype or, epigenetically, from the natural phenotype to the social phenotype. From such a generic possibility to the formulation of 'theories' on natural/biological genetic determinism on economic behaviour was not too difficult to pass. In this regard, we make the following considerations:

- there are positions that state that there are (or may be, i.e., they are not prohibited in principle) 'specialized' biological genes for different behaviours, attitudes, values and so on, which concern the economic phenomenon, so that these genetic endowments act as predictors for the identification of preferences and even some *modi operandi* (Lehrer & Ding, 2016). This biologically originated predestination is obviously very similar to the Calvinist predestination in the field of religion—somehow, the genetic structure of a person forces that person to a certain behaviour;
- what is omitted, in our opinion, in these attempts (we can call them attempts to *naturalize the social*) to introduce necessary economic/social behaviours, in the logical sense, that is, inescapable, is the fact that, mainly, social action—first of all, the economic action—is normatively conditioned, not biologically. Of course, certain natural predispositions (e.g., talents) cannot be ignored—thus, we also consider that preference is an objectified or objectifiable manifestation of an idiosyncratic propensity of the individual/person, a propensity that originates mainly in biologic, in native—but it is quite obvious that these predispositions (which have their 'root' in the genetic structure) acquire a form of social manifestation. Moreover, it is the social conditioning that can increase or annihilate, as the case may be, the respective predisposition. For example, let's say that a rare (in fact, almost unlikely[28]) genetic mutation causes a person to have a significantly higher than average lung capacity, making him or her a potential runner-up in the Olympics. If the family forbids him to do sports (e.g., s/he is instructed to become an economist), this predisposition will never be objectified. Analogous examples can easily be found for so-called economic predispositions (i.e., economic behaviour), so

we can conclude that the existence of genes specialized in certain forms or types of economic behaviour is just a conjecture that (according to our information) fails to be factually corroborated. One of the most ingenious investigations in this regard concerns the examination of the social path of some twins—twins have the same genetic dowry, so the same natural predispositions, but different social contexts make these predispositions manifest differently or even be completely inhibited (De Neve et al., 2012);

- in our opinion, the most important, relevant and significant aspect of the 'natural determinism of economic behaviour' is that of propensity which, being mostly subconscious in nature, retains this natural or biological determination. *Nota bene*: from the perspective of the objectives of this study, investigations such as neuroscience, which would develop this suggestion, are impossible;[29]

• less obvious is the inverse causal relationship, from social to natural. In this regard, the ways and degrees in which economic behaviour and social conditions (e.g., the normative framework) accentuate the genetic differences of human individuals are studied (Benjamin et al., 2007). However, in order for the social effect on the biological individual to persist, that is, to be transmitted to his/her genetic device, a number of additional assumptions must be made:

- in order the economic (or, equivalent, social) behaviour to result in genetic mutations, certain properties of this behaviour should affect the genetic device. Let us look at the 'available' possibilities:

  first of all, the mutation in question must have taken place at the physical level, that is to say at the level of the genetic device (physically affecting the genes of the biological individual). It is obvious that such a phenomenon is practically impossible, if we seek to detect a direct causal line economic behaviour—biological genes;

  secondly, namely, indirectly, economic behaviour being, like any other behaviour, an objectification of the biological individual's propensity (in which genetic dowry plays an important role), it can accidentally (i.e., randomly) generate genetic mutations—for example, in the case of a person working in a toxic or radioactive environment, an environment that is likely to cause changes in the genome. However, being entirely accidental, we consider that such a causal line should not be taken into account. In other words, this possibility must be framed in the general impact of the environment on biological evolution, because economic action is simply a behaviour of the biological individual in his/her environment;[30]

- however, we can also examine the case where the social impact on the biological entity is realized at the population level, that is, not directly, physically, at the genome level:

  a certain economic activity, which requires certain skills[31] (e.g., the activity of a player on the stock market, requires personal abilities of fast reaction or reaction automatisms or dexterities of mathematical modelling) can retain, in its field, only those persons who hold those abilities. Being efficient, those people will acquire a superior quality of life, they will be able to have biological offsprings, which, over time, will change the population structure in the direction of having, at the biological level, the biological dowry 'suitable' for that economic activity. It is immediately obvious that this path of causing biological selection in the social way is, on the one hand, extremely unlikely, and, on the other hand, it has a completely insignificant share in natural evolution;[32]

  social specialization is not always and in mass proportion (and, above all, it is not preserved throughout the life of an individual) a cause of population selection. Especially, as the technologically conditioned civilization develops, the change of occupations and/or fields of specialization becomes more frequent, which makes this conditioning, in terms of population restructuring from the perspective of having a certain genetic endowment, become insignificant, remaining more of a theoretical possibility.

In summary, our position in this matter is as follows:

(a) the conditioning of natural selection on social selection cannot be neglected, but it must be considered as 'wrapped' by the socialization of the biological individual: certain native endowments/predispositions (such as talents) that are or can be granted to the biological are always used through instruction and education, so the biological causality of social selection always remains in the background, as a substrate more or less activated. Even when this activation occurs (e.g., when the individual 'guesses' his/her native skills and chooses a social career in line with these skills), s/he uses always use, in fact, the social 'vehicle';

(b) the conditioning of social selection on natural selection is much less possible (we probably have real black swans here), but we do not rule out a certain impact that, only from a population (not physical) perspective, the social can have—so, also at a potential level—on natural selection;

(c) there is, however, a cultural phenomenon (in fact, a technologically conditioned cultural phenomenon) called transhumanism, which, from a social perspective, has or may have an increasing impact on natural selection. Genetic engineering, that is, the deliberate intervention (thus assuming a purpose) in the human genome, an intervention that has a rather saltationist character, overlaps predominantly with the natural evolution of the human individual.[33]

Short Discussion

Prima facie, it could seem that the syntagm social selection is artificially imported from the biology (natural selection) into financial field, *mutatis mutandis*. Such imports were, indeed, often made in the history of science (including social science),[34] and they were not always beneficial for the import destination (generally it was ignored the presence of the free will inside the social field). In fact, the social selection neither needs to be imported as a 'species' from the genus called selection, because, really, a selection (that cannot be named than as social one) happens in the social field (especially in the financial field). Below we provide some facts which ground the 'entitlement' to say that there is a social selection in its own right. We will do that by examining the two basic (logical and chronological as well) moments of the general concept of selection, as they objectify in the financial phenomenology.

- regarding *mutation*
  - information is, certainly, the most volatile entity in the financial field, no matter its nature, origin or presumptive impact;
  - as a consequence, information, which grounds the decision (and, so, the action on the financial market) has the potential to generate modifications in the agents' behaviour;
  - that potential to generate mutations has a necessary character, not a contingent one; even if, for example, an agent decides to ignore

the information change, that information has already modified the behaviour in that case;
  - we consider the implicit information (information 'translated' by agents from the observed behaviour of other contemporary or non-contemporary agents) is the main source of mutation in the financial behaviour, but other types of information, as well—although with less frequency and, probably, less impact—generate mutations in the financial gene (*Nota bene*: in our opinion, the financial gene is the preference or, better said, the proference—i.e., a preference conducted by propensity);
  - to be mentioned that the mutation in the financial field happens under the free will auspices.
- regarding *cumulative selection*
  - by either prudence or resolutory incompetence, the economic agents in the financial field do not react immediately or proportionally with the happened mutation;
  - this leads to the conclusion that, inherently, by the own way of reacting to the mutation, agents in the financial field 'wait' the mutations to accumulate over an established threshold (as shown in the book) before adopting a new behaviour (new decisions and new actions);
  - it is, again, clear that the cumulative selection in the financial field is performed through the free will dominance (*Nota bene*: not necessarily in a rational way, of course);
- regarding *saltationist selection*
  - much more obviously than in the natural world, the saltationist selection is possible (and, probably, dominant) in the social field (again in either rational or irrational way).

The specific of the social selection is already discussed in the economy of the book, so we will not repeat them here.

Formal Selection Versus Functional Selection
The distinction between formal selection and functional selection is significant (i.e., it has a referential) for both natural selection and social selection. The predicate *formal* has, here, its Aristotelian meaning, of formal cause, that is, of constraint of the 'program' type of a process under the control of that 'program'.

Formal and Functional in Natural Selection

The formal component of natural selection refers to the content of the DNA to be transcribed (along with the random mutations that have occurred in the meantime) in the messenger RNA which, in turn, will make the translation that will determine which amino acid/protein is to be synthesized/produced. Despite the accidents, which start with the genetic mutation, which is completely random,[35] it continues with transcription (where mutation transcription errors can occur) and ends with translation (where errors are also possible, in the sense of commanding some amino acids 'wrong'), this formal component of natural selection is quite safe. The problem of errors—in all three episodes mentioned above—is an ambivalent one: in essence, it is precisely these errors[36] that underlie the evolution of the biological/natural individual. Indeed, if there were no mutations (and still no transcripts or 'wrong' translations), then each natural phenotype would reproduce as a simple clone, perfectly identical to itself, which, in turn, would produce an identical individual, and so on, so that the *statu quo* of that species would be preserved for an indefinite time horizon. Therefore, with a certain abuse of language, it can be said that, in fact, the evolution is based on the errors that appeared, on the one hand, at the level of the phenotype (within the process of its development) and, on the other hand, in the course of genotype replication (transcription, respectively translation).[37]

Regarding the functional component of natural selection, we can say the following:

- its content refers, on the one hand, to the adaptation of the phenotype to the environment—that is, to small contextual transformations of the individual in the process of living in the environment, transformations that do not manifest at the genotype level and therefore are not inter-generationally transmitted by the natural reproduction of phenotype;
- it should be mentioned (as it has been done before, where appropriate) that the genetic mutation, integrated into the fitness of the biological offspring, is tested by the environment—so, either accepted or rejected—exactly in the process of functioning of the individual (feeding, intra-species or inter-species competition, reproduction, etc.);

- the functional component of natural selection achieves, in fact, the predominance, at the population level, of a certain fitness carried by the genetic dowry, which faces the challenges of the environment;
- through the functional component, the phenomenon of co-evolution also occurs: within the functioning of the individual, it influences the environment which, in turn, adapts to the individual.[38] Adapting the environment to the individual (more precisely to the population of individuals concerned) changes, of course, the way, intensity and directionality with which the environment thus adapted achieves the subsequent selection of fitness.

Formal and Functional in Social Selection

Formal and functional aspects in social selection are much less discussed in the literature. Perhaps, two were the main causes for this state of affairs: (a) *operational* cause: the incomparably greater difficulty of this problem, given the quasi-impossibility of experiments; (b) *conceptual* cause: the presence of free will, given by the presence of the cultural being who is the human being, greatly complicates the process of social evolution (starting with mutation, continuing with transcription/translation and ending with testing/selecting social fitness). Although there is, of course, a continuity between natural and cultural, the cultural is 'imperialist' in the matter of social selection, so it is necessary to build a solid theoretical infrastructure on which to build the specific theory of social selection. In the following, we will briefly present our opinion on this matter.

Formal Aspects of Social Selection

It is good to repeat a statement already made: social selection refers to symbolic species (or, equivalently, logical species) that function in human society—for example, one of these symbolic species is the financial market—not to natural species. For the time being (until transhumanism probably will perverts this state of affairs) the human individual is a biological 'object', so social selection will not consider the human individual at all, but his/her artefacts. Regarding artefacts, it is also useful to make the following statement: we refer to institutional artefacts, not material/products artefacts. For example, a material/product artefact is a numerical calculator (a computer) or a wind power plant—these are not subject to social selection.[39] Instead, social conditions, that is, the institutions[40] that allowed or made possible or caused or conditioned the realization of material/products artefacts, are (or can be) the subject of social selection.[41]

Therefore, what we want to call the formal component of social selection refers to the situational framework of society, a framework that, on the one hand, generates symbolic/logical species and, on the other hand, exerts the action of social selection on these species. A completely general typology and of significance rather exemplary of the formal component of social selection can be the following:

- spontaneous axiological matrix: traditions, customs, identity;
- deliberate axiological matrix (basic structure of society): constitution, laws, codes (institutional or procedural);[42]
- organizational institutions of the state: legislative institutions, executive institutions, judicial institutions, institutions of (coercive) force—police, gendarmerie, army;
- organizational institutions of the civil society;[43]
- mass media: written, spoken, video (current and/or archived): especially through opinion leaders or opinion formers;
- direct public opinion.[44]

Regarding the formal component of social selection, there is a peculiarity (compared to the formal component of natural selection) on which it is useful to make further investigations: it is about the fact that this component is both the genotype of the symbolic/logical species and the selector environment. This particularity is, moreover, the basis of the preponderance of Lamarckism (over Darwinism) in social evolution in general. We therefore make the following considerations in this regard:

- since any symbolic/logical species is a (non-material/non-product) artefact, it results that it can only appear as an objectification/implementation of the situational framework, as outlined above. This causal determinism obviously has a formal meaning, so the generation of the phenotype of the symbolic species is made/allowed/conditioned by the situational framework which, through this, constitutes the (social) genotype;
- mutations—either accidental or deliberative[45]—occur at the level of the situational framework (i.e., at the level of the social genotype), and this way modifying, directly and immediately, the corresponding phenotype or, as the case may be, creating a new phenotype within a given species or creating, at the same time, a new species;

- regardless of the way in which a phenotype instituted/modified by the social genotype appears, the phenotype in question must 'plead' its fitness also in front of the generating genotype, that is, in front of the situational framework or, more directly, in front of the cultural geodesic of that situational framework;
- therefore, there is a double functionality of the situational framework within the society: as generator (cause, condition) of the phenotype or its modification, respectively as court for testing the fitness of the social phenotype in question and of selection decision (acceptance vs. rejection);
- one of the immediate and very strong consequences of this double functionality of the situational framework is the self-evolution of symbolic/logical species. In fact, it was this state of affairs that led us to formulate the hypothesis/conjecture that will be developed by the research: the hypothesis/conjecture of the social autopoieticity. One of the authors developed a proposal for social autopoieticity, based on his own concept, namely, the concept of a *living logical system*, a proposal that will be adapted to the case of the symbolic species called financial market (Dinga, 2021).

Functional Aspects of Social Selection

The functional aspects of social selection refer, in analogy to the case of natural selection, to the real manifestation (objectification) of the formal 'program' which, precisely through this manifestation, exposes to the selector environment the (social) fitness that will be the object of the selection process. Like so many other concepts, which we referred to earlier (growth, evolution, progress), the concept of selection is ambivalent: both the acceptance/validation and the rejection/invalidation of an individual (more precisely, of a fitness that the symbolic individual in cause exhibits) are both selections—we can say positive or affirmative selection in case of acceptance/validation, respectively negative selection in case of rejection/invalidation but, in any case, we speak also about selection.

In addition to the difference in mechanism, which we referred to above (namely, in the case of social selection, the selector coincides with the genotype, as opposed to the case of natural selection), there is also a difference between the two types of selection: if, in the case of natural selection, the adequacy of fitness (both in terms of mode and grade) was 'examined' exclusively from the perspective of the success that fitness entails in the functioning of the biological individual, including in terms of intra- or inter-individual or species competitiveness, in the case of social selection there are two social courts against which social fitness is examined: (1) the court of institutional adequacy and (2) the court of performative adequacy.

The Court of Institutional Social Fitness

The instance of the institutional adequacy of social fitness means the consistency of the last with the institutional framework (i.e., the compliance/conformity component of the cultural geodesic, see Fig. 1.2). This court works in a mechanical way, by applying the formal grid on the social fitness in question: the overlap of the two parts means corroboration, their non-overlap means refutation. Of course, here the important and thorny issue of the threshold arises: to what degree/percentage of non-overlap of fitness with the formal framework (cultural geodesic) is enacted the 'decision' to refute? We formulate, below, our opinion in this matter:

- the degree of non-compliance must be considered, here, a hierarchical concept: the more the violated norm is situated towards the genus norm than towards the species norm, the more recommendable the refutation of fitness;
- thus, if fitness violates (i.e., is inconsistent with) a constitutional norm, its refutation is indisputable (e.g., a trading strategy that has the drug or human person as the object of the transaction). If, however, the violated rule is below the constitutional norm—for example, it is at the level of primary/institutional legislation—its refutation retains a small chance of not being objectified, and if the violation concerns a procedural norm—for example, at the level of secondary legislation—the chance of being refuted is even lower;
- this descending ordering of the chance of refuting a fitness according to the hierarchical place on which the violated norm is positioned is, somehow, in opposition to the classic test of Popperian falsifiability, where any non-conformity leads, without degrees, to refuting the hypothesis/conjecture. The explanation is immediate here: in the case of Popper's falsifiability, the truth correspondence is taken into account, while in the case here discussed we are dealing with a 'truth-adequacy'.[46] The quotation of the term truth indicates that it is not, in fact, truth (i.e., an epistemic category), but an appropriate adequacy[47] (i.e., a praxiological category);

- in assessing the adequacy of social fitness (achieved by social genotype) there is no longer a specific 'authority', identifiable as such, as is the case in natural selection, where this authority is the environment, but we are dealing with the case of a diffuse selection authorities, although identifiable: thus, any of the six formal courts mentioned above can formulate the decision of refutation[48] and, in most cases, the publicly formulation of the refutation decision by one of these courts can lead other courts to agree (or not[49]) with that decision.

Nota bene: It is interesting to discuss here, briefly, the significance and impact of inadequate social fitness which, for various reasons (e.g., due to corruption or incompetence of formal selection boards), is not rejected.[50] It is therefore possible that fitness, which should be formally rejected but is not actually rejected,[51] should functionally produce beneficial effects that could ultimately lead to (even) the modification of some norms of the selection courts that would accept, in the future, that fitness that was (or at least, seemed) inadequate from the perspective of the current norms. We are dealing here with a signal to the legislators regarding the inadequacy, this time, of the selection rules. This double selection—so to speak—or the selection of the selector is, of course, not a novelty, because even in natural selection the environment is somehow 'selected' by the phenotype.[52]

The Court of Performative Social Fitness

While the court of institutional/formal adequacy of social fitness is one that acts mechanically or automatically[53] (somehow, in the 'grid' system), the court of performative adequacy of the social fitness is the case of a court that acts pragmatically, that is, decides on the success/failure of social fitness concerned. It is immediately obvious that the instance of performative social fitness is perfectly analogous to the cumulative selection of natural selection, but with an important difference (already mentioned above): directionality takes a teleological form—namely, there is a purpose both from the perspective of the bearer of social fitness in question and from the social environment (of society as a whole). We will briefly discuss the main issue that arises in the matter of the court of performative adequacy of the social fitness, namely, the issue of the coincidence between the individual purpose and the social purpose.

- A first assurance of this coincidence (which, obviously, is not necessarily punctual, complete and permanent, but rather approximate, i.e., more related to compatibility, consistency and convergence) is given by the first instance of adequacy, the institutional/formal one. Indeed, cultural geodesic essentially contains the formalization of the social purpose, of what society aspires to (or allows to) achieve. The fitness that is rejected[54] by this first instance is that fitness that deviates, through its particular purpose, from the general (societal) purpose;
- therefore, the performative adequacy is examined only for that fitness that has passed the first 'control', that is, the formal one. At the second check, it is checked (so to speak) whether the particular purpose incorporated in the fitness in question is compatible, consistent and convergent with the social purpose from an action point of view, not a formal one. If the institutional/formal court has found a potential acceptability of social fitness concerned, the performative court is interested in a current acceptability. For example, suppose a particular social fitness refers to the monopolization of a good or service. Such fitness will still be rejected by the institutional/formal court. However, if the potential for monopolization is well disguised, this first instance will not notice the formal incompatibility of that fitness and will corroborate it from its point of view. In practice, however, monopolization will be done (or can be done) in the insidious form of collusion. The factual finding of this functioning of the fitness will make it be rejected by the court of performative adequacy. The reason for this rejection is this: if cultural geodesic has incriminated monopolization (symmetrically, and monopsonization, of course), this means that society aims at consumer protection (and, conversely, in the case of monopsonization, where the social purpose is to protect the producer). As collusion has the same effect as monopolization (being a disguised monopolization), it follows that the particular[55] purpose (more precisely, the private one) is inconsistent with the social purpose, so there will be a rejection of that fitness from the perspective of performative adequacy.

Directed Selection Versus Projected[56] Selection
From the above, the idea has already emerged that, unlike mutation (which is random, in the natural case, respectively hybrid, in the social case), the selection is at least directed. Being *at least* directed means it can

be designed as well. We will operate the necessary delimitations in this matter:

Directed selection (*DS*) is found in both the natural and the social case. The content of directed selection consists in the existence of an automatic evolutionary arrow (a concept we referred to in *Financial Market Analysis and Behaviour. The Adaptive Preference Hypothesis*, hence FMAB-APH (Dinga et al., 2022)). The automatic evolutionary arrow can be defined by the following predicates of sufficiency (*PS*):

- $\left(PS_1^{DS}\right)$: it is *intrinsic* to the evolutionary process, that is, it is internal to it; we specify that the evolutionary arrow is placed (located) in the environment of the phenotype subject to selection;[57]
- $\left(PS_2^{DS}\right)$: it is *constitutive* of the evolutionary process, that is, it has a necessary character. The evolutionary arrow could not be missing from the mechanism of evolution, under the sanction of the disappearance of the evolutionary process itself (*Nota bene*: we will see next what 'remains' of the phenomenology of change if there is no evolution);
- $\left(PS_3^{DS}\right)$: it is *unidirectional*, that is, prohibits reversibility. This is an issue that can raise some questions. First of all, what is meant by the reversibility of fitness? From a terminological point of view, it would mean dealing with an involution, but (as we have shown before) involution is an … evolution, just as a decrease is an increase or a regress is a progress. Suppose that, after a certain fitness (as nature and/or grade) has been validated by the selector, a change in the fitness in question occurs in the next period which can be evaluated as a logical negation of the previous change, already validated (in other words, the result of the change in question is to bring fitness to the level—as nature and/or grade—prior to the first change that was validated). Obviously, we cannot say that the evolutionary arrow has the opposite meaning, so it produced a reversibility of fitness, because time (it is about a clock time, in this case) continued to 'move forward';
- $\left(PS_4^{DS}\right)$: it is *an-axiological*, meaning there is no second-order directionality, so to speak, aimed at guiding the first-order directionality: the directed evolutionary arrow is not based on value criteria—the best fitness has only a performative significance. Needless to say, this conclusion results from the fact that deliberation cannot be accepted in nature, deliberation occurs only in culture;

- $\left(PS_5^{DS}\right)$: it implies a *coincidence between logical and chronological.*[58] At the macroscopic level (*Nota bene*: we understand by macroscopic the supra-atomic level of the world—the sub-atomic level being the domain of the quantum world or, by terminological symmetry, the microscopic level of the world) there is an arrow of time which places a world within the effect occurs *after* the world within the cause occurs.[59] Based on the above, it immediately follows that in the evolutionary process, there is a coincidence between the evolutionary arrow and the temporal arrow, that is, a coincidence between logical (causal) and chronological (temporal).

From a formal point of view, directed selection (DS) is therefore generated by the logical conjunction:

$$DS \leftarrow \left(PS_1^{DS}\right)\wedge\left(PS_2^{DS}\right)\wedge\left(PS_3^{DS}\right)\wedge\left(PS_4^{DS}\right)\wedge\left(PS_5^{DS}\right)$$

- projected selection (*PS*) is met only in the case of social selection,[60] it being a teleological type selection. Its sufficiency predicates are as follows:
  - the first three predicates of sufficiency mentioned in the case of directed selection are also kept in the case of the projected selection, that is, we have:

$$PS_1^{PS} \equiv PS_1^{DS}$$
$$PS_2^{PS} \equiv PS_2^{DS}$$
$$PS_3^{PS} \equiv PS_3^{DS}$$

  - $\left(PS_4^{PS}\right)$: it is *axiological*, that is, it implies a background that controls the selection (we have, therefore, a directionality of order 2)[61] from the perspective of values. As we have shown above, the background values are integrated into the cultural geodesic itself. Also, the indistinguishability between genotype and environment in the case of social selection makes the values operate relentlessly in the selection process. *Nota bene*: it is obvious that the projected selection involves deliberativeness, but by virtue of Ockham's principle and based on logical inference, we will accept that deliberativeness is contained, predicatively, in axiology—indeed, neither setting nor choosing values, in cultural geodesic, nor their operationalization in the direct process of selection, could not be done in the absence of deliberation;

- $\left(PS_5^{PS}\right)$: it implies the *non-coincidence between logical and chronological*. This predicate represents not only the negation of the corresponding predicate in the case of directed selection, but also an extension of its sphere. The characterization of this suffix can be done as follows:

  being a deliberative selection, the projected selection can determine the return of a social fitness to a state (as nature and/or degree) previously had from a chronological point of view, so we have an opposition between logical and chronological. This decision—operated by the social fitness adequacy courts in question—is of the resilience type;[62]

  being a deliberative selection, and this deliberation being of teleological type, the projected selection can consider not only a predetermined goal (in which case a feedback acts), but also an intentional goal for the future (in which case a feed-forward acts). Again, we are dealing with a logical and chronological non-coincidence.

It should be noted that, as will be seen later, the projected selection can even use visionary or fantasy to introduce selection-purpose criteria into social evolution.

Cumulative Selection Versus Saltationist Selection

In addition to the distinction between directed selection and projected selection, there is another important distinction in the selection process: that between cumulative selection and saltationist selection. Cumulative (or uniform or gradual) selection means selection that validates (corroborates) relatively small changes that, over time, occur in a manner consistent with previous ones, so that they are, in fact, additional (or, as stated, cumulative). It is not to be understood, of course, that all these small changes are necessarily consistent with each other in the series of changes that follow one another over time. Some of them are inconsistent with the previous changes already (a)cumulated and, as a result, are invalidated by the selection—whether directed or projected—but those incremental changes that are consistent with the past series of such changes are selected from the perspective of the stage reached by the (a)cumulation concerned. This view is dominant in the scientific community in the field of evolutionism (especially biological, that is, natural evolutionism) but, as we know, there is an alternative proposal. This is called the saltationist (or punctuated) selection and was proposed by Stephen Jay Gould (Gould, 2007) under the name of *punctuated equilibrium*.[63] The punctuated equilibrium considers that the selection (*Nota bene*: the concept in question refers to natural selection) occurs suddenly, at a large size—so not gradually and with relatively small increments. This is an inductive inference (in fact, an abduction) based on a rather controversial phenomenon that occurred, according to fossil evidence, in the Pleistocene.[64]

Regarding the connection between this dichotomy of selection and the two types of selection of interest (natural selection, respectively social selection), it must be said that both types of selection—both gradual/cumulative and saltationist[65]—meet in both categories of selection (to make a terminological distinction between types and categories).

Ethics and Morals in Social Selection

The concepts of situational framework and cultural geodesic, respectively, are well known from our previous analyses. Among the selective components (as, by the way, among the components of the social genotype) are also those norms (either codified or not) that refer to the principles of ethics, respectively, of morals. We adhere, in this matter, to the position according to which ethics represents the idiosyncratic moral structure of the individual, and morals is the generalized/communized ethics at the level of society as a whole.

Conceptual Elements Regarding Ethics and Morals

The deepest need of people is the justification of life (some call it finding the meaning or sense of life). The justification of life can be made before two courts: (a) the external (social) court—the *social rule*—which requires *accountability*; (b) the internal (individual/subjective) court—the *ethical rule*—which requires *responsibility*. While accountability is governed by *positive laws*, responsibility is governed by *ethical laws*. When the common core of individual ethical rules is generalized/communized, the moral normative network of society is obtained. Also, legitimacy/legitimation of legality can turn legal laws into moral laws, that is, it can replace accountability with responsibility. Finally, ethics is necessary to legitimize (more precisely, to justify) our actions (acts or abstentions) that affect (or could affect) ourselves or others (regardless of the good or bad significance of those actions). (*Nota bene*: the significance of our actions should be assessed only from the perspective of the actors, not from the perspective of those who bear the effects of the actions of the actors—i.e., the dominant sign to be deciphered in action is the *intention*.) Figure 1.3 presents a synopsis of the conceptual elements of the 'inferring' of ethics (the fundamental element in this inference is the non-utilitarian character of ethics):

There is the question of the existence of a sense of ethics. The roots of a possible ethical meaning are located in the cultural dimension of the human being, not in its natural (genetic) dimension. However, even in the cultural environment (involving the social environment), there is a sense (the most common sense) that dominates the ethical sense: the sense of survival—which is natural/genetic (*Nota bene*: we remember that in the financial market, really, dominates a *second best* criterion—of survival—while the *first best* criterion—of the optimal—is completely accidental). In other words, it can be said that meeting human needs can be filtered ethically only after ensuring physical and biological survival.[66] Being of a cultural nature, the ethical sense must be instilled in individuals, either unintentionally (accidentally) or deliberately (systematically), because the individual is not naturally (i.e., natively) endowed with an ethical sense.[67] Therefore, the following can be noted about the ethical sense (or the sense

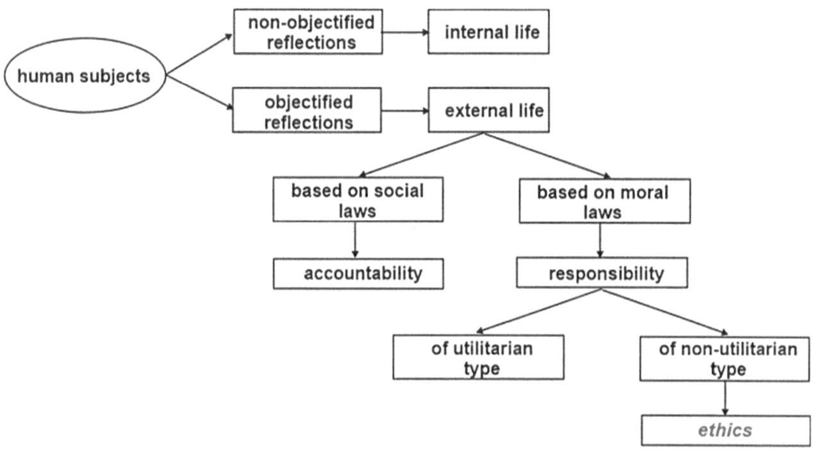

Fig. 1.3 Ethics generating. (*Source*: Authors)

of ethics): (a) the ethical sense is necessarily acquired within the social interactions; (b) the ethical sense is attributed only individually, it is never attributed to groups; (c) no individual who has passed his/her instinctual age lacks an ethical sense;[68] (d) like the general instruction, the ethical sense is the result of the life of the social groups, either deliberately or non-deliberatively; (e) ethics belongs to education, not instruction. Figure 1.4 systematizes the above discussion.

Ethics can be examined as an *ex-ante* ethics or as an *ex-post* ethics in relation to action. Regarding this dichotomy, we note the following:

- being a non-utilitarian concept, ethics is, in essence, an *ex-ante* concept; more precisely, ethics is a concept driven by two imperatives:[69] (a) intentionality (not in the sense of Husserl, but simply based on an intention in the sense of action/practical motivation,[70] not cognitive); (b) non-contextual values (i.e., principles[71]);
- authentic ethics is always *ex-ante* and can never be *ex-post*;
- the consideration of (a possible) *ex-post* 'ethics' is analogous to Popper's falsifiability (*ex-ante* ethics is the hypothesis, while *ex-post* ethics is the factual that can corroborate or reject the hypothesis)[72] (*Nota bene*: we could have here a practical version—more precisely, a praxiological one, to be rigorous—of the cognitive factual testing of scientific theories: we could call it *factual actional testing*);

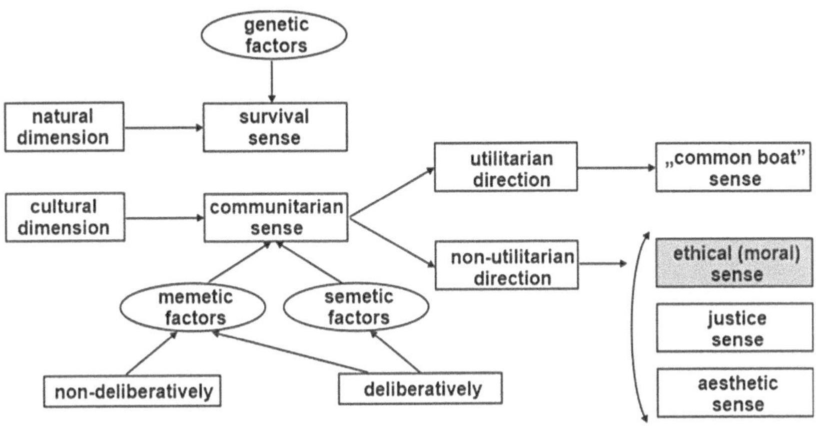

Fig. 1.4 Genealogy of the ethical sense. (*Source*: Authors)

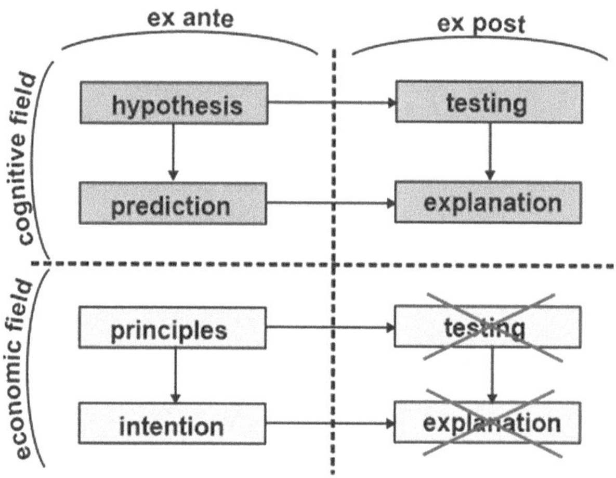

Fig. 1.5 Relationship between ex-ante and ex-post ethics. (*Source*: Authors)

- since ethics has nothing to do with truth (more clearly, with the correspondence-truth), *ex-post* ethics is a meaningless concept;[73]
- any consideration of *ex-post* ethics leads us directly to utilitarianism.

We represent, in Fig. 1.5, the (theoretical) relationship between *ex-ante* ethics and (a possible, although praxiologically unacceptable) *ex-post* ethics.

Impact of Ethics/Morals in the Social Selection

Prima facie, it seems that the value grid of ethics/morality should act in a similar way to the one in which the other norms of cultural geodesic act, as it being one of the components of the latter. However, we believe that a more detailed examination of this issue is needed:

- *firstly*, there is a reason why ethics/morality contained in cultural geodesic should generate (as a genotype) and then filter—corroborate/reject—(as a selector) the social fitness. The justification for this statement is that ethical/moral values are a priori principles of social evolution, more precisely, what we usually (or should) call the symbolic utility[74] of the agent/actor in question;

- *secondly*, there is, symmetrically, a reason why the ethical/moral norms in cultural geodesic should have priority, both in the genesis of fitness and in its selection. The justification for this statement is that the an ethical/a-moral norms are, by law, mandatory, so they are of a necessity for the social agent/actor in question;
- to distinguish between the two categories of norms in the structure of cultural geodesic (of course, from a general or average perspective, so to speak) does not seem to be a theoretical issue, but a strictly empirical one. For this reason, at the end of this paragraph we will mention only a few opinions[75] that we share in this matter:
  - the ethical/moral norms in cultural geodesic have not only a logical (and chronological) priority in social selection, but also have the greatest force of discrimination (*Nota bene*: in addition, we appreciate that they have the highest accuracy in the discriminatory process, given the general dichotomous (i.e., relatively uninterpretative) nature of this category of rules);
  - somehow, the ethical/moral norms apply to a first selection (the one made by the an-ethical/a-moral norms). Here it is appropriate to return to the pair of legal-legitimate concepts: we can consider that the first selection of social fitness (the one made by the an-ethical/a-moral norms) confers the 'legality'[76] of fitness, by selecting it, and the second selection of social fitness (the ethical/moral one) confers the 'legitimacy' of that social fitness.[77] Therefore, legality takes precedence over legitimacy.

Social Selection and Typology of Change

Social selection is a stage/phase in the social evolutionary process, that is, in the evolution of society as a whole. The questions are (a) Which is the logical nature of evolution and (b) What is its place in all possible forms of change? So, in fact, a first issue that needs to be clarified is the typology of change in the world, a typology in which evolution will have to appear, possibly with its distinct forms.

In the following we will make some considerations regarding the two questions. To form a basis for discussion, we present Fig. 1.6.

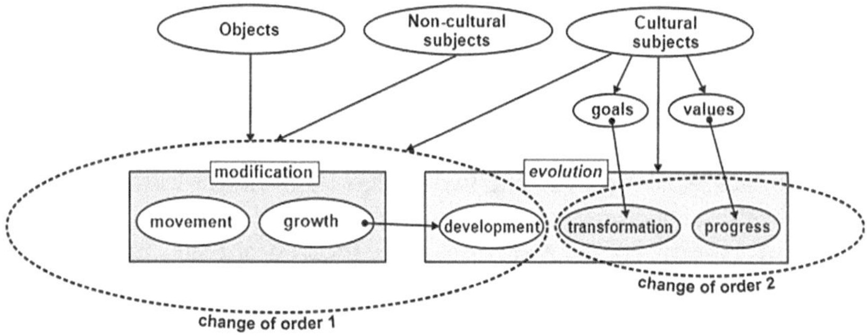

Fig. 1.6 An abstract typology of change. (*Source*: Dinga et al., *Co-evolution of symbolic species in the financial market. A framework for economic and political decision-making*, Springer, 2023, Chap. 1, Fig. 1.11)

Short Discussion

(1) Change is of two types: (a) first-order change—which affects both objects and subjects (both non-cultural and cultural); (b) change of order 2—which targets only cultural subjects.
(2) Evolution is a genus of motion that contains three species (or, equivalently, a species of motion that contains three individuals): (a) development—a first-order change generated by growth; (b) transformation—a second-order change generated by the purpose; (c) progress—a second-order change generated by values.[78]

There are, therefore, three cases of evolutionary processes in which selection is operational. Let us look at some features:

- in the case of evolution *as development*,[79] quantitative accumulations can lead to structural changes of the 'object' under development. For example, if we consider the financial market as a symbolic species (as we agreed earlier), then increasing the number of trading strategies (purely dimensionally/quantitatively) can lead to a change in the structure of the financial market from a monopolist to a financial market closer to the competitive type. In this case, the social selection will take place in the direction of favouring those structures that better serve, as a reward, the economic agents participating in the financial transactions;

- in the case of evolution *as transformation*, social selection will focus on accepting those transformations that are compatible or imposed by the common goals of private economic agents and society as a whole. As a result, the transformation of the symbolic species in question will follow this teleologically projected evolutionary direction;
- in the case of evolution *as progress* (the most performative form of evolution), social selection will take into account those changes that validate the fundamental values of the axiological matrix of the society in question. As we have already hinted, values are primitive in relation to purpose, so, in general, it can be said that the progress in society is part of a 'tunnel' of values. With the necessary caution, it can also be stated that a responsible society (first and foremost, free and democratic) will always select those social fitness that aims at or guides society in a progressive way.

Notes

1. We are not tired of reminding the reader not to confuse the random with the stochastic (e.g., only the stochastic can be assigned probability distributions).
2. We will see that, in the social field, there is a logic living (this concept will be developed in the right place).
3. The term *natural biological individual* is not pleonastic, because, as we will see below, there is also a *social* biological individual (as it seems, there are also technological individuals, based on AI—artificial intelligence—or, in the mixed case, trans-human biological individuals—combination of natural/social biological individual and technological individual).
4. Unless we accept the hypothesis of the divine project of creation—a case that will not be the subject of this investigation.
5. See, for example, the authors' books: (1) (Dinga et al., 2022); (2) (Dinga et al., 2023).
6. It is easy to show that, for the subject, the randomness does not exist, because it cannot be observed in the absence of a pattern of observation. But a pattern of observation means to *ex-ante* accept a distribution of those observations, which transform the randomness into stochasticity.
7. B.F. Dowling localizes the latent information in the so-called bytes from which the memes are derived, based on either intuition or rationality models more or less elaborated (Dowling, 2005).

8. We remind you that the system/set of sufficiency predicates associated with any concept must simultaneously verify the following logical conditions (a kind of sufficiency predicates of … sufficiency predicates): (a) consistency (non-contradiction); (b) coherence; (c) completeness (the principle of sufficient reason).
9. Sometimes (and perhaps more semantically justified) we will use, instead of the phrase *symbolic species*, that of *logical species* or, still, of logically living species. Although the literature prefers the name of symbolic species, it should be noted that the symbolic or symbolist aspect—as treated by general semiotics—requires much more complicated conditions (predicates of specific sufficiency). However, the expressions symbolic species, respectively, logical species (or logically living species), must be considered, in this study, as semantically equivalent, so as having the same reference/denoted.
10. As will be seen below, the two selective polarities will be combined in a hybrid selection (which, in fact, will also call for the 'hybridization' of Darwinism with Lamarckism).
11. The absence of social selection (or, equivalently, the presence of a pseudo-social selection) occurs under the logical condition:

$$\overline{SS} \leftarrow \left[\left(\overline{PS}_{SS}^{1}\right)\wedge\left(PS_{SS}^{2}\right)\wedge\left(PS_{SS}^{3}\right)\wedge\left(PS_{SS}^{4}\right)\right]\vee\left[\left(PS_{SS}^{1}\right)\wedge\left(\overline{PS}_{SS}^{2}\right)\wedge\left(PS_{SS}^{3}\right)\wedge\left(PS_{SS}^{4}\right)\right]$$
$$\vee\left[\left(PS_{SS}^{1}\right)\wedge\left(PS_{SS}^{2}\right)\wedge\left(\overline{PS}_{SS}^{3}\right)\wedge\left(PS_{SS}^{4}\right)\right]\vee\left[\left(PS_{SS}^{1}\right)\wedge\left(PS_{SS}^{2}\right)\wedge\left(PS_{SS}^{3}\right)\wedge\left(\overline{PS}_{SS}^{4}\right)\right]\vee$$
$$\left[\left(\overline{PS}_{SS}^{1}\right)\wedge\left(\overline{PS}_{SS}^{2}\right)\wedge\left(PS_{SS}^{3}\right)\wedge\left(PS_{SS}^{4}\right)\right]\vee\ldots\vee\left[\left(\overline{PS}_{SS}^{1}\right)\wedge\left(\overline{PS}_{SS}^{2}\right)\wedge\left(\overline{PS}_{SS}^{3}\right)\wedge\left(\overline{PS}_{SS}^{4}\right)\right].$$

12. By functioning is meant all the attributes that aim at the occurrence, existence, manifestation (e.g., action) and evolution of the symbolic individual, respectively, of the symbolic species in question.
13. In the literature regarding the motivations/intentions of the human subject, we talk about affections, which are three in number: (a) needs; (b) desires; (c) propensities (*Nota bene*: this is the same propensity that we used in defining and describing the preference). A proposal on the expectations of the human subject can be found in Welton (2012).
14. We are of the opinion that, in line with the 'list' of expectations of the individual/species towards the environment, the expectations of the environment (in this case, of the cultural geodesic) towards the individual/species should also be specified. We propose the following categories of expectations from cultural geodesic part: (a) compliance; (b) participation; (c) commitment.

15. In fact, this is how we described the concept of law—when the norm concerns a particular case, it becomes, instead of law, a privilege, that is, a private law, unacceptable in a free and democratic society.
16. Please note that by commensurability we mean comparability, from any point of view, not necessarily quantitative (*Nota bene*: often, even in articles with scientific claims, this term receives the meaning of … measurability, as with the term quantification or quantifiability, also credited with properties of … measurement/measurability).
17. We mention the conceptual family of which the way of life is part: (a) *standard of living*—the quantitative aspect (material, economic) of the fulfilment of expectations; (b) *quality of life*—the qualitative aspect of fulfilling expectations; (c) *way of life*—the communitarian/social aspect of fulfilling expectations. (*Nota bene*: although the literature distinguishes between way of life and lifestyle, we consider that these distinctions are somewhat overly pedantic and have a relatively low added value, from a cognitive point of view.) (d) *lifestyle*—the subjective/idiosyncratic aspect (at the level of personal perception) of fulfilling expectations. We mention that the meaning of life occurs in the sphere of lifestyle, even if the causal origin of these meanings is in the way of life (Durant, 2005).
18. With a certain amount of imagination, one can obviously conceive also of a way of life of cultural geodesic (or even of the situational framework).
19. The absence of social fitness (or, equivalently, the presence of a pseudo-social fitness) occurs under the logical condition:

$$\overline{FS} \leftarrow \left[\left(\overline{PS}^{1}_{FS}\right) \wedge \left(PS^{2}_{FS}\right) \wedge \left(PS^{3}_{FS}\right)\right] \vee \left[\left(PS^{1}_{FS}\right) \wedge \left(\overline{PS}^{2}_{FS}\right) \wedge \left(PS^{3}_{SS}\right)\right] \vee$$
$$\left[\left(PS^{1}_{FS}\right) \wedge \left(PS^{2}_{SF}\right) \wedge \left(\overline{PS}^{3}_{FS}\right)\right] \vee \left[\left(\overline{PS}^{1}_{FS}\right) \wedge \left(\overline{PS}^{2}_{FS}\right) \wedge \left(PS^{3}_{FS}\right)\right] \vee \ldots \vee$$
$$\left[\left(\overline{PS}^{1}_{SS}\right) \wedge \left(\overline{PS}^{2}_{SS}\right) \wedge \left(\overline{PS}^{3}_{SS}\right)\right].$$

20. For example, the current migration phenomenon of labour (especially in the economic space of the European Union, as a direct result of one of the economic freedoms of this space—freedom of movement of population and labour—functions as a *sui generis* selection that it does so with regard to its environment, more precisely with regard to the fitness that another environment can offer it. As a (rule of) reaction, the original environment can be modified so as to acquire the characteristics of the destination environment, in order to cause labour re-migration, so the selection made by the species on the environment determines (causes) the environment of origin to adapt to the fitness requirements of the species and, thus, to co-evolve with it.

21. Although co-evolution involves two co-species, we have previously shown that, in some cases, the environment of a species can be assimilated with a co-species, so that co-evolution can be accepted for the *species-environment* pair.
22. Of course, the judiciary justice also characterizes social fitness, because it refers to the *rule of law*.
23. It is obvious that evolution cannot be assessed from an axiological point of view (e.g., whether it is 'moving' progressively or regressively, since the progress involves values, which are external and autonomous in relation to evolution), it is a fact, randomly generated, and with a directional arrow. In this sense, terms such as involution or regress, applied to the evolutionary process, are meaningless—what we may be willing to call an involution is, in fact, always an ... evolution. Of course, in the social field, the axiological aspects of the evolution of symbolic species are different. In the latter field, the deliberative nature of the evolution of symbolic species, based on social fitness (customized for each symbolic species), creates conditions for progress, that is, for a guided evolution by values (see Fig. 1.6).
24. The selection generates, from a populational point of view, and in a trans-generational order, a positive feedback (self-catalyst or self-escalator).
25. The mixed character of the selector environment (an-anthropic and anthropic) in the case of the two types of selections can be controversial. However, we consider that there is no alternative in this matter, since the human (biological) individual is also the material carrier of the symbolic species called the financial market (and, indeed, of all other symbolic species that exist or can exist in the society).
26. This is, as we have already pointed out, a conceptual issue that we need to pay attention to. A solution that eliminates the need for this specialized attention could be the following: to consider the individual transaction as a phenotype of the financial market species and to consider the trading strategy as a kind of super-individual (or aggregate individual, given that individual transactions are logically inferred from the trading strategy), so that SS at the populational level can be achieved in two steps: (a) reaching the critical threshold in the trading strategy by selecting the individual transaction; (b) selection of the trading strategy. For the time being, we will not apply this suggestion, but it remains in the portfolio of further (possible) developments of our evolutionary model of the financial market.
27. In a more pretentious and generalizing expression (but which is, in fact, the basic definition of the economy), the need for low entropy from the environment.
28. In other words, a black swan in the genome.
29. There is even an (intentional) bi-disciplinary branch in this field, called *Genoeconomics*, which shows, once again, how much terminological inflation the economic research field is capable of.

30. Otherwise, we should invent all sorts of other terms or branches of economic theory, related to all sorts of human activities: Genointernet, Genopolitics and so on.
31. We refer here to innate skills (talents) not to skills acquired through instruction and/or exercise. However, the innate/acquired distinction should not be exaggerated, as the acquisition and preservation of skills also depends on the dowry of innate abilities.
32. In the history, there are cases in which natural selection at the populational level is carried out, systematically, from a social perspective: in the military-fortress state of Sparta (around 650 BC), in the Mediterranean basin (Laconia, in ancient Greece) children who presented, at birth, with physical malformations that would have prevented them from becoming successful soldiers, were sacrificed.
33. As far as non-human plants and animals are concerned, since the invention of agriculture (about 11,000 years ago), more or less systematic interventions have been made in natural selection but mainly from a populational perspective (increasing the share of individuals with the desired characteristics in the total population concerned).
34. See, for example, B.F. Dowling's work *Evolutionary Finance* (2005) where the financial behaviour is modelled based on the molecular replication—a summary of our position to that book is provided in authors' book entitled *Co-evolution of Symbolic Species in the Financial Market—A Framework for Economic and Political Decision-Making*, Springer, 2023.
35. We ignore, for the time being, the genetic engineering framed, according to some authors, in the wider cultural-technological movement, called transhumanism.
36. The term error is, of course, a circumstantial term, because, in order to categorize a phenomenon or process or event as an error, there must be a benchmark (validation criterion) whose verification indicates the correctness versus error in question. As natural evolution is not projected (but only directed by fitness), it cannot be determined whether an error leads to better fitness than the absence of that error (obviously, the 'proof of truth' is found in the factual/empirical selection which the environment performed on objectified fitness, i.e., actually manifested). As we will show later, in the social field, errors have a very different meaning from the natural case.
37. To an even greater extent, errors (of understanding, experimentation, evaluation, etc.) are also the basis of (saltationist) advances in knowledge, especially in scientific knowledge.
38. Of course, all these processes occur from a statistical perspective, so, on average, there are oscillations, deviations or exceptions for 'private' individuals, both in terms of environmental impact on them and the impact of individuals on the environment.

39. In fact, the state of affairs is a bit more nuanced: there is also a selection here (which is also social), which refers to another symbolic species, not discussed in our study but obviously of at least as great interest—it is about the symbolic species that can be called a *technological market*, whose concrete, particular hypostases are precisely the material artefacts (of the product/service type).
40. It is clear that the term *institution* must mean any entity, as a rule, generally opposable to all members of the society which are eligible for that entity, in the broadest sense: norms (codified or not), organizations, procedures, mechanisms, social structures, codes, instructions and so on, that is, with a term that we introduced earlier, the situational framework (which generates cultural geodesic) of the society.
41. If we were to exaggerate the pedantry of our approach at this point, we would say that social selection is exerted over the institutional/cultural web in which all the objectifications generated by social action are 'caught' (*Nota bene*: a kind of inverted Husserlian *hýle* that interposes between subjectual intentionality and objectual reality).
42. The fact that the spontaneous axiological matrix is listed before the Constitution (which can be considered the projected axiological matrix) is significant from the following perspective: the Constitution (and all subsequent logical and chronological norms) should, in principle, be consistent with the spontaneous axiological matrix, which expresses the fundamental historical identity of society, people, nation in question. In addition, if the Constitution (and the norms 'under' it) are inconsistent (contradictory) with the spontaneous axiological matrix, the real/effective behaviour of individuals and communities will favour the spontaneous axiological matrix (here we have the old wisdom of the people who says that the alley in a park must be built exactly on the path that people walked before the alley was built, which also includes the more elaborate precept of Kotarbiński's praxiology, that breaking codified norms is a peremptory signal to lawmakers of inadequacy of those violated norms).
43. So-called NGOs (non-governmental organizations).
44. Especially in small communities. There are opinions about the maximum number of individuals in a community which still allows direct and informed contact between individuals—it seems that there are about 150 individuals (although there are opinions that 'widen' this limit). This is the so-called Dunbar number (Dunbar, 1992). Of course, the expansion of virtual space nowadays considerably expands the possibility of 'direct' (but how genuine?) inter-individual contact.
45. Regardless of the type of mutation—accidental/random or deliberative—it is always contingent. Otherwise, we should accept the laws of history (in the way Marx tried this—*Nota bene*: Romanian historian and philosopher

of history A.D. Xenopol also tried to introduce a certain historical necessity through the concept of *serial succession*, in order to avoid effective causality in history).

46. However, the 'truth' of the adequacy type is more appropriate to natural selection, in fact. In social selection, the 'truth' targeted by the selection is of the performing type (we will emphasize this nuance when we propose and examine the autopoietic model of the financial market).
47. Elsewhere, one of the authors of this research even proposes that, in the economic (more general, social) field, a tetravalent logic should be constructed (as opposed to the now dominant bivalent logic, including in the case of Popperian falsifiability), which refers to adequacy, not to correspondence-truth.
48. We specify that, as in the case of Popper's falsifiability, this time, the corroboration does not take an explicit form, in fact, only an explicit form takes the refutation.
49. The case of a conflict between formal courts of social selection is not unlikely, and, in this case, our position is that the credibility of a decision to refute social fitness is also directly proportional to the place occupied in the hierarchy by the selection court in question.
50. It is worth noting that such an eventuality is, in principle, impossible in the case of natural selection, because the DNA 'program' does not allow deviations in implementation—of course, transcription or translation accidents are possible here, as in the case of social selection—but, as lacking free will, in the natural selection the 'institutional' adequacy is not problematic.
51. A functionally equivalent situation of non-rejection is that situation in which a social fitness is explicitly rejected but it continues to exist (or co-exist) fraudulently (e.g., by masking, dissimulation or other methods of avoiding visibility or observability).
52. A more striking case of beneficial inadequacy can be found in the field of knowledge (including scientific)—a misunderstood theory can lead to the opening of research or development or application directions that would have been impossible in a correct understanding framework (i.e., how the author of that theory desired). A peremptory example, in this context, is that of Planck: having to harmonize the theory with the experiment, Planck introduced a coefficient of correction (Planck's constant) which later proved to be the cornerstone of the whole quantum mechanics. It seems that the introduction of the cosmological constant (Einstein) in his theoretical model of gravity (general relativity) must be interpreted in the same way—this constant later proved to be fundamental for explaining the dynamic behaviour of the Universe.
53. The suggestion that institutional adequacy could be categorized as an automatic formal stabilizer is immediate.

54. We remind you that, at the most fundamental level (constitutional norms), this is about the basic structure of society, as formulated by John Rawls.
55. The term particular can be relatively unclear, as it can be read in the context of the general-particular relationship, in which the particular is an instantiation of the general. In the case discussed, it is a public (social)–private relationship. *Nota bene*: at the limit, the public–private relationship could be analogous to the general–private relationship, however.
56. We want to use the term projected instead of the term designed, because the former term includes the meaning of the purpose/goal, while the latter does not do that (so clear). Somehow, the term projection here has similar connotations to the term projection used by Quine.
57. As we have seen before, in the case of social selection, the social environment is identical with the social genotype—which is the cultural geodesic. In the case of this selection, we have an overlap or indistinguishability that occurs between the environment and the genotype, both of which oppose the phenotype.
58. Note that this predicate of sufficiency does not 'parasitize' (is not redundant with) the predicate of sufficiency which refers to unidirectionality: it is the fact, generally accepted in the macroscopic world, that the effect follows the cause both logically and chronologically (of course, given the clock time, which is a mechanical, uniform time, independent of the measured phenomenon/process).
59. The time arrow, which 'distributes' the succession of worlds and the corresponding causes and effects, is given by the kinematics of global entropy: according to the second law of thermodynamics, in a closed system (such as the Universe) the entropy—that is, the unavailability of bound energy—grows spontaneously, permanently, continuously and irreversibly.
60. Of course, a theologian (perhaps, a fundamentalist one) will argue that even in the field of natural evolution we have a projected selection, namely, projected by God. From a technical point of view, to paraphrase Laplace, we do not need this hypothesis here.
61. In fact, if we want to save terms/concepts (generally, means of verbal expression), we can call the projected selection a second-order directed selection.
62. From a very broad perspective, this is the case, for example, with social counter-reforms or social counter-revolutions.
63. Historically, as we mentioned previously, the idea of the saltationist selection has been proposed to the scientific community by Stephen Jay Gould and Niles Eldredge since 1972. Five years after Gould's death, in 2007, this idea was resumed in *Punctuated Equilibrium* and published by HUP.

64. The Pleistocene (also known as the Ice Age) is a geological period estimated to have stretched from 2,588,000 years ago to 11,700 years ago, being the last stage of the Paleolithic.
65. Which thus 'refutes' the famous principle of natural philosophy: (lat.) *natura non facit saltus* (nature does not make jumps) which, before appearing in Darwin, was mentioned by Leibniz as an axiom in connection with the invention of infinitesimal/differential calculus. Of course, from an ontological point of view, at least in one respect, this maxim proved to be false: it is about the fact that neither time, nor space, nor mass are indefinitely decomposable—they have a lower limit and certain corresponding Planck values.
66. Here, of course, Maslow's pyramid of needs correctly perceived the order of priority of their satisfaction (Marxism also noted this prioritization that comes from ancestral times, namely, from the days when man was an animal that technology had not yet come to place it at the top of the food chain).
67. This issue—of the innate character versus acquired character—of the ethical sense is a particularly difficult one. It will not be developed more in this study, as its relevance in the context of the main research interest (as we designed it) is relatively low.
68. That is, the ethical sense is of the nature of necessity (it is closely related to what we call, rather vaguely, the character of the person).
69. Both imperatives are obviously of an *ex-ante* nature.
70. We specify that the relations governed by ethics are of a practical type (subject–subject relationships), not of a praxiological type (subject–object relationships).
71. On the role of principles in action (especially the rational one), or, what is equivalent, on the role of symbolic utility, see the synthesis provided by Robert Nozick (Nozick, 1994).
72. However, the analogy is completely external here, because in the matter of ethics (i.e., principles) we cannot speak meaningfully about the concept of correspondence-truth.
73. This statement is not pejorative, but simply expresses the absence of a referential (or referent or denoted).
74. See the relatively extensive discussion in this book on symbolic utility.
75. Here, expressly in the original sense of the term, that is, of *doxa* (which is the opposite of *epistemé*, without being the negation of the latter. *Nota bene*: logically, therefore, the two concepts are related of contrariety, not of contradiction).
76. This is obviously about what we call positive norms or positive law—that is, those norms that objectify the principles established by the social contract.

77. On the legal–legitimate relationship in the matter of public norms, see also Dinga et al. (2022).
78. The question of a certain (possible) overlap (or non-independence) between purpose and value is a good question. In principle, we accept the non-independence between purpose and value (even a certain primitivity of value in relation to purpose) but we ignore, for the moment, this difficulty.
79. Not to be confused the term development, used in this context, with the term development used for the phenotype of natural evolution—the process of reaching the stage of adulthood, that is, reaching the physiological capacity of biological reproduction. This second case is opposite, conceptually, to evolution, while the first case is a type of evolution.

References

Benjamin, D., Chabris, C., Glaeser, E., Gudnason, V., Harris, T., Laibson, D., Launer, L., & Purcell, S. (2007). *Genoeconomics*. Biosocial Surveys.

De Neve, J.-E., Christakis, N. A., Fowler, J. H., & Frey, B. S. (2012). Genes, Economics, and Happiness. *Journal of Neuroscience, Psychology, and Economics, 5*(4).

Dinga, E. (2021). *Logically Living System: A Generative "Machine" for Autopoietic Systems* (pp. 73–97). IGI Global.

Dinga, E., Oprean-Stan, C., Tănăsescu, C.-R., Brătian, V., & Ionescu, G.-M. (2022). *Financial Market Analysis and Behaviour. The Adaptive Preference Hypothesis*. Routledge, Francis & Taylor Group.

Dinga, E., Oprean-Stan, C., Tănăsescu, C.-R., Brătian, V., & Ionescu, G.-M. (2023). *Co-Evolution of Symbolic Species in the Financial Market—A Framework for Economic and Political Decision-Making*. Springer.

Dowling, B. F. (2005). *Evolutionary Finance*. Palgrave Macmillan.

Dunbar, R. I. M. (1992). Neocortex Size as a Constraint on Group Size in Primates. *Journal of Human Evolution, 22*(6), 469–493.

Durant, W. (2005). *On the Meaning of Life*. Promethean Press.

Gould, S. J. (2007). *Punctuated Equilibrium*. Belknap Press of Harvard University Press.

Lehrer, S., & Ding, W. (2016). Are Genetic Markers of Interest for Economic Research? *IZA Journal of Labor Policy, 6*.

Lo, A. (2019). *Adaptive Markets: Financial Evolution at the Speed of Thought*. Princeton University Press.

McGene, J. (2013). *Social Fitness and Resilience: A Review of Relevant Constructs, Measures, and Links to Well-Being*. RAND Corporation.

Nozick, R. (1994). *The Nature of Rationality*. Princeton University Press.

Peters, E. E. (1994). *Fractal Market Analysis. Applying Chaos Theory to Investments and Economics*. John Wiley and Sons, Inc.

Welton, D. (2012). *Bodily Intentionality, Affectivity, and Basic Affects*. The Oxford Handbook of Contemporary Phenomenology.

CHAPTER 2

Social Selection in the Financial Market: Logical Mechanism

General Mechanism of Social Selection

Preamble

In the literature, social selection is treated, in most cases, also as a natural selection but which is socially conditioned, namely, in co-specific phenotypic interactions (i.e., between individuals of the same species). Social conditioning means that, for a given phenotype, of a given species, the environment is considered to be not only the context in which the species in question operates but, for a given individual/phenotype, the environment also includes other individuals of the same species, with which the individual in question (which the research is exercised on), often called the focal individual, interacts within its own functioning. In other words, the environment in which a species operates is separated, from the perspective of the focal individual, into two components: (a) the component of the non-co-specific environment and (b) the component of the co-specific environment (Wolf et al., 1999).[1] Therefore, in most approaches to the concept (and process) of social selection, we do not have an analysis of social selection from the perspective of human society, but one of socially conditioned natural selection. In our opinion, the idea of separating the environment of a species into two distinct components, as shown above, is productive and scientifically necessary,[2] instead, to name the selection examined in this context as a social selection (or a hybrid

E. Dinga et al., *Economic and Financial Market Behaviour*, https://doi.org/10.1007/978-3-031-31702-6_2

selection)—natural/genetic and social/interactive—is exaggerated. The interaction of phenotype with its environment is a commonplace in the theory of selection of living organisms, and the fact that the environment also contains individuals of its own species does not bring anything new—for any adult individual (i.e., phenotype), the interaction takes place simultaneously with the non-co-specific environment and the co-specific environment, even if, from the point of view of empirical research and so on,[3] this separation is useful, allowing the partitioning of the effects (by calculating the corresponding partial regressions). However, from the theoretical/conceptual point of view it is not very relevant. In our opinion, simply the environment of a given phenotype of a given species is all that is not that (focal) phenotype. Moreover (and this is a relatively uncommon aspect in the literature), if co-specific interaction is accepted, then trans-specific interaction should be introduced, that is, the impact of a given phenotypic trait on the focal individual also as a result of the interactions of this individual with individuals of other species which are operating in that environment (as proximate or accessible nearness) of the focal individual. (*Nota bene*: in this case, the environment of the focal individual would acquire a third component: (c) the component of the trans-specific environment.)

In any case, our interest in this research focuses on the concept of social selection that takes place in human society, on the one hand, and that is exerted on symbolic species, on the other hand. These two particularizations introduce two constraints or commands: (a) a reduction of the sphere to be examined—only the social selection that takes place within the human society—what we call societal space; (b) a limitation of the action of social selection to the symbolic species—therefore not on the human species.[4]

Forming and Variation of the Social Fitness

We resume the conditions (predicates) of sufficiency of social selection, respectively of social fitness, previously introduced.

- Social selection:
  - ($\boldsymbol{PS}_{SS}^{1}$) the phenotype subject to selection belongs to a *symbolic* (not biological) species;
  - ($\boldsymbol{PS}_{SS}^{2}$) the selector (or selector environment) is the *cultural geodesic*;

- (PS_{SS}^{3}) the selection criterion is the *social fitness*;
- (PS_{SS}^{4}) the phenomenology of selection is *bi-polar*: directed and projected.

- Social fitness:
  - (PS_{SF}^{1}) *mutual* verification of the expectations of the individual/species and of the cultural geodesic;
  - (PS_{SF}^{2}) the expectations, both of the individual/species and of the cultural geodesic, must be *generical*;
  - (PS_{SF}^{3}) the measurable expression of social fitness is the *way of life*.

The first important remark about social fitness is that it does not form unidirectionally (as happens in the formation of biological fitness), that is, starting from the variation of some features of the phenotype, as they are caused by mutation (be it random, as in the biological case, or hybrid or bi-polar—see (PS_{SS}^{4})—as in the case of human society). Therefore, the variation (or, more generally, the updating, with its three processes[5]) of certain traits that will lead to the variation of the phenotype occurs in a doubly conditioned way, and this conditioning must be considered in its causal significance.[6] As previously and partially suggested, the genotypic mutation in the field of human society (*Nota bene*: hereinafter, by the term *social* we mean the social/societal in human society, and by the phrase social selection we mean the selection of symbolic species produced in human society) occurs both accidentally and projected/programmed, and the projecting/programming factor is the normative framework (cultural geodesic). Therefore, the social genotypic mutation occurs as suggested in Fig. 2.1 (*cSI* means co-specific inter-action, i.e., between individuals of the same species; *GV* means genotypic variation of the focal individual; *tSI* means trans-specific inter-action, i.e., between individuals of two different species that share the same environment; *pSC* means pre-selection conditioning by cultural geodesic; *SS* means social selection exerted by cultural geodesic). (*Nota bene*: the focal individual is considered the 1/A individual.)

Short Discussion

- A given individual (called focal individual, i.e., the individual on whom the analysis is explicitly focused)—noted in the figure above as 'individual 1/A', that is, individual 1 of species A—will suffer, outside

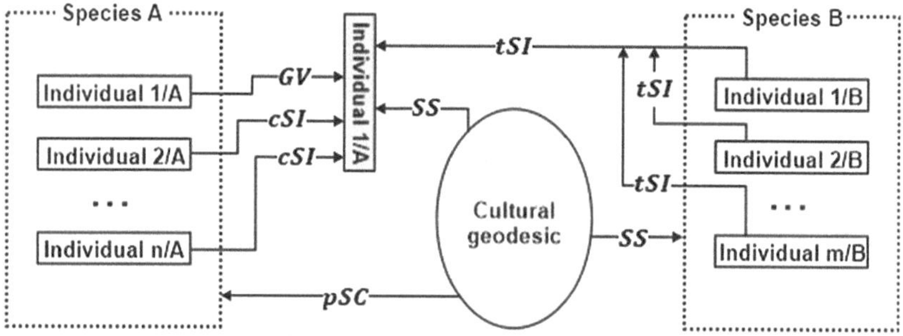

Fig. 2.1 A general scheme of social fitness formation of the focal individual. (*Source*: Authors)

the genotypic influence (which is not shown in the figure), three types of phenotypic influences:

- the influence of interactions with individuals of their own species (individuals k/A, where k = 2, …, n); we call these interactions *co-specific*;
- the influence of interactions with individuals of other species (e.g., with individuals k/B, where k = 1,2, …, m, of species B);[7] we call these actions *trans-specific*;
- the influence of cultural geodesic, which manifests itself both *ex-ante* (in the form of pre-selection conditioning) and *ex-post*[8] (in the form of social selection itself);[9]

• the social fitness acquired by the focal individual will be, therefore, the result of the integration of the three mentioned causal/conditional influences, with the implicit synergy effects. As a result, this social fitness will not be an algebraic sum of influences but,[10] so to speak, a logical sum.

Signification of the Sufficiency Predicates of Social Fitness

Although the issue of social fitness is addressed in the literature, as we have shown above, especially from the perspective of 'societies' of non-human animals, through a more or less adequate adaptation of phenotypic evolution based exclusively on genotypic mutation and environmental selection (the latter being different from the phenotype in question) to the case where other phenotypes of the same species (co-specific phenotypes) interact with the focal individual, the suggestions are interesting and useful for examining social selection (and, consequently, evolution) in relation to human society. In this paragraph we will develop a more analytical discussion of the predicates of sufficiency of social fitness, for a better understanding of the concept of social selection in this particular framework—human society.

- (PS_{SF}^{1}) *mutual* verification of individual/species expectations and cultural geodesic.

This predicate aims, so to speak, at both a temporal and a spatial reciprocity (the two perspectives result immediately from Fig. 2.1).

- Temporal (or kinetic) reciprocity:
  - it refers to the fact that, as far as the projected mutation of the genotype of the analysed symbolic species is concerned, it will be carried out (at least as an attempt) within the cultural geodesic, from the perspective of an *ex-ante–ex-post* combination of influences between the two parties. This means that the change will be designed in such a way as to ensure a functional degree of compliance with the applicable regulatory basis of the society;
  - we can highlight the following possible degrees of compliance, in descending order of their 'strength':

    self-eligible mutation (*PM*0): mutation that conforms exactly ('without rest') to the normative content of cultural geodesic;[11]

    formally tolerable mutation (*PM*1): mutation that conforms to the letter but not necessarily (also) in the spirit of the norms of cultural geodesic;[12]

    factually acceptable mutation (*PM*2): mutation that conforms to the spirit but not necessarily (also) to the letter of the norms of cultural geodesic;

    sustainable non-compliant mutation (*PM*3): mutation that flagrantly violates the rules of cultural geodesic but based on the cost–benefit analysis performed by the cause of the mutation (the human individual who is the carrier of the individual of the intended symbolic species) is (at least) covered by the benefit of this non-compliance[13]—this is the case, for example, in tax evasion or the production of negative externalities (in both cases we have standardized internalisations, at the level of cost/sanction, of non-compliance);

non-conforming mutation (*PM*4): mutation that violates cultural geodesic 'without rest', not even justified by cost-benefit analysis;

- we can speak here, from a methodological point of view, of a certain *elasticity* of cultural geodesic: although, *ex-ante*, cultural geodesic directs/drives/guides the implementation of the projected mutation, except for *PM*3 and *PM*4 mutations, its non-conformity with cultural geodesic does not lead to the rejection of the mutation in question (obviously, we exclude the case *PM*0 in which we have a ... tautology between the *ex-ante* indication and the *ex-post* selection executed by the cultural geodesic);
- if the cultural geodesic undergoes changes precisely as a result of the behaviour of the projected mutations (e.g., a critical mass of non-compliances, of different degrees, may suggest to the legislator to make changes that increase the permissiveness of the cultural geodesic exactly in the direction of observations)—this could be called the *plasticity* of cultural geodesic. After all, the co-evolution of symbolic species represents a continuous and permanent mutual adjustment of the elasticity and plasticity of cultural geodesic.

- Spatial (or topological) reciprocity:
  - it refers to the fact (mentioned above also from a temporal perspective, by the way) that social selection is made from both directions: from the cultural geodesic, respectively from the projected mutation. This means that the construction of social fitness is a co-construction, in which both the *object* of construction (the projected mutation) and its *subject* (cultural geodesic) participate;
  - as in the case of temporal reciprocity, spatial reciprocity in the formation and variation of social fitness implies the mechanism of fetal reaction norms previously discussed, applied, of course, to generic symbolic species that are created and function in human society.

The functioning of PS^1_{SF} can be represented as in Fig. 2.2.

- ($\boldsymbol{PS^2_{SF}}$) the expectations of both the individual/species and the cultural geodesic must be *generical*.

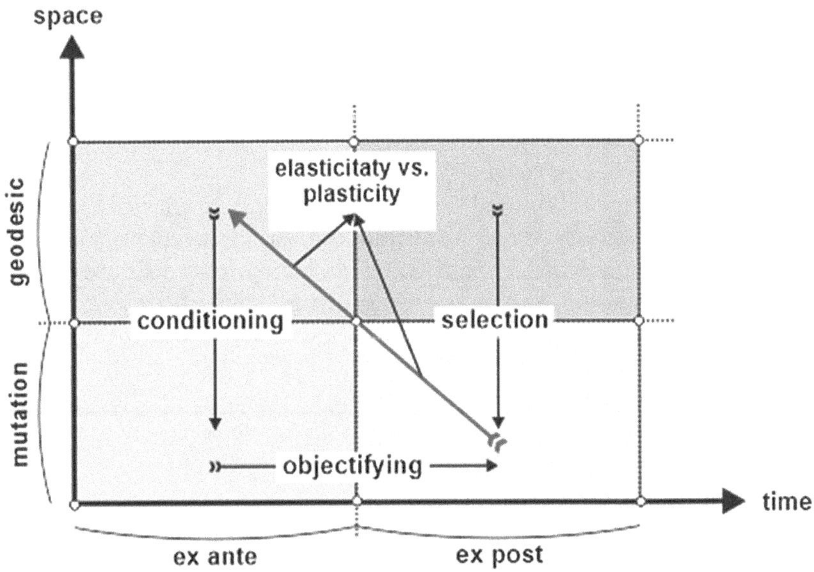

Fig. 2.2 Elasticity versus plasticity in cultural geodesic kinematics. (*Source*: Authors)

This predicate of sufficiency is claimed from two commandments that are valid (are applied) both in the case of the symbolic individual (symbolic species), more precisely, on the genotypic mutation, and in the case of cultural geodesic.

- Perspective of mutation:
  - for a mutation, occurring for an individual of the symbolic species in question (e.g., in an individual financial transaction—*IT* in the notation adopted by us—within the financial individual called trading strategy—*TS* in our notation) to have an impact on the formation/variation of social fitness, that mutation must have the potential to be generalized at the level of all possible hypostases of the financial individual, otherwise it will be 'extinguished' or amortized in the social mechanism involved. This generalization is possible through the memetic mechanism, which involves the concept of implicit information introduced by us in FMAB-APH—in this case it is an implicit information at the level of the

human individual that implements the financial individual called trading strategy (this information will be used to adjust all individual hypostases of that trading strategy, obviously, if the mutation that customizes those hypostases brings financial success—namely, net gain).

- The perspective of cultural geodesic:
  - in the case of cultural geodesic, the generical character is even more pronounced and justifiable. Indeed, for a geodesic norm to be a proper 'rule' of behaviour—including in terms of social fitness formation/variation—it must be of a general nature, that is, to apply to an unspecified category (than, possibly, by eligibility criteria for the applicability of the norm in question, criteria that must also be general[14]) of particular hypostases of the symbolic individual (e.g., in our concrete case, the financial individual which is the trading strategy).

Of course, there is no infallible 'litmus paper' for establishing or identifying the generical nature of the mutation or the norms integrated in cultural geodesic, but this genericity is necessary to achieve the real interaction between the projected mutation and the cultural geodesic. However, this property of genericity will be decided by the practice/praxiology of effective actions and behaviours within society;

- ($\boldsymbol{PS^3_{SF}}$) the measurable expression of social fitness is the *way of life*

This predicate of sufficiency is the most important (i.e., more significant and relevant) from the perspective of formation, respectively of variation of social fitness, as we conceive it in this research. We have previously shown the meaning (definition) of the way of life: the communitarian (i.e., social or, more precisely, societal) way of fulfilling expectations of individuals. It should be noted that expectations are always expectations of the human (biological) individual[15] in relation to the ability (potential or actual) of a particular social fitness to meet these expectations which, as we have shown, are objectifications of quality of life. The exact way in which the human individual links the way of life to the social fitness in question is a matter dependent both on the models of rationality of the human individual[16] and on psychological aspects, that is, the idiosyncrasy which is the most inaccessible to the analyst. For the moment (but we will try, later, to improve the approach in the matter) the handiest, although not infallible, tool for identifying or establishing this way of causal-functional connection remains Samuelson's revealed preference.[17] In this context, we make the following considerations regarding this predicate of sufficiency regarding social fitness:

- the way of life, in its current meaning, refers to the human individual, but social fitness refers to the symbolic individual (respectively the symbolic species),[18] so it presupposes a way of life specified for the latter type of individual;
- therefore, a concept must be introduced to link the two categories of individuals, so as not to confuse the social selection (evolution) of the human individual[19] with the social selection (evolution) of the symbolic individual;[20]
- the solution we propose is to define the way of life from the perspective of the symbolic individual. Like any definition, it must be based on its own predicates of sufficiency, as follows:
  - (α) *convertibility*: symbolic social fitness (SSF) must be able to be converted into an effect (or effects) that is part of the human individual's set of expectations—for example, a positive monetary effect or a positive effect such as social prestige and so on;[21] in other words, the symbolic way of life must be convertible into the real way of life (of the human individual/group);
  - (β) *replicability*: symbolic social fitness must be able to be maintained over a reasonable time horizon, that is, it cannot be a singular property or a singular phenomenon; this predicate of sufficiency can also be called quasi-semantically equivalent with terms such as sustainability and reliability;[22] this means that symbolic social fitness must have some stability/continuity;[23] as we will see in the final part of the research, the autopoieticity of the financial market uses the phrase *adaptive replicability*, which also integrates the results that were obtained in FMAB-APH (Dinga et al., 2022) on the adaptive preference hypothesis of financial market;
  - (γ) *axiological compatibility*: symbolic social fitness must be compatible, in terms of the values involved, with the belief, propensity or, more precisely, with the proference of the corresponding human individual. Although social selection is carried out, as we have shown, by the selector called cultural geodesic, which is somehow external (transcendent) in relation to the human individual, nevertheless, what is 'offered' to the respective selector is a result already filtered by the human individual. Therefore, this

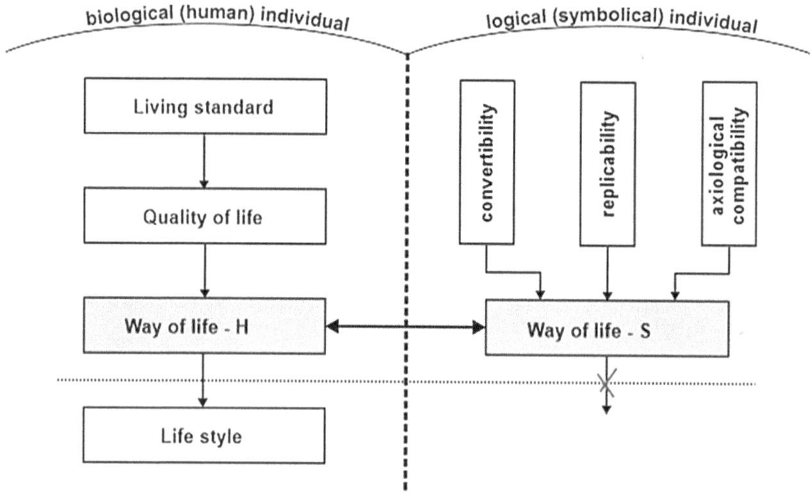

Fig. 2.3 Correlation human individual–symbolic individual: the way of life. (*Source*: Authors)

predicate of sufficiency assures that symbolic social fitness has the potential to generate the satisfaction of the communitarian expectations of the human individual precisely as a result of the fact that it is part of its value grid;[24]

- therefore, the symbolic way of life, as a sufficiency predicate of social fitness, is to be measured from the perspective of the three own sufficiency predicates (α, β, γ), when comparative approaches are needed, either over time or over space.

A synoptic representation of the connection between the way of life of the real (biological) individual and the way of life of the symbolic (logical) individual is given in Fig. 2.3. (*H* marks the human 'version' of the way of life, and *S* marks the symbolic 'version' of the way.)

Selection of Social Fitness

Figures 2.1, 2.2, and 2.3 give relevant suggestions regarding the mechanism to select social fitness—fitness associated with the symbolic/logical individual, respectively associated with the symbolic/logical species within human society. In this paragraph we will summarize/integrate the results already obtained previously in this matter, in order to provide a complete mechanism of social fitness selection.

General Considerations

- The fundamental aspect in the problem of symbolic social fitness (SSF) is its deliberative or projected character. As we have shown, the genotype of a symbolic species is, in overwhelming proportion, the cultural geodesic which, in turn, is an emanation of the propensity or proference of human individuals, respectively of social groups formed within society;[25]
- cultural geodesic is, mainly,[26] a deliberative, programmatic artefact which, in addition, is claimed from a solid, unambiguous basis and with a high degree of stability and acceptability—the Constitution; this makes the projected nature of cultural geodesic unquestionable;
- the construction and reconstruction (updating) of cultural geodesic[27] is generally done by the legislative structure of the society (Parliament) but, exceptionally, the executive structure (Government, respectively the presidential administration[28]) can intervene (most often, only in emergencies) for this updating;
- in a 'curious' way, as it has already emerged from the above, in the social field, the genotype coincides, from an institutional point of view, as well as from a logical point of view, with the selector (selector court) or the selector environment—that is, cultural geodesic, on the one hand, generates (to a large extent), deliberately, projected, programmed, the formation/variation of social fitness and, on the other hand, it selects what it has already 'guided as formation/variation' (*Nota bene*: this results in a certain institutional tautology or a tautology of the institutional logic) specific to social selection and evolution.

The Mechanism of Social Fitness Formation/Variation

- The first preliminary issue that needs to be clarified in this matter[29] is the one regarding the concept of symbolic individual; the second issue is that of symbolic species that can co-exist (and, of course, co-evolve) in society;

- the *first* problem: the symbolic social individual
  - the best-known proposals in this regard are: (1) the proposal of *routine* (Nelson & Winter, 1985): refers to a procedure or behaviour that is operationalized at the organizational level (especially in the economic field, but, of course, the concept can be generalized to any type of social action); (2) the proposal (Luhmann, 2012) of *communication*: the social phenotype is communication, not the human individual (which, in fact, is ignored in his model); (3) one of the authors (Dinga et al., 2020) proposed the concept of *norm* as a generic phenotype of the social domain;[30]
  - in this context, therefore, we must identify a generic concept for the symbolic social phenotype from which, through subsequent particularizations, we obtain phenotypes (symbolic social individuals) for different sub-domains of the social domain, that is, for different symbolic social species;
  - our proposal for the concept of generic symbolic social phenotype is *transaction*.[31] A brief argument for supporting/justifying this proposal is provided below:
    - the fundamental aspect (eidetic one, as an inveterate phenomenologist would say) of the existence and functioning of human society (i.e., the sociality[32]) is the interaction,[33] and a kind of interaction is precisely the transaction;
    - of course, in this case, we could use the term interaction directly. The problem that arises here, however, is this: interaction does not logically imply contemporaneity, while the transaction does involve it; thus, there may be an interaction between a researcher in the matter of metaphysics and (the works of) Aristotle, but there can be no transaction (in this case, of an intellectual type) between the two parties;
    - the interaction may result in a zero impact, whereas the transaction involves a non-zero impact for both parties participating in that transaction.[34] For example, the interaction between two people looking at each other at the same time may have a null result in terms of the impact on one or both parts engaged in the interaction, while a transaction (involving at least one incidental flow from one part and which is excidental to the other part[35]) cannot result in zero impact;[36]

- the *second* problem: the typology of symbolic social species[37]
  first of all, note that the term transaction does indeed have the semantic potential to be so general (despite all its specificity, given the requirement of non-zero impact) that it 'covers' the terms used, in various particular cases already highlighted by the literature: thus, the term routine is obviously a kind of transaction, just like the term communication, both mentioned above. Some semantic coverage may exist in the case of the term norm—but given that the norm is a potential rule that, if applied, would necessarily lead to transactions (from the most concrete to the most abstract), we can conclude that we do not have, in this case, an exception to the general applicability of the transaction term;
  secondly, in order to extract a (proposal for a) typology of symbolic social species, we obviously need at least one classification criterion. From a logical point of view, the choice of a classification criterion needs, in turn, a … criterion (of course, there is an *ad infinitum* regression here). As a result, we will consider that this classification criterion is the very nature of human activity in society—in other words, for every type of human activity of a social nature (e.g., personal reverie will not be considered a human social activity) it will be 'allocated' a symbolic social species;
  therefore, the general list of human activities of a social nature is as follows:
  theoretical activities: *object–object* relationship (refers to the action aimed at exclusively transcendent relationships; the subject is positioned externally and autonomously to objects,[38] and their focus is mainly in the form of objective knowledge—the active factor in initiating the activity is, of course, the subject);
    <u>symbolic social species</u>: *objective/phenomenological paradigms*—the term paradigm is considered here in the well-known sense given by Thomas Kuhn[39] but, obviously, having a much wider scope than the exclusively scientific one, as it is practiced by the mentioned author. Therefore, at the level of society, there may be several such species (several objective paradigms). It is obvious that this species retains the transactional character that calls the generic symbolic social species.

Nota bene: theories can be considered, ***mutatis mutandis***, either individuals of objective paradigms or sub-species within those paradigms. The rationale for this proposal is as follows: a paradigm 'brings together' under its auspices several theories which, however, have a common core (or, in any case, have sufficiently numerous and relevant interferences) to ensure the personality/uniqueness of the paradigm in question—this common core ensures that the theories contained in a paradigm can be considered as individuals of the species in question;

- example:
  - mechanistic/deterministic paradigm;
  - the evolutionary/institutionalist/autopoietic paradigm;
  - stochastic/random paradigm;
  - quantum/entangling paradigm and so on.

    Practical activities: *subject–subject* relationship (refers to the action concerning exclusively inter-subjective relations, without interference of objects, the latter remain passively in the background of these relations; the aim in question is manifested mainly in the form of social construction);[40]

    symbolic social species: ***relational/structural paradigms***—these paradigms build and re-build the normative structure of society (so-called basic structure) that provides the framework for its organization and functioning, allowing causality, stability, sustainability/replicability and control/piloting it, from the perspective of the social contract;[41]
- example:
  - liberal-democratic paradigm;[42]
  - dictatorial paradigm (which can be either liberal or non-liberal);
  - closed society paradigm;
  - open society paradigm and so on.

    Praxiological activities: *subject–object* relationship (refers to the interaction between subject and object/thing in the co-evolutionary process,[43] a process in which both the subject and the object undergo co-adaptive transformations; the targeting is manifested with especially in the form of the transformation of the non-anthropic environment according to the needs—first of all, the survival needs—of the subject, and in this case, the active factor in initiating the activity is the subject);

symbolic social species: *actional/drásistic paradigms*[44]—these paradigms are 'responsible' for the human–environment inter-action (the latter understood both as a non-anthropic environment and as an artefact environment). The main inter-action of this type is economic (or of economic-type[45]) inter-action, with its specific categories of sub-inter-actions (e.g., financial inter-action, which is of particular interest to us in this study);

- example:
  - paradigm of stationary action (of stationarity);
  - paradigm of optimal action (of optimality);
  - paradigm of sustainable action (of sustainability);
  - paradigm of viable action (of viability) and so on.

The Mechanism of Social Fitness Selection

The selection of social fitness depends, in its particularities, on the symbolic social species involved; therefore, in the following, we will examine the general case of the social fitness selection mechanism. We consider that the main structural and functional elements of such a mechanism are the following:

- the filter through which the social environment (i.e., cultural geodesic) will examine the nature and degree of social fitness of the individual of the symbolic social species in question is the *way of life* of this individual, as stated above;
- the fundamental element of the way of life of the symbolic social species is, of course, the *axiological compatibility* of that way of life with the cultural geodesic concerned;
- in principle, the verification of this axiological compatibility is relatively mechanical, because, in fact, the values that the society in question accepts, supports, promotes and defends are already specified (often and for the most part, explicitly verbal and formally codified) by the cultural geodesic related to the examined symbolic social species;
- consequently, also in principle, we consider that the testing of the way of life of the symbolic social species is of dichotomous[46] type (yes vs. no), without the possibility of intermediate degrees, possibly of fuzzy type,[47] of acceptability, respectively (by 'difference to 1') of refutability;

- the selection of social fitness remains, apparently, simply directed, only that the direction has a teleological character, included in the cultural geodesic (which is an artefact product 'endowed' with purpose or, in any case, with deliberately established values);
- as for the cumulative nature of social selection, it cannot be completely ruled out, because, even if the selected mutations may have a saltationist character, these mutations themselves can be extended additions over long periods of time, so, on a 'macro' scale, they also exhibit a cumulative character;
- unlike natural selection, social selection is reversible: this is a particularly important feature because it eliminates evolutionary rigidity in the social realm (a rigidity that is present in the non-symbolic living world, including the biological human individual). Of course, the reversibility of social fitness—which essentially means that once a social fitness has been selected by a geodesic, the subsequent, possibly radical enough, change of that geodesic can establish that the previously selected (accepted) fitness is, according to the new geodesic, rejectable.[48] Of course, the reversibility of the selection of social fitness is a serious praxiological and practical problem, as it greatly reduces the predictability of the human activity of the type to which the symbolic social individual (respectively the symbolic social species) belongs—while this predictability is one of the conditions for the very success of that social fitness;[49]
- regarding the sufficiency predicate of the way of life of the symbolic individual, called *replicability*, it is ensured together with the selection of the predicate axiological compatibility;
- a particular problem is the third predicate of sufficiency of *convertibility*: indeed, in this matter, cultural geodesic has no power, because the human individual, the one who designs the formation/variation of social fitness, presumed as rational (or, in any case, acting on the basis of a model of theoretical rationality, i.e., on the basis of a rational belief) will 'take care' that the fitness in question has this potential for convertibility, as described above. In fact, therefore, cultural geodesic, as stated above, only selects the axiological compatibility of the social fitness in question.

Based on the above, the selection of social fitness could take the synoptic form in Fig. 2.4.

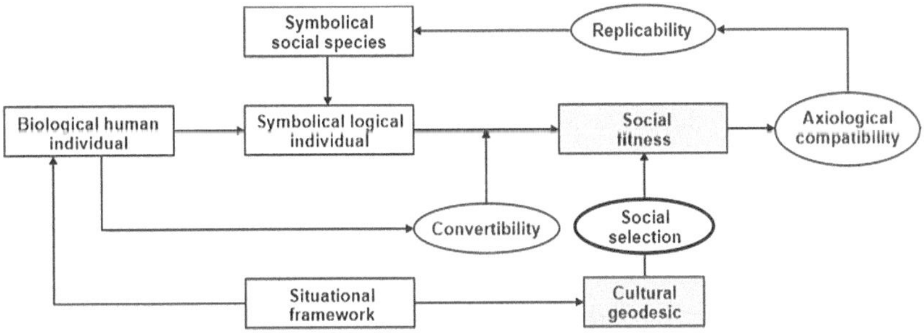

Fig. 2.4 Correlation human individual–symbolic individual: the social fitness selection. (*Source*: Authors)

Financial Market Models and Financial Fitness

Financial Market Models

The concept of the model, as it has gained 'citizenship' in the scientific community, is almost equivalent to that of theory—a set of theoretical/conceptual, methodological and instrumental principles, regarding a field of knowledge (in natural sciences, in spiritual sciences or in social sciences). In FMAB-APH, we presented the abstract/general aspects of the model and modelling of a domain of reality (Dinga et al., 2022). It is now useful to detail those general considerations for the particular case of the financial market:

1. *conceptually*, of the three categories of possible models (of discovery, of corroboration, of refutation), financial market researchers have constructed only corroboration/refutation models.[50] Although it is possible that in each researcher's personal laboratory, discovery models had also worked—absolutely idiosyncratic—they were not made available to the scientific community or, if they were made, they do not prove to be anything else than corroboration/refutation models;
2. *formally*, of the four classes of possible models (opaque/black-box, functional/evolutionary, behavioural/impact, decision/choice), two categories are proposed and used in the financial market analysis: (a) behavioural/impact models; (b) functional/evolutionary models. Thus, the Efficient Market Hypothesis (EMH) model is a behavioural/impact model: any available past information is necessarily embedded

in the price (or in the variable of interest in the financial market). The Behavioural Market Hypothesis (BMH)[51] model is also a model of this category. As for the Adaptive Market Hypothesis (AMH) model, it is a functional/evolutionary model. From a practical (more precisely, praxiologically) point of view, analysts—either theorists or actual players in the financial market—use many methods and techniques that, however, claim to be (or may be subsumed to) models or theories as such.[52] The hypotheses proposed by this research[53] are belonging to the category of models called functional/evolutionary;

3. from the point of view of the principles/axioms on which the financial market models are based, we can say the following:
   - even if they are sometimes conceptually diametrically opposed approaches,[54] financial market models are based, either explicitly or implicitly, on a single principle;
   - a brief examination of the two categories of models currently developed leads us to identify (or formulate, if we are dealing with an implicit treatment) the following principles or maxims.

Behavioural/Impact Models[55]

1. **EMH (Efficient Market Hypothesis)**: the fundamental principle is explicitly formulated by the initiator of the model (Fama, 1965): *the future price is independent of the past price, it is equal to the current price.* The basis of this principle lies in the very assumption of the informational efficiency of the (financial) market—all past information (available and of interest/impact) is necessarily, immediately and without cost integrated in the price (or in the command variable in the financial transactions in question).[56] All other behavioural/impact regularities of the model represent logical inferences from this principle (respecting, of course, the rules of valid inference).[57]
2. **FMH (Fractal Market Hypothesis)**: the fundamental principle is explicitly formulated by the initiator of the model (Peters, 1994): *the level of risk,*[58] *scaled at different time horizons, is the same.* One of the direct consequences[59] is that *the liquidity of the financial market is stable, that is, smooth and continuous*, which makes the frequency distribution of the market return the same for different time horizons. The foundation of this principle lies in what we can call (*Nota bene*: Peters did not provide such a wording) *the liquidity efficiency of the financial market*[60]—the large number and different waiting horizons of investors

ensure the smoothness and continuity of liquidity in the financial market.[61] Although Peters strongly insists that FMH rejects the Gaussian distribution associated with time series, a closer look will reveal a fissure in this insistence: the large number of investors (or players), as well as the large number of different waiting horizons (i.e., trading horizons), required for the operation of the fractal market hypothesis, involves, in principle (in the background), although indirectly, the hypothesis of perfect competition, that is, the phenomenal Gaussian distribution. However, FMH is much more empirically testable than EMH.[62]

3. **CMH (Costs Matters Hypothesis)**: this model was proposed by John Bogle (Bogle, 2005) who explicitly formulates its fundamental principle as follows:[63] *investors as a whole will gain the gross return of the total stock market before costs, but will share only the amount of that yield that remains after costs.* The model emphasizes the important fact that the success in the financial market depends not only on the return obtained (e.g., the price) but also on … the price of obtaining that return, that is, the cost involved in the transaction in question. In our opinion, this model is superfluous, only emphasizing one aspect of the cost–benefit analysis, which is, however, a commonplace in the investment decision. However, the CMH indicates a certain change in perspective in assessing the causality and conditionality of financial market behaviour:
    - *firstly*, it should be noted that, unlike EMH, CMH does not refer to the gross return (e.g., price) brought about by a financial market trading strategy, but to the net return, that is, the profit (difference between price and cost);[64]
    - *secondly*, this model is perfectly compatible with EMH (i.e., with the *homo œconomicus* model generated by neoclassical economic theory), although the author insists on the idea that CMH should replace EMH.[65] Consequently, the informational efficiency of the market is accepted, but the validation (or selection) of a certain trading strategy is no longer external (i.e., at the level of the financial market)—where, as a result of informational efficiency, economic agents are indistinguishable from each other from the point of view of price—but becomes internal, at the level of cost–benefit analysis of each economic agent;
    - *thirdly*, the model is consistent (but only superficially) with our proposal (see APH below) because *ex-post* cost–benefit analysis of each trading strategy will lead to a change in the cost associated with that trading strategy, in the sense of reducing it;[66]

- *fourthly*, based on the point immediately above, CMH interferes (but also superficially) with Andrew Lo's proposal (see below AMH), as the change in cost associated with a trading strategy that can only get the average market return will lead to a change in that strategy, that is, to a negative selection by the selector (*Nota bene*: as mentioned above, Lo considers the financial market itself as a selector, which introduces some logical inaccuracies regarding the evolutionary aspect);
- *fifthly*, the model is not continuously operational: for example, if there is no informational efficiency of the market,[67] there is no need to change the cost associated with the trading strategy in question (unless there is an improvement in the net return of that strategy, independent of the functioning of the market);
- CMH can be said to be a simple and credible explanation for the fact that EMH cannot function in a real financial market—thus representing the second argument, in addition to the Grossman–Stiglitz paradox, against the EMH model (*Nota bene*: there is, however, a significant difference between the two arguments—while the Grossman–Stiglitz argument highlights, especially, on the inconsistency, i.e., the self-contradiction of EMH, the CMH argument highlights the incompleteness of EMH).[68]

Functional/Evolutionary Models

1. **AMH (Adaptive Market Hypothesis)**: this model is (relatively) developed, in particular, by Andrew Lo (A. W. Lo, 2019), as a reaction, not too radical, to EMH, which he aspires to combine with behaviourism.[69] The fundamental principle of this model (not explicitly formulated by the author, however) can be the following (in our formulation): ***the price is dependent on the path (it has memory) and is established at the level of satisficing provided by the financial environment***. Some clarifying comments are needed here:
   - the concept of *satisficing* is that created by Herbert Simon from the combination of the terms *satisfy* and *suffice* or to a sufficient extent;
   - *satisficing* no longer represents a price level either at the *fair* or *fair best price* level or at the level of *best price*[70])—the latter involving optimization, that is, maximizing sales, respectively minimizing when buying—but represents the price that ensures, as a rule, the economic survival[71] of the agent in question (trader);[72]

- it is quite obvious that the formulation of the fundamental principle of AMH, as done above, leads, *prima facie*, also to the idea of an efficient market—that state of the market in which no one can get more from the market than s/he needs for survival. However, we urge the reader to notice a conceptual difference in market efficiency (or, equivalently, efficient market) between EMH and AMH: EMH refers to informational efficiency, according to its own fundamental principle, while AMH refers to behavioural efficiency.[73]

2. **APH (Adaptive Preference Hypothesis)**: this model is (the first of) the authors' proposal of the present research on the functioning of the financial market, by 'escaping' this functioning from the constraints of the *homo œconomicus* model and placing it in an evolutionary market paradigm (Dinga et al., 2022). However, unlike the AMH model, we also propose a structural mechanism—the variation of adaptive preference (generated by propensity in the form of proference), under the impact of the selection of symbolic social fitness made by cultural geodesic. The fundamental principle of this model can be formulated as follows: *the distribution of the financial market return on trading strategies primarily follows the distribution of the proference* (*Nota bene*: which obviously leads directly to the co-evolutionary concept and process in the financial market—where co-evolution takes place between the return on a trading strategy and the propensity that generated the preference for that trading strategy). We present some clarifications regarding this model:
    - although it seems to be a commonplace that the economic operator chooses on the basis of his/her own preference (as modelled as proference in our proposal), the qualifier *primarily* used in formulating the fundamental principle peremptorily shows that the cost–benefit analysis is secondary (or, if you will, complementary in logical and chronological order) to the proferential 'analysis';[74]
    - therefore, far from denying the rationality of choice or, more precisely, making the choice on the basis of a model of rationality, APH emphasizes even more on this rationality, indicating as its ground the very theoretical rationality, based on belief (or, in terminology used by us, on propensity that turns preference into proference), not the practical rationality, based on cost–benefit analysis;
    - obviously, the proposed model calls for a permanent interplay between theoretical rationality and practical rationality, which is, moreover, the essence of the hypothesis itself;

- this clarification is consistent with and underpins the construction of the behavioural efficiency of the financial market, as opposed to the informational efficiency proposed by neoclassical economic theory; not even AMH focuses on this key issue of economic decision-making, but in the financial market's choice of trading strategy.

3. **APMH (Autopoietic Market Hypothesis)**: this model is the second proposal that the authors make in the context of this research. The fundamental principle of this model could be formulated as follows: *the distribution of the return of the financial market on the trading strategies primarily follows the distribution of the replicability of the fitness of those strategies*. The following considerations develop, in a more analytical way, this fundamental principle:
   - APMH does not need either EMH or CMH to explain (justify) the distribution of return on active trading strategies in the financial market;
   - conceptually, APMH is part of the evolutionary model, like AMH, but unlike the latter, it goes beyond evolution (and even co-evolution), namely, it aspires to model the financial market as a self-evolutionary system or, using a term that appeared in biology but later extended to almost all fields of science that claims to be evolutionary, an autopoietic system;
   - the autopoietic model of the financial market takes over the self-organization, considered proper to biological systems and 'imports' it into the economy (Foster, 1997, 2021; Vromen, 2007). *Nota bene*: two crucial hypotheses are also retained for the functioning of economic systems/processes: the continuity hypothesis, respectively the autonomy hypothesis. Of course, this approach requires what has been called a generalized theory of Darwinism—all these elements, together with the concept of entropy and their interconnection, will be convened later;
   - the autopoiesis of the financial market requires two interconnected 'circuits' (although with a certain mutual autonomy) of validation/adjustment—one at the level of the phenotype–environment relationship, another at the level of the internal environment–external environment relationship.

Short Discussion

1. All financial market models, discussed above, aim at or relate to the efficient financial market or, equivalently, to the efficiency of the financial market—of course, each model comes with its own definition or significance of the attribute of efficient (or of efficiency), as follows:
   - EMH: information efficiency
   - FMH: scale efficiency
   - MHC: structural efficiency
   - AMH: behavioural efficiency
   - APH: adaptive efficiency
   - APMH: reproductive/replicative efficiency
2. With regard to testability (in the sense of factual falsification), we make the following statements:
   - testability can be ensured both from the perspective of theoretical rationality (or rational belief or simple belief, equated by us with the propensity that generates the proference) and from the perspective of practical rationality (equated by us with the cost–benefit calculation);
   - therefore, in order to be able to test, financial market models must provide at least a methodological anchor (either of the nature of theoretical rationality, or of the nature of practical rationality, or of both natures) that underlies the issuance/formulation of conjectures—which to function as predictions or predictive statements;
   - from this perspective of testability, the six models considered for the functioning of the financial market are characterized by the following:
     - *EMH*: this model is not testable—in its fundamental principle there is no reference to theoretical rationality or practical rationality. Moreover, the literature clearly notes this feature of the EMH model—that is, its empirical non-testability (Berk, 2008)—the underlying explanation for this non-testability is, of course, the very substance of the hypothesis underlying this model: a hypothesis not only unrealistic but, in many respects, erroneous;
     - *FMH*: this model is testable—on the basis of its fundamental principle, conjectures can be issued which, then, by careful organization of the experiment or observation,[75] can be either corroborated or rejected. It should be noted that the rationality on the basis of which it is possible to formulate predictive state-

ments is a practical one (it does not refer to the possibly rational beliefs of the economic agents);

- *CMH*: this model should logically be part of an extended EMH model that addresses the informational efficiency of the financial market not from the perspective of price (i.e., gross return), which has no meaning for the economic agent, but from the perspective of net income/gain—that is, the difference between price and cost. In the absence of this 'merger', the model is a warning of the need for a more in-depth analysis than that allowed for the exclusive examination of price. From the point of view of testing, we consider that the model is non-testable, because the fundamental principle, although aimed at practical rationality (cost–benefit calculation, in other words), does not offer the possibility of formulating conjectures that can be tracked and evaluated empirically;[76]
- *AMH*: this model is testable based on the arguments that any evolutionary model is testable. Its fundamental principle requires theoretical rationality, because satisficing is directly related to the (possibly rational) belief of the subject. Of course, from a technical point of view, designing, organizing, conducting and observing an experiment (whether *in vitro* or *in vivo*) require much more care for the correct capture of the co-evolutionary relationships that take place in the financial market. Although, in the vast majority of cases, the tests performed in the literature are also performed from a perspective that we can call 'objective' (i.e., one that focuses on facts, not behaviours), the model allows a test of behaviour, namely, by capturing the aspects of choosing second-best solutions;
- *APH*: this model is currently in its infancy (Dinga et al., 2022). However, its fundamental principle allows testing, from the perspective of a theoretical rationality, because the adaptation of preference is done by changing the propensity (i.e., as we proposed, the proference as dyad propensity–preference). Therefore, the formulation of conjectures (or predictions) should be made from the perspective of comparing distribution of the proference, with distribution of return of the financial market;[77]
- *APMH*: this model, as such, is just being developed in this book. However, the approach of autopoieticity in economics is quite rich in the literature, especially in the field of conceptual transfer

from biology, with the founding contributions of Maturana and Varela (Maturana & Varela, 1980). Its fundamental principle is claimed both in theoretical rationality (originating in belief or propensity) and in practical rationality (cost–benefit analysis—also at the level of second-best solution, as in the case of AMH or APH). Therefore, there is a wide possibility of formulating conjectures/predictions to test this model of the financial market.

Nota bene: the third model of the financial market, which will be developed by the authors of the present research (in addition to APH and APMII, respectively), namely, the *Natural Price Hypothesis* (NPH) will be (probably) the subject of another book.

Financial Fitness

The Concept of Financial Fitness

We have seen, previously, what social fitness essentially refers to, associated with the social phenotype that we have called with the general term of transaction. Now is the time to develop, in a more detailed way, the concept of financial fitness, as a logical species (or customization/application) of the concept of social fitness.

First of all, it must be said that to the symbolic social individual (or the symbolic social phenotype), we have called as transaction, corresponds, from the perspective of the financial market, the financial individual (we can add the predicate symbolic—that is, symbolic financial individual—if there is a risk of confusion). I called it trading strategy. Therefore, the phenotype (adult individual) of the financial market (as a symbolic species) exactly is the trading strategy.

Secondly, we have seen that generic social fitness is the way of life of the symbolic social individual, that is, of the transaction. Translating this result to the case of the financial market, we will have to specify, by particularization,[78] what is the meaning of the *way of life* phrase for the case of the financial phenotype. In order to limit (or eliminate) the connotations by which the expression way of life refers to the human (biological) individual and, therefore, to eliminate possible confusions between the biological human individual and the symbolic financial individual, we will replace the expression way of life, in the case of the financial market, with the expression *performative depth* (PD). In what follows in this paragraph, this will be the goal that we will pursue.

The Concept of Performative Depth of Financial Fitness

By performative depth (PD) of a trading strategy (TS) we mean its following capabilities:

- (*PD1*) compatibility[79] with the propensity of the human individual: this is a *proferential corroboration* and is defined as the efficient/efficacy cause of TS;
- (*PD2*) compatibility with cultural geodesic: this is a *normative corroboration* and is defined as the formal cause of TS;
- (*PD3*) positivity of the return captured from the financial market: this refers to the positive difference between the effect of TS and the effort (cost) of TS, represents a *factual/empirical corroboration* and is defined as the final cause of TS.

As the PD needs to be measured, we believe that we need to keep the following in mind in this regard:

- given the three benchmarks to be checked simultaneously, the PD of a TS can only be measured positionally. This means that a state vector will have to be constructed, dated and located (to ensure comparability in time, respectively comparability in space) of that positional vector;

$$PD_{ij}^{TS_k} = \begin{pmatrix} PD1_{ij}^{TS_k} \\ PD2_{ij}^{TS_k} \\ PD3_{ij}^{TS_k} \end{pmatrix}$$

where: *i* is a time (or moment) counter; *j* is a spatial (locality) counter; *k* is a distribution (assignment) counter;

- *PD1* and *PD2* are qualitative-type capabilities of TS, while *PD3* is a quantitative (or dimensional)-type capability;
- the qualitative capacities are of dichotomous/dyadic type (accepted–rejected, respectively yes–no), while the quantitative capacity is of a polyadic type (the positivity coefficient can take any real value);

- however, for computational reasons, $PD3_{ij}^{TS_k}$ may be subjected to a normalization process within the real range $[0,1]$, as follows:

$$\overline{PD3}_{ij}^{TS_k} = \frac{PD3_{ij}^{TS_k} - PD3_{\min}^{TS_k}}{PD3_{\max}^{TS_k} - PD3_{\min}^{TS_k}} = \frac{G_e^{PD3}}{G_{\max}^{PD3}}$$

where $\overline{PD3}_{ij}^{TS_k}$ is the normalized value of the value $PD3_{ij}^{TS_k}$; $PD3_{\min}^{TS_k}$ is the minimum value of the positivity coefficient; $PD3_{\max}^{TS_k}$ is the maximum value of this coefficient; G_e^{PD3} is the effective gap of $PD3_{ij}^{TS_k}$; $G_{\max}^{PD3}$ is the maximum gap of $PD3_{ij}^{TS_k}$.

Measuring Performative Depth: A Topological View
Therefore, financial fitness, measured by performative depth, has two components: (a) the nominal component—the cumulative verification of the predicates *PD1* and *PD2*, that is, the logical conjunction $\left(PD1_{ij}^{TS_k}\right)\Lambda\left(PD2_{ij}^{TS_k}\right)$; (b) dimensional component—verification of the predicate *PD3* ($PD3_{ij}^{TS_k}$). While the nominal component *absolutely* selects a certain TS (either as corroboration or rejection), the dimensional component makes a *relative* selection. As discussed previously, this relativity can be examined from two perspectives or, more precisely, by referring to two benchmarks: (1) the average of the financial market (i.e., the financial species whose individual is the trading strategy, whose position dated and localized is the individual transaction); (2) the best competitor (champion) in the financial market. From the perspective of the dimensional component of the performative depth, we have, therefore, a wide range of positions of a certain economic agent (more precisely of a trading strategy), in relation to each of the two mentioned benchmarks.[80]

If we operate with non-normalized values of performative depth, then we have the following possible gaps, from the perspective of *PD3*:

- non-normalized gap with the market average:

$$G_{e/med}^{PD3} = PD3_{ij}^{TS_k} - PD3_{med}^{TS_k}$$

where

$$PD3_{med}^{TS_k} = \frac{1}{n} \cdot \sum_{k=1}^{n} \left(PD3_{ij}^{TS_k}\right)$$

- non-standard gap with the best competitor (champion) on the market:

$$G_{e/c}^{PD3} = \max_k \left(PD3_{ij}^{TS_k} \right) - PD3_{ij}^{TS_k}$$

We can also build the normalized values:

- normalized gap with the market average:

$$\bar{G}_{e/med}^{PD3} = \frac{PD3_{ij}^{TS_k} - PD3_{med}^{TS_k}}{G_{\max}^{PD3}}$$

- normalized gap with the best competitor (champion) on the market:

$$\bar{G}_{e/c}^{PD3} = \frac{\max_k \left(PD3_{ij}^{TS_k} \right) - PD3_{ij}^{TS_k}}{G_{\max}^{PD3}}$$

A graphical picture of the concept and measure of the performative depth of financial fitness is shown in Fig. 2.5 (notations were made: E1—non-survival positioning; E2—tense positioning; E3—indifferent positioning; E4—successful positioning).

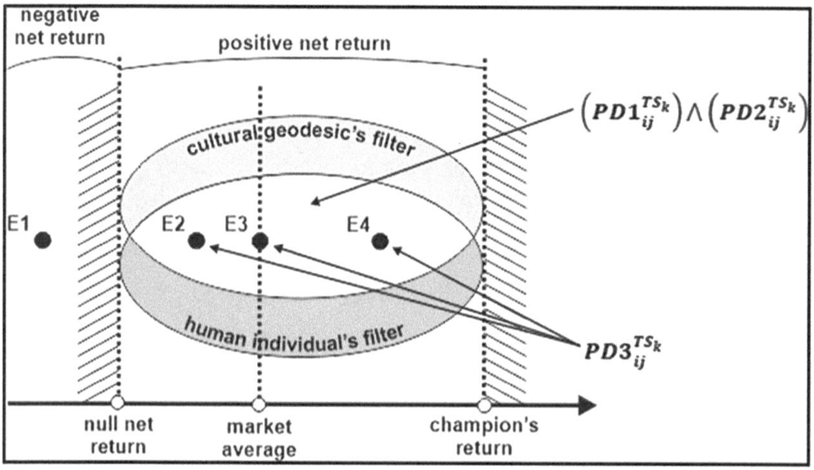

Fig. 2.5 A conceptual topology of the performative depth of financial fitness. (*Source*: Authors)

Typology of Financial Fitness

A typology of financial fitness is of the greatest importance and relevance in the perspective of the following research, dedicated to the construction of the APMH hypothesis. In the following we make a proposal regarding this typology.

Financial Fitness Classification Criteria

First of all, it should be noted that all the predicates of sufficiency of symbolic social fitness (hence also of financial fitness) act to establish the fitness class in question. Therefore, a first classification criterion must be the *predicates of sufficiency* of financial fitness.

Secondly, if the 'decision' of classification is dichotomous with respect to the predicates of sufficiency *PD1* and *PD2*, we will have to adopt a non-dichotomous impact on the classification of the predicate of sufficiency *PD3*.

Thirdly, a second criterion for classifying financial fitness should be *the trend*. Although, *prima facie*, examining the trend from the perspective of financial fitness classification seems relatively superfluous (because static classification might be considered as sufficient), our view is that a kinematic classification is not only simply complementary to static classification, but contains an obvious logical necessity. We put forward some arguments in support of this view:

- from one point (or static position) a fitness can develop either negatively (by decreasing the performative depth) or positively (by increasing this depth) or to show an inertial tendency to maintain the position. Therefore, it is relevant which of the three trends the fitness in question is located on, so it is not enough to know its static position;[81]
- in the competitive economic game in the financial market, three characteristics of financial fitness are important, from a kinematic perspective: (a) direction (and orientation/sense) of change, (b) speed of change and (c) acceleration of change. Therefore, a given fitness must be able to be associated with these three parameters, in addition to the static positioning;[82]
- we have shown, above, the relevance of the kinematic parameters of a given fitness, from the perspective of the fitness in question (i.e., of the reflexive or temporal comparability). But this relevance is maintained also from the perspective of spatial (non-reflexive) compara-

bility, that is, comparability with other fitness, possibly statically positioned at the same point. It can therefore be rightly said that two fitnesses, relative to two different trading strategies (or the same fitness at two different times), are not equivalent (or identical) only if they occupy the same static position from the perspective of performative depth, but also requires kinematic evaluations.

Based on the above, we propose the following criteria to classify the financial fitness:

1. (*PO*) the criterion of ***propensive organicity***: refers to the verification/non-verification of the compatibility of fitness with the propensity of the human agent in question—that is, refers to the first compatibility filter (an internal compatibility filter);
2. (*CO*) the criterion of ***cultural organicity***: refers to the verification/non-verification of the compatibility of fitness with the valid/operational cultural geodesic at that moment—that is, refers to the second compatibility filter (an external compatibility filter);

Nota bene: these first two criteria may together form the ***nominal eligibility*** criterion for financial fitness, as suggested above by the logical conjunction $\left(PD1_{ij}^{TS_k}\right) \wedge \left(PD2_{ij}^{TS_k}\right)$.

3. (*SP*) the criterion of ***static positioning***: refers to the performative depth of financial fitness, as this concept was introduced above. It is a distributive criterion, unlike the first two criteria which, being nominal, are not distributive. This criterion includes two sub-criteria:
   - 3.1. (*SPm*): sub-criterion of static positioning compared to the *market average*;
   - 3.2. (*SPc*): sub-criterion of static positioning towards the *market champion*;
4. (*KP*) the criterion of ***kinematic positioning***: it also refers to the performative depth, but not from a distributive perspective, but from a vectorial one. This criterion contains three sub-criteria:
   - 4.1. (*KPd*) sub-criterion of the direction/direction of financial fitness (ascending vs. descending);

4.2. (*KPs*) sub-criterion of financial fitness speed (derived from the first order of the financial fitness function is positive/negative in relation to time);
4.3. (*KPa*) sub-criterion for accelerating financial fitness (the second-order derivative of the financial fitness function is positive/negative over time).

Financial Fitness Classes

Based on the proposed classification criteria, we will now proceed to identify the eight classes of financial fitness that may, in theory, exist:[83]

- (class *F1*): *erroneous* (or inauthentic) financial fitness—that financial fitness that violates the *PO* criterion. The term erroneous refers to the fact that it is not inferred—more or less rationally—from propensity, that is, it is not an effect of the proference;[84]
- (class *F2*): *non-compliant* (or illegal) financial fitness—that financial fitness that violates the *CO* criterion. The term non-compliant refers to the fact that it is not compatible or consistent with cultural geodesic. The name illegal is also a proper name, because the norms contained in the cultural geodesic constitute the normative framework of the society in question, that is, its legal/positive structure;[85]

Nota bene: classes *F1* and *F2* will not enter into the following discussion because they are not eligible, either in terms of their authenticity or in terms of their legality.[86]

- (class *F3*): *risky* financial fitness—that financial fitness which, from the perspective of the *SPm* criterion, is located in the negative zone of the net return in the financial market:
  - (subclass $F3^{+}$): risky, *positively oriented* financial fitness—that risky financial fitness that tends to approach, from left, to the net zero return;[87]
  - (subclass $F3^{-}$): risky, *negatively oriented* financial fitness—that risky financial fitness that tends to move away, to left, from zero net return;
  - (subclass $F3^{0}$): risky, *unfocused* financial fitness—that risky financial fitness that is stationary (inertial) in the occupied risky position;

- (class *F4*): ***indifferent to zero*** financial fitness—that financial fitness that is exactly at the point where the return of the trading strategy in question equals the cost incurred to form and implement that strategy:
  - (subclass $F4^+$): financial fitness regardless of zero, ***positively oriented***—that financial fitness regardless of zero that has the tendency to move to right from the position occupied;
  - (subclass $F4^-$): financial fitness regardless of zero, ***negatively oriented***—that financial fitness regardless of zero that has a tendency to move to left from the position occupied;
  - (subclass $F4^0$): financial fitness regardless of zero, ***non-oriented***—that financial fitness regardless of zero that is stationary (inertial) in the zero-occupied position occupied;
- (class *F5*): ***underperforming*** financial fitness—that financial fitness that is in the positive net return area but does not yet get the average financial market:
  - (subclass $F5^+$): underperforming, ***positively oriented*** financial fitness—that underperforming financial fitness that tends to move to right from the underperforming position occupied;
  - (subclass $F5^-$): underperforming, ***negatively oriented*** financial fitness—that underperforming financial fitness that has a tendency to move to left from the underperforming position occupied;
  - (subclass $F5^0$): underperforming, ***non-oriented*** financial fitness—that underperforming financial fitness that is stationary (inertial) in the occupied underperforming position;
- (class *F6*): ***regardless of average*** financial fitness—that financial fitness which, from the perspective of the *SPm* criterion, is positioned at the level of the market average:
  - (subclass $F6^+$): financial fitness regardless of average, ***positively oriented***—that financial fitness regardless of average that tends to move to right compared to the financial market average;
  - (subclass $F6^-$): financial fitness regardless of average, ***negatively oriented***—that financial fitness regardless of average that tends to move to left compared to the average financial market;
  - (subclass $F6^0$): financial fitness regardless of average, ***non-oriented***—that financial fitness regardless of average that is stationary (inertial) in the position indifferent to the occupied average;

- (class *F7*): ***competitive*** financial fitness—that financial fitness that is placed with a performative depth above the market average and, of course, below the value associated with the market champion:
  - (subclass $F7^+$): competitive financial fitness, ***positively oriented***—that competitive financial fitness that tends to move to right from the position occupied;
  - (subclass $F7^-$): competitive financial fitness, ***negatively oriented***—that competitive financial fitness that tends to move to left from the position occupied;
  - (subclass $F7^0$): competitive financial fitness, ***non-oriented***—that competitive financial fitness that is stationary (inertial) in the occupied competitive position;
- (class *F8*): ***maximal*** financial fitness—that financial fitness that is at the fitness level of the financial market champion:[88]
  - (subclass $F8^+$): maximal financial fitness, ***positively oriented***—that maximal financial fitness that tends to move to right from the champion position;
  - (subclass $F8^-$): maximal financial fitness, ***negatively oriented***—that maximal financial fitness that tends to move to the left from the champion position;
  - (subclass $F8^0$): maximal financial fitness, ***non-oriented***—that maximal financial fitness that is stationary (inertial) in the maximal position occupied.

Figure 2.6 provides a synoptic representation of the financial fitness typology.

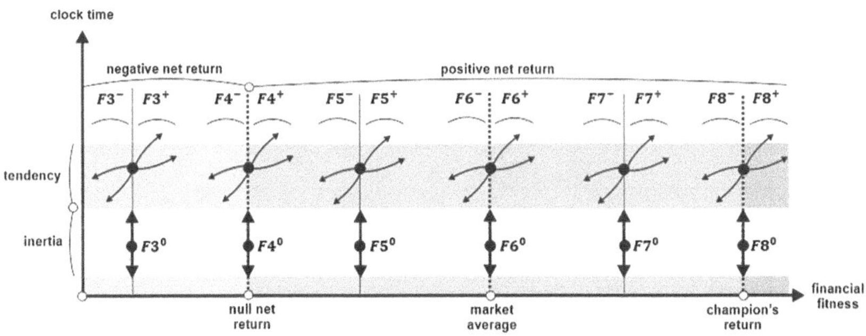

Fig. 2.6 A conceptual typology of the performative depth of financial fitness. (*Source*: Authors)

Short Discussion

- Both the left shift (with negative significance) and the right shift (with positive significance) of the financial fitness positions of a given trading strategy can take place either accelerated (concave curves) or decelerated (convex curves);[89]
- of course, a position occupied by a given (observed) financial fitness can show inertia, that is, it can be maintained, at least for a period of time—this inertia is represented in the form of 'movements' (up-down) exclusively on the time axis.

'Assigning' Financial Fitness Classes to Financial Models

The financial fitness classes established above are of general abstract applicability. However, it is useful to examine how these classes are compatible with the six financial market models identified in this study. In this context, in Table 2.1 there is proposed such an 'allocation' of the (possible) financial fitness classes in the financial models in question.

Table 2.1 Financial fitness classes and financial market models

		Financial market models					
		EMH	FMH	CMH	AMH	APH	APMH
F1							
F2							
F3	*F3*$^+$						
	F3$^-$						
	F3^0						
F4	*F4*$^+$						
	F4$^-$						
	F4^0						
F5	*F5*$^+$						
	F5$^-$						
	F5^0						
F6	*F6*$^+$						
	F6$^-$						
	F6^0	?					
F7	*F7*$^+$						
	F7$^-$						
	F7^0						
F8	*F8*$^+$						
	F8$^-$						
	F8^0						

Source: Authors

Nota bene: The compatibility between the financial fitness class and the financial market model is expressed by shading the intersection cell of the line with the corresponding column, the sign '?' expresses indecision about this compatibility, and non-completion of the cell means incompatibility between the financial fitness class and the financial market model.

Notes

1. The evoked authors call natural selection with the expression ecological selection, in order to distinguish it from social selection. They probably want to say what we proposed in the main text, namely, natural selection is 'conferred' by the non-co-specific component of the environment and social selection is 'conferred' by the co-specific component of the environment—this because, conceptually, any selection is ... ecological, that is, it is exerted/realized by the environment of the focal phenotype under analysis.
2. Which we also did, separating the financial market environment into two components: normative geodesic, respectively operational geodesic (see above).
3. Quantitative aspects are generally based on equations derived from the Price equation (i.e., using statistical covariances).
4. This means that we will not examine the force and mechanism of social selection that is exerted on the human (biological) individual but those that are exerted on the social individual—the latter can take different 'forms': individual or economic phenotype, individual or political phenotype and so on. Given the specifics of our research, the focus of the analysis will be the financial individual, that is, the trading strategy, which is part of the symbolic species called financial market.
5. We mention them here: (a) deleting; (b) modifying; and (c) adding.
6. The problem of distinguishing between causes and conditions is still disputed in the literature. In our opinion, the conditions (favourable or inhibiting, as the case may be—*Nota bene*: neutral conditions are obviously superfluous, here) must enter, logically, into what is called a ***multiple cause*** or, perhaps more properly expressed, ***general cause***. In Annex 1.1 we present an opinion developed in this matter by one of the authors of this study (Dinga, 2014).
7. The basic interactions with individuals of other species (called by us trans-specific interactions) are (a) cooperation interactions and (b) competition interactions. Of course, in reality, the two types of interactions are not 'pure', but always represent combinations between them, sometimes dominating the interactions of the type of cooperation, sometimes those of the

type of competition. For example, if there are enough resources (of any kind), then the interactions of cooperation (or sometimes mutual 'ignorance' will predominate), and, if the resources become scarce, then the interactions of competition will predominate. These clarifications are valid, *mutatis mutandis*, for both co-specific and trans-specific interactions (*Nota bene*: as in the case of human society, increasing the danger of cross-specific competition can strengthen co-specific cohesion, and vice versa, reducing that danger can strengthen co-specific competition—perhaps a more appropriate term for co-specific would be intra-specific).

8. From a logical point of view, the problem of tautology arises here: indeed, the pre-selection conditioning (e.g., some norms do not allow, from a legal point of view, some trading strategies, to use the field in which this study is made, therefore, when applying social selection to *ex-ante* permitted trading strategies, exactly these strategies will be found, so the social selection in question is superfluous or pointless). In reality, however, the *ex-ante* conditioning of the selection cannot 'solve' all the problems of social fitness, on the one hand, and, on the other hand, there are always cases of ineffectiveness of the *ex-ante* conditioning of the selection—simply, some individuals of the symbolic species considered ignore that conditioning, of course taking the risk based on a cost–benefit analysis (in the way in which Gary Becker approached these issues).
9. Social selection is symmetrically exerted on any symbolic species considered, of course, but in Fig. 2.1 we considered mainly species A and, more precisely, the focal individual 1/A.
10. As can be seen, most of the quantitative approaches in the literature on social selection use exactly algebraic additionality, without, therefore, taking into account the synergistic effects. Of course, quantitative modelling of synergy is particularly difficult, requiring special assumptions which, in turn, need to be tested—see, here, the significance of Duhem-Quine's thesis on testing and empirical testability—but the results of considering the synergy effect can bring many scientific benefits, especially in terms of veracity.
11. We remind you that cultural geodesic contains both positive (codified) norms and informal norms, such as traditions, customs and morals.
12. For example, if the norm in cultural geodesic requires that the product sold be produced by the seller himself, s/he can import the subassemblies of the product, which s/he then assembles, gives them the certificate of origin on the final product and thus falls under the letter of the norm.
13. A particular marginal analysis can even lead to 'maximizing' the net gain from practicing this non-compliance (Gary Becker would be delighted with the idea!).

14. As we mentioned above (see note 12), a norm that is not general enough is called privilege—but the privilege is forbidden from the point of view of legitimacy.
15. Even if, almost always, the human individual is integrated in micro-communities (family, socio-professional group, locality, etc.), these integrations occur on the basis of psychological and/or economic-social affinities, so, in the last resort to a representative (or average) individual.
16. Rationality models refer to belief (s) or, with a term we have adopted throughout the research, to the propensity of the human individual (*Nota bene*: the propensity that is shown in preference has been called, as we remember, proference).
17. We recall that our proposal in this issue was the concept of implicit information, that is, information that is acquired not by the analyst (as in the case of Samuelson's revealed preference) but by the economic agent participating in the market (financial in our case)—way to acquisition is the inference of the information in question, based on its own hermeneutic device (which can be, e.g., a model of rationality), from the behaviour of other economic agents on the market.
18. In fact, the previous two predicates of sufficiency of social fitness refer more explicitly to the symbolic individual (or symbolic species).
19. At no moment or point in the discussion did our research refer to the social selection of the human individual (an extremely delicate and difficult issue from many perspectives), but to the social selection of the financial individual (symbolic individual, even if it is an artefact of human individual).
20. The selection (evolution) of the human individual refers to fitness traits of biological nature, while the selection (evolution) of the symbolic individual refers to fitness traits of a symbolic nature.
21. From an abstract point of view, even if, in most cases, without explicit verbal wording, expectations are focused on high layers of Maslow's pyramid of needs—some (psychologists, sociologists or anthropologists) call it social recognition, others (political scientists or political philosophers) call it power.
22. Of course, exceptions are not ruled out (which in this case even confirm the rule in a genuine way): this is what is called, in slang, 'cannons'—actions/strategies that are operated only once, under exceptional conditions, with extraordinary effects, too (see the financial operations carried out by George Soros or Warren Buffett).
23. The idea of replicability (although not using exactly this term) in the evolutionary ideas ventilated in the field of economics is not new. As early as 1985, Richard R. Nelson and Sidney G. Winter introduced, in their work *An Evolutionary Theory of Economic Change* (a somewhat ... pleonastic title), the concept of *routine*, operated at the level of the organization, in

the sense of procedure (either technological, managerial or cultural) which is repeatedly applied under the rule of the selection operated by the market on it.

24. With a slightly rebarbative expression, this is a connection between the transcendental of propensity and the transcendent of selection (of cultural geodesic).
25. The main human group that is formed in society from the perspective of the dynamics of cultural geodesic is of the type of political party—but, of course, also refers to other structures of civil society (*Nota bene*: political parties are also structures of civil society—NGOs) which have their role, more or less direct/explicit in this dynamic.
26. The (only) predominant character results from the fact that cultural geodesic also includes many emerging elements/components, caused by the 'impersonal' functioning of society (see, e.g., the invisible hand, which acts not only in economics—at the suggestion of Adam Smith—but also, in general, in the society.
27. From a conceptual point of view, cultural geodesic, together with its basis—the Constitution—forms the situational framework of a society. This is the meaning in which, throughout our research, we have said that cultural geodesic is an 'emanation' of the situational framework. The situational framework, moreover, can be considered a propensity (or a proference) of substrate, that is, a fundamental base of a certain society.
28. In societies where the president (head of state) is one of the components of executive political power.
29. For the moment, we refer to the society as a whole, and we will later customize the entire discussion on the case of the financial market (or the financial field of the society).
30. In the evoked paper, three other categories of symbolic social species phenotypes are proposed (*Nota bene*: the syntagm *symbolic social species* seems pleonastic because, as we said, symbolic species can only be artefacts, i.e., can only be generated within the social inter-action: we add, here, in our 'defence', that, in reality, there may be a category of symbolic species, specific to the human individual, but which no longer has a proper social character, although it still contains a strong social conditioning: these are individual or, more specifically, personal, idiosyncratic symbolic species: e.g., productions specific to the individual/person and which are not yet shared with other members of the community; in other words, we are dealing with 'individuals' or 'species' in Popper's second world, who 'inhabit' the psychic world and who may or may not migrate to Popper's third world, that is, in the world of inter-subjective objectification, from to which belong all of symbolic social species), namely, (1) *thought*, in the

psychic field; (2) *idea*, in the field of theory; (3) *way of doing*, in the field of praxiology (or of the actional paradigm).

31. *Prima facie*, such a term refers to the idea of economic exchange (which is the common, 'civil' meaning of the term in question), so here we will present a brief 'defence' in the matter: (a) the transaction denotes (has as reference) any inter-action between two non-solitary individuals (i.e., an inter-action in their quality as members of a society), which allows any nature of such a transaction (*Nota bene*: for example, there is a prestigious scientific publication of the British Royal Society, called ... *Philosophical Transactions*—established in 1665); (b) the conversation is often considered a verbal transaction (i.e., an interaction); (c) the transaction can be defined, in the most general way, as a *quid pro quo*.
32. But, of course, also of any society of imaginable living beings.
33. Here is a kind of primacy of the relationship in relation to thing, respectively in relation to property—in a way, the relationship generates both property and even thing (since we are talking about symbolic species, i.e., artefacts).
34. We must not particularize on this point until we assume an impact of equal quantity and opposite sign on those parts of the transactional event (as does, e.g., the theory of zero-sum games—*Nota bene*: the correct name is, in our opinion, games with zero amount of mutual impacts). We should probably even weaken the condition, namely, to stipulate the existence of a non-zero impact on at least one of the trading parties.
35. We mention here a problem discussed in cosmology, in connection with the principled upper limit of light passing through an empty space. So, the question is: does a thought that 'arrives' right now on the star Proxima Centauri (located about four light-years away from our planet) travel through that space at a super-light speed? The answer is that it must be shown that the thought actually reaches the star in question, and the proof for that is of an empirical type (in the terminology we use here, it is of the ... transactional type): namely, it must be proved that the thought that reaches there produces a small disturbance of the target, that is, produces a non-zero impact (in this case only to one of the 'parties' involved).
36. Recall that, for example, in the economic field, a market-type exchange (such as selling/buying) of a good against currency, even if we consider an equivalent exchange (provided that a fair or natural price works), is not neutral in terms of impact—the two utilities exchanged (good, respectively currency) produce different marginal utilities for the two parties (we leave the demonstration of this result to the reader).
37. Our opinion on solving this problem is only outlined here, and a thorough treatment will be done in another context.
38. In literature, especially in philosophy, objects are also called things.

39. A *modus operandi* of a scientific community that acts, both in terms of principles and procedures/methodology, dogmatically, within normal science (*Nota bene*: the property of dogmatic refers to non-critical positioning, from the point of view of reflective view of the paradigm in question—in FMAB-APH (Dinga et al., 2022), this issue is discussed in detail, in connection with financial market theories/models).
40. We specify that by the phrase *social construction* we mean the generation of culture in the narrow sense of the term, that is, of spiritual culture, which does not include civilization, as the latter is understood from the perspective of a material culture. We recall that the idea of social construction, as a result of purely subjective inter-action, is a commonplace in social philosophy and epistemology.
41. As this concept was built by Rawls, Nozick (1994), Sen and Nussbaum (following Locke, Rousseau and Kant).
42. Even today (including some states in the European Union) attempts are being made to combine iliberalism with democracy.
43. Of course, in relation to the object, in the first instance, the relationship also occurs between the subjects, but the final goal is not the relationship between the subjects (this is the middle, so to speak) but the acceding to the object, in this case, the transformation of the object. A more analytical examination of the three categories of relations discussed in this paragraph, from the perspective of a typology of science (but the analysis can be generalized for the case of a typology of paradigms), is given in Annex 1.2.
44. The name drásiste comes from the term (gr.) δράση (drási) which means action.
45. We do not insist here with semantic details on the concept of economic, we only emphasize that its essence (its eidos) is the entropic exchange with nature. This predicate of sufficiency (which is also a predicate of necessity) distinguishes the economic relationship in society from any other type of human relationship with nature.
46. Note that, also in natural selection, the selection of social fitness is also done in dichotomous mode, even if, in the case of this type of selection, we have a cumulative (i.e., gradual) selection—namely, accepting a small degree of variation is also done in *yes* versus *no* (or, with an economic game equivalent: all or nothing).
47. The fuzzy theory is a polyvalent logic (but with a set of truth values of the power of the continuum, included in the range of real numbers [0,1]—i.e., having the cardinal $\aleph_1$), proposed by Lotfi A. Zadeh in 1965. On its basis has also developed a fuzzy algebra (which also contains the related arithmetic), as well as other research directions: fuzzy semantics, fuzzy probability and so on.
48. This includes institutional reforms, either autonomous in relation to symbolic species or as an effect of the latter.

49. For example, in the case of fiscal-budgetary geodesic, it is forbidden for the amendment of a norm to enter into force earlier than six months after the announcement of that change. Of course, other conditionalities can be imposed, so that the number of cases of reversibility of the selection of social fitness is minimized.
50. It should be noted that the distinction between corroboration models and refutation models is somewhat pedantic, because a model that has the ability to corroborate hypotheses has, *eo ipso*, and that of refutation. Popper's falsifiability implies either one result or another (but it never implies an indecision—if we disregard the Duhem–Quine thesis, according to which we cannot, in principle, have an undoubted decision from factually testing a hypothesis/conjecture).
51. Which, in our opinion, is not completed in a 'round' form (*Nota bene*: based mainly on perception, we believe that the phenomenological approach should be the methodological basis of such a model).
52. All the 'circulating' variations in financial theory and analysis can be subsumed under one of the two approaches. Thus, the so-called fractal approach to the financial market (*Nota bene*: some even call it the Fractal Market Hypothesis—FMH, a name we also used here), introduced by Edgar E. Peters in 1994 (*Fractal Market Analysis: Applying Chaos Theory to Investment and Economics*, Wiley), is an extension of EMH, trying, like the latter, to identify predictors in the 'hope' that the kinematics of the financial market (more precisely of the records in the time series in question) behave fractally—it should be noted that we are dealing here, in fact, with a chaotic approach, in the sense of chaos theory, of the functioning of the financial market. It should be noted also that the fractal approach is maintained in the neoclassical 'paradigm' of economic theory. Even the famous Black–Scholes model is based on martingale (or fair game theory), that is, it proceeds similarly to EMH. In essence, all these techniques (in addition to CAPM—Capital Asset Pricing Model—as well as Modern Portfolio Theory) built under the 'umbrella' of neoclassical economic theory are claimed from the principle of equilibrium (imported from mechanics Newtonian) (Dinga, 2021) and presupposes the equivalence between investment and speculation, maintaining the analysis of the financial market in the gaming area (Peters, 1994).
53. Our research proposes two new hypotheses (or models) of the financial market: (a) Adaptive Preference Hypothesis (APH)—see FMAB-APH (Dinga et al., 2022); (b) Autopoietic Market Hypothesis (APMH). In fact, as it will turn out, the second hypothesis incorporates the APH one, the latter becoming not a particular case, but a logical/behavioural sequence of the autopoietic hypothesis.
54. And, by the way, metaphysical.

55. Some authors (Lo, 2019) consider that the theory of rational expectations (the concept of rational expectation was introduced by Muth in 1961) is part of … the paradigms of the financial market (theory). In our opinion, although EMH seems to verify the criteria of the model *qua* paradigm (see FMAB-APH), we consider that the theory of rational expectations which, like EMH, is a necessary consequence of neoclassical economic theory, based on equilibrium, has a lower scope than required by a paradigm (*Nota bene*: however, the equilibrium theory is a paradigm). As is well known, the theory of rational expectations (*Nota bene*: in our opinion, it should be called the theory of rational anticipations) has at least four deviations from its own assumption (Lo, 2019): (a) aversion to loss; (b) overlap on probability—that is, on the behaviour of the environment (see, here, our proposal on implicit information); (c) the law of small numbers; (d) heuristic representativeness (introduced by Kahneman).
56. As we have said before, the typology of market informational efficiency (weak, semi-strong, strong) is not relevant here, although, from an empirical perspective, the testability may be different in the three cases.
57. The logic considered here is a bivalent epistemic logic, with two values of truth: true and false, respectively.
58. The author maintains the standard deviation as a risk measurement variable, although he also points out that this indicator varies faster than the square root of time (standard deviation is the square root of the variance, which is actually considered to 'generate' volatility). It should be noted that, unlike the EMH model, the FMH model is testable empirically in the exact way in which it formulates its guiding principle (*Nota bene*: logically, for a financial market model to be scientific—i.e., empirically testable, which is the same thing—the guiding principle, or, alternatively, a 'theorem' inferred from this principle, must allow the experiencing or experimentation, as the case may be, of the conjecture in question). *Nota bene*: this conjecture has, of course, the form of a prediction (predictive statement).
59. Which can therefore also be a field for issuing conjectures for factual testing.
60. Such liquidity efficiency is fractal due to the self-similarity of the frequency distribution of the return of the financial market to different time horizons (or waiting horizons) of investors.
61. This phenomenon is in turn based on the essential feature of the fractal model of the financial market, namely, that there is, at all times, a structural functional combination between microeconomic (local) randomness and macroeconomic (global) determinism. *Nota bene*: obviously, this idea is an application of the Prigoginian principle of the generation of order (macroscopic aspect) from fluctuations (microscopic aspect).

62. One of the most convenient conjectures that can be made here is to change the frequency distribution of the return, when the distribution of time horizons becomes uniform (i.e., market liquidity decreases). This does not mean, *eo ipso*, that FMH is a paradigm—in fact, verifying that it is (or is not) a paradigm is a next research task of authors.
63. In original: *Investors in aggregate will earn the gross return of the total stock market before costs, but share only in the amount of that return that remains after costs.*
64. In this context, it may be interesting to examine the issue of financial market efficiency in terms of cost—for example, the question may be asked: how does the financial market trend towards its informational efficiency in terms of price and its informational efficiency in term of cost?
65. He says, *expressis verbis*, that in the analysis of the financial market, we do not need EMH but ... CMH.
66. The superficial aspect of this consistency (or, rather, similarities of ... family) consists in the following: while, in the case of CMH, it operates with practical rationality, in that of APH it operates with theoretical rationality (*Nota bene*: but, as known, any practical rationality implies a theoretical background rationality).
67. As is well known, the informational efficiency of the market is 'forbidden' by the Grossman–Stiglitz paradox.
68. From another perspective, it can be said that the Grossman–Stiglitz argument examines the functioning of the EMH from inside, while the CMH argument examines the functioning of the EMH from outside.
69. In this regard, Lo is ambiguous: sometimes he says that AMH makes a mix between EMH and behaviourism, other times he states that AMH is a generalization of EMH. In our opinion, EMH with any theory that leaves the canons of neoclassical economic theory (such as behaviourism) are ... conceptually immiscible. However, behaviourism, in itself, is compatible with an evolutionary approach, as AMH is trying to do.
70. As we will see later, the fair price can be equated with the natural price, that is, the price generated by economic fundamentals.
71. The informed reader will immediately find here Smith's concept of *natural price*, at which we will refer in a (possible) vol. 3 of this research, focused on the natural economic values and their modelling.
72. It is obvious that, through this assertion, we have already created at least one extremely difficult problem (which Simon also faced in his time): how do we determine the level of satisficing if we do not have a benchmark? This benchmark could have been the optimal (i.e., a first best) level. If this is no longer possible (of course, from the perspective of the economic operator, not the financial market observer/analyst), then we need a criterion external to the financial market (but one of the unintended conse-

quences of looking for such an external benchmark is the introduction, almost necessary, of the elements of social justice, which, in a predominantly positivist analysis—at the stage of which we are at the moment—introduces possible insurmountable complications). This is a fundamental reason why financial market theories (and economic theories in general) should be based on political economics, not positive economics.

73. In fact, we believe that the very replacement of informational efficiency with behavioural efficiency essentially expresses the basic pattern of our research.
74. We can identify, here, a very interesting aspect regarding the economic choice, namely, that this choice is one of the type of theoretical rationality, not practical. Indeed, the theory of choice shows that theoretical rationality is based on belief (*Nota bene*: some authors consider that these are rational beliefs, based on justification or justifiability, while practical rationality is based on calculation) (Welton, 2012).
75. *In vivo* observation is also called a *natural experiment*.
76. Perhaps a theoretical and methodological effort to combine EMH with CMH would be much more productive than trying (only announced, not yet realized, in our opinion) to combine EMH with AMH (or, even, only with behaviourism).
77. Either the gross return or the net return, according to the most relevant significance in the context of the particular experiment considered.
78. As is well known, particularization (or speciation or individuation, as appropriate) is obtained by adding at least one predicate of sufficiency in addition to the genus (or species) against which the species (or individual) is particularized.
79. Of course, this qualitative requirement can be supplemented, on a case-by-case basis (especially in conditions of … internal competition between the trading strategies of a given human individual), by degrees of compatibility which, for example, we might call *degrees of propensive adherence*.
80. It is implicit that both the financial market average and the best competitor in the financial market refer exclusively to the trading strategies that have already verified the nominal component of the performative depth.
81. The usefulness of assessing the dynamic position of financial fitness is addressed not only to the analyst, but also to the economic agent in question, respectively to the economic agents co-participating in the transactions in the financial market. We recall, for example, that our proposal on the concept of implicit information (information inferred by economic agents from observing/interpreting the behaviour—decision, respectively action—of other financial market participants) is based precisely on the possibility to identify not only the static behavioural position of these other participants, but also that of identifying trends in their behaviours (usually in the short term).

82. In the short term, the parameters in question are quite relevant even in the form of constants, but, obviously, the identification of functions of dynamics of the parameters in question raises the financial analysis to a higher level. The identification of such functions is all the more necessary (and relevant) as, for example, speed and acceleration can be determined using (for the continuous case) first-order and second-order derivatives, respectively (or, for the discrete case, absolute differences of order 1, respectively order 2).
83. Please note that all fitness is considered from the perspective of the net gain brought by the trading strategy whose fitness is examined (i.e., from the perspective that integrates CMH).
84. One important point to note here is that an erroneous fitness is not necessarily a 'bad' fitness—for example, it can be in any of the positions around the market average (including at the level of the market champion). The term erroneous refers only to the fact that the fitness in question has no justification/'rationality' in the context of the proference of that economic agent. Consequently, all the following financial fitness classes can be both erroneous fitness classes and non-erroneous fitness classes.
85. See note immediately above, *mutatis mutandis*.
86. In a simple logical formalization, we have, for a given financial fitness, from the perspective of nominal eligibility, the following cases: (a) non-compliant fitness: $\left[\left(\overline{OC}\right)\wedge\left(\overline{OP}\right)\right]\vee\left[\left(\overline{OC}\right)\wedge\left(OP\right)\right]$, when the OC criterion is violated; (b) erroneous fitness: $\left[\left(OC\right)\wedge\left(\overline{OP}\right)\right]\vee\left[\left(\overline{OC}\right)\wedge\left(\overline{OP}\right)\right]$, when the OP criterion is violated; (c) non-compliant and erroneous fitness: $\left[\left(\overline{OC}\right)\wedge\left(\overline{OP}\right)\right]$, when both criteria are violated.
87. In empirical analysis, this trend can be examined, of course, from the perspective of the speed, respectively the acceleration with which the financial fitness in question approaches the average of the financial market—here we do not develop this analysis.
88. Here is a problem that we will only enunciate, without making a more in-depth examination of it: the maximum (champion) value of fitness in the financial market can be seen either from an empirical perspective or from a theoretical perspective. From an empirical perspective, it is about the maximum financial fitness actually reached by a certain trading strategy operated on the market, while, from a theoretical (or potential) perspective, it is about the financial fitness that can/could be achieved. Of course, given that our research avoids abstract evaluations of the *homo œconomicus* model, we only consider the maximum financial fitness from an empirical perspective.
89. We take into account that the dependent variable is represented on the abscissa, so the association of the convexity (respectively concavity) with the abscissa is inverse than if the dependent variable is represented on the ordinate (usual case).

References

Berk, J. B. (2008). *A Critique of the Efficient Market Hypothesis*. University of California, Berkeley, and NBER.

Bogle, J. C. (2005). The Relentless Rules of Humble Arithmetic. *Financial Analysts Journal, 61*(6), 22–35.

Dinga, E. (2014). *Correlation and Causality. Revista OEconomica, 1.*

Dinga, E. (2021). Institutionalism as a Species of Evolutionism. *Management of Sustainable Development, 13*(1), 49–54.

Dinga, E., Oprean-Stan, C., Tănăsescu, C. R., Brătian, V., & Ionescu, G. M. (2022). *Financial Market Analysis and Behaviour: The Adaptive Preference Hypothesis.* Routledge & CRC Press.

Dinga, E., Tănăsescu, C.-R., & Ionescu, G.-M. (2020). Social Entropy and Normative Network. *Entropy, 22*(9), 1051.

Fama, E. F. (1965). The Behavior of Stock-Market Prices. *The Journal of Business, 38*(1).

Foster, J. (1997). The Analytical Foundations of Evolutionary Economics: From Biological Analogy to Economic Self-organization. *Structural Change and Economic Dynamics, 8*(4), 427–451.

Foster, J. (2021). In Search of a Suitable Heuristic for Evolutionary Economics: From Generalized Darwinism to Economic Self-organisation. *Munich Personal RePEc Archive (MPRA), 106146*, 24.

Lo, A. W. (2019). *Adaptive Markets: Financial Evolution at the Speed of Thought.* Princeton University Press.

Luhmann, N. (2012). *Introduction to Systems Theory.* Wiley.

Maturana, H., & Varela, F. (1980). *Autopoiesis and Cognition. The Realization of the Living.* D. Reidel Publishing Company.

Nelson, R. R., & Winter, S. G. (1985). *An Evolutionary Theory of Economic Change.* Harvard University Press.

Nozick, R. (1994). *The Nature of Rationality.* Princeton University Press.

Peters, E. (1994). *Fractal Market Analysis: Applying Chaos Theory to Investment and Economics.* Wiley.

Vromen, J. (2007). *Generalized Darwinism in Evolutionary Economics: The Devil Is in the Details.* Papers on Economics and Evolution, No. 0711, 1–27.

Welton, D. (2012). Bodily Intentionality, Affectivity, and Basic Affects. In D. Zahavi (Ed.), *The Oxford Handbook of Contemporary Phenomenology.* Oxford University Press.

Wolf, J. B., Brodie, E. D., III, & Moore, A. J. (1999). Interacting Phenotypes and the Evolutionary Process. II. Selection Resulting from Social Interactions. *The American Naturalist, 153*(3), 254–266.

CHAPTER 3

Autopoietic Market Hypothesis: The Concept of Autopoiesis

Autopoiesis—A Propaedeutic

The Concept of Biological/Natural Living

Basic Considerations

The elaboration of the concept of the living is a problem still quite controversial in the literature. Of course, such a concept could not be developed except from the perspective of the perception of the human body, as it is possible on planet Earth, and having as prototype the biological living (BL) which is based, as we know, on carbon.[1] Although the concept of biological living is not an objective of this research, we will make a small analysis of it to create a basis for discussing the defining of logical/symbolic living. Specifically, we will try to establish the predicates of sufficiency that can conceptually separate the living[2] from the non-living, at the biological level.

In our opinion, the predicates of sufficiency (*PS*) of biological living (*BL*) are the following:

- $\left(PS_1^{BL}\right)$ physical membrane, which separates the living entity from the environment

This predicate of sufficiency refers to the distinction[3] to be made between the biological living system (hereinafter *BLS*) and its

E. Dinga et al., *Economic and Financial Market Behaviour*,
https://doi.org/10.1007/978-3-031-31702-6_3

environment. The consequence of its operation is that *BLS* is always 'visible' as being exclusively within a physical boundary. Of course, there may be systems of systems in the case of *BLS*, that is, more and more comprehensive membranes, in which lesser comprehensive membranes enter, which generates hierarchies of organisms that are increasingly complicated structurally and functionally, but, as we mentioned, it is always possible that *BLS* can be inventoried by tracking physical membranes.[4] Although, in some cases, *BLS*s may be indistinguishable from each other, even then their distinct existence is (or may be) 'proven' by the very existence of the membrane.

- $\left(PS_2^{BL}\right)$ functioning away from thermodynamic equilibrium

This predicate of sufficiency is the fundamental,[5] crucial predicate of biological living. The thermodynamic equilibrium of a system refers to its entropic state. Specifically, the thermodynamic equilibrium is obtained when the entropy[6] of the system in question is maximum. As is well known, the second law of thermodynamics 'requires' that, in a closed system, the entropy be permanently increasing (consequently, it never decreases and is not even invariant and, as a consequence, its increase is irreversible). However, there are systems (and this is obviously exactly *BLS*) that not only do not reach or remain in the thermodynamic equilibrium state, but even move away from it or stay away from it once they have moved away from it. This is achieved by the property called ***dissipativity***,[7] which ensures the extraction of negative (low) entropy from the environment and the dissipation of positive (high) entropy into the environment.[8] Moreover, the property of self-organization (culminating in the concept of autopoieticity) is, in turn, a logical consequence of this predicate of sufficiency.

- $\left(PS_3^{BL}\right)$ identitary self-replicability

This predicate of sufficiency refers to the property of a system to contain internal principles (devices, structures, functions, etc.) capable of replicating that system in a (quasi) identitary way. In the case of *BLS*, it is the DNA–RNA structures that contain the information (chemically encoded) about the identity of the system and which, through a specific process,[9] replicates the system in an (almost) identical one,[10] not in its final form, but in one which develops programmatically, necessarily, in the direction of reaching that final form which is identical with the form which caused the replication. One of the logical consequences of this predicate of sufficiency is the concept of development, which means a process that the new individual appeared through replication goes through to reach the stage at which, in turn, it can replicate itself.

- $\left(PS_4^{BL}\right)$ cognitive-reactive capacity in relation to the environment

In examining this predicate of sufficiency, we must first say that the term cognitive or cognition[11] is considered here in the sense given to it by Humberto Maturana and Francisco Varela (Maturana & Varela, 1980), that is, it refers to the ability of a *BLS* to adapt to its environment. A logical consequence of this predicate of sufficiency is that of a double capacity of *BLS*: sensitive capacity, that is, perception[12] of environmental actions/reactions, respectively reactive capacity (of any kind) through which *BLS* responds (by reaction) to environmental actions/reactions.

Therefore, the logical formalization of the definition of the concept of biological living is as follows:

$$BLS \leftarrow \left(PS_1^{BL}\right) \Lambda \left(PS_2^{BL}\right) \Lambda \left(PS_3^{BL}\right) \Lambda \left(PS_4^{BL}\right)$$

In connection with this definition, there are at least three issues that will be assessed, briefly, at the end of this paragraph: (a) the issue of automata; (b) the problem of crystals; (c) the problem of the distinction between cognition in general (in the sense of the Santiago school, i.e., on the line established by Maturana and Varela) and the cognition of the human being.

(a) The problem of automata

The automata check three of the four predicates of sufficiency of the living: $\left(PS_1^{BL}\right)$—they are delimited by the environment through a physical membrane;[13] $\left(PS_3^{BL}\right)$—they can be programmed to replicate/reproduce themselves (there are, e.g., factories where robots/automatons work to produce ... robots/automata); $\left(PS_4^{BL}\right)$—automata can obviously be made sensitive to the environment (of course, in the sense of the concept of cognition proposed by the Santiago school). However, automata do not check the second predicate of sufficiency $\left(PS_2^{BL}\right)$—they do not function far from thermodynamic equilibrium, that is, they are not dissipative systems regarding thermodynamic entropy. As the sufficiency predicates must be checked cumulatively, it follows that the automata are not *BLS*s.

(b) The problem of crystals

Crystals have been (and still are) the subject of intense scientific discussion about the possibility of being considered living beings. The phenomenon that has generated, in particular, these debates is that of growth: put in the right conditions, the crystals grow like a living entity. Note, however, that among the predicates of the sufficiency of biological living, there is none that refers to growth.[14] It can be easily shown that, as in the case of automata, the crystals check only three of the four predicates of sufficiency—they do not check the same predicate $\left(PS_2^{BL}\right)$.

(c) The problem of human cognition

It is obvious that Maturana and Varela have proposed such a broad concept of cognition (or cognitive ability) that this includes any potential, however small, of reactivity, that is, adaptation to the environment. In the sense of this meaning, cognition exists everywhere in nature.[15] We will discuss, in this context, two issues: (i) the concept of cognition and (ii) the specificity of human cognition (more precisely, of the cognition associated with representation).

(i) Adjusting the concept/term of cognition

Cognition, as a term for general reactivity (or, equivalently, for general ability to interact[16] with the environment), does not imply the meaning. An entity that is sensitive to the environment and has the ability to adjust its behaviour (or, sometimes, only its state[17]) in relation to (or in response to) what is perceived as an action/reaction of the environment does not make an interpretation of which is noticeable, although obviously, in regional cases, such an interpretation is also made. We propose to introduce, at this point in the discussion, the pair of necessity-contingency concepts. In our opinion, a necessary reactivity to the action/reaction coming from the environment is a state-modifying reactivity, while the contingent reactivity is a behaviour-modifying reactivity. If we agree to give the concept of sensation or sensory capacity a very wide sphere of reference, then perhaps it would be more appropriate to replace the term cognition (in the sense of Santiago school) with the term *cogsation*.[18]

(ii) The peculiarities of human cognition

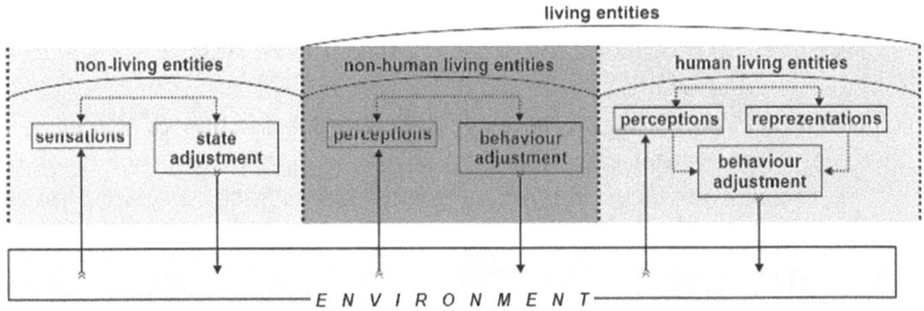

Fig. 3.1 Sensation, perception and representation in the cognition matter. (*Source*: Authors)

Human cognition is, of course, a species of cognition as it is defined, as a genus, by the Santiago school. Its main feature is that it moves from perception to representation, through two psychic instances that are present only in the case of organisms considered (in terms of brain capacity and function) as 'superior': the intellect (which generates the concepts from perceptions), respectively reasoning (which generates judgements from concepts). It is obvious, from the context just described, that, in the case of the human being, we are dealing with giving meaning (first of all, the meanings of veracity—true vs. false) to the sensations that come from the environment. Before making some further considerations in the matter, we present, in Fig. 3.1, an overview of the typology of cognition.

Therefore, the difference between human being and the non-human living, from the perspective of the concept of cognition, is of degree, not of quality, which largely justifies the generality of the concept of cognition, proposed by the Santiago school and which is 'glued' of the concept of autopoiesis which we will discuss in detail in the following.

The Nature of BLS

One of the issues that is still discussed in the literature, although more from a philosophical perspective (more precisely ontological, so metaphysical), is the nature of a *BLS*—is it a substance (e.g., a cell), or a state/property (e.g., excitability), or a process (e.g., growth or replication)? Our position on this issue is as follows:

- *BLS* is a taxonomic species, of an ontological nature, with a real and objective character;[19]

- instead, the living or, more precisely, livingness is a property, which is therefore assignable to different categories of systems (in the case discussed above, biological systems were considered);[20]
- therefore, the living is a broader logical category than *BLS*, that is, it is a property that can describe also the livingness of other types of systems (*Nota bene*: further, we will discuss such another type of system, namely, living systems in a logical sense or, equivalently, in the symbolic sense);
- from the way *BLS* was defined, it follows that it is a substantial-energy unit (here the term energy is used in its comprehensive sense, that is, associated with the concept of entropy). From this perspective, a *BLS* is consistent, albeit in a still informal way, with the suggestion of the theory of special relativity that mass/substance and energy are equivalent.[21]

The Concept of Logical/Symbolic Living

Basic Considerations

We will abbreviate the logical/symbolic living system by *LLS* (logically living system). As in the case of *BLS*, we will look for the predicates of sufficiency that could define, by their conjunctive cumulation, this type of entities. A 'mirror' examination, parallel to that performed in the case of *BLS*, can only be helpful. Therefore, we consider these predicates to be the following:

- $\left(PS_1^{LL}\right)$ membrane that separates the living entity from the environment

A *LLS* must be, like the *BLS*, distinct from its environment because otherwise it is indistinguishable from the environment and, as a result, it logically does not exist. Therefore, this predicate requires the existence of a membrane, but it no longer has to be, of exclusive necessity, of the physical type, although it can also be physical. Thus, we extend the sphere of possible membranes that can separate an entity (a system) from its environment, accepting any type of membrane[22] that achieves such a distinction or observability. We mention that the distinctiveness, ensured by the membrane, is considered from a criterial perspective, which means that there must be at least one operational criterion based on which to perceive (in the phenomenological sense or, at least, psychologically one) the distinction in question.[23]

- $\left(PS_2^{LL}\right)$ dissipative functioning

This predicate of sufficiency is analogous to the functioning away from the thermodynamic equilibrium (*Nota bene*: see, here, the well-known concept of Prigogine) of *BLS*. It implies the following peculiarities, however, with respect to $\left(PS_2^{BL}\right)$:

- it is integrated into and interacts with the environment also from an entropic perspective, but it is a behavioural entropy, while in the case of *BLS* we are talking about a thermodynamic entropy or an energetic entropy;[24]
- the concept of behavioural entropy (hereinafter BE), which we introduced (Dinga et al., 2021) regarding the functioning of the financial market, must now be generalized to refer to any *LLS*. We consider that a description of this concept, sufficient for its inclusion in the discussions that follow in this study, could have the following coordinates:
- maintaining a range of choice from the perspective of *LLS* on the interaction with its environment. This coordinate has the following procedural significance: a system has a certain cognitive capacity[25] on the basis of which it perceives the action/reaction of the environment, exerted on it. Perception is then the basis of *LLS* action/reaction and this cycle resumes indefinitely as long as the system in question is working;[26]
- the larger this range of choice (which can also be formulated as follows: the higher the number of degrees of behavioural freedom), the smaller the *LLS* entropy and vice versa;
- it should be noted that this definition is perfectly compatible with both the definition of thermodynamic entropy (we can say: the higher the temperature gradient between the elements of a system, the lower the thermodynamic/energetic entropy and vice versa—*Nota bene*: at zero gradient, entropy in question is maximum) and the definition of informational entropy (we can say: the more probabilities in Shannon's formula have different values, the lower the informational entropy—*Nota bene*: at equal values, the entropy in question is maximum);[27]
- conceptually, even in the case of behavioural entropy, it can be said that the entropy and homogeneity[28] of the system in question are

directly proportional, more precisely, they have a directly proportional kinematics;

- however, the assessment of the behavioural entropy of a given system only on the basis of its property (in our case: the property of having 'access' to that range of choices[29]) seems to ignore the fact that the range of choice available to the system does not depend only on cognitive and reactive capacity of that system, but also of the general relationship between system and environment. At this point in the discussion, we will introduce the concepts of observability, accessibility and controllability,[30] both from the perspective of *LLS* and from the perspective of its environment;[31]
- *observability* of an entity is not an absolute concept, it must always be related to the entity called the observer—in this case, observability is the property of an entity to produce sensations (sensitive variations) in the observer, so it is a relative concept. Of course, this implies a certain sensational[32] compatibility between the observed and the observer, namely, a compatibility between the ability of the observed to present/suffer variations and the observer's ability to notice these variations;
- *accessibility* of the variation of the observed represents a property also generated by the relationship between the observed and the observer, regarding the closing of the 'chain' of action/reaction. Specifically, from the set of sensational variations of the observed that are observable from the perspective of the observer, only for a part of this set the observer will have reactions. The reasons for this restriction are very different: either the observer has no reason to react (e.g., s/he has no interest if it is a human individual who observes a change in the price in the financial market) or s/he does not have the capacity (resources) to react—for example, it needs a longer reaction time than the one required by the observed aspect—or it makes an error in reacting. Therefore, accessibility has a smaller choice range (at most equal) to the observability choice range;
- *controllability* of the observed variation represents that property (generated by the observed–observer synergy) that allows the kinematic fetality of the 'action/reaction–reaction' pair between the observed and the observer, which implies the continuation of this process from the perspective of a *win–win*[33] final result. Obviously, the requirement of controllability restricts, in turn, the range of accessibility;

- consequently, it can be said that behavioural entropy is, in principle, subject to the condition of *OAC* (observability–accessibility–controllability). The 'thread' of a behaviour that reduces entropy can be 'broken' from the perspective of any of the three conditionalities. Of course, the experience gained by the human individual (which is, as we have shown, the ultimate/ground support of *LLS*[34]) as well as the existence and use of formal rationality models greatly reduces the risk (or likelihood) of excessive narrowing of successive ranges of choice we have spoken before;
- the dissipative phenomenon, in the context of the concept of behavioural entropy, can be described as follows:
- *first of all*, we must remember that we have three types of behavioural entropies: (a) at the level of observability, (b) at the level of accessibility and (c) at the level of controllability;[35] if we denote by BE^O: behavioural entropy related to observability, BE^A: behavioural entropy related to accessibility, BE^F: behavioural entropy related to controllability/fetality, then, from the perspective of set theory, we can write:

- $BE^F \subseteq BE^A \subseteq BE^O$

from which, obviously:

$$BE^F \cap BE^A = BE^F$$

$$BE^F \cap BE^O = BE^F$$

$$BE^A \cap EB^O = BE^A$$

$$BE^F \cup BE^A = BE^A$$

$$BE^F \cup BE^O = BE^O$$

$$BE^A \cup BE^O = BE^O$$

secondly, the reduction of a type of behavioural entropy (by extending the range of choice) does not necessarily imply an extension of the type of behavioural entropy contained in the reference, although it does neither necessarily prevent such an extension;

thirdly, the reduction of a type of behavioural entropy necessarily implies the reduction of the type of behavioural entropy in which it is referentially content. Thus, if we denote by $BE_{\downarrow}^{(x)}$ the decrease of the behavioural entropy of type (x), respectively with $BE_{\uparrow}^{(x)}$ the increase of the behavioural entropy of type (x), respectively with $BE_{\leftrightarrow}^{(x)}$ the stationary behavioural entropy of type (x) (where $x \in \{O, A, F\}$), we can write the following formal relations:[36,37]

$$BE_{\downarrow}^{(O)} \rightarrow \left(BE_{\downarrow}^{(A)}\right) \vee \left(BE_{\leftrightarrow}^{(A)}\right)$$

$$BE_{\downarrow}^{(A)} \rightarrow \left(BE_{\downarrow}^{(F)}\right) \vee \left(BE_{\leftrightarrow}^{(F)}\right)$$

$$BE_{\downarrow}^{(O)} \rightarrow \left(BE_{\downarrow}^{(F)}\right) \vee \left(BE_{\leftrightarrow}^{(F)}\right)$$

$$BE_{\uparrow}^{(A)} \rightarrow \left(BE_{\uparrow}^{(O)}\right) \vee \left(BE_{\leftrightarrow}^{(O)}\right)$$

$$BE_{\uparrow}^{(F)} \rightarrow \left(BE_{\uparrow}^{(A)}\right) \vee \left(BE_{\leftrightarrow}^{(A)}\right)$$

$$BE_{\uparrow}^{(F)} \rightarrow \left(BE_{\uparrow}^{(O)}\right) \vee \left(BE_{\leftrightarrow}^{(O)}\right)$$

In connection with the predicate of sufficiency PS_2^{LL}, the question arises regarding the relation between the internal behavioural entropy of *LLS*—let us denote it with $BE_{LLS}^{(x)}$—and the internal behavioural entropy of the environment—let us denote it with $BE_{E}^{(x)}$. As is well known, in the case of *BLS's* specific thermodynamic (energetic) dissipation, maintaining or reducing the internal entropy of *BLS* is due to the faster[38] increase in the environmental entropy of that system. Let us examine this aspect from the perspective of behavioural entropy:

(i) *firstly*, let us see what kind of entropy is the behavioural entropy. This issue is relevant because, depending on the qualification that could be made, the concerned functionality can also be designed. Thus, it can be said that thermodynamic/energetic entropy is *transactional* (*BLS* 'changes' negative entropy, which it receives from the environment, with positive entropy, which it sends to the environment), while behavioural entropy is *relational* (*LLS* confronts his cognitive capacity, on the one hand, and the choice range, conditioned by *OAC*, offered by the environment, on the other hand);[39]
(ii) *secondly*, and based on the previous qualification of behavioural entropy, let us see if the phenomenology of behavioural entropy

needs to involve a closed system, as it happens in the case of thermodynamic/energetic entropy. Our opinion is as follows:

- as not involving transaction (or, more generally, transactionality), behavioural entropy does not 'aspire' to a homogenization of a given system (within which there may exist, of course, different subsystems, together with their associated environments);
- moreover, if, in the case of thermodynamic/energetic entropy, the system can exist independently of its environment—to which it is closed both substantially, energetically and informally—in the case of behavioural entropy, this entropy does not make sense, as we have shown, unless the system is related to its environment (which obviously can be considered, in turn, as a system against which the considered system is an environment);
- in conclusion, behavioural entropy necessarily presupposes, as a *conditio sine qua non*, precisely the openness of the system in question;

(iii) *thirdly*, it can be shown (we will do this later in this study) that in the case of behavioural entropy, the system and its environment co-evolve. Moreover, the previous formal–logical relations regarding the kinematics of behavioural entropy unambiguously suggest precisely this co-evolutionary phenomenology.

- $\left(PS_3^{LL}\right)$ identitary replicability

We believe that this predicate should be modified in the case of an *LLS*, which should be given the possibility of identitary replication, but not exclusively that of identitary self-replication. Therefore, in the case of an *LLS*, it can (must) be replicated (either by external principles or by internal principles—as in the latter case, in autopoiesis—or by a combination of the two categories of principles[40]). As in the case of the predicate PS_1^{LL} , here too we are dealing with an extension of the scope of the corresponding predicate of *BLS*, because identitary self-replicability is obviously a kind of identitary replicability. Based on this predicate of sufficiency, the following conclusions can be drawn:

- the replication of an *LLS* is a decisional, that is, deliberative replication (compared to the *BLS* replication, in which case the replication is non-decisional/non-deliberative[41]), namely, it occurs as a result of a pre-existing justification for the replication itself. Usually such a justification is inferred from a model of rationality, that is, based on a deliberative pair 'purpose–means';

- as it results from the extension/generalization of the replication concept, replication can be performed both as a result of an internal decision (in which case we have self-replication[42]) and as a result of an external decision. The self-replication of *LLS* has a feature that is not found in *BLS*: the immortality of *LLS*. *LLS* self-replicates exactly by its operation. This type of replication is radically different from *BLS* replication, as follows:

  replication of a *BLS* necessarily involves another membrane-distinct replicator entity,[43] whereas in the case of *LLS* replication does not refer to another membrane-distinct replicator entity but, as we shall see below, to the replicator itself;

  it is not useful to introduce, for the case of *LLS*, a concept parallel to the life cycle, that is specific to *BLS*, and which is denoted by the term generation—in the sense that *BLS* replication is of the type of generational replication. The reason for this uselessness is that, in the case of *LLS*, the replicability, and, therefore, the replication, is 'distributed' in the current functioning of that *LLS*: as long as it works according to the procedures in force (which we will refer to in detail later), exactly through this functioning the *LLS* in question is reproduced.[44] We note, therefore, that there are two differences between *LLS* and *BLS* in terms of replicability or replication: (i) in the case of *BLS*, replication is of the quantity type, while in the case of *LLS*, replication is of the quality type; (ii) in the case of *BLS*, the (complete) replication requires a duration (reaching the replicator stage—phenotype, which is called development), that is, it is duration-dependent, so we have to do with a non-reflexive replication, whereas in the case of *LLS*, (complete) replication does not need such a length, because the replicator and the replicate coincide, they are concomitant, thus dealing with reflexive replication, which excludes the development process in this latter case;

  a curious (but logically necessary) consequence is that, in the case of *LLS*, the indistinguishability between replicator and replicate, evoked above, makes the idea (and process) of replication somewhat vague. In other words, the performing of the *LLS* replication is somehow presumed until the 'contrary evidence', that is, until the moment when the *LLS* functioning ceases.[45] We have, here, as it seems, a phenomenon of continuous replication (or continuity of replication). The idea of continuous replication (not to be confused with permanent replication, because we also have permanent replication in the case of *BLS* although, in the latter case, replication is obviously discontinuous or discrete) is very interesting and can be useful in modelling quantitative changes in the evolution of *LLS*;[46]

- *LLS* does not manifest the phenomenon of growth, at least not in the sense that this phenomenon is encountered in *BLS*. *LLS* is able, from the very moment of its genesis, both to function at its maximum parameters and to reproduce (as shown below) precisely by this func tioning. The non-existence of growth (as well as the non-existence of development) is a crucial difference from *BLS*, which we will take into account in examining the autopoieticity of *LLS*;[47]
- given the (observational, perceptual) indiscernibility between replicator and replicate, the question arises: to what extent is this indiscernibility maintained? In other words, is there a threshold above which that replication loses its identity? Let us take an example: suppose that the *LLS* examined is an institution, for example, ANAF.[48] The functioning of the institution in question indicates to us, as stated above, that the associated *LLS* (identitarily) replicates itself every time it function. Now, suppose there is a refinement of the fiscal control methodology (and procedures) in order to increase the efficiency of the institution. So, the institution is still functioning, that is, is it still replicating, but do we still have an identitary replication? When we move from the old methodology to the new, improved one, do we still have to deal with the same institution? The issue deserves some special comments:

  the issue of identity also arises in the case of *BLS*, of course, not with regard to generational replication, but with respect to the development of the phenotype. Thus, it is known that all the cells of a biological living individual are replaced in a certain duration—is the individual resulting from this replacement still identical to the existing individual before the replacement? The question is relevant, first of all, from a philosophical point of view, but it is also significant from an anatomical-physiological point of view and even (in the case of *BLS*s endowed with psychic experience) from a psychological point of view;

the solution comes from the call to the structure. Since the functions are generated by the structure (a principle accepted in the case of *BLS* and which is consistent with the paradigm of natural evolutionism[49]), our opinion is as follows: as long as the structure remains unchanged, regardless of differences in structural components (differences that cannot be radical, since the same functions[50] must be provided), replication remains identitary, so the loss of identitary character of replication (for both *BLS* and *LLS*) occurs only when the structure itself changes,[51] case in which we have also non-identity at the functions or functioning level;

therefore, in line with the previous discussion on the non-existence of growth in the case of *LLS*, a pseudo-growth (generated by structural change) that would exceed a certain threshold of significance would, *eo ipso*, lead to a change of identity—we therefore have to deal with another *LLS* that, in turn, is an adult individual, capable of immediately replicating of the new identity.

$\left(PS_4^{LL}\right)$ cognitive-reactive capacity in relation to the environment

For the general case, which we are discussing here, for the time being, the concept of cognition will retain the significance given to it by the Santiago School, that is, the most general significance of sensitivity of any kind (from purely vegetative one to ones which involve perception). However, for the *LLS* case, some clarifications are needed:

- both the cognitive and reactive capacity of *LLS* are deliberately determined by the human individual (which is a species of *BLS*);[52]
- as a result, these capabilities (which are themselves in a co-evolutionary relationship) are subject to programmatic variations, either of the discretionary type or of the automatic type;[53]
- the question arises whether this deliberative nature of the establishment and variation of the cognitive/reactive capacity of *LLS* extends (or can be extended) also to the environment of the system in question. In this regard, our opinion is as follows:

  most of the environment of an *LLS* is of the *LLS* nature, because the functioning of the society is, in part (but more and more extensive, as the society develops more both from a cultural point of view and from a civilizational perspective), a functioning of the artefacts relationship. Consequently, the environment of an *LLS*

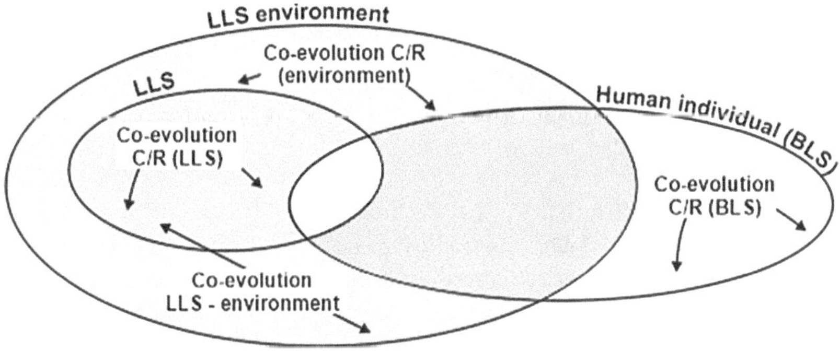

Fig. 3.2 Four co-evolutions in LLS functioning. (*Source*: Authors)

will have, predominantly, cognitive-reactive capacities of a deliberative nature;

therefore, usually, when the cognitive-reactive capacity of an *LLS* varies, it varies, in a correlated way (more or less, depending on the competence of the human individual or individuals involved in the introduction of these variations) the cognitive capacity-reactive of the environment of that system as well.[54]

Figure 3.2 provides an image of the four possible (and necessary) co-evolutions in the case of *LLS* (with *C* the cognition was noted, with *R* the action/reaction was noted).

Short Discussion

(i) The human individual can be in three hypostases at the same time: (a) integrated in *LLS* (e.g., as an economic agent in the financial market);[55] (b) integrated in the *LLS*'s environment (e.g., as a regulator of the functioning of the financial market); (c) integrated in the social/societal space outside the *LLS*'s environment (e.g., as a researcher of financial phenomenology);

(ii) there is a co-evolution outside the *LLS*'s environment, that is, at the level of the human individual (more precisely, at the level of human society). The other three co-evolutions take place within the *LLS*'s environment (one outside the *LLS*, another even in the *LLS* in question, and the third in the form of the *LLS*–environment relationship);

Nota bene: of course, an appropriate formalization can take over the interactions between the four co-evolutions that occur in the phenomenology of behavioural entropy related to *LLS*.

- $\left(PS_5^{LL}\right)$ scale distributivity[56]

*LLS*s have a feature that we do not find in *BLS*. It is about the possibility that a certain *LLS* (who, as it shown, is always 'adult', even from the moment of its appearance) to have 'children' or representatives. For example, *LLS* such as a country's medical system or tax system may have (geographically) local subdivisions.[57] This feature raises the issue of *LLS* identity, so we will make the following considerations:

- conceptual considerations
  - if in the case of *BLS*, such 'copies' are just the own children, the descendants, who are in the process of development, in the case of *LLS*, the copies are fully developed as adults but differentiated from the original *LLS* by size;[58]
  - the dimensional (or scale) difference refers to the sphere, which is smaller than for the original *LLS*: the occupied social/societal space, the degree of structural (and, therefore, also functional or of role) particularization;
  - the copies are not ontologically[59] different individuals from the original *LLS* (unlike the *BLS* case), so we will have to find a term for them: we propose to call them *projections*. The reason for this name lies in at least two characteristics: (a) a copy of *LLS* is actually the same as the original; (b) a copy of *LLS* is always obtained by translating (either in time or in space) of the original (see typology, below);
- typology
  - *spatial* scale distribution: there are decentralized or, as the case may be, deconcentrated *LLS*s, which are small-scale copies of the *LLS*, and which are distributed from a spatial perspective, from the 'centre'. These copies work identically (i.e., have the same structure, of course, adapted to the scale in question) as the central *LLS* functioning;
  - *temporal* scale distributivity: it is possible to have *LLS*s that have a discontinuous (albeit permanent) existence/functioning. This means that at certain intervals (periodically or a-periodically ordered) that existence or functioning manifests itself in an

observable/perceptible way. In this case, it is also not about different *LLSs*, but about the same original *LLS* but which is distributed on a temporal scale.[60]

The Nature of LLS
From the above, it peremptorily follows that an *LLS* has an ontological character—more precisely, it is an objectification of the inter-subjectivity present in human society.[61] In this sense, it is a completely cultural product (i.e., it is generated by the cultural component of human society), an artefact that is ideal, although in some cases it also needs a material 'ground' (usually of organizational type), for its functioning.

Autopoiesis and Autopoieticity

The hypothesis we want to build regarding the functioning of the financial market is the hypothesis of autopoieticity or, in other words, the hypothesis of the autopoietic market. To this end, in this paragraph, we will make an overview of the concept of autopoiesis which will later be customized to the financial market.

The concept of *autopoiesis* consists of the Greek terms αὐτο (self) and ποίησις (poiesis) and means a property of a system of self-perpetuation in many ways: conservation, repair, organization, reproduction and so on, all based on their own principles (structural and functional), although in the context of interactions with the environment. As we will see, the interplay between system and environment is seen at the most general and abstract level, namely, through the concept of cognition as a simple sensory-reactive capacity, according to the proposal of the Santiago school of this concept.

Short History
The theme of autopoieticity was, as is well known, triggered by the inspired book of Chilean biologists Humberto Maturana and Francisco Varela (Maturana & Varela, 1980). The new idea, which brings an ingenious explanation of the (functioning of the) living entities, then generated, as expected, many other takeovers. The concept of autopoiesis seeks to bring together the basic elements of continuous life ensuring, based on the internal principles of systems (in this case, living systems) and in the interactions with the environment. All the intellectual efforts made in the

matter are meant to provide the foundations of the living fact. A brief introduction to the issue of autopoiesis is presented below:[62]

(i) the concept of autopoiesis has its origin in living biological entities (organisms), namely, at their basic level (cell). Not only did the two Chilean biologists not extend the concept of autopoieticity beyond biological life, but they rejected the very idea of such an extension (e.g., to social entities);[63]
(ii) the concept of autopoiesis and the concept of knowledge (cognition) are put together and, in fact, are considered logically equivalent. But such an equivalence needs some clarification:
- knowledge is no longer attributed to consciousness, but to any way of perceiving/recording what needs to be done for an entity that, only on the basis of that knowledge (perceptions), could repeat the experience of knowledge (i.e., could survive as a result of the cognitive action in question);
- the very idea of reproducing the entity, based only on internal principles and mechanisms (operations), is seen as the essence of autopoieticity; all the sufficient conditions that ensure such reproduction by internal principles constitute the basis of the autopoietic property;
- although knowledge is attributed to the observer of biological life as autopoieticity, such an attribution does not change anything in the idea that autopoieticity is conditioned by knowledge (of course, in the general, non-anthropomorphic sense mentioned);
- survival in the process of reproduction means that the interactions of the system involved with its environment are 'chosen' by that system so that those interactions are appropriate for survival and reproduction; in fact, the main body of knowledge is to 'know' which interactions are allowed and which are forbidden; it should be noted that Maturana calls such a set of allowed (or appropriate) interactions as forming a *niche* in the wider environment;[64]
- whereas, however, knowledge, understood as associated with consciousness, is not denied, then the extension of autopoieticity to non-biological entities of life (as is the case with our concept of *LLS*) is open, despite the scepticism of the two creative biologists;

(iii) the fundamental ideas, examined or suggested by the two scientists, even if they were taken up by other scientists interested in the topic of autopoieticity, remained quasi-invariant:
- the operational closure (through the membrane) of the system and the interactional (or relational,[65] as we prefer to say) openness of the system to its environment (in fact, to its niche);
- an evolutionary behaviour of the autopoietic system, that is, a cognitively based selection of appropriate interactions with the environment, capable of ensuring the identitary invariance of the system and, at the same time, its reproduction within such an identity;
- a (somewhat) structural determinism of the autopoietic system, that is, the Darwinian idea that functions arise from the structure and never the other way around.

The generality of Maturana and Varela's approach has encouraged other scientists to examine the concept of autopoieticity. One of the most original was the German sociologist, Niklas Luhmann. He tried to abstract and further extend the results obtained for living systems to apply them to social systems (note that those systems are human social ones). As in the case of Maturana, we do not examine the whole social theory of Luhmann, but only those elements that interfere with our intention to clarify the concept of autopoieticity in the financial market. Luhmann's main goals were:

(a) the identification and definition of the phenotype of social systems, that is, the entity that has three predicates of sufficiency: (a) is self-replicable; (b) is reflective; (c) retains its specific identity when reproduced;
- <u>solution provided</u>: *communication* (with some specifications that distinguish it from information or statement, or customize it for different subsystems in the social system—either organizations or interactions); it should be noted that Luhmann considers the event as a unit of reproduction (more precisely, he argues that a communication is an event), which eliminates the duration of the 'equation' of reproduction—that is, a communication is reproduced exactly when it is produced.[66] The similarity of this treatment with our specification that, in the matter of *LLS*, we do not have growth/development of the phenotype is obvious;

(b) identifying and defining the genotype of social systems, that is, the entity that can change (over time or even through its own functioning) and thus influence the reproduction of the phenotype;
   - solution provided: *existing social programmes* that include the 'list' from which only the communications to be made must be selected; as programmes change, so do communications;[67]

(c) the identification and definition of the environment, that is, the system with which the system involved (the system of interest) interacts in order to reproduce/replicate;
   - solution provided: Luhmann does not accept that the social system can have its (social) environment, because any environment of the social system is (in his conception) also of the nature of the social system, so it cannot be outside the social system involved, that is, it cannot be an environment for the social system; consequently, he is obliged to introduce an internal environment, which is considered to be, in fact, widespread within that social system.[68] He called this medium as *understanding of communication*; such an understanding is, of course, different for different individuals and can mean either accepting or rejecting a particular communication. More precisely, the environment of the social system is considered the *psychic system*, which belongs to individuals understood as external sensors of communications.[69]

The Conceptual Family of Autopoieticity[70]

Conceptually, autopoieticity is a property of systems. The concept of autopoieticity is integrated into a true conceptual family regarding the organization and functioning of systems (of any kind, not only of logical/symbolic systems, which we are mainly interested in here). In our opinion, this conceptual family includes the following individuals:

- *stationarity*: is the property of the system which, in terms of its state vector, is absolutely invariant. A stationary system therefore replicates its structure, *punctually*[71] and for an indefinite period of time. For example, stationary economic systems existed in the human communities that preceded the technological civilization—those systems did not produce more than necessary consumption (there were no stocks of products, no production for sale/exchange) and they were rather characterized through autarchy; the principle of behaviour in stationary systems is *current survival*;

- *stability*: is the property of the system which, in terms of its state vector, is relatively invariant. A stable system therefore replicates its structure in an *interval* mode[72]—the system remains stable if the variation of its state vector falls within a pre-accepted range. For example, stable economic systems can exist at any stage of human society's development. However, the interdependencies of economic systems, which today have reached a global dimension (networks), make stability vulnerable, as we will show in the following; the principle of behaviour in stable systems is *anticipated survival*;
- *optimality*: it is the property of the system that, in terms of its state vector, extremizes the potential of the system in question. Extremization that takes place under a set of restrictions/constraints of any kind (material, normative, behavioural, etc.) is called optimization; the principle of behaviour in optimal systems is to obtain the *first best* solution;
- *sustainability*: it is the property of the system which, in terms of its state vector, perpetuates the potential of the system in question, more precisely ensures the replication of its structure, provided that this replication contains sufficient attributes to continue replication (theoretically) indefinitely; the principle of behaviour in sustainable systems is *continued survival*;
- *viability*: can be considered as a stage that will continue that of sustainability, namely, by introducing values (axiological grid) in the design of the structure of the system involved (*Nota bene*: as noted above, sustainability is axiologically 'blind', if we do not consider survival as a value[73]); the principle of behaviour in viable systems, which can also be called logically living systems (Dinga, 2021), is *adequate survival*;
- *autopoieticity*: can be considered as a stage that will continue that of viability, namely, by ensuring the regulatory principles exclusively from within.[74] The concept of autopoiesis (Maturana & Varela, 1980) makes a *sine qua non* connection between the self-organizing capacity of a system and its cognitive capacity—cognition means, in the broadest sense, the perception of actions/reactions that come from the environment to the system in question, and on the basis of which the system either reacts to the environment (based on reaction norms) or changes its structure (and therefore its functions) in accordance with those actions/reactions. Of course, self-organizing

actions/reactions can also come from within the system. The principle of behaviour in autopoietic systems is *self-survival*.[75]

Figure 3.3 shows a synoptic systematization of the conceptual family of autopoieticity.

We mention that, from the point of view of the actional paradigms in the history of humanity, they have 'settled' quite accurately, exactly on the properties discussed—for example, nowadays, the capitalist paradigm based on the property of optimality predominates, being emerging the paradigm (which does not yet have a name) that will be grafted onto the sustainability property.[76]

In order to obtain a logical definition of autopoieticity, it is necessary to establish/choose the predicates of sufficiency which, through their conjunction, provide the content of that definition. To do this, we will first identify the predicates of sufficiency of sustainability—the actional

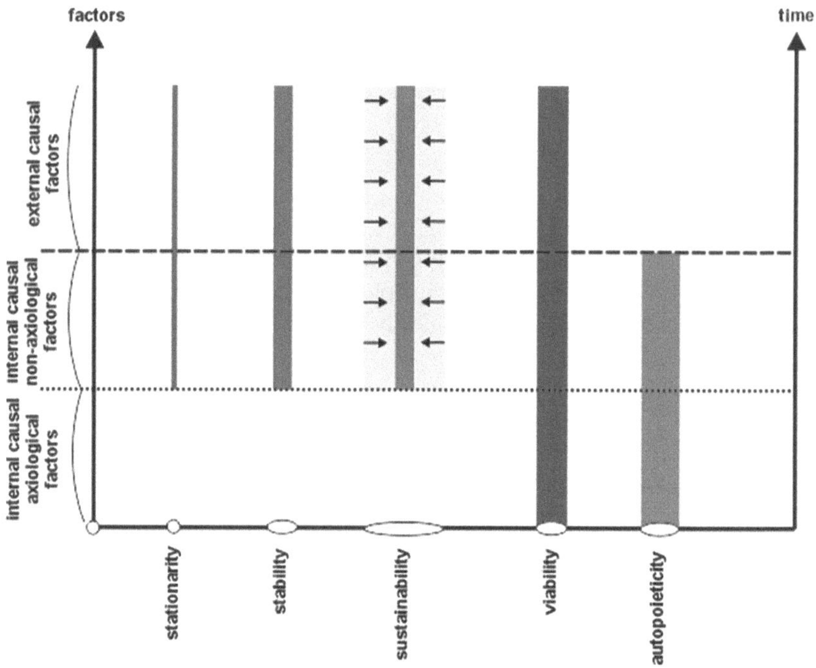

Fig. 3.3 Causal factors of master properties of systems. (*Source*: Authors)

paradigm closest, in essence, to that of autopoieticity. In our opinion, a system is sustainable if and only if it contains the following properties/attributes, which we call sufficiency predicates:

- (S_1): *structural replicability*: identity preservation through structure reproduction;[77]
- (S_2): *operational openness*: regulating of structural replicability involves both internal and external (environmental) principles;
- (S_3): *relational openness*: the system is open in relation to its environment, that is, there is an exchange of substance, energy and information between the system and its environment;
- (S_4): *processual closure*:[78] the system can ensure substantial and energetic recovery of the input based on its own output.[79]

Therefore, as a logical formalization, the sustainable system (SS) can be described as follows:

$$SS \leftarrow (S_1) \wedge (S_2) \wedge (S_3) \wedge (S_4)$$

While an unsustainable system can be described as follows:

$$\begin{aligned} \overline{SS} \leftarrow & \left[(\overline{S}_1) \wedge (S_2) \wedge (S_3) \wedge (S_4)\right] \vee \left[(S_1) \wedge (\overline{S}_2) \wedge (S_3) \wedge (S_4)\right] \\ & \vee \left[(S_1) \wedge (S_2) \wedge (\overline{S}_3) \wedge (S_4)\right] \vee \\ & \vee \left[(S_1) \wedge (S_2) \wedge (S_3) \wedge (\overline{S}_4)\right] \vee \left[(\overline{S}_1) \wedge (\overline{S}_2) \wedge (S_3) \wedge (S_4)\right] \\ & \vee \ldots \vee \left[(\overline{S}_1) \wedge (\overline{S}_2) \wedge (\overline{S}_3) \wedge (\overline{S}_4)\right] \end{aligned}$$

We can establish some logical consequences ('theorems'[80]), based on the definition of the sustainable system.

Every Sustainable System Contains at Least One Sustainable Subsystem

Proof: if the system is sustainable, then, according to (S_4), at the system level the input (of all types) used in an operating cycle of that system will be reproduced (quantitatively, structurally and qualitatively) through that system's output. This means that regardless of the interactions within the system (among which some or more will fail to reproduce the input using the own output), there is at least one interaction (i.e., a subsystem) that succeeds to reproduce the initial input from the final output. Q.E.D.

Reciprocal: if a system contains at least one sustainable subsystem, then it is sustainable, *is not true*—it is always possible that, although at the level of a subsystem, the input is reproduced by the own output, other subsystems fail this, so that, at the level of the system, the sustainability property is not registered.

A System That Contains Only Sustainable Subsystems Is Sustainable

Proof: if each subsystem succeeds in reproducing the input it uses through its own output, it is obvious that there will be no subsystem that fails to do so. As a result, at the system level, the global input will be reproduced/re-constructed by the global output (because the sum of the inputs will be rigorously reproduced/reconstructed by the sum of the outputs) so the system is sustainable. Q.E.D.

Reciprocal: a sustainable system contains only sustainable subsystems, *is not true*—it is always possible for an unsustainable subsystem to be neutralized by another unsustainable system in terms of the gap between the sum of the inputs in the two subsystems and the sum of their outputs (e.g., one of the subsystems produces, through its output, the exact difference, of the opposite sign, which the other subsystem fails to produce, from their own relative output, their own input).

A System That Contains Only Unsustainable Subsystems Can Be Either Sustainable Or Unsustainable

Proof: the proof (which we leave to the reader) can be constructed using the proofs for the two direct theorems or for their reciprocals, given above.

Reciprocal: a system that is undecidable in terms of sustainability (or unsustainability) contains only unsustainable subsystems is obviously *false*. We also leave the proof of the falsity of the reciprocal to the reader.

The Logical Conditions of Autopoieticity

Before we establish the logical conditions (more precisely, the predicates of sufficiency) of autopoiesis, we must distinguish between autopoiesis and autopoieticity. Autopoieticity is a property of a system, while autopoiesis is a process that is made possible by autopoieticity and that results in autopoieticity—(re)confirmation and strengthening of autopoieticity.[81] On the basis of this conceptual dissociation, it becomes obvious that, firstly, the predicates of sufficiency for property, that is, for autopoieticity, must be established.

The Predicates of Sufficiency for Autopoieticity

The sufficiency predicates of autopoieticity are a list of attributes that if a system has cumulatively verified, then it possesses the property of autopoieticity. Some preliminaries are useful in this context:

- the existence of a system, either real or ideal, is presumed;
- the observability of that system is presumed;

Nota bene: in the case of logical/symbolic systems, the system contains, as an internal component, the human individual (or human group or human society).

In our opinion, autopoieticity is a sustainability that is operationally closed. Therefore, if we note an autopoietic system with *APS*, then the predicates of sufficiency for autopoieticity are as follows:

- (AP_1): structural replicability
- (AP_2): operational closure
- (AP_3): relational openness
- (AP_4): procedural closure

Consequently, compared to a sustainable system, the autopoietic system shows a change at the level of the second predicate of sufficiency: the replacement of the operational opening with the operational closure—(AP_2).

The logical construction of an autopoietic system (*APS*) is therefore:

$$APS \leftarrow (AP_1) \wedge (AP_2) \wedge (AP_3) \wedge (AP_4)$$

While a non-autopoietic system can be described by the following conjunction disjunction:

$$\overline{SAP} = \left[\left(\overline{AP_1}\right) \wedge (AP_2) \wedge (AP_3) \wedge (AP_4)\right] \vee \ldots \vee \left[\left(\overline{AP_1}\right) \wedge \left(\overline{AP_2}\right) \wedge \left(\overline{AP_3}\right) \wedge \left(\overline{AP_4}\right)\right]$$

Nota bene: obviously, $S_1 \equiv AP_1$, $S_3 \equiv AP_3$, $S_4 \equiv AP_4$.

We will examine in more detail the sufficiency predicates of the autopoietic system, given that the purpose of this study is to develop an autopoietic model of the financial market.

- (AP_1): ***structural replicability***: identitary preservation by reproducing one's own structure

The identity of a system (more precisely, the preservation of the identity of a system, in time and space) is a rather delicate issue, as it must be indicated on the basis of which criterion/measure can be made the statement that the structure of the system in question has been replicated in such a way we are dealing with the same system after the replication in question. In our opinion, the structural replication (and replicability) of a system must be aimed at its *formal structure*. It is therefore necessary to define or at least describe the meaning of the phrase formal structure. We consider that the formal structure of a system is replicated (or, equivalently, preserved by replication) if the following two conditionalities are verified:

- (C_1) preservation of the number of internal components—by replication, the system must neither lose nor gain structural components;
- (C_2) preserving the hierarchy of internal components—by replication, command relationships versus reporting relationships (i.e., relationships between leading components vs. executing components) must be maintained;

Nota bene: we did not say anything about the nature of the internal components of the system. Is structural replicability hermeneutically indifferent to the changing nature of these components? Our answer is, in this respect, affirmative: the change in the nature of the internal components following structural replication preserves the identity of the system—of course, if the conditionality (C_2) is further verified. The justification of this answer is provided by the very phrase that is analysed here: formal structure—a formal structure allows 'filling' each structural component/form with any type of 'substance', this can be material, ideal/logical, energetic, equational and so on.

- (AP_2): *operational closure*: the regulation of structural replicability involves only internal principles

This predicate of sufficiency is the one that casually distinguishes the autopoietic system from the sustainable one and which (as we will show immediately) generates the property of self-organization. It can be said that this predicate of sufficiency is the very mark of autopoieticity. Of course, the very mechanism of self-organization is to be described and explained (which we will do in the following). Operational closure generally means that the autopoietic process takes place without the need for environmental intervention (which, therefore, should pass through the membrane). These external interventions can refer to resources (substantial, energetic, informational), principles, actions/forces and so on. Of course, all these potential external interventions (which are forbidden by the predicate of sufficiency discussed here) interact with the given system, but only in the form and with the finality of their own input–output relations.[82] The problem of distinguishing between a simple input–output relationship output (I/O) and an external intervention on the kinematics of the system in question (K) is also difficult, because in both cases the transit of the system membrane is allowed, so we suggest, below, some criteria to help their differentiation:

- an I/O flow depletes its potential for influence after a single operating cycle[83] of the penetrated system, while K lasts, in principle, for the duration of the system itself;
- a logical consequence of the characteristic of a K-type flow is that, although at one point it came from the system's environment, the fact that it later remains in the system makes this flow to be considered internal[84] in nature or, more precisely, internalized in nature;
- however, the consequence inferred above is of the nature of Achilles' heel: indeed, at any moment, the membrane of a system can be penetrated by a K-type flow (later it is internalized) but, given this repeatable possibility, can we still talk about operational closure of the system? In this regard, we make the following considerations:
  the K-type flow must not have a causal nature/function, but only a conditional one. Thus, it must 'dictate' only the margin within which the action/reaction of the system must be framed to the action/reaction of the environment, in such a way that the action/reaction of the system is fetal in relation to the environment; this restriction on K-type flow is general and permanent;

the possibility that K-type flows (of an exclusively conditional nature regarding the fetality of the norms of action/reaction, as we mentioned) exist permanently does not violate, therefore, the predicate of sufficiency regarding the operational closure of the autopoietic system;

- (AP_3): *relational openness*: the system is open in relation to its environment, that is, there is an exchange of substance, energy and information between the system and its environment;

  there are no controversial or delicate issues regarding this predicate of sufficiency, as it is required by the quality of the system to be dissipative;

  relational openness to the environment ensures that the system can maintain or reduce its internal entropy (inside the membrane) by extracting negative entropy (neg-entropy, or low entropy) from the environment and spilling high entropy (or positive entropy) into the environment;[85]
- (AP_4): *processual closure*: can ensure substantial and energetic recovery of its input based on own output;

  this predicate of sufficiency also defines sustainable systems;[86]

  processual closure is not implied by operational closure, so the two predicates of sufficiency are not redundant with each other;

  procedural closure is, in our view, a dimensional mark of systems, whether sustainable or autopoietic, in the sense that the membrane of the system in question extends to cover the entire minimum space in which the processual closure occurs;[87]

  processual closure can be thought of both serially—concatenated subsystems in such a way that the output of the system (k) is the input of the subsystem ($k + 1$), provided (called final condition or closure condition) that the output of the subsystem (n) to be the input of the subsystem (1)—and parallel, based on the same relationship between outputs and inputs.

The most important logical consequence of the property of autopoieticity is that of self-organization. It results from the predicate of sufficiency (AP_2)—operational closure—which prohibits processes within the autopoietic system from being caused/conditioned by principles external to that system (i.e., principles within the system's environment), as permitted, from the point of view of logical view, in the case of sustainable systems. For example, a tax system may be sustainable but not autopoietic, because it must be constantly updated from outside (by the Government, which is not structurally part of the tax system).

A problem that arises at this point is that of cognition associated with autopoietic systems. As mentioned above, Maturana and Varela build autopoieticity/autopoiesis bundled with the concept of cognition, understood in its broadest sense (known today as the position of the Santiago school). But in its broadest sense, cognition includes the most mechanical sensitivity, that is, a property that is common to every system imaginable, not only autopoietic systems (and not only, even, living systems[88]). This is why, in the list of predicates of sufficiency for the conceptual definition/delimitation of autopoieticity, there is no predicate that claims the cognitive capacity of the system.[89]

At the end of this sub-paragraph, we will examine the possibility of the functioning of some theorems regarding autopoietic systems (from the perspective of the property of autopoieticity). In this sense, we propose the following theorems:

The Behaviour of an Autopoietic System Is a Function of Its Functionality

Proof: the functionality of a system consists of the relationships (either potential or actual) between its components. These relationships generate the functions (and, by their interpretation, i.e., more precisely, by giving them meaning, generate the roles) that the system is able to perform or actually perform. The behaviour of a system consists of the relationships (either potential or actual) between the components of that system and its environment. If the functionality remains inside the system membrane, the behaviour can only be actualized by transiting this membrane. So, of the functions generated by functionality, some will pass through the membrane and interact with the environment (in the form of actions/reactions)—this is the meaning in which the statement in this 'theorem' must be understood. *Nota bene*: of course, the entry from the environment, through the transit of the membrane, of some actions/reactions also enters the behaviour of the system, from the perspective of the fact that some functions ensure precisely this penetration of the actions/reactions from the environment. More generally, it can be said that behaviour should be discussed only in the plural: system behaviour is a reflective projection of the interference between one's own behaviour and environmental behaviour, just as environmental behaviour is a reflective projection of this interference, this time on the environment. Q.E.D.

Reciprocal: the functionality of a system cannot be said to be an effect of its behaviour. However, an influence of behaviour on functionality (i.e., actualizing the set of functions, especially on those intended to generate the behaviour) must be accepted, at least from the perspective of adaptation.[90]

Any Autopoietic System Is a Sustainable System

Proof: given that the operational closure, specific to autopoietic systems, is of the nature of restricting the operational sphere, and not of its extension,[91] it follows that sustainability is not affected (denied) by the elimination of the open operational part. Q.E.D.

Reciprocal: any sustainable system is an autopoietic system is obviously *false*, because the part of the operationality of the system that has an open character (as allowed by the definition of sustainability) violates the predicate of sufficiency (AP_2).

Lemma: any autopoietic system contains at least one sustainable subsystem. The proof is immediate if we consider, for example, the subsystem as the system itself.[92]

A Set of Autopoietic Systems Always Form an Autopoietic Supersystem

Proof: if all systems are autopoietic, so, if each of them verifies the four predicates of sufficiency for autopoieticity, then the (logical) sum of those systems cannot violate any of these predicates, which means that they will form an autopoietic supersystem.

Reciprocal: an autopoietic supersystem contains only autopoietic systems, it is *not true*, because inside the supersystem there may be two systems that are not autopoietic, each separately, but their cooperation to generate, at the level of the membrane that comprises them, an autopoietic system.[93]

Autopoiesis and Autopoieticity in the Financial Market

The Genesis of Autopoietic Systems

Membranation

The relationship between autopoiesis and autopoieticity[94] is of the nature of the relationship between process and property. In the previous section we discussed in detail about the autopoietic property of a system, highlighting the sufficiency predicates of such a property. Following this discussion, two other issues arise: (a) how the property of autopoieticity arises or, in other words, the question arises whether there is a propensity of the system[95] (or the environment of the system or both entities) in the direction of acquiring this property; (b) how may be lost the property of autopoieticity.

The Concept of Membranation

In general, the appearance of the membrane[96] (of any of the three possible types: physical, logical, institutional) is an effect of an inherent propensity for autonomy or individualization (Maturana & Varela, 1980). When an entity, [97] of any kind, surrounds itself with a membrane, it lays the foundations for a filtering of both inputs and outputs in its relationship with what, from the moment the membrane is formed, becomes an environment for it. This filtering or, in other words, individualization of life, is the decisive step in generating the conditions of autonomy.[98] On the other hand, the appearance of the membrane creates, in the supra-system, a differentiation, that is, a reduction of homogeneity, which is equivalent to saying that, in the supra-system, there is a reduction of entropy—more precisely, the system just 'membranated' becomes a dissipative system that will create an ontological breaking between the system and its environment: while, inside the membrane, the entropy will decrease or, at least, will remain constant, outside the membrane (namely, in the environment) entropy will increase.[99] This (we could call it) entropic bubble is, in fact, the first sign of life which, in essence, manifests itself as an entropic individualization[100] in the environment. The explanation for this propensity for entropic individualization must be left to biologists or the philosophy of biology, we will take it here as a given. Moreover, we will leave the realm of biological life and species and focus, in the following, on the realm of logical life and species or, equivalently, of symbolic life and species.

In the case of logical/symbolic autopoietization, we have (of course, in terms of membrane), a propensity analogous to that in the case of biological autopoietization. Since, however, the symbolic individual is an artefact, this propensity will have a double source: (i) a non-deliberative source and (ii) a deliberative source.

(i) Non-deliberative membranation

Non-deliberative membranation (which is of the nature of what has been called the invisible hand of the formation of the social order, especially the economic one) occurs, as the name implies, impersonally, by the simple interaction between social agents (individual human beings) who pursue exclusively[101] their own objectives (interests). This non-deliberativeness is, of course, a macroscopic one, because, at the microscopic level (i.e., at the level of each economic agent) there is the individual deliberativeness—purpose, rationality and so on.[102] In the case of non-deliberation, the principle of self-organization enunciated by Prigogine and Nicolis (1977) is maintained: order from/through fluctuations. For example, if we restrict the discussion to the field of the financial market (as a symbolic species), the trading strategy (which is the financial individual) becomes autonomous in relation to the financial environment (it acquires a membrane, logical in this case) which delimits it both from other strategies of the given human individual (economic operator) involved and from the other trading strategies that operate throughout the aggregate financial market. In this way, a symbolic individuality is created, representing, in turn, an entropic bubble (this time, not of a thermodynamic or informational type, but of a behavioural type in relation to the environment). The standard case for non-deliberate financial market membranation could be considered the emergence of a trading strategy through the memetic mechanism, which produces the type of information we have called implicit information (Dinga et al., 2022).

(ii) Deliberative membranation

Although non-deliberative membranation should not be ignored, the overwhelming share of membranation in society, and therefore in the financial market, is deliberative. The most important factor of deliberative membranation is, of course, the normative factor that takes over, within the institutional framework of society, the common (or supposedly common), social objectives of the individuals that configure the society in question. In this sense, most of the artefact membranes in society are of the institutional type.[103] In the deliberative case, the principle of self-organization enunciated by Prigogine can no longer be applied to autopoiesis, *tale quale*, because the macroscopic order is not only the result of microscopic fluctuations, but also (in the majority scale, as mentioned above) of a directly established order at the macroscopic level. A possible principle of self-organization in the case of human social systems should

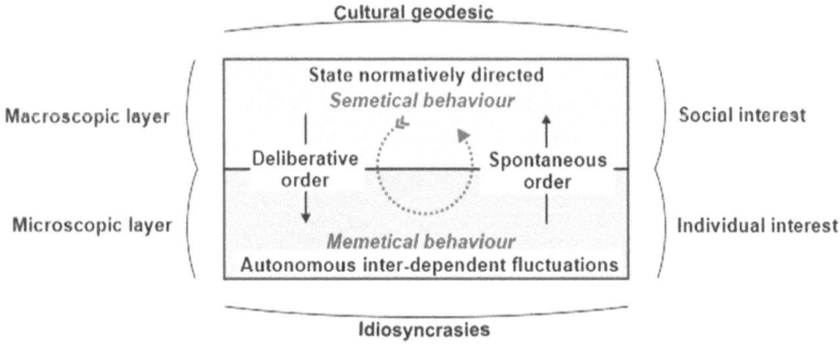

Fig. 3.4 Self-organization in the financial sphere. (*Source*: Authors)

refer to a synergy between a non-deliberative or freely fluctuating microscopic, based on *causa eficiens*, and a deliberative or programmatic (anticipatory) macroscopic, based on *causa finalis*.

Figure 3.4 illustrates the new 'principle of self-organization' that works in the process of membranation in the financial or financial market.

Autopoiesis

Autopoiesis is the process by which, after the completion of the membrane, the four predicates of sufficiency that define the property of autopoieticity are established. Therefore, autopoieticity is the end result of autopoiesis. In the following, we present, briefly, a (possible) description of the autopoiesis, only in the case of artefacts, namely, of the financial market.

First of all, we have to solve a very important problem, namely, the problem of cognition. In the above, the concept of cognition was used in its sense proposed by the Santiago school: that is, as a mechanical reactive sensitivity of the most general type.[104] However, a type of non-mechanical cognition or reflexive cognition may also exist. A reflexive cognition is a cognition (or cognitive capacity) that can be exerted, as cognition, on itself, that is, it is a cognition of cognition,[105] or, equivalently, a reflexive cognition. Reflexive cognition is also called awareness or, with a term that goes beyond both physiological and psychological, acquiring cultural connotations, consciousness. *Nota bene*: because the term consciousness has come into general use—especially in the field of English literature—we will use, in the following, in a non-discriminatory way, the term consciousness, although sometimes we will refer to, in fact, awareness.

The floor of reflexive cognition, namely, of consciousness, is, it seems, specific to human being,[106] who, though the subject of any artefact,[107] is not himself an artefact.[108] In this context, it is probably useful to distinguish between three types of autopoiesis:

- type of *alpha-autopoiesis*: refers to natural systems (non-living or non-human-living), characterized by non-reflexive cognition (i.e., with a cognition within the meaning of the Santiago school);
- type of *beta-autopoiesis*: refers to living human natural systems, characterized by reflexive cognition;
- type of *gamma autopoiesis*: refers to artefactual systems (non-living or living).[109]

Nota bene: we should, perhaps, also distinguish a *delta autopoiesis*, specific to a single system, namely, divinity (the only system characterized by the *cause sui*). Obviously, in the latter case we will also have a relational or inter-actional closure. As far as cognition is concerned, reactivity will probably exist only in the case of deism.[110] Regarding the cognition of delta autopoietic systems, this should probably be called absolute, infinite and self-caused cognition. Alpha-autopoiesis is out of the realm of artefact, so it will not be examined further here.

Based on the above reasoning, for the case of beta-type autopoietic systems,[111] we will have to introduce an additional predicate of sufficiency (we will note it with AP_0^{β}) to those already mentioned, which will contain, explicitly, the cognition. Let us therefore examine systems with beta-autopoiesis and gamma autopoiesis, respectively.

Figure 3.5 shows a graphical summary of the types of autopoiesis we propose.

Beta-autopoiesis

- $\left(AP_0^{\beta}\right)$ *spontaneous internal cognitive reflexivity*

This cognition is generated spontaneously, as a result of natural evolution, being an effect of non-human living. It has a reflexive character because, as we assume, the appearance of human being, on the evolutionary path, is accompanied, as a *conditio sine qua non*, by the emergence of consciousness (in fact, awareness).

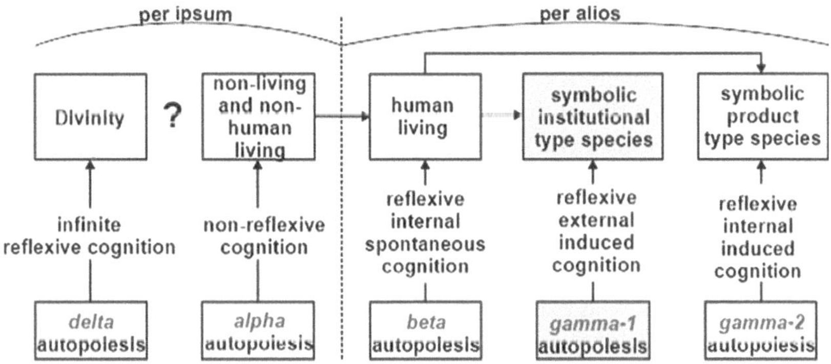

Fig. 3.5 A typology of autopoiesis from the perspective of cognition. (*Source*: Authors)

- $\left(AP_1^{\beta}\right)$: *structural replicability*

Structural replicability in the case of beta-autopoiesis refers to the biological reproduction of the human phenotype, based on the morphological construction instructions contained in DNA, which reproduce what we call the anatomy of the human body.

- $\left(AP_2^{\beta}\right)$: *operational closure*

The operational closure of beta-autopoiesis systems refers to the fact that such systems (biological human individual) contain exclusively internal mechanisms of functioning (including structural replication)—what we call the physiology of the human body.

- $\left(AP_3^{\beta}\right)$: *relational openness*

Relational openness is imposed by the dissipative nature of systems with beta-autopoiesis (biological human individual)—entropic exchange with the environment is not possible outside of relational openness. This relationship refers to all three fundamental flows that can cross the membrane (in one direction or another): substance, energy, information.

- $\left(AP_4^{\beta}\right)$): *processual closure*

The processual closure in the case of beta-type autopoietic systems is relatively ambiguous, at least in the light of the following considerations:

- defecation (both in terms of feeding and breathing) is not an output that is (as such) an input to the next functioning cycle of the system in question (e.g., expired carbon dioxide can no longer serve as input in the next act of breathing, that is, the next inspiration, because the human body needs to inhale oxygen). In this sense, there is no processual closure of its own or, more precisely, it is a processual closure that involves relational openness—which is the case with beta-autopoiesis systems; this processual closure obviously occurs in the context of dissipation;[112]
- therefore, the processual closure does not imply, in any case, an invariance of the total entropy (internal entropy of the system plus the entropy of the environment), but even necessarily implies a non-invariance of it—but it must be ensured, at the level of the system–environment pair, this processual closure.[113]

Gamma-autopoiesis

In the case of gamma-autopoiesis we will also have to introduce an additional predicate of sufficiency (denoted by AP_0^{γ}) which explicitly contains the cognition (*Nota bene*: obviously, here we are dealing with an induced cognition or a secondary cognition—secondary cognition is induced by primary cognition[114]). This type of autopoiesis has two sub-cases: (b1) the gamma-1 autopoiesis of the symbolic/logical systems of *institutional* type and (b2) the gamma-2 autopoiesis of symbolic/logical systems of *product* type. Category (b1) includes the institutional artefacts which constitute, in fact, the structure of the societal system (of human society), of which, for example, the financial market is a part, and category (b2) includes the product-type artefacts which include, for example, products based on artificial intelligence. In the following we will discuss only the autopoiesis of category (b1). Therefore, gamma-1 autopoietic systems of institutional type must be generated by the following sufficiency predicates:

- $\left(AP_0^{\gamma 1}\right)$): *improper internalized cognitive reflexivity*[115]

Here arises the important problem (including from a philosophical perspective, especially ontological one) of the existence of cognitive reflexivity (i.e., of consciousness) outside the human biological organism/body. Our position in this regard is that of the unacceptability (due to impossibility), as we believe, of the existence of consciousness (or awareness, as the case may be) at the level of an entity other than that of the human biological organism/body. In this context, therefore, in the case of symbolic/logical artefactual entities of institutional type, we will only accept cognitive reflexivity in the form of an external one, which can be only internalized and, therefore, inappropriate. This cognitive reflexivity is an internalized one, because such cognitive reflexivity remains localized exclusively at the level of human individuals involved (structurally integrated) in that institutional system, although it is considered (e.g., by organization chart) as internal—so it remains external but is, somehow, internalized—and inappropriate because even though apparently the symbolic institutional system in question makes decisions and takes action, in fact these decisions and actions are made/taken exclusively by human individuals—for example, the decision making system of such a system simply sets out how the people involved in making that decision do so. Of course, through abuse of language and, as a rule, to shorten verbal expression, we can say 'this institution has decided this and that' but, in fact, we are always aware that it is just an abbreviated form of expression.

- $\left(AP_1^{\gamma 1}\right)$: *structural replicability*

Structural replicability must be 'programmed' in the functionality of the symbolic individual (respectively of the symbolic species) in question, by ensuring a continuity property—ensuring of the continuation of the functions involves maintaining/replicating the structure. It is true that, unlike in the case of beta-autopoietic systems, in the case of gamma-1 autopoiesis the replication of the structure refers to its formal aspect, not to the material one (the latter happens in beta-autopoieticity). Somehow, the material aspect of the structure does not need to be maintained, it can take other substances, provided that the formal structure is preserved. For example, as a result of digitization (or, more broadly, digital transformation[116]) a structure whose function was to receive balance sheet documents from economic firms at the Ministry of Public Finance can be organized as an online activity (based on electronic signature): so, although, materially, that structure no longer exists, formally it is, in fact, replicated.

- $\left(AP_2^{\gamma 1}\right)$: *operational closure*

Operational closure retains its full significance in the case of gamma-1 autopoiesis, in the sense that the structural replication, respectively the assigned cognitive reflexivity (internalized and improper, as said), must be achieved by its own 'forces', that is, based on internal principles.[117] In our opinion (but this aspect will be discussed in detail later), in the field of gamma-1 autopoietic systems, sustainability is much more widespread than autopoieticity, hence the emphasis that this research focuses on the building up of an autopoietic system (and not simply sustainable[118]) of the financial market.

- $\left(AP_3^{\gamma 1}\right)$: *relational openness*

The need for relational openness in the case of gamma-1 autopoiesis no longer needs special argumentation, given that this predicative condition is general as soon as we start talking about sustainability.

- $\left(AP_4^{\gamma 1}\right)$: *processual closure*

As in the case of beta-autopoiesis, processual closure in gamma-1 autopoiesis systems is correlated with relational openness, so it must be seen, interpreted and, of course, implemented in such a conceptual and methodological horizon: processual closure depends on the horizon (spatial, structural and temporal) of relational openness. We specify that there is always such a horizon in order to processually 'close' a gamma-1-type autopoiesis system.

Short Discussion

Before to put into evidence some conceptual correlations between autopoieticity and other (macro)hypotheses launched in the financial theory and modelling, it is useful to show the (logical) correspondence between the autopoiesis in the natural world (following Maturana and Varela positioning) and the cultural one (i.e., the economic field and, more specifically, the financial markets):

(a) in the natural world (of living entities, however) the autopoieticity is programmed into the genetic code, so it is, somehow, automatic, although this automatism is conditioned by the environment (either other natural living entities or the natural non-living environment);
(b) autopoiesis implies the niching, that is, finding of the environment which is the most appropriate for the entity plenary surviving. This finding is conditioned by a species of knowledge (which does not presuppose consciousness or reasoning) consisting in identification of the best context for the evolution of the entity in

case (*Nota bene*: we remind the reader that this concept of knowledge is supported by the Santiago School);

(c) *a fortiori*, autopoiesis in the financial (i.e., cultural) world can be associated with the niching based on knowledge, this time, a con scious knowledge, which goes from the intuition to the most sophisticated models of rationality;

(d) consequently, there is a continuity between the autopoiesis in the natural living world and the cultural world, even if a jump in the knowledge performance is recorded in such a 'transition' between the two worlds;

(e) to be mentioned that it cannot be said with certainty that the conscious knowledge (within the cultural world) is more efficacy than the unconscious knowledge (in the natural world). Many times, the free will, in the cultural case, can be less performative than the necessary automatism in the natural world—but, of course, in both worlds, failures are possible; [119]

(f) in conclusion, we think it is perfectly natural to accept the autopoiesis in the financial field, exactly based on the definition of the concept as it was formulated regarding the natural living entities by Santiago School—searching the niche in the environment, based on knowledge; the difference between the knowledge efficacy in the two worlds has a quantitative character, not a qualitative one.

Some Conceptual Correlations of Autopoieticity

Autopoieticity and Automatic Stabilizers

About Automatic Stabilizers[120]

Since automatic social stabilizers are designed and implemented in a normative way, that is, through public policies, it is useful to make a brief examination of the concept of public policy, as well as its mechanism of functioning.

Public policy (*PP*) generally means a policy that verifies the following sufficient attributes:

- it is instrumented by a public institution/organization empowered as such, by law (usually by the fundamental legal/positive law—the Constitution);
- pursues a public goal (or coherent set of public goals);

- the public objective pursued is relevant at macroeconomic or macrosocial level;[121]
- it is permanent and continuous;
- it contains a computational mechanism[122] (of algorithmic type) that describes the input–output relationship (or, more generally, the cause–effect relationship), which accompanies its instrumentalization;
- there is a procedure that triggers the above-mentioned computational mechanism;
- there is a procedure associated with the computational mechanism that triggers this mechanism.

Public policy can be qualified from the perspective of two fundamental criteria: (a) the causal criterion and (b) the formal criterion. According to the causal criterion, a *PP* can be of two types: (a1) direct *PP*; (a2) indirect *PP*. According to the formal criterion, a *PP* can also be of two types: (b1) explicit *PP*; (b2) implicit *PP*. We will briefly characterize the four types of *PP*.

Direct PP is that *PP* that causes the variation of the target variable directly, without the intermediation of any control variable. For example, the administrative setting of a price for a particular good or service (the reasons for such an intervention do not matter here) simply means changing that price.[123]

Indirect PP is that *PP* which causes the variation of the target variable mediately, through a control variable. Of course, some methodological clarifications are needed here: (1) it is assumed that the theory that establishes the causal link between the variation of the command variable and the variation of the target variable, with a pre-accepted probability, is given (accepted); (2) the channel (mechanism) for transmitting the influence of the variation of the control variable on the target variable is known, observable, accessible and controllable (under all necessary aspects: amplitude of shock transmission, various lags or leads, etc.). For example, obtaining the change in the tax base by changing the tax rate (see also the Laffer curve) or changing the bank interest rate by changing the monetary policy interest rate.

Explicit PP is that *PP* that obtains the variation of the target variable through a formal action (following a decision) of the institution/organization responsible for that *PP*. For example, if the central bank finds an excessive decrease in the exchange rate (which means an excessive appreciation of the currency against the reference currency), then it may decide to lower the required minimum bank reserve ratio. Or, if the government finds an increase in the share of the underground economy, then it can decide to reduce the fiscal pressure (or the convenient restructuring of general taxation). In other words, an explicit *PP* involves making a formal decision (and, of course, implementing it) in the desired direction.

Implicit PP is the *PP* that obtains the variation of the target variable without a formal action (following a decision) of the institution/organization responsible for that *PP*. How is this possible? By implementing, in the causal mechanism, some institutional devices that are triggered automatically, when certain preconceived conditions are verified and, as a result, produce the variation of the target variable—such institutional devices are called *automatic stabilizers*.

Let us make a few comments on the above:

(1) it should be mentioned that the listed criteria act simultaneously, realizing a double characterization of any concrete *PP*. In other words, a certain *PP* will be qualified, at the same time, according to both the first and the second criteria. We would thus have, in principle, four distinct categories of *PP*: (a) explicit direct *PP*; (b) implicit direct *PP*; (c) explicit indirect *PP*; (d) implicit indirect *PP*. Note, however, that the implicit direct *PP* is an inconsistent *PP*. Indeed, if *PP* is direct, this means that the target variable is targeted immediately, that is, without the intermediation of any control variable. Or, the implicit character means the existence of such a command variable that acts on the target variable. Therefore, according to the condition of consistency, we will have only three distinct types of *PP*: (1) explicit direct *PP*: *PP-de*; (2) explicit indirect *PP*: *PP-ie*; (3) implicit indirect *PP*: *PP-ii*;
(2) an explicit *PP* is what we will call a discretionary *PP* because, as we mentioned above, it involves the 'conscious' intervention of the institution/organization responsible for that *PP*, at a time, with a range, and in a way which are established together with the decision to intervene (usually formally); therefore, we have two types of discretionary *PP*, namely, *PP-de*, respectively *PP-ie*;
(3) an implicit *PP* is what we will call a non-discretionary *PP* because, as we mentioned above, it does not involve the 'conscious' intervention of the institution/organization responsible for that *PP*. According to

the typology already identified, there is only one type of non-discretionary *PP*: *PP-ii*;

(4) according to the above, both discretionary and non-discretionary *PP* imply the pre-existence of a top-down algorithm.[124] Therefore, both deliberate intervention and automatic intervention on the target variable occur in a computational way that excludes both the need for intuition (i.e., understanding) and the need for axiological evaluation (it is assumed that both were considered in the top-down algorithm design). We will return to the features of this algorithm in the following.

By public policy adjustment[125] (*PPA*) we mean that *PP* in which we do not find the direct character of public intervention. According to the above, it follows that there can be only two such *PPAs*: *PPAs*, which are discretionary, and *PPAs*, which are non-discretionary. The best known *PPAs* are those available to the government (fiscal-budgetary policy) or to the central bank (monetary policy), respectively, with the role and functions of intervening in market economic mechanisms in order to implement (induce, stimulate, maintain, correct, etc.) those economic and social processes and phenomena and so on, which are supposed to lead to the achievement of the fundamental objectives of the government, respectively of the central bank. In the following we will only be interested in *PPA*.[126]

If, as mentioned, semantics no longer play a role in the application of a *PPA*, once the algorithm has been designed, whether it is a discretionary or a non-discretionary algorithm, instead the syntax of the interventions of *PPA* is of decisive importance.

From a syntactic point of view, we can have extremely different adjustment 'discourses'.

Firstly, there are simple adjustment discourses or compound adjustment discourses. A simple adjustment discourse is that *PPA* intervention that is mono-typical: either an intervention of type 'de' (de0 - de1 - de2 - … - dek), or one of type 'ie' (ie0 - ie1 - ie2 - … - iek), or one of type 'ii' (ii0 - ii1 - ii2 -… - iik). A compound adjustment discourse is that *PPA* intervention that is poly-typical: a concatenation of different mono-typical interventions.[127]

Secondly, there are atomic adjustment discourses (or singular, i.e., adjustment discourses that contain a single *PPA* intervention) and molecular adjustment discourses. The latter can fall into two categories:

periodical adjustment discourses (contain groups of *PPA* interventions that reappear, in the same configuration, periodically) and a-periodical adjustment discourses (contain groups of non-recurring *PPA* interventions, such as two or more times).

Thirdly, it is important whether the initial intervention is discretionary or non-discretionary. In this sense, if the initial intervention is of discretionary type but then involves only non-discretionary interventions, this initial intervention can be called *discretionarily initiation of a non-discretionary process.*[128] If the initial intervention is non-discretionary, but then involves only discretionary interventions, this initial intervention may be called a *signalling message*. Of course, a more meticulous analyst might extract from this a multitude of other classifications that may be interesting from a conceptual, methodological and even instrumental[129] point of view, but for the purposes of this paragraph, we consider that what we have already established is sufficient.

Fourthly, the more elaborate a *PPA* is (both conceptually and methodologically or instrumentally), the more poly-typical adjustment discourses predominate, and the more complicated[130] they are syntactically.[131]

Therefore, by the structure of a *PPA* we will understand, in fact, the syntactic structure of that *PPA*. This is not a coincidence if we consider that the mechanism of transmitting the impulse of any kind in the economy is, in the last resort, a matter of syntax. Therefore, we note that we have a *logical equivalence* between the transmission mechanism of an impulse and the syntax of a *PPA*. Therefore, when we have to discuss one of them, we can very well discuss the other one, *mutatis mutandis*. This qualitative result is particularly important, from a methodological point of view, because it allows us to move the centre of our analysis from one aspect to another, as this choice serves better or more directly the purpose pursued by those analyses.

Based on public policy considerations, we can now introduce the concept of *automatic stabilizer* (*AS*). An automatic stabilizer is a sequence of public policies that has the following properties:

- is initiated by a *PPA-de* in a single episode/stage;
- is followed (exclusively) by *PPA-ii* in an indefinite number of episodes.

From a quantitative point of view, the effectiveness of an *AS* is a function of two parameters: (1) the *action rate*—the intensity with which the *AS* actualizes its scheduled action; (2) the *action basis*—the economic support on which the action rate is exerted. Let us examine, in turn, the two components and make some logical and methodological considerations:

- the *rate of action* (k) refers to the 'step' that the *AS* takes, once the 'path' conditions that automatically trigger its action are met;[132]
- the *basis of action* (B) refers to the range of the 'action cell' for which a certain rate of action is given;
- the quantitative dimension of the efficacy of *AS* (E) refers to the product between the rate of action and the basis of action: $E = -k \cdot B$. It is immediately noticeable that the rate of action and the basis of action are substitutable. In this case, a curve of indifference to the effectiveness of the *AS* can be defined, setting the differential condition:
- $dE = 0 \rightarrow dk \cdot B + dB \cdot k \rightarrow Rms = \frac{dk}{dB} = -\frac{k}{B}$
- where with *Rms* the marginal rate of substitution between the rate of action and the base of action was noted.

Nota bene: in connection with *AS*, we introduce its concept of *granularity*, which is a concept regarding the fineness of the 'grid' related to both the rate of action and the basis of action. The finer the two 'grids', the lower the granularity of the *AS* and vice versa. The granularity of the *AS* is important from the perspective of the sensitivity with which the *AS* reacts to the change of economic conditions which is, as we said, its efficient cause.[133] It is understood that just as we have nominal substitutability between the rate of action and the basis of action of an *AS*, so the same can we speak about the substitutability between the granularity of the rate of action and the granularity of the basis of action.[134] It is, of course, another matter whether the efficacy of *AS* depends more on one granularity or another.

According to the definition of a non-discretionary *PPA*, including the institutional device called *AS*, this is an indirect and implicit entity. From the point of view of the concrete action in the economy, however, *AS* can have an impact characterized by a certain *economic lag*.[135]

Based on the above, we can say, at a more analytical level, that an *AS* is a device of *institutional* type, of *normative* origin, with *structural* character, with *macroeconomic* sphere, with *anti-cyclical* action and with *implicit* (automatic) triggering, with the aim of reducing the volatility of the field to which it is addressed.

Let us try to identify the list of sufficiency predicates of an *AS*.[136] We consider these to be the following:

- *AS* is an ***institutional*** type construct, that is, it is generated normatively. This is an obvious attribute of the nature of sufficiency, because if it is not met, we may be dealing with self-stabilizing mechanisms (also based on the principle of negative feedback) but generated by the economic process itself.[137] We will note this attribute (predicate) of sufficiency with (S_I);
- *AS* is a ***structural*** construct—a permanent construct with a discontinuous action. The argument for the sufficient nature of this predicate is the following: being a construct that must behave non-deliberatively (automatically), this non-deliberativeness can only be ensured if the *AS* is a component part of the economic process concerned, that is, it is structurally endogenized.[138] If not, then its activation would require an assessment of the effective cause of action and, following that assessment, would require a deliberative decision to activate its specific re-action (i.e., exactly how to activate a discretionary public policy measure); we will note this predicate of sufficiency with (S_S);
- *AS* is a ***macroeconomic*** construct, that is, its action is relevant to the dynamics of macroeconomic variables. Although *AS* acts effectively at the microeconomic level, the relevance of this action is always macroeconomic (i.e., aimed at reducing the volatility of output at the target area—such as the financial market in the case of interest in this study, e.g., to reduce volatility of price or, relatively equivalent, of profit). This predicate has the nature of a sufficient predicate because if the *AS* construct does not verify the predicate in question, the purpose of the construct—that of reducing the volatility of macroeconomic output—is not actualized;[139] we will note this predicate of sufficiency with (S_M);
- *AS* is ***anti-cyclical***,[140] that is, it acts in the opposite direction of the variation of the variable it controls. This predicate is also clearly of the nature of sufficiency because, if we did not impose this, any such institutional device could have an impact on the escalation of the volatility of the structurally controlled variable (i.e., being procyclical), undermining, therefore the very concept of *AS*; we will note this predicate of sufficiency with (S_A);

- the action of the AS is *supra-proportional* in relation to the variation of the controlled variable. This predicate is obviously of the nature of sufficiency because, if the action were proportional (or, worse, sub-proportional), then the dynamics of the process would not be influenced but only maintained, preserved or even increased in a pro-cyclical sense. It should be noted that the verification of the predicate of supra-proportionality does not depend on the direction in which the controlled variable varies: if it increases, then *AS* will decrease it more than it increases, and if it decreases, then *AS* will increase it more than it decreases. In other words, we are talking here about the supra-unitary value of the marginal variation of *AS*. If we note with dV the variation of the controlled variable generated by the evolution of the economic process in question, with dV_{AS} the variation of the controlled variable generated by the action of the *AS* construct, and with AS_m the marginal effect of *AS*, then we must have verified the algebraic condition:
- $AS_m = -\dfrac{dV_{AS}}{dV} < -1$

This is, in fact, what we propose to call the *AS multiplier*. Of course, the extent to which the *AS* multiplier is supra-unitary (in absolute value) even gives the very measure of its effectiveness;[141] we will note this predicate of sufficiency with S_P.

Note that these predicates meet, taken in pairs, the conditions of independence (neither is a logical result of the other), consistency (neither is contradictory to another) and completeness (simultaneous verification of the five predicates generates a construct that will function as an *AS*).

$$AS \leftarrow (S_I) \wedge (S_S) \wedge (S_M) \wedge (S_A) \wedge (S_P) \text{SFA}$$

Relationship Between Autopoieticity and Automatic Stabilizers

Having, on the one hand, the sufficiency predicates of autopoieticity and, on the other hand, the sufficiency predicates of the automatic stabilizer, the functional relations between the two categories can be represented synoptically as in Fig. 3.6.

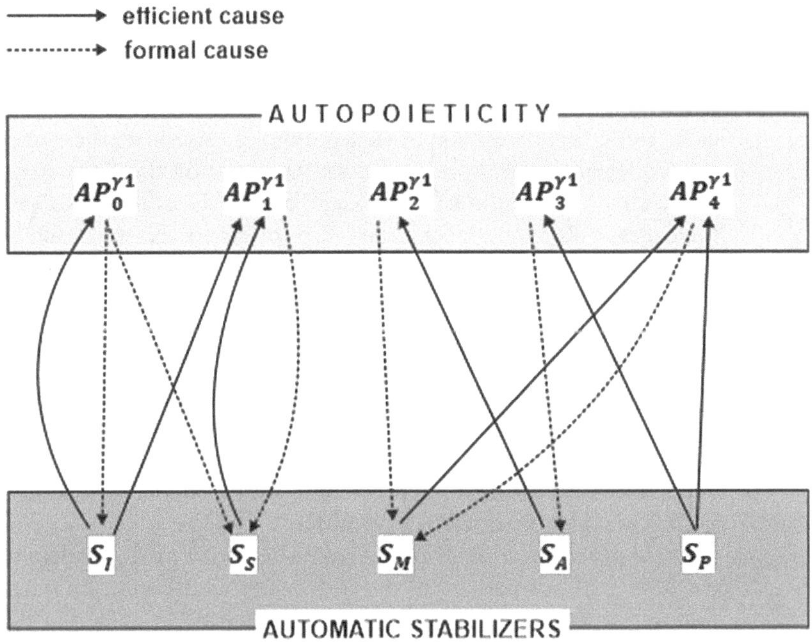

Fig. 3.6 Logical relationships between autopoieticity and the automatic stabilizer. (*Source*: Authors)

Autopoieticity and Behavioural Entropy

A General Framework

The concept of behavioural entropy is not discussed in the literature, where only the concepts of thermodynamic (or energetic) entropy, respectively informational entropy,[142] are found. Consequently, in this subparagraph, we will outline this concept exclusively from the perspective of the financial market,[143] which is of particular interest to us here. The main ideas are those already published by the authors (Dinga et al., 2021), so they will be used, according to the requirements of this study, in the ones below.

- Any type of entropy is based on the ratio between homogeneity and heterogeneity of the system under analysis—of course, from the perspective of each criterion specific to that type of entropy:

- the case of ***thermodynamic*** entropy: the degree of homogeneity/heterogeneity is determined by the ratio between available (or bound[144]) energy and free energy (unavailable for use), usually in the form of heat dissipated in the environment of that system or even inside the membrane of that system; in this sense, the entropic model of the economic process, proposed by the Romanian-American economist Nicholas Georgescu-Roegen (Georgescu-Roegen, 1971), explicitly refers to this ratio which aims at the availability/unavailability (or accessibility/inaccessibility) of related energy;
- case of ***informational*** entropy: degree of homogeneity/heterogeneity refers to the probability distribution of the series that are transmitted, in a communication, through the channel linking the sender to the recipient—in this case, the probability of transmitting a character from the language used in the communication depending on the previous character (or immediately preceding, as the case may be) already transmitted;
- the case of ***social*** entropy: in our opinion, social entropy refers to the degree of normativity of the society (societal system) in question. Since this type of entropy is relatively little discussed in the literature (the most present is, from this perspective, the concept of informational entropy—including the famous but so unrealistic EMH model), we will add some clarifications related to the profile of social entropy (Dinga et al., 2020):
  - must be related to the social order;
  - its connection with the social order must be inversely proportional;
  - must have the connotations (either quantitative or qualitative) of the relationship between homogeneity and heterogeneity of a system/process, as shown above—in this case, the relationship between homogeneity and heterogeneity refers to the social order;
  - is fundamentally based on normativity;

• the concept of behavioural entropy
  - the authors of this study define the concept of behavioural entropy by referring to behavioural efficiency (Dinga et al., 2021). Behavioural efficiency, as opposed to informational efficiency (inherent in neoclassical financial market models such as EMH and, to a large extent, FMH), refers to the ability to access behav-

iours that 'exit' the average of financial market behaviour (or, in general, within the social field of interest[145]). In other words, the more similar the market behaviours are—or suggest, by interpreting the implicit information,[146] similar behaviours that could be followed by market-watching economic agents—the lower the behavioural efficiency. Therefore, simply, by behavioural entropy is meant the inverse of behavioural efficiency: the higher the behavioural efficiency, the lower the behavioural entropy, and vice versa;[147]

- behavioural entropy does not yet have a specific formalization (*Nota bene*: as well as social entropy), as has thermodynamic (or phenomenological) entropy, respectively informational entropy, so one of the tasks of the authors is to develop such formalizations for the two concepts (but, however, in subsequent communications, namely, in another book, which is dedicated to building the hypothesis of the natural price of the financial market: Natural Price Hypothesis—NPH).

The Relationship Between Autopoieticity and Behavioural Entropy

As mentioned earlier, the behaviour of a system refers to the relationships between the components of that system and the system's environment, that is, refers to the flows (of any kind: substantial, energetic, informational) that pass through the membrane of the system, either as inputs or outputs. Based on the descriptions of the two concepts—autopoieticity and behavioural entropy—the relationship between them could be presented as in Fig. 3.7.

Short Discussion

- The relationship between behavioural entropy (as an exogenous variable) and autopoieticity (as an endogenous variable) is of a decreasing logistic curve type. The logistical allure is explained by the fact that the increase in behavioural entropy is expected to generate a strong shock, at first, on the decrease in autopoieticity, but later the autopoieticity will find (local or temporal) possibilities to mitigate the impact, so the further increase of behavioural entropy has the effect of decelerating the decrease in autopoieticity;[148]
- the relationship between behavioural efficiency (as an exogenous variable) and behavioural entropy (as an endogenous variable) is, as

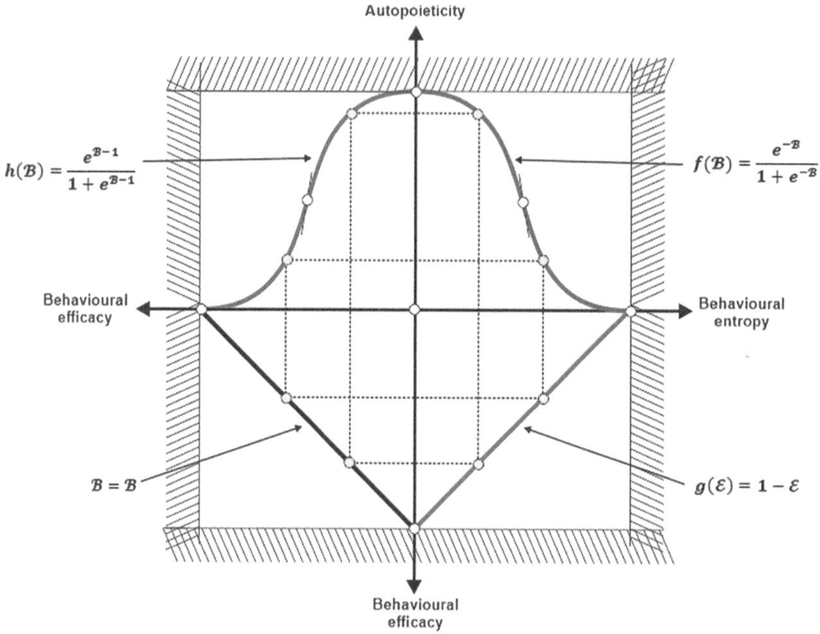

Fig. 3.7 Autopoieticity curve related to the behavioural entropy. (*Source*: Authors)

shown above, a relationship of inverse proportionality. We consider that this relationship should also be formalized through a logistic curve (function), symmetrical to the second bisector, that is, while the curve of autopoieticity starts concave and ends convex, the behavioural entropy curve begins convex and ends concave;[149]

- if we denote with $\mathcal{A}$ the autopoieticity, with $\mathcal{B}$ the behavioural efficiency and with $\mathcal{E}$ the behavioural entropy, we can write, successively: $\mathcal{E} = f(\mathcal{B})$, $\mathcal{A} = g(\mathcal{E})$, $\mathcal{A} = g(f(\mathcal{B}))$, $\mathcal{A} = h(\mathcal{B})$, where $h = g \circ f$;

- as $f(\mathcal{B}) = \frac{e^{-\mathcal{B}}}{1+e^{-\mathcal{B}}}$, and $g(\mathcal{E}) = 1 - \mathcal{E}$, it follows that:

$$h = g \circ f = g(f(\mathcal{B})) = h(\mathcal{B}) = \frac{e^{\mathcal{B}-1}}{1+e^{\mathcal{B}-1}}$$

Autopoieticity and Constructal Law

The Concept of Constructal Law

The concept of constructal law was introduced into the literature by a Romanian American researcher—Adrian Bejan (2007). Constructal law aspires to be more primitive than the laws of thermodynamics[150] (especially than the second law of thermodynamics—the law of entropy or the law of irreversibility of exergy[151]).

The construction law has the following wording: 'for an open system, of finite dimensions, to persist over time (to survive) it must evolve in such a way as to provide easier and easier access to the flows that pass through it'.[152] *Nota bene*: in constructal theory, any finite system is considered thermodynamically imperfect.

The main features of the construction law are the following:

- it is placed in the position of principle of evolution;[153]
- it targets both non-living and living nature;
- restricts its scope to systems that are characterized by flows, more exactly, by flows that have a physical objectification[154]—both within the membrane of the system and in relation to its environment; moreover, another reduction in scope refers to the fact that the systems in question must move or live generating physical/materials supports for flows,[155] the so-called dendritic tubes;[156]
- constructal evolution involves choice (either non-deliberative or deliberative, as the case may be);
- in constructal evolution, choice involves cognition;[157]
- the application of the constructal law to evolution (at least in the case of living nature) provides quantitative regularities from an allometric perspective;[158]
- constructal law rejects optimization in systems configuration;
- the constructal law is considered a law of physics but as applicable everywhere, including in the social field, engineering, innovation or psychology;
- the constructal law acts completely holistically—the evolutionary solution is formed at the level of the system which, thus, may contain subsystems that have not been regulated by the constructal law (Bejan, 2007);
- the constructal law offers a new arrow of time, compared to that provided by the second law of thermodynamics: time flows in the

direction in which the access to their own life support flows of systems is greater.[159]

Relationship Between Autopoiesis and Construction Law

It is quite obvious that there may be both similarities and differences between the autopoieticity (A) of a system (S) and the impact of the constructal law (CL) on the system (or directly on the property of autopoieticity and even on the process of autopoiesis— $\tilde{A}$ —associated with the system), on the one hand, as well as structural–functional relationships, on the other hand.

(b1) Similarities

We think that there are at least the following four similarities:

- both $\tilde{A}$ and CL aspire to be principles of organization, construction and functioning of evolution; [160]
- in our opinion (which differs from that of Maturana and Varela, in terms of autopoieticity, and that of Bejan, as well, in terms of constructal law), both $\tilde{A}$ and CL function, rather, as mechanisms than as principles, that is, both answer the question 'how' rather than the question 'why'/'which is reason'. Thus, the $\tilde{A}$ mechanism is the hypercycle,[161] and the CL mechanism is the self-designing. *Nota bene*: here we may be asked the following objection: both answer, in fact, the question 'why', and the answer is the same: ***survival***. In connection with this possible objection, we make the following analytical considerations:
  - *first of all*, survival is an end in itself,[162] so it cannot be an efficient cause. *Nota bene*: the question 'why' obviously refers to the efficient cause. Not being an efficient cause, it cannot be of the nature of a principle, but of the nature of a mechanism;
  - *secondly*, it may seem strange, of course, to argue that finality/purpose does not answer the 'why' question. Indeed, when the question 'why' is asked, most of the time, it can be reformulated as 'for what purpose', 'for what reason', so it is obvious that, thus reformulated, the question aims at the finality/purpose. However, the original (and rigorous) meaning of the question 'why' is what leads to the efficient cause;[163]

- therefore, survival cannot be a principle of evolution, but only its mechanism;[164]
- both $\tilde{A}$ and *CL* pursue a ***second best*** solution (or survival solution, as we have already shown above) rather than a ***first best solution*** (or optimal solution);
- both $\tilde{A}$ and *CL* have the potential (already, partially, demonstrated) to 'migrate' from the fields in which they were initiated (*CL* appears in physics, respectively $\tilde{A}$ appears in biology) in other fields, including psychology or sociology, although, as is well known, Maturana and Varela expressed some scepticism about the (scientific) legitimacy of extending the scope of autopoiesis.

(b2) Differences

- We consider that there are at least the following three differences:
  - a first difference concerns the sphere: while *CL* targets any evolving entity[165] (living or non-living), $\tilde{A}$, respectively *A*, targets only living entities (from the molecular level to the human level)—this limits $\tilde{A}$ in relation to *CL*, that is, we can write $\tilde{A} \subset CL$;
  - a second difference also refers to the sphere, but from a different perspective: while *CL* explains only the entities that, in their evolution, develop the so-called dendrites—that is, a self (re)design generated by the flows passing through the entity in cause, $\tilde{A}$, respectively *A*, refers also to the entities that are not characterized by this configuration of 'dendrites', so, we can write $\tilde{A} \supset LC$;[166]
  - while *CL* no longer maintains a logical connection with thermodynamics (neither with the first nor with the second law), $\tilde{A}$ maintains a (background) connection with these two laws (especially with the second one).

(b3) Structural–Functional Relationships

- The structural–functional relations between $\tilde{A}$ and *A*, on the one hand, and *CL*, on the other hand, can be represented synoptically as in Fig. 3.8.

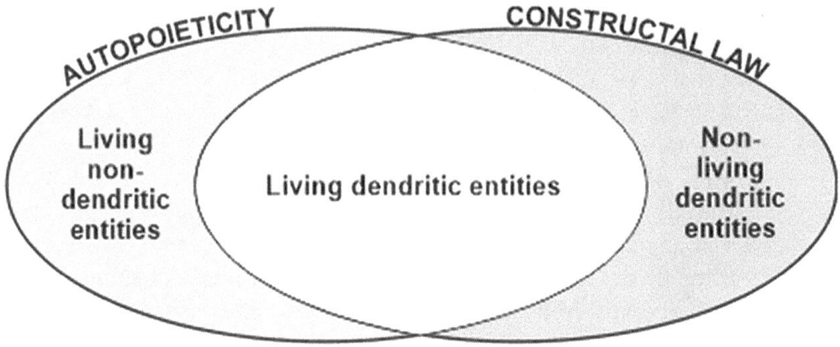

Fig. 3.8 Logical relationships between autopoieticity and constructal law. (*Source*: Authors)

Autopoieticity and Minimal Entropic Interaction

The Concept of Minimal Entropic Interaction Law

Suppose that in Universe 0 (the initial Universe), several dissipative systems appear simultaneously (of course, this set of dissipative systems can be constituted in a successive way, as well, not necessarily in a concomitant one, it is important that, at some point, in Universe 1 we have several such dissipative systems, both of '1α' rank and '1β' rank).[167] In this context, the notion of complementary environment becomes, so to speak, multi-relative (it was, however, relative even in the conditions of the existence of a single dissipative system, as is immediately observed, based on the use of the concept of distinction generated by membranation). This means that, given a certain dissipative system, say *A*, another dissipative system, say *B*, becomes a relatively anti-dissipative complementary environment for system *A*.[168] That being the case, we wonder how entropy will evolve in system *B*, given its certain evolution in system *A*. In other words, the question is whether we have an entropic impact of one dissipative system on another dissipative system.[169] As we realize, in order to formulate an answer, it is necessary to admit that dissipative systems 'recognize', at the level of the membrane (i.e., at the level of their border), the entropic gradient between them and the complementary environment.[170] Assuming such a capacity, how do dissipative systems 'choose' to achieve 'entropic exchange' (i.e., to procure low entropy in exchange for high entropy, with which they 'pay' for the acquisition of low entropy)? Put another way, the question is: will a certain dissipative system 'prefer' to perform the entropic exchange with the complementary environment (which, as is already obvious, includes all other existing dissipative systems) at the maximum entropic gradient or at minimum level? Perhaps, a principle similar to that of the minimum path in physics[171] will have to be postulated here, namely, that *entropic exchange takes place at the level of the minimum entropic gradient.*[172] This principle, once accepted, generates the relativity of the complementary environment but, on the other hand, it also necessarily generates a matrix (here the term necessarily has its logical meaning) of entropic interactions. This means that if we had a 'map' of the entropic gradients in Universe 1, we could tell exactly[173] what entropic interactions would take place.[174] Therefore, the complementary environment can only be defined in a multi-relative way (in fact, in a contextual way, even, as it seems to us, in a practical or empirical rather than theoretical way). The 'chain' of entropic interactions based on the principle of choosing the minimum entropic gradient indicates a necessary acceleration of the global entropy of the Universe, namely, an autocatalytic entropic acceleration: the more dissipative systems, the greater the rate of global entropy. Moreover, the more evolved the dissipative systems (in the entropic sense of the term, i.e., the slower the rate of local entropy), the greater the rate of global entropy. Or, as it has been shown in the specialized literature, dissipative systems have a necessary tendency of entropic evolution. We can summarize, therefore, the following: (a) any variation of the speed of the local entropy is equivalent to an inverse and supra-proportional variation of the entropy of the complementary environment; (b) the principle of choosing the minimum entropic gradient for the entropic exchange between dissipative systems further accelerates the global entropy. The last assumption needs, however, a specific argument: suppose we are in a Universe 1 in which there are two dissipative systems, A, with the speed of the local entropy λ_S^A, and B, with the speed of the local entropy λ_S^B, so that $\lambda_S^A < \lambda_S^B$. We will note the speed of entropy in the complementary environment relative to the two dissipative systems with $\lambda_C^{A,B}$ (the notation mode means that the appearance of the two dissipative systems has led to an increase in the speed of entropy in the complementary environment—according to the proposed explanations in the present discussion—so that $\lambda_C^{A,B} > \lambda_E$). Obviously $\delta^{A,B} = \left|\lambda_S^A - \lambda_S^B\right| < \left|\lambda_S^A - \lambda_C^{A,B}\right|$ (where with δ the entropic gradient was denoted), so the entropic exchange for a further reduction of the entropy velocity in the dissipative system A will be made between the latter and the dissipative system B.[175] Given the order relation between the speeds of the local entropies of the dissipative systems, the entropic exchange will consist in the taking over by system *A* of a low amount of entropy from system *B* and, conversely, the taking over of a high amount of entropy by system *B* from system *A*. Now the basic significance of the selection criterion results of the minimum entropic gradient: this selection criterion ensures a minimum transfer of low entropy from the less evolved system to the system more evolved from an entropic point of view. Indeed, it is quite obvious that in order to achieve a certain local entropy speed differential, system *A* should consume more low entropy from the complementary environment itself than it should from system *B*.[176]

Here is one last question that we would like to address: is the choice of the minimum entropic gradient to achieve the entropic exchange necessary for a dissipative system consistent or not with the Prigoginean principle of minimum entropy production? If we take the behaviour of natural systems as an argument, we should give an affirmative answer.[177]

A synoptic picture of the above considerations could be the one in Fig. 3.9 (with the notations: G-CE: general complementary environment; CE-A: complementary environment for the dissipative system *A*; CE-B: complementary medium for the dissipative system *B*; A-E: entropic interaction of the dissipative system *A* with the environment; B-E: entropic inter-action of the dissipative system *B* with the environment; A-B: entropic inter-action between the dissipative systems *A* and *B*).

Nota bene: developed to its last consequences, this propensity for minimal entropic interaction can be not only an explanatory model of the functioning of the financial market, but could also be a *sui generis* predictor (of behavioural type, not informational!).

Relationship Between Autopoieticity and Minimal Entropic Interaction

In our opinion, the law of minimum entropic gradient interaction (*LMEGI*) is more fundamental than autopoiesis ($\tilde{A}$) and autopoieticity (A).[178] The main relationships between the two concepts are the following:

- the minimal entropic gradient interaction seems to be necessary, while the autopoiesis/autopoieticity seems to be contingent. In other words, it is impossible for the interaction between two systems to take place in violation of the principle of minimum entropic gradient interaction, although some dissipative systems may not be autopoietic;[179]

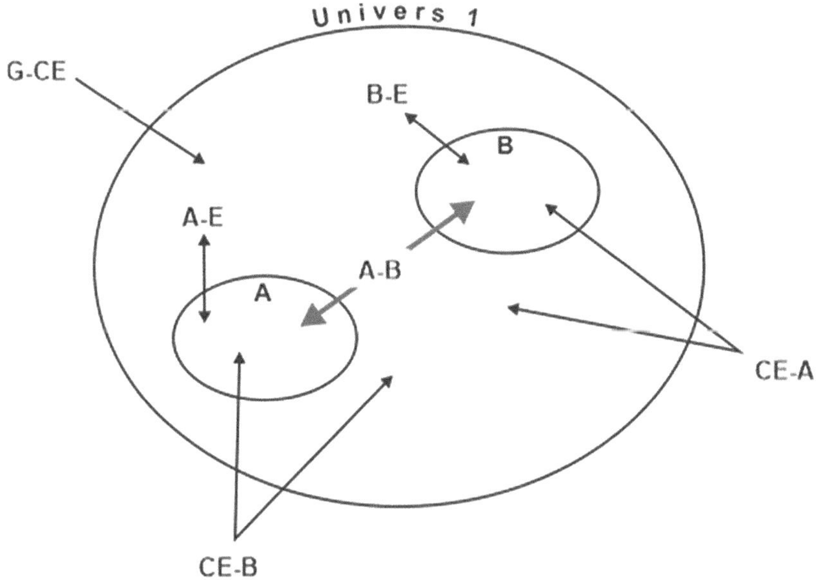

Fig. 3.9 Inter-actions between dissipative systems is 'preferred' to inter-actions with the environment. (*Source*: Authors)

- the question arises as to whether minimal entropic gradient interaction has an impact on autopoiesis/autopoieticity and vice versa. Our opinion on this matter is as follows:

  since the minimum entropic gradient interaction is consistent (and convergent) with the minimum entropy output in the general complementary environment (G-CE) in Fig. 3.9), and the minimum entropy output 'feeds' the autopoieticity, it follows that we can 'prophesy' a trend, for example, long term, to increase the share of autopoietic dissipative systems in the total dissipative systems, under the impact of the law of minimum entropic gradient interaction;

  autopoieticity, by its simple operation (based on the self-organization sustained by hypercycles) reduces the intra-membrane entropy, increasing (by more than this reduction) the entropy from the general complementary environment. This leads to an increase in the entropic gradient between the other dissipative systems existing in the general complementary environment and the entropy of the general complementary environment, which strengthens the propensity of other dissipative systems to behave according to the 'law' of minimum entropic gradient interaction;[180]

therefore, a *sui generis* hypercycle seems to form between autopoieticity (or autopoiesis) and the law of minimal entropic gradient interaction;[181]

- the propensity for minimal entropic gradient interaction can, of course, be further examined (which will be done in a later communication, separate from this book), as it is possible to allocate probabilities[182] generated by this propensity, which would allow more analytical modelling (including predictive value) for the functioning of the financial market;
- the relationship between autopoieticity and minimal entropic gradient interaction can be developed from the perspective of the autopoietic market hypothesis—a hypothesis that follows and completes, logically and methodologically, the hypothesis of adaptive preference, already discussed in FMAB-APH (Dinga et al., 2022).

Autopoieticity and Network

The Concept of Network

The concept of network is considered here in its well-known sense in geometry (or topology) as well as in algebraic formalizations in graph theory, that is, it represents a collection of nodes connected by arcs (which also implies loops, i.e., arcs at which the source node and the destination node coincide[183]), the latter constituting flows between nodes (of substance, energy, information).[184] Logically, the network has a number of features that we will refer to below:[185]

- matrix structure (or grid structure)—the network no longer has a hierarchical (which is specific to systems) organization, namely, with a leading or 'legislative' subsystem and one (or more) operational (or 'executive') subsystem(s);
- in connection with this feature, of course, the question of the logical relationship between the network and the system arises—our view on this issue is as follows:

- the network can no longer be considered a system, as it is no longer structurally organized vertically, but exclusively horizontally;
- however, a network has, like the system, a membrane, which differentiates the network from its environment; in this way, the behaviour of the network in the environment is analogous (though not similar) to the behaviour of the system, based on a functionality generated by the interactions between nodes;
- therefore, we consider that the network should be considered a *quasi-system*, by which we mean a horizontal system (the 'genuine' systems are always vertical ones);
- of course, from a conceptual point of view, we can have systems of systems, network of systems, systems of networks and networks of networks; moreover, each of the four 'pure' types of structural organization can have a mixed structure: that is, there can exist systems of systems and networks, respectively networks of systems and networks,[186] which brings the number of possible types of structural organization to six, including the *LLS*s, as the financial market is as well;

• in networks it is possible for the *hub effect* to occur: the hub effect is one generated by the positive feedback that occurs (either accidentally or normatively) at a node that has (either accidentally or deliberately) several arcs at a time; the existence of this connection imbalance tends to self-catalyse (Barabási, 2002) so that, paraphrasing the assertion of the evangelist Mark (4; 25),[187] the node with many arches will be granted with more arches[188] while the node with few arches will cancel the arches it has;
• what can be said about the network node: is it a system? If it is not a system, what is it? Our position on this issue is as follows:

- based on what has just been established regarding the possible (theoretically) types of structural organization, we consider that the node of a network can be either a system or a network;
- however, if we continue the analytical decomposition of the node, regardless of the type of organization to which it is associated, we will eventually reach a component that will have to be considered as the last;
- this last component can only be a system. To the presumptive question: why cannot there be a network, we answer:

  a network must, by definition, comprise at least two components (of any type), while a system may contain a single com-

ponent (itself)—in which case the leading system and the operating system coincide; [189]
therefore, the simplest network (consisting of exactly two components) can be broken down into two systems, so the 'indivisible' component (or, to use a scientific term, the atomic[190] component) is always a system and cannot be a quasi-system (i.e., a network);

- the production and consumption of entropy within the network (i.e., through substantial, energy or information flows between nodes) is free,[191] in the sense that each node is free to design and target its own needs for such flows, either input or output or loop type;[192]
- of course, as in the case of systems, in that of quasi-systems (networks) there may be spontaneous networks, respectively deliberate networks (e.g., established and implemented in a normative way). Taking the case of the economic market again, it is always a combination of spontaneity (or automatism) and deliberation, one side domi-

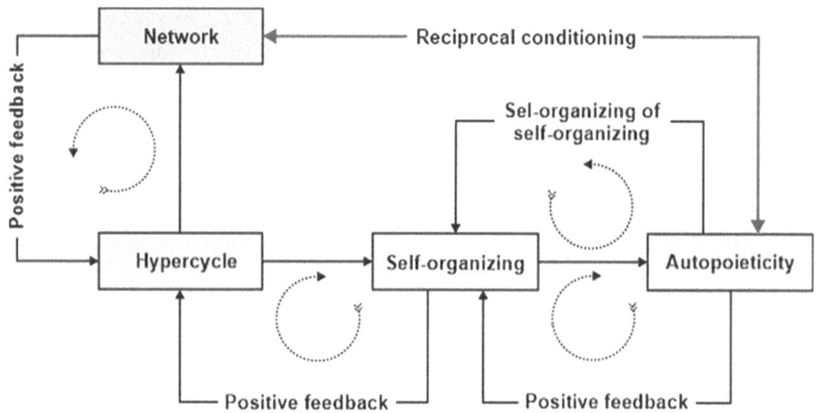

Fig. 3.10 Relationship between autopoieticity and network. (*Source*: Authors)

nating the other depending on the political regime or form of government in the society in question.

Relationship Autopoieticity—Network
The relationship between autopoieticity and the network can be examined, in a peremptory way, with the help of the hypercycle concept, mentioned above, a concept that is common to autopoieticity and the network. We will present this relationship in a synoptic form, in Fig. 3.10.

Notes

1. The scientific basis for the fact that biological life on our planet is based on carbon is that this chemical element—carbon—has the greatest ability to form combinations with other elements, which gives it the highest probability of initiating and maintains such combinations (*Nota bene*: it is obvious that here we are dealing with a propensity type of probability, as this concept was previously defined in this research (Dinga et al., 2022)). From a technical point of view, carbon (located in the Mendeleev periodic table in the second period, the fourth group) has two layers of electrons, and the second layer (outer layer) has four electrons. As this layer allows eight electrons, carbon can form four more co-valent bonds (i.e., it is tetra-valent) with other elements—four single bonds or two double bonds or a triple bond. However, in the second period there is another element, also tetra-valent—silicon—which, theoretically, could be the basis of life. Moreover, the water molecule, used as a solvent in the case of carbon, can be replaced (with the same functions) by ammonia, in the case of silicon, which, like water, is a polar molecule. At the same time, DNA–RNA information structures could be replaced by other structures containing the 'plan' of the future living phenotype. Exploration of exo-planets is already bringing these ex-carbon possibilities to the attention of researchers.
2. It is estimated that there are the following living components of ecosystem on our planet: (a) plants; (b) animals; (c) mushrooms; (d) algae; (e) bacteria (Nota bene: viruses, which are non-cellular entities, do not fall into the category of biological living).
3. The issue of distinction is much more important, relevant and significant than the current meaning (in common/civil language) of the term distinction indicates. We would direct the reader, in this matter, to the ingenious (though largely ignored, today) work of mathematics of logic (i.e., the opposite of what Bertrand Russell did—namely, a logic of mathematics) by George Spencer-Brown, *Laws of Form* (Spencer-Brown, 1994).

4. To paraphrase a famous formula, to find a *BLS* the maxim must be applied: *cherchez la membrane*.
5. Here the term fundamental refers to the importance/relevance/significance of the sufficiency predicate in question, and not to any logical priority of it in relation to the other three predicates. Specifically, the other three predicates cannot be inferred from it, all four predicates of sufficiency are independent of each other.
6. Thermodynamic entropy (a macroscopic quantity) refers to the degree of binding (or availability/accessibility) of energy in that system—for example, heat is a form of free (unbound) energy that can no longer be used to perform an action (a mechanical thing, in the terminology established by Newtonian physics). In an approximately similar sense, the concept of entropy is taken over in economics, through the pioneer of the entropic economic model, the Romanian-American economist Nicholas Georgescu-Roegen (Georgescu-Roegen, 1971).
7. The concept of dissipative systems was introduced into the literature by Ilya Prigogine (Prigogine & Stengers, 1984).
8. It is shown that dissipative systems accelerate the production of global entropy, which 'shortens' the lifespan of the Universe.
9. Which we call reproduction, either (1) *sexual*, with two cases: (a) sexuated or 'normal', when the female sexual cell is fertilized by the male sexual cell; (b) asexuated or by parthenogenesis, when the new individual appears from the female sexual cell without it being fertilized, or (2) *asexual*, with four cases: (a) by *spores* (reproductive cells develop in new organisms without fertilization); (b) by *binary fission* (an individual reproduces and divides by mitosis creating two individuals); (c) by *budding* (an individual grows from/on its parent's body); (d) by *regeneration* (the detached part of an individual forms another individual).
10. The use of the qualifier *quasi* is meant to take into account replication accidents caused by mutations that occur at the genetic level (these issues have been addressed, in general, in FMAB-APH (Dinga et al., 2022)).
11. Maturana and Varela developed the concept of cognition as a *conditio sine qua non* of autopoiesis—thus, cognition is defined as the ability to adapt to the environment. Cognition is acquired through bilateral perturbations (what we have called: through mutual reaction norms) and it is present regardless of whether or not the entity in question has a nervous system.
12. Here the term perception refers exclusively to the physiological aspect (because cognition, according to the Santiago school—as Maturana and Varela's theory of cognition is called—does not necessarily imply a nervous system, so it does not necessarily imply the psychological or phenomenological aspect of perception).

13. There are also logic automata, called cellular automata (*Nota bene*: discrete automata), but they have logical membranes, not physical ones (initially studied by Stanislaw Ulam and John von Neumann, they were intensely examined, especially in one-dimensional space, by Stephen Wolfram—see the latter's work: *A New Kind of Science* (Wolfram, 2002); also the Darwinist biologist Richard Dawkins uses cellular automata in modelling the processes of natural evolution).
14. As is well known, bacteria (which verify the sufficiency of biological living sufficiency) do not grow.
15. It can be shown (we will do, to some extent, this, in what follows) that cognition, in the sense of the Santiago school, is proper to non-living entities as well.
16. It should be noted that the concept of interaction is even broader than that of adaptation, used by Maturana and Varela. Thus, the adaptation denotes only the one-way action (the examined entity adapts to its environment), but it has been shown, and we have shown before, that the environment also adapts to the given entity. Somehow, the inter-action is a reciprocal adaptation (and perhaps of a cumulative/gradual character) (*Nota bene*: the reader who follows us closely remembers, of course, that we used the concept of co-adaptation, which we related to co-evolution).
17. For example, an iron bar that expands as a result of an increase in internal temperature (as in the case of keeping it in a flame) gives no significance to the 'observation' that its temperature rises, and even more so does no significance to the cause of this increase, but it reacts, so to speak, a-noematic (from the Greek nóημα, nóima—which means sense, understanding). The iron bar does not change, in the usual sense of the term, its behaviour, instead changes its state (its state vector).
18. *Cogsation* is a morphological combination of two terms involved: *cognition*, respectively *sensation*.
19. We remind you that reality has three components: (a) physical or objective reality; (b) ideal or subjective reality; (c) hybrid or objectified reality (*Nota bene*: the content of the latter component is the following: the objectification of inter-subjectivity). This is also the configuration of reality on Popper's three worlds. Imagination/fantasies are added to reality, together with which they form what is called *datum* (see, here, the point of view of phenomenology, especially in Heidegger).
20. If living entities (in the sense defined here) were discovered on an exoplanet which is not based on carbon, but on silicon, respectively, not on water, but on ammonia, those entities would still have to be called biological.
21. In Physics, that is, in a discipline that studies the non-living, the factor of proportionality between mass and energy is represented by the square of the speed of light ($E = m \cdot c^2$). Perhaps it would not be uninteresting, especially

from the perspective of unifying knowledge, to find, for the case of the living, such an equivalence.

22. In principle, there can be three categories of environmentally separating membranes: (a) *physical* membranes, as discussed in the case of *BLS*; (b) *logical* membranes—for example, the definition of concepts by the proximate genus and the specific difference only introduces a logical membrane between genus and species; (c) *institutional* membranes—although this type of membrane could be considered a kind of logical membrane, we prefer to consider it distinct from the latter for the following reason: the institutional membrane is not inferred from a model of rationality, as is the case of the logical membrane, but it is established by decree (it is a normative decree)—for example, the establishment of an organization involves the establishment of its purpose, and/or the means it can legally use. These delimitations are not the consequence of syllogisms, but of desideratum whose foundational justification has no relevance.
23. Which makes there are as many distinctiveness as distinctiveness criteria can be operationalized. Of course, distinctiveness, in the most general sense, is causally dependent on the perceptual and representational 'endowments' of the observer subject.
24. Shannon's concept of informational entropy represents an intermediate level between thermodynamic (or energetic) entropy and behavioural entropy, although it is also projected from the perspective of behaviour—in this case from the perspective of communication 'behaviour'.
25. We specify that we are still in the interpretation of the Santiago School regarding the concept of cognition or cognitive capacity.
26. It should be noted that, in the case of *BLS*, this pair of 'action/reaction–action/reaction' also occurs between the system and the environment, but in addition in the case of these systems, there is also the non-behavioural pair 'action/reaction–action/reaction', based on thermodynamic entropy.
27. At this point an interesting and (possibly) useful discussion can be developed on the allocation of Bayesian probabilities to a distribution of events (or hypostases of an event) under conditions of absolute uncertainty—that is, by allocating the same numerical value to each of the probability in question—as required by Laplace's principle of insufficient reason—but respecting the Kolmogorov conditionalities (e.g., for a set of n events, any probability will have the value $1/n$).
28. The criterion against which the homogeneity of a system is assessed can be any, depending on the research interest.
29. The set (range) of accessible choices must be imagined from a monadic perspective—that is, we do not differentiate between these choices, for example, based on the expected utility or other possible benefits—for now, only the number or quantity of these possible and accessible choices to the

system in question matters, which means that the 'individuals' of this set of choices are performatively indistinguishable from each other (but this preliminary hypothesis will, of course, be relaxed when finer behavioural analyses are needed).

30. We remind the reader that, from an informational perspective, the three concepts—observability, accessibility and controllability—were also discussed in FMAB-APH (Dinga et al., 2022).
31. In principle, there is no essential difference between system and environment (whether we are talking about *BLS* or *LLS*): what is environment for the system, when viewed from the environment, becomes system, while system becomes environment. So, from a qualitative point of view, the system and the environment are simply interchangeable.
32. Obviously, the term *sensational* has, here, a precise meaning, without any connection with its meaning in the common (civil) language—in the latter case it denotes an event or a property or a relationship or a thing out of the ordinary.
33. For example, the reaction of human society as a whole (or of individuals or groups of individuals) to signals received from the phenomenology of climate change (such as global warming), which should be beneficial to both humans and planet as a whole.
34. This aspect will become much more obvious when we discuss selection in the case of *LLS* (i.e., autopoietic selection).
35. The controllability component of behavioural entropy could also be defined, according to the semantic content of the concept of controllability, as a fetal component of behavioural entropy.
36. However, $BE_{\uparrow}^{(A)}$ cannot occur, because the extension of the choice range from the point of view of observability cannot narrow the range of choice from the point of view of accessibility (*Nota bene*: as we shall see below, the same reasoning also applies to the case of the choice range from the perspective of fetality).
37. The case $BE_{\leftrightarrow}^{(O)}$ occurs when the reduction of the choice range from the point of view of observability is made exclusively on account of $(BE^{O}) \setminus (BE^{A})$ (*Nota bene*: the same reasoning applies also to the case of increasing behavioural entropy such as observability).
38. Faster in relation to the growth rate (inexorable, according to the second principle of thermodynamics) of the global entropy, that is, in principle, the entropy at the level of the largest closed system (logically, it can only be the Universe, in its entirety).
39. Note that if we want to find an analogous predicate for informational entropy, the most appropriate would be its *positional* character—which involves neither transaction nor relationship.

40. For example, sustainability is replicable by principles external to the system in question, so, sustainability is replicable by a combination of external and internal principles, while autopoieticity is replicable exclusively by internal principles.
41. Although, of course, in the case of humans, there may be a decision (i.e., a deliberative choice) to reproduce (to have biological offspring), in general, in the case of *BLS*, the replicability and, consequently, the replication/reproduction of the individual is non-decisional—we could call it quasi-necessary, given its instinctual determinism which is very close to necessity, on the one hand, but also the presence of free will, on the other hand (*Nota bene*: in the case of non-human living entities we believe that it is not wrong to consider that we are facing necessity, not quasi-necessity, because, as it seems, there is no free will here, i.e., the possibility of opposing necessity).
42. We mean autopoiesis.
43. We make a certain abuse of language here, because by replicator is meant, in biological theory, the genome—the genome is the one that replicates and will form, in the process of growth/development, the phenotype in question. Here, by referential extension, we call as replicator the very symbolic phenotype.
44. This is the genealogical (and, in fact, etiological) basis of bureaucracy—as is well known, one of the principles of bureaucracy (which should, in our view, be considered the fundamental principle or fundamental axiom) is: 'any bureaucrat works in the purpose of producing/maintaining the work front of another bureaucrat'.
45. This indeterminacy or, rather, undecidability is (as can easily be seen as) extremely similar to that which refers to the factual falsifiability of scientificity—and, in that case, the non-rejection of a prediction/conjecture, so its corroboration, was inconclusive, so, only rejection having the power to be conclusive. Therefore, if a parallel were to be drawn between the corroboration of a predictive statement and the replicability of a *LLS*, they are, logically, equivalent, *mutatis mutandis*, of course.
46. A collateral consequence of this finding is that, from the observer's perspective, replication (and, implicitly, the replicability property) is not observable exactly as long as it occurs, while becomes observable exactly when it no longer occurs.
47. In some cases (but, in principle, in all cases), given the deliberative, artefact nature of the *LLS*, there is a substitute for growth (which consumes an extremely short period of time), namely, the simulation of the *LLS* functioning in question.
48. ANAF is the abbreviation for the Romanian National Agency for Fiscal Administration.

49. As we pointed out before, in the case of social evolutionism we will have a different perspective.
50. It is useful to note that the improvement of the same function does not generate a qualitative difference, but only a degree one. In other words, the variation of the degree preserves the nominal function—perhaps it would be of theoretical utility to further develop this idea of 'nominal protection' of the function in the matter of the *LLS* evolution.
51. The fact that the change in the structure itself can be the effect of changes in the degree of function should not surprise us—it is the all-pervading issue of the significance threshold, that is, the fact that in any quantity there is always a potential quality (obviously, in the most abstract way, we find, here, the Hegelian idea of the leap in quality as a result of the accumulation, or dis-accumulation, of quantity).
52. We remind you that any *LLS* is considered an artefact (i.e., an inter-subjective objectification) generated by the *BLS*s of the human species.
53. Logically, a decision is discretionary if and only if it is explicit (either formal or informal), while it is automatic if and only if it is implicit (either formal or informal). It is obvious that an automatic decision was, previously and necessarily, a discretionary decision that established precisely its automatic character (but, obviously, not every discretionary decision establishes a subsequent automatic decision, there are discretionary decisions that subsequently require discretionary decisions as well). Therefore, the meaning of the term discretionary, as it is conveyed in the common (civil) language, where it often has the connotation of arbitrary, is excluded here.
54. In a sense, what is the cognitive-reactive capacity of the *LLS* corresponds to the range of choice offered by its environment and vice versa: what is the cognitive-reactive capacity of the environment of an *LLS* corresponds to the range of choice of this system. Of course, Maturana's niche concept fits perfectly with this kind of ideas.
55. We recall that, in our opinion, the financial market is not the environment (as considered, e.g., in AMH) of *LLS*, but is the financial species (whose environment is cultural geodesic).
56. We recommend abstention from the (possible) tendency to qualify this distributivity as … fractal, because this is not the case at all.
57. This distributive aspect of *LLS* should not be confused with its event aspect—for example, a trading strategy (as a financial individual) manifests itself in concrete, particular situations called individual transactions. In the latter case, therefore, we do not have a distributive aspect.
58. In general, in the case of *BLS*, the size of the offspring is preserved (although, in the very long run, the environment may select individuals that differ in size from their ancestors).

59. The consequence is that the 'population' of *LLS* does not increase as a result of replication, while in the case of *BLS*, we have a population increase following replication. Of course, from a conceptual point of view, here appears the important problem of populational selection in the evolutionary process, which we will refer to in detail below.
60. Of course, a special case in this category of distributivity of *LLS* is the cyclicity (either of existence or of operation) of that *LLS*. Such manifestations of time-scale distributivity can be observed in the case of macroeconomic kinematics.
61. We remember that these inter-subjectively objectified entities are part of Popper's third world.
62. This paragraph represents partly a takeover and partly a development of the article of one of the authors (Dinga, 2021) dedicated to the abstract concept of autopoiesis as a generative 'machine' of *LLS*.
63. This rejection is, of course, strange, given the intellectual and creative openness shown by the two biologists. In our opinion, the form of behavioural entropy, which we introduced above (in order to replace thermodynamic entropy and, in part, informational entropy) is even more suitable for the use of the concept of autopoiesis—which we will continue to do, by the way.
64. As we have already shown, the interactional niche of a system with its environment is simply formed by the totality of fetal reaction norms (which 'enter', respectively 'exit', from the system concerned).
65. From a logical point of view, the relationship is more extensive than the inter-action, because it can also refer to unidirectional actions/reactions that are obviously not of the nature of the inter-action (the latter implies bi-directionality).
66. The influence of Shannon entropy, which is of the communication type, is not difficult to observe here.
67. Here Luhmann makes an obvious analogy with Lakatos' concept of research programmes, trying to sketch a paradigmatic version of social evolution.
68. Again, the analogy between Luhmann's solution and our solution of the identity between the social genotype and the social selector (i.e., the idea that the environment is … inside the phenotype) is obvious.
69. The fact that the psychic environment is considered outside the social system is somewhat curious, though not too much, because it can be correlated with the distinction between Popper's three worlds: the psychic world is the second world, while society, as an objectification of inter-subjectivity, is the third world.
70. This subparagraph is a processing of an excerpt (Chap. 5) from the book *Economy and Society*, currently in course of publishing, under the coordination of one of the authors (Dinga, 2023—manuscript).

71. Punctuality accepts accidents of non-punctuality if the system has the potential to return to the point (resilience of point or punctual resilience).
72. Stability accepts instability accidents if the system has the potential to return in the interval (resilience of interval).
73. We consider that survival, as a goal, is not grafted on a value, precisely due to the fact that survival is the existential condition of any value (*Nota bene*: this argument follows, somewhat, the way in which Kant rejected existence as a property/attribute, in the attempt to overturn the conclusion of Anselm of Canterbury's famous argument about the existence of God—a failed attempt, just like Descartes' attempt in the same matter).
74. That is, as is the case with systems known as second-order cyber systems (those cyber systems in which the observer/controller is itself a component of the system concerned, as opposed to first-order cyber systems, where the observer/controller is outside the system concerned).
75. An equivalent expression, which we will use mainly in the following, is adaptive replicability (or replication).
76. The concepts of 'green economy', 'circular economy' and the like are, in fact, terms that refer to the concept of sustainability.
77. Obviously, we refer to the formal, logical structure, regardless of the substantive/material nature of the components that 'fill' that formal structure.
78. We did not call this predicate of sufficiency as functional replicability because, as we know, structure generates function. However, since the system replicates structurally, it turns out that it also replicates its functions, which is why the predicate was called operational replicability.
79. Thus, a sustainable system can contain either sustainable subsystems (in the sense defined here), unsustainable subsystems (systems that violate at least one of the sufficiency predicates of sustainability) or, as the case may be, both sustainable subsystems and unsustainable ones.
80. The term theorems is not risky, because the four predicates of sufficiency can be considered axioms and a logical consequence inferred from one or more axioms is called, as it is known, a theorem.
81. Autopoiesis can also be understood in a different sense (analogously to the understanding of semiosis in relation to semiotics or, more precisely, to the sign): as the process that produces the property of autopoieticity.
82. It is easy to see that operational closure (AP_2) is not contradictory to relational opening (AP_3)—in fact, no system can be dissipative unless it is relational open (substantially, energetically, informationally) in relation to its environment.
83. The identification of an operating cycle is made on the basis of establishing the resumption of the need for input—thus, an operating cycle (which is, of course, different as depending on the nature of the analysed system) has a

duration that stretches between two consecutive inputs (immediately successive).

84. This external origin which is internalized will become even more evident when the issue of automatic stabilizer is discussed, below, in the context of autopoietic systems.
85. The literature shows that the balance sheet of such an entropic exchange is always in favour of the dissipative system: global entropy (i.e., at the level of the Universe, which is the only system that can be considered genuinely closed) is accelerated by the dissipation of component systems.
86. However, we cannot say that the autopoietic system is a self-sustaining system, because autopoieticity contains, in addition to the exclusivity of the internal principles of kinematics/dynamics, the potential for self-organization, which cannot be imposed on simple sustainable systems.
87. Here, we have a peremptory illustration of the implicit concept of economic space (a concept in the mirror of economic time): the economic space of a system is the physical space in which that system develops interactions with the environment, that is, manifests itself behaviourally.
88. We will find, below, that the so-called *constructal law* (proposed by the Romanian-American researcher Adrian Bejan) also targets the whole world, not just living systems.
89. It is obvious that between mechanical sensitivity and more efficient types of cognition there is only a difference of degree, not of quality. However, a qualitative leap seems to occur in the case of conscious cognition or, in other words, in the case of the humans and, consequently, in the case of logical/symbolic species. We will take this matter back to the right place. We will perhaps have to introduce, on that occasion, the concept of reflexive cognition, which is not present (as far as we know, in biology studies) in the case of non-human living entities.
90. Moreover, it is obvious, for example, that selection is not possible without behaviour, that is, without an environmental reaction to the externally manifestation of the functions of the system.
91. It is clear that operational opening includes operational closure, while operational closure does not include operational opening: in other words, in any operational opening we have operational closure, but in no operational closure do we have operational opening.
92. According to set theory, any set is a component of the set of its parts.
93. Obviously, a very important logical problem arises here, namely the problem of the degree of analyticity of a system from the perspective of its subsystems. A system can be made up of subsystems which, in turn, are made up of subsystems and so on. When judging autopoieticity (or sustainability, as the case may be), we need to determine the level of subsystems we go to, because (although not always) it is possible that by packing two non-auto-

poietic systems we obtain an autopoietic system—in this case, for example, we continue packing until we get the operational closure. Therefore, when discussing or applying this theorem it is necessary to establish in advance the degree of analyticity of the subsystems of a system—this degree usually depends on the research interest or, in some cases, on the praxiological or practical interest, being therefore either a methodological problem or an empirical one, but by no means a theoretical question.

94. Which is, for example, perfectly symmetrical with the relationship between semiosis and semioticity.
95. The concept of propensity considered here is the one discussed at length in FMAB-APH (Dinga et al., 2022), that is, the one proposed by Popper (in the Aristotelian tradition, by the way).
96. So, as Spencer-Brown points out, membranating means introducing a distinction, and introducing a distinction is the act of 'creating' two entities that are hanging from each other: the system and the environment, respectively. More generally, a distinction generates, as companion of each other, an interior and an exterior.
97. This 'inherent propensity' is, of course, a mere label or statement, because the existence of such a propensity, in turn, implies a metaphysical principle (i.e., a principle that does not allow for a factually verifiable justification). We will not, however, develop this regression *ad infinitum*.
98. The property of autonomy is not absolute, but relative, which means: (a) it is dependent on the nature of the environment in question and (b) it involves degrees of autonomy.
99. Of course, the reasoning can continue symmetrically (some would say: in a … fractal way) if the environment is, in turn, a system and the environment of the latter system is a system and so on.
100. In other words, the propensity of non-life to life (without entering Bergson's vitalism, of course).
101. We ignore, for the moment the radicalism of the term 'exclusive' which is an avatar of the insidious *homo mathematicus* model.
102. As is well known, a logical equivalent, but applicable in non-deliberative systems, is that of the order from fluctuations, which refers to the emergence of the macroscopic order from the spontaneous interaction of microscopic disorders (Prigogine & Stengers, 1984).
103. In fact, a significant part of the normative-institutional construction of society is nothing but the codification of implicit norms or background values that characterize the behaviour of individuals and social groups.
104. It should be noted that the most natural systems (non-living or living) have a mechanical cognition or cognitive ability. By mechanical cognition we mean a pre-programmed cognition in the structure (hence, in the functioning) of the systems in question and which is non-reflexive; in a more …

'technological' expression, mechanical cognition is a hard-type cognition, while reflexive cognition is a soft-type cognition.

105. In the theory of knowledge, it has long been noted that consciousness can be described by the phrase *know that you know*, which expresses exactly the reflexivity of cognition.
106. The dedicated research also identified, in the case of animals considered as superior (i.e., having a life, brain-based, relatively rich), some aspects related to memory/experience, 'intentional' cooperation, emotion/affectivity and other psychic feelings. Psychism is a necessary condition, but not sufficient for consciousness, that is, for a reflexive cognition, therefore (given that our study touches only tangentially and without the claim of scientificity, this issue) we will consider that only humans possess this type of cognition called reflexive cognition (or consciousness).
107. The constructions that some animals make in nature (nests, dens, dams—as in the case of beavers—nets—as in the case of spiders) cannot be considered artefacts, because they are not 'endowed' with the final cause (purpose), being simple effects of instinct, on the one hand, or (most frequently) of memetism, on the other hand.
108. Of course, transhumanism—which we have referred to on other occasions—will be able to adjust this assertion.
109. In our opinion, artefacts cannot have reflexive cognition although artificial intelligence (*AI*) can learn from its own functioning (from its own 'experience'—the quotation marks used here are intended to indicate that experience requires consciousness, i.e., feelings, what *AI* lacks). Learning (which is possible and real, e.g., by updating one's software, either biologically or mechanically) does not necessarily involve consciousness (here is an example where the appropriate term is, of course, awareness), as in the case of non-human animals. *Nota bene*: the possibility of learning is contained in the 'software' of the system concerned: the laws of physics in the case of non-living and non-artificial systems, DNA in the case of living systems and computer programmes (also based on the laws of physics) in the case of *AI*.
110. In the case of theism, there is no need for reactivity, because all the interventions of the Divinity are of the action type, never of the reaction type.
111. For the case of the alpha-type autopoiesis, we propose to maintain the concept of cognition proposed by Maturana and Varela—so, cognition in the sense of the Santiago school.
112. It is therefore obvious that the term *procedural closure* is another name for the same concept, namely, the concept of dissipation.
113. The non-invariance of total entropy (as consequence of the second law of thermodynamics) cannot be preserved in what we want to call (without developing further here), the *invariance of total complicatedness*: the invariance of the (logical) sum between the complicatedness of a system and the

complicatedness of its environment. The export of simplicity from the system and the import of complicatedness from the environment make a relative parallel (because it is symmetrical) with the export of high entropy from the system and the import of low entropy from the environment (which is, as it is known, asymmetric).

114. The primary cognition is the natural cognition, specific to the human individual.
115. We specify that, for the case of gamma-2 autopoiesis (which, for obvious reasons, we do not treat in this study), the predicate of sufficiency $AP_0^{\gamma 2}$ must be called: ***induced internal cognitive reflexivity***.
116. As we know, in this matter, there are three 'floors': digitization, digitalization and digital transformation—in an increasing order of informational, technological, social and general cultural scale and sophistication.
117. Under the sanction (as we have shown above) that the violation of this predicate of sufficiency 'degrades' the system from the quality of autopoietic system to that of sustainable system, the latter being characterized by operational openness.
118. We recall, at this point in the discussion, the scepticism expressed by Nicholas Georgescu-Roegen about the possibility of a sustainable economy (more precisely, sustainable economic growth) in discussing the entropic model of the economic process—we will return to this issue.
119. As known, in general, the failures (e.g., in the reproductive process) are bifurcation points for evolution.
120. This paragraph is a processing of some considerations from the work of one of the authors (Dinga, 2012).
121. The macroeconomic relevance of an objective can be assessed from at least two points of view: (a) as *significance*—the objective is significant for the vast majority of the population; (b) as *impact*—the objective contains emerging principles of generating processes at macroeconomic level. If these conditions are not met, or are met without continuity or are partially met, then macroeconomic relevance is compromised.
122. The computational feature of the mechanism means that it can be run on a universal Turing machine. In other words, aspects such as understanding (comprehension) the mechanism or framing it in some axiology are not relevant here, although, without a doubt, any *PPA* is generated by a theory that also contains aspects of understanding or values.
123. A concrete example could be the establishment of the guaranteed minimum nominal monthly minimum wage in payment on the economy.
124. By ***top-down*** algorithm is meant (in systems theory and especially in computational theory), an algorithm that contains the entire protocol to be followed by a universal Turing machine, without the possibility for the Turing machine itself (although it may exist, obviously for the programmer but, in

this case, we remain within the top-down) to modify this protocol through experience (or learning). On the contrary, an algorithm that allows this learning (i.e., modification of the protocol) through the very process of running the algorithm concerned, that is, by the Turing machine itself, will be called a *bottom-up* algorithm. The logical consistency between bottom-up algorithms and emergency phenomena is immediately noticeable.

125. Note that a public policy of adjustment can only be a macroeconomic policy (i.e., a policy with targets that are relevant to the macroeconomic level, even if the underlying effects most often occur—or are expected to occur—at the microeconomic level). Therefore, macroeconomic adjustment policies (especially monetary policy—available to the central bank—and fiscal policy—available to the government) must be causally, structurally and functionally correlated in what is called the *fiscal-monetary policy mix*, so that the aggregation of effects at macroeconomic level leads to the convergent achievement of the set targets, including through the synergy effect between the fiscal and the monetary factors.
126. Obviously, according to those mentioned, $PPA \subset PP$.
127. The syntactic rules according to which the poly-typical adjustment discourses are formed are, of course, incorporated in the mentioned top-down algorithm and depend, as we have shown, on the relevant (accepted) theory in the matter.
128. We refer to the less improved stages of public policies of adjustment, since this is the typical case (we do not take into account the situation in which the initial discretionary intervention is followed only by interventions of discretionary type). However, as public policies of adjustment improve, a dominance of initial non-discretionary interventions is established, which are followed also by non-discretionary interventions.
129. For example, the case of the circular adjustment discourse, which extends the periodicity to the initial intervention as well.
130. The presence of the human factor also introduces complexity (as shown above), not just complicatedness.
131. We propose that the degree of complexity of a poly-typical adjustment discourse be determined by the number of mono-typical discourses involved. This obviously involves the introduction of a dedicated institutional metric.
132. Let us observe, here, the necessary discrete character of the rate of action. Let us observe, at the same time, another property (which we will resume and develop further), namely, that according to which there is, on the one hand, an administrative constraint (administration of tax revenues) regarding the number of 'cells of action' (income tranches in our example above), and, on the other hand, an economic constraint on the actual size of the action rate (see Laffer curve).

133. Obviously, the sensitivity of an *AS* is directly proportional to its granularity. However, the *effectiveness*/efficacy of an automatic stabilizer is not unconditionally directly proportional to the sensitivity (or granularity) of the *AS*. Likewise, the *efficiency* of an automatic stabilizer depends, in a relatively non-intuitive way, on this sensitivity/granularity.
134. The substitution effects mentioned above (both between the rate of action and the base of action and between the granularities of the two) can act as a *sui generis AS*.
135. So, this is not a temporary lag, because any *AS* acts 'instantly', once the conditions that form the effective cause of that *AS* are met, but an economic lag, that is, a lag regarding the mechanism of transmission of the *AS* action on the variable of command that needs to be changed (economic lag is generated by economic theory accepted as governing the economic process concerned).
136. This reversal of the order in which the definition of a concept is treated and its predicates of sufficiency is more rhetorical—since, in order to state the definition, in fact, exactly the predicates of sufficiency were taken into account.
137. For such a case, we have given, elsewhere, the example of the free exchange rate, which is an automatic monetary stabilizer spontaneously generated by the foreign exchange market.
138. Here we want to warn the reader that by this we do not mean at all that *AS* is an endogenous (resultant) variable of the logical model of the economic process in question. Rather, it must be considered that *AS* is a parameter (it cannot be a variable, because its fixation was made from the very beginning, through the predicate of being institutional, i.e., normative) of control or, rather, a gap analyser.
139. For example, we may have institutional constructs with a stabilizing effect at the firm or microeconomic market level, but their final impact is not found in reducing GDP volatility. Although the theory of microeconomic substantiation of macroeconomics may argue that, in fact, by aggregation, such constructs can have the expected effect on GDP, we reject these arguments by invoking the composition fallacy and claim that such a construct should aim, from the very beginning, that is, from the design phase, as a goal (final cause), exactly the macroeconomic impact.
140. Note that the counter-cyclic predicate is 'stronger' than a possible predicate that would retain only the feedback behaviour. As is well known, feedback can also act pro-cyclically (positive feedback), if the analysis of the output of a black box indicates that achieving the finality of that black box requires a pro-cyclical variation of the input. By specifying a predicate of the counter-cyclicity type, we ensure that the *AS* always acts in the opposite direction of the variation of the controlled variable, that is, in the sense of smoothing

volatility, which is the very *raison d'être* of an *AS* (and which obviously has the nature of a negative feedback).

141. The extent to which the *AS* multiplier is supra-unitary obviously depends on the granularity of the action rate, respectively on the granularity of the action base, as well as on the admissibility range of the substitutability between the two quantities, respectively between the two granularities. It is easy to notice the logical and methodological connection between the concept of granularity and the concept of capillarity—which we do not develop here yet (the common element can be, of course, the concept of institutional grid).
142. We mention that, in the literature, the concept of social entropy is discussed, although not very intensely but, in our opinion, through an excessively mechanical analogy with the thermodynamic or informational entropy.
143. Of course, it can be extended to the whole social field, under the name of *social entropy* (Dinga et al., 2020).
144. The qualifier of *bound* refers to the fact that the energy in question is integrated, naturally or artificially, into a material support that preserves it, while ensuring accessibility to its use—for example, coal or wood are such material support for 'binding', that is, for storing the caloric energy.
145. Possibility that would materialize only if the price were still sensitive to information (past or present), in other words, if it did not already include this information available to the economic operator. Of course, lovers of neoclassical economic theory and frequential probabilities develop, here too, variants in which informational efficiency goes through values in the continuous range $[0, 1]$.
146. The concept of *implicit information* is a concept introduced by the authors and refers to information that does not exist *per se* but is inferred (by idiosyncratic models of rationality and hermeneutics) by economic agents, based on observing the behaviours of other economic agents in the market.
147. Note the reversal of the relationship between behavioural efficiency and behavioural entropy compared to the relationship between informational efficiency and informational entropy (in the case of EMH): while in the first case we have a relationship of inverse proportionality, in the latter case we have a direct proportionality relationship (the informational efficiency of the financial market—which means the exactly maximum informational efficiency—also expresses the maximum informational entropy of the financial market).
148. Of course, the inflection point of the autopoieticity curve will be determinable empirically in the analytical specifications and then at the level of parameters, as made for the function of autopoieticity in relation to the behavioural entropy.

149. These statements are easy to prove, rotating in the plane the curve *behavioural efficiency– behavioural entropy*, so that on the abscissa is the behavioural efficiency and on the ordinate is the behavioural entropy.
150. As it is known, the laws of thermodynamics (*Nota bene*: so far, it seems that four laws of thermodynamics have been formulated) do not give any answer about the way or the rule according to which the systems are configured (i.e., acquire their shape and structure).
151. Exergy is the name for useful, available or bound energy.
152. The original formulation is: *for a finite-size open system to persist in time (to survive) it must evolve in such a way that it provides easier and easier access to the currents that flow through it*) (Bejan, 2007).
153. In our opinion, the constructal law is not of the power of a principle (or a … law of nature), as it is presented by the author, but it has the features of a mechanism (like the Darwinian theory of the evolution of life, which is a mechanism, not a principle—e.g., Darwinism cannot explain the origin of life, but only its evolution after it appeared; *Nota bene*: neither Physics can explain the singularity from the moment of the big bang, but only everything that happened later). The difference between principle/law and mechanism is as follows: principle/law answers the question 'why', that is, 'based on which cause', while the mechanism answers the question 'how'.
154. Which, obviously, detracts from the justification of its universal character.
155. But there are cases in which either there are no such material support for configuring the shape and structure to allow flows (e.g., cactus), or the movement of the systems in question is very slow (e.g., turtle) (Freire & Andrade, 2021).
156. Although the emphasis (and the examples given) refers to physical flows, it is obvious that, from a conceptual point of view, any type of flows can be accepted: informational, entropic, ideational, axiological and so on. However, such a generalization is not yet achieved, constituting, in our opinion, a challenge for researchers who consider that the constructal law is a productive direction in epistemology (*Nota bene*: we are not among these researchers, since we have our own fundamental 'law' on behaviour, i.e., in a more general sense, interaction, namely, the *law of the minimum entropic gradient*—which will, however, be developed later).
157. It is a cognition that has an even wider scope than the one proposed by the Santiago School, because it also includes non-living (non-animated) nature.
158. Allometry (or allometrics) studies the relationships of determination between the body dimensions of living entities and the shape and dimensions of their somatic organs (either internal or external), their internal structure, functions and behaviour.
159. In addition to these two arrows of time (which are logically consistent with each other), there is also the psychological arrow of time: time increases

from the point where the feelings (or lived events) in memory are less numerous to the point where those feelings are more numerous.

160. Although autopoieticity has been developed (and examined) for living nature, it is easily extensible to non-living nature, thus gaining the same frame of reference as constructal law.
161. Recall that the concept of hypercycle was introduced by Manfred Eigen and Peter Schuster (1979) and means, in the most general sense, a catalytic network (including self-catalysis). Although the concept was developed to explain the transition of molecules (more precisely, a molecular complex, integrated precisely by the action of the hypercycle) from the pre-biotic phase to the biotic phase (i.e., in order to explain the origin of life), its abstract meaning can be taken also by other scientific fields, including financial market issues (more generally, *LLS*).
162. Or purpose, if we consider human individuals, knowing that the purpose is a conscious finality. However, both finality and purpose are of a *causa finalis* nature.
163. Some authors consider that all causality is covered by the effective/efficacy cause, which is a simplification but not a logical error, however.
164. Regarding the principle of evolution (which will cover both the second law of thermodynamics and autopoieticity, respectively the constructal law), we will make a proposal in the following.
165. In this sense, Adrian Bejan also published the work entitled *The Physics of Life: The Evolution of Everything* (Bejan, 2016).
166. It is understood that the conclusion is not valid here: $[(A \subset B) \bigwedge (B \subset A)] \rightarrow A = B$, because the two inclusions refer to different parts of the referential sphere. Therefore, *CL's* claim to be the most fundamental 'law' of evolution is debatable, at least from an extensive point of view.
167. Dissipative systems can be classified as follows (Dinga, 2012): (1) dissipative systems of rank ' -1 '—in which the speed of entropy in the system (λ_S) is higher than the speed of entropy in the environment (λ_E), that is, $\lambda_S > \lambda_E$; (2) dissipative systems of rank ' 0 '—where $\lambda_S = \lambda_E$; (3) dissipative systems of rank ' 1 '—in which $\lambda_S < \lambda_E$. Dissipative systems of rank ' 1 ' can, in turn, be of two types: (a) dissipative systems of rank ' 1α ' (these are non-human systems), provided that $0 \leq \lambda_S^{1\alpha} < \lambda_E$; (b) dissipative systems of rank ' 1β ' (these are human-type systems), provided $0 \leq \lambda_S^{1\beta} < \lambda_S^{1\alpha} < \lambda_M$.
168. Obviously, 'A' and 'B' are interchangeable without changing the reasoning, although, as we shall see, it may be necessary for the membranes of dissipative systems to be endowed with the ability to recognize the entropic gradient between the dissipative systems concerned and the complementary environment (including other dissipative systems, with different rates of local entropy).

169. We consider only the case of 'contemporary' dissipative systems. The alternative case, in which the dissipative systems in entropic interaction are not contemporary, is reduced to the previous case, given that the existence of a dissipative system leaves an 'entropic trace' in the complementary environment in which it 'lived', a trace that will be taken into account on the occasion of the appearance of a new dissipative, non-contemporary system, in terms of the level and speed of entropy (in other words, the Universe is brought to 'zero' every time).
170. Among the 'functions' of the demon that replaces Maxwell's demon will obviously be that of 'calculating' the entropic gradient between the dissipative system concerned and the genuine complementary environment (or between the dissipative system concerned and other dissipative systems).
171. As it is known, for example, light always follows the shortest path between two points (in general, the shortest path is the path that follows the geodesic generated by the curvature of space–time, as indicated by non-Euclidean geometries, respectively the general theory of relativity). But, as we mentioned in the content of this study, the dissipative systems generate, in their turn, a sui-generis *entropic curvature*, although in a different sense than the one referring to the physical space–time. Specifically, dissipative systems generate 'geodesics' that indicate that the entropic interaction will occur between dissipative systems with the minimum entropic gradient (the principle also works in the particular case where in Universe 1 there is only one dissipative system: indeed, in this last case, the minimum entropic gradient is just that between the dissipative system and the genuine homogeneous anti-dissipative complementary medium, so the principle is held).
172. The principle is suggested, moreover, by the sublunary experience (and, until proven otherwise, we should consider it valid for the whole Universe, that is, to make a transition, under the sanction of Popper's falsifiability, from contingent to necessary) regarding, for example, the genuine food (trophic) chain: carnivorous animals at the top of the food chain do not procure low entropy directly from the plant environment, but 'prefer' to do so indirectly by consuming herbivorous animals. But this only means 'choosing' the entropic exchange based on the principle of the minimum entropic gradient.
173. Laplaceanism in this expression is not too difficult to recognize.
174. Of course, this deterministic enthusiasm should be substantially tempered by the fact that, instrumentally, for the moment, it is impossible for us to measure these entropic gradients. Note that, from an epistemological point of view, we have here exactly the same problem that arose in the matter of the theory of cardinal utility (in the latter case, however, we have the 'solution' of recourse to the theory of ordinal utility, generating, however, in turn, so many inconsistencies between predictions and their updating). Let

us note another important thing here: the entropic gradient has not only a scalar but also an algebraic sign: the entropic exchange will occur in such a way that the low entropy will 'flow' from the system that has the highest entropy to the one that has the lowest entropy, never the other way around. However, this statement must be substantiated. Here is our argument: we have 'established' that the finality of Universe 0 (and therefore of any possible Universe 1) is to reach the state of thermodynamic equilibrium. As the appearance of dissipative systems (systems far from equilibrium) accelerates this process, it 'results' that this appearance of dissipative systems is (from the 'point of view' of the Universe) 'rational'. Now, if we were to assume that the entropic exchange, in the case of a given entropic gradient, would be done in such a way that high entropy would flow from the higher entropy system to the lower entropy system, then, as stated above, low entropy should be consumed from the higher entropy system to achieve this exchange; consequently, this would produce high entropy in the system that has just 'delivered' high entropy, which would nullify, for example (or decrease, in any case), the entropic 'gain' obtained by 'exporting' high entropy. This result does not fall within the rationality mentioned above. Consequently, the entropic exchange will occur exactly the opposite: the system with higher entropy will 'pump' to the system with lower entropy, lower entropy, which will consume additional low entropy from the system with higher entropy. This time, the result is consistent with the 'rationality' of the Universe in question.

175. Logically, as soon as there are at least two dissipative systems in Universe 1, there are no direct entropic exchanges with the genuine complementary environment, but only between existing dissipative systems, based on the principle of choosing the minimum entropic gradient. It is obvious, at the same time, that the indirect entropic exchange will take place between the two dissipative systems, following that, based on the same principle of the minimum entropic gradient, the dissipative system with the entropy speed closest to that of the complementary environment will nevertheless achieve direct entropic exchange with this environment.

176. It is as if we were dealing with a kind of entropic 'productivity': the amount of low entropy needed to increase by a given size the entropic differential between two dissipative systems (or between the dissipative system and the complementary environment, if in Universe 1 there is only one dissipative system). Therefore, the principle of the minimum gradient of choice of entropic interaction can also be expressed in the form, logically equivalent, of the principle of maximum productivity of variation of the entropic gradient. Here, a suggestion for economists dealing with total factors productivity might arise: perhaps, along with the Solow residue, a residue (this time with a negative sign) generated by entropic processes in economic activities

should also be considered, so that we have a *global* factors productivity of the issue and not only a *total* one. But we consider the most important suggestion at this point in the discussion to be the following: there is a natural tendency for low entropy to flow spontaneously in the direction of a negative entropic gradient and high entropy to flow spontaneously in the direction of a positive entropic gradient, analogous to that the heat (as a macroscopic quantity) flows spontaneously in the direction of the negative temperature gradient and 'non-heat' (cold) flows spontaneously in the direction of the positive temperature gradient.

177. For example, in the case of economic systems, the emergence of specialization, based on the productive advantage (absolute or relative), which led to exchange, makes, in fact, trade relations to take place on specific 'geodesics' generated by the degree of economic development. In this sense, it can be stated (but remains, of course, to be developed in a complete and coherent way) that economic flows (of goods or factors of production) follow a kind of minimum gradient of the level of economic development (the gradient may refer to either competitiveness, productivity or opportunity, etc.). More talented analysts may find suggestions here to replace the current national specialization criteria (absolute advantage, relative advantage, competitive advantage, endowment with factors, level of average of national productivity, niches, etc.) with a more general criterion: that of... economic geodesic. A suggestion, completely general, in this sense, is made in Emil Dinga, *The inertial phenomenon in the economic process* (Dinga, 2001).
178. The authors believe that *LMEGI* is more fundamental than *CL*, but this assumption will be examined elsewhere.
179. For example, they can be simply sustainable.
180. This conjecture is one of the clearest ways of empirical testability of the minimum entropic interaction hypothesis, which gives scientific character to this hypothesis.
181. This interesting result will not be further developed here, where we will only specify that the hypercycle can be of two types: (a) positive hypercycle—based on positive feedback—and (b) negative hypercycle—based on negative feedback (combinations of the two categories of hypercycle being, of course, possible).
182. It is obvious that the type of probabilities that 'qualifies' in this case is neither that of objective frequential probabilities nor that of subjective Bayesian probabilities but, most ... probably, that of propensity-type probabilities (*Nota bene*: which are, in essence, possibilities, not probabilities—except if we do want to call with the term probability exactly the degree of possibility).
183. For example, a loop can be formalized as feedback (either positive or negative).

184. Of course, in the most general sense, these flows can be considered entropy flows, based on an appropriate formalization.
185. But, for the needs of this study, we do not further develop the network analysis.
186. Obviously, for research on the organization and functioning of the financial market it is important and relevant to identify precisely the type of structural organization concerned.
187. The assertion, also mentioned previously, is: '*For to him who has will be given more, but from him who has not, even what s/he has will be taken away!*'.
188. It seems possible to calculate a 'gravitational acceleration' in this regard, by analogy with the gravitational acceleration generated by mass in cosmology.
189. This case occurs, for example, in the *LLS* called family—family members are, at the same time, legislators and executors regarding the tasks and actions carried out in that *LLS*.
190. In Lebniz's terminology, the monadic component, although not exactly in the Lebnizian sense, in which monads are qualitatively indistinct/indistinguishable from each other.
191. This is the exact meaning in which the phrase (which has the value of a mechanism, although not of principle as well) 'invisible hand', which appeared in connection with the functioning of the so-called free market, is used in reasoning and modelling (*Nota bene*: however, neither more fierce and dogmatic libertarian parents of economic theory do not support the existence of a (completely) free market, because this is a logical and functional impossibility).
192. Perhaps a criterion for segmenting the action of the constructal law could be extracted from this: the constructal law is proper (although, as we will show in another communication, currently being prepared, not necessarily) to quasi-systems (networks), because the networks are the ones that develop flows with material support, that is, they have dendritic spatio-temporal configurations.

References

Barabási, A.-L. (2002). *Linked-the New Science of Networks*. Perseus Books Group.

Bejan, A. (2007). *Constructal Theory of Social Dynamics*. Springer.

Bejan, A. (2016). *The Physics of Life: The Evolution of Everything*. St. Martin's Press.

Dinga, E. (2001). *The Inertial Phenomenon in the Economic Process*. Economică Publishing House.

Dinga, E. (2012). *Rebuilding Economics: Logical, Epistemological and Methodological Approaches*. Lambert Academic Publishing, Saarbrucken, Germany.

Dinga, E. (2021). Logically Living System: A Generative "Machine" for Autopoietic Systems – Chapter 4. In *Handbook of Research on Autopoiesis and Self-Sustaining Processes for Organizational Success – Chapter 4 – Logically Living System – A Generative Machine for Auto-Poietic Systems* (first, p. 25) IGI Global.

Dinga, E. (2023). *Economy and Society. Theoretical, Methodological and Empirical Approaches – In progress.* Economică Publishing House.

Dinga, E., Oprean-Stan, C., Tănăsescu, C.-R., Brătian, V., & Ionescu, G.-M. (2021). Entropy-Based Behavioural Efficiency of the Financial Market. *Entropy, 23*(11), 1396.

Dinga, E., Oprean-Stan, C., Tanasescu, C.-R., Brătian, V., & Ionescu, G.-M. (2022). *Financial Market Analysis and Behaviour: The Adaptive Preference Hypothesis* (Vol. 1). Taylor and Francis Ltd. – Routledge.

Dinga, E., Tănăsescu, C.-R., & Ionescu, G.-M. (2020). Social Entropy and Normative Network. *Entropy, 22*(9), 1051.

Eigen, M., & Schuster, P. (1979). *The Hypercycle: A Principle of Natural Self-Organization.* Springer-Verlag.

Freire, L. O., & de Andrade, D. A. (2021). Novel Aspects of Constructal Law: Four Distinct and Competing Goals in Flow Channels Design. *Open Journal of Applied Sciences, 11*(6), 647–664.

Georgescu-Roegen, N. (1971). *The Law of Entropy and the Economic Process.* Harvard University Press.

Maturana, H., & Varela, F. (1980). *Autopoiesis and Cognition.* Living. D. Reidel Publishing Company.

Prigogine, I., & Nicolis, G. (1977). *Self-Organization in Non-Equilibrium Systems.* Wiley.

Prigogine, I., & Stengers, I. (1984, Romanian edition). Noua alianta. Metamorfoza stiintei (Engl: New alliance. The metamorphosis of science). Editura Politică.

Spencer-Brown, G. (1994). *The Laws of Form.* Cognizer Co.

Wolfram, S. (2002). *A New Kind of Science.* Wolfram Media.

CHAPTER 4

Autopoietic Market Hypothesis: The Financial Autopoiesis

Autopoietic Selection in the Financial Market

Autopoietic Mutation in the Financial Market

The evolutionary (respectively co-evolutionary) model of the financial market as a financial species[1] has already been described and assumed previously, from the perspective of the hypothesis of the adaptive preference regarding the functioning of the financial market (Dinga et al., 2022). At this stage of the research, given the objectives set for the overall research, we need to examine the functioning of the financial market from the perspective of another hypothesis: the (financial) market autopoieticity hypothesis or the *Autopoietic Market Hypothesis* (APMH).[2]

Regarding the concept of autopoietic mutation related to the species called financial market, we will discuss the following issues: (a) the possibility/necessity of autopoietic mutation; (b) the mechanism of the autopoietic mutation; (c) genetic autopoietic mutation versus epigenetic autopoietic mutation.

The Possibility/Necessity of the Autopoietic Mutation

The examination of this aspect of the autopoieticity of the financial market will be made on the basis of the predicate of sufficiency of autopoieticity (discussed above) called operational closure. This predicate refers to the fact that any 'decision' within the system in question is made exclusively

E. Dinga et al., *Economic and Financial Market Behaviour*,
https://doi.org/10.1007/978-3-031-31702-6_4

within the membrane of that system,[3] which can of course also be called decision-making autonomy. In connection with this assertion, several aspects are important:

- Is decision-making autonomy really possible in the case of trading strategy? The trading strategy (as a financial individual) is obviously inalienable in relation to the human individual (as a biological individual), that is, the trading strategy (TS) is thought, designed and objectified (through the set of individual transactions inferred from the TS) by a human individual. The immediate conclusion (suggested, by the way, also earlier, albeit rather implicitly) is that the TS genome is the propensity of the human individual, in the sense that TS does not have an authentic genome, but one 'borrowed from the human individual', that is, it is a genome assumed by transfer. Therefore, any adjustment of the genome called propensity (i.e., any mutation) can be, in essence, only autopoietic, since the human individual is autonomous and sovereign in deciding (consciously or not—*Nota bene*: as already shown, any individual decision is a result of the emotion-rationality mix[4]) if, in what sense, to what degree and with what lag/lead s/he will change his/her propensity associated (variation) with that TS. Consequently, the possibility of decisional autonomy (i.e., operational closure) in the occurrence of the mutation is clear;
- Is decision-making autonomy relevant/significant? The answer is obviously yes, because there is no alternative to self-adjustment of propensity, as already shown above. Here, however, another problem arises, namely, the problem of normativity. Indeed, although the human individual is autonomous in his/her decision to adjust the propensity associated with a given TS, yet (to a large extent) the adoption and objectification of the TS is subject to normative constraints which, by definition, come from outside the human individual, through relational openness. In a very direct sense, normativity 'adjusts' from the outside (so by a heteronomous decision) the propensity of the human individual in relation to a given TS. However, given that the human individual may (on the basis of a cost–benefit analysis or for other reasons) oppose, that is, not respect the external norm,[5] assuming, of course, the associated costs, it can be concluded that, even in the case of normative constraints, one cannot speak, in fact, of an operational opening. Therefore, decision-making autonomy is relevant, that is, it has significance;

- a conclusion can be drawn of the utmost importance for the construction of the autopoietic model of the financial market, namely that, in fact, the financial market can only function (in an) autopoietic way, that is, there is an intrinsic (structural) need for the autopoieticity of the financial market—we will call this conclusion the *ontological condition of the autopoieticity of the financial market* (this condition will be used massively in the design of the APMH model of the financial market further).

Autopoietic Mutation Mechanism
Let us examine, in a more analytical way, the mechanism by which the autopoietic mutation occurs with respect to a TS. To examine the occurrence of the autopoietic mutation is to examine the endogenous adjustment of the propensity of a human individual in its relationship with the TS to which that propensity[6] is associated. We consider that the main aspects in this matter are the following:

- there is a *structural inertia of propensity*, of a purely psychological (i.e., idiosyncratic[7]) nature, which makes the propensity associated with a given TS to resist, to some extent, the temptation to adjustment, as the latter is induced by the information (taken as such, or inferred from observing the behaviour of other participants in financial market transactions—i.e., information that we have called implicit information—or taken over by normative enforcement) processed by the human individual;[8]
- there is, at the same time, an *inertia of the irreversibility of the propensity*, once, under certain conditions, that propensity has been adjusted. In fact, the two inertial properties can be considered as one, acting under different conditions—one on the propensity adjustment, the other on the cancellation of the adjustment (i.e., in the latter case, a negation 'without rest', otherwise it is just a new adjustment);[9]
- the autopoietic mutation (genetic type, here, because it refers to propensity adjustment) is done, as already shown, in our model $RE^{(1)}E^{(2)}$ (reason/rationality–experience–emotion). Therefore, this modal filter (described in FMAB-APH), in making the decision to adjust the propensity, cannot be modelled, in principle, analytically, because it contains at least one weightless component (emotion $E^{(2)}$), although the experience ($E^{(1)}$) is debatable, as well, in terms of the possibility of its quantitative measurement. Note that by measurement we mean an

ex-ante measurement (since *ex-post* measurement does not pose any problems, neither methodological nor epistemological[10]), and, more than that, by *ex-ante* measurement we mean prediction—in this sense, the highest predictability, with the inherent cautions, of course, is exhibited by the rationality component R, on the second place in this ordering is the experience $E^{(1)}$, and on the last place is the emotion $E^{(2)}$.

Figure 4.1 indicates a suggestion of this mechanism (where with '*1*' the adjustment of the propensity was noted—i.e., an adjustment generated by the modal filter[11]—and with '*2*' the adjustment of empirical type, i.e., rule of thumb, was noted).

Genetic Autopoietic Mutation Versus Epigenetic Autopoietic Mutation
In connection with this problem, the possibility (or impossibility) of the existence of the epigenetic autopoietic mutation should be shown, given that the possibility of the genetic autopoietic mutation has been shown above. Our reasoning is this:

- epigenetic autopoietic mutation refers to a mutation that occurs directly in the phenotype (in our case, directly in the trading strategy), without any propensity adjustment. Such a mutation obviously involves influences on TS that come from the environment but come out of the area that the human individual can control in terms of decision;[12]

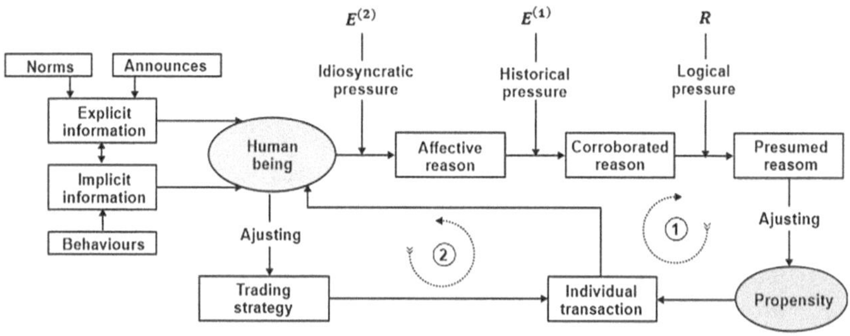

Fig. 4.1 Mechanism of autopoietic mutation. (*Source*: Authors)

- of course, it could be objected that the economic operator can always avoid or violate this type of constraint (assuming the associated costs, regardless of their nature and amplitude) and that, therefore, there can be no epigenetic mutation. We will reply to this position that, although it is true that the economic operator has, in theory, the ability to ignore any constraints (most often on the basis of a cost–benefit analysis[13]), s/he may, in some cases, decide on the TS adjustment without that this implies an adjustment of the propensity—here we have, obviously, the exact operational definition of an epigenetic autopoietic mutation;
- to accept the epigenetic autopoietic mutation—and we see no decisive reason for rejecting the possibility of such a mutation—at the TS level implies, logically, some consequences to which we will refer, briefly, in the following:
  - *firstly*, it confirms (in terms of the coherence of the discourse in this research) our position that individual transactions do not directly and necessarily lead to the adjustment of the TS and that it is necessary to exceed significance thresholds in this regard; as long as the quantitative impact is below the significance threshold, it is possible to adjust the TS without it going through the adjustment of the propensity;
  - *secondly*, it is possible for the economic operator concerned to make changes to the TS without any environmental influence in the direction of that change[14]—for example, a superstitious person who has made a profit from using a TS through its three operationalizations in the form of individual transactions, based on the mystical meaning of the number three, can change the TS in question both without an external impulse or without having adjusted the propensity when s/he has to perform the fourth attempt (*Nota bene*: of course, the example is a marginal one, but the exceptions are always marginal, are they not?).

Classes of Autopoietic Mutations

There are two basic criteria for classifying autopoietic mutations: (a) the *structural* criterion—refers to the foundational aspect of the mutation; (b) *functional* criterion—refers to the operational aspect of the mutation.

- According to the structural criterion, there can be two types of autopoietic mutations:
  - *strategic* autopoietic mutations: those autopoietic mutations that change the propensity of the economic agent in question (of course, as we have shown above, exclusively through the decision of that economic agent, namely on the basis of theoretical rationality);
  - *tactical* autopoietic mutations: those autopoietic mutations that modify individual transactions (within a given TS), obviously, without this implying the adjustment of propensity;[15]
- according to the functional criterion, there can be three types of autopoietic mutations:
  - *autonomous* autopoietic mutations: those autopoietic mutations that, whether they adjust the propensity or not, are decided by the idiosyncrasy of the economic agent, for whatever internal reason (i.e., not came from the environment): cost–benefit calculation, intuition, lottery, adventurism, chance and so on;
  - *tracking* autopoietic mutations: those autopoietic mutations which are, logically and economically, obligatory to be performed following an autonomous mutation (or of any other type), in order to ensure the coherence of the general behaviour of the economic operator concerned;
  - *induced* autopoietic mutations: those autopoietic mutations which, although carried out by the economic operator (*Nota bene*: this is, of course, the precise meaning of the qualifier autopoietic, which implies the operational closure, as already shown) come, more or less imperatively, from environment (most often from the regulatory system regarding the functioning of the financial market).

Therefore, there are four types of autopoietic mutations:

- $(\mathcal{M}_1)$ Strategic autonomous autopoietic mutations
- $(\mathcal{M}_2)$ Strategically induced autopoietic mutations
- $(\mathcal{M}_3)$ Autopoietic tactical tracking mutations
- $(\mathcal{M}_4)$ Tactically induced autopoietic mutations

Nota bene: any of the three types of autopoietic mutations according to the functional criterion can be any of the autopoietic mutations according to the structural criterion, so by simultaneously applying the two classification criteria, we can have four distinct autopoietic mutations.[16]

Theoretical Rationality and Practical Rationality in Autopoietic Mutation

The rationality of a manifestation (decision, action—either act or abstention—pattern of behaviour, etc.) means the property of that manifestation to be inferred from or consistent with a model of rationality. The model of rationality is a model of justification.[17] In this sense, it is obvious that rationality is 'anchored' to the model of rationality in question, which means that rationality is always relative, although, from the perspective of the individual, the model of rationality is usually absolute.[18] In this conceptual context, to reason means to extract a logical consequence from a model of rationality,[19] while to rationalize means to demonstrate the consistency and coherence of a certain manifestation with a given model of rationality.

Rationality can be a theoretical rationality, respectively a practical one. Theoretical rationality aims at the prominence of belief—more precisely, it aims at the interest of the individual so that his/her manifestation is concordant (consistent, compatible, coherent) with his/her belief system. Practical rationality aims at the prominence of the manifestation as such—more precisely, it aims at the interest of the individual for the manifestation to take place, that is, to make a decision, to carry out an action or to manifest a certain behaviour.

Applying these conceptual delimitations to the issue of autopoietic mutation in the financial market, we can draw the following main conclusions:

- the autopoietic mutation is governed by both theoretical and practical rationality, because the human individual (economic agent) is interested both in the consistency of his/her manifestations with his/her own belief system (theoretical rationality) and in the objectification of these manifestations (practical rationality);
- of course, the dominance of one type of rationality over the other is a function of the specific behaviour of the economic agent in question—for example, it is plausible to consider that the design or choice of a TS implies a dominance of theoretical rationality, while the design

or choice of an individual transaction within a given TS implies a dominance of practical rationality;
- it is perhaps correct to consider, at the same time, that practical rationality lies rather in the origin of tactical autopoietic mutations, while theoretical rationality lies rather in the origin of strategic autopoietic mutations.

Autopoietic Selection

The Concept of Autopoietic Selection in the Financial Market
The concept of autopoietic selection can be understood in at least two ways: (a) autopoietic selection at the phenotype level and (b) autopoietic selection at the species level. As we are talking here about the financial market, we are reminded that the phenotype (the 'adult' financial individual) is the trading strategy (TS), and the financial species is the financial market (FM). *Nota bene*: the environment of this species is cultural geodesic. At the same time, the main meaning of autopoiesis (or the property of autopoieticity) should be (re)specified: the operational closure, as defined by this predicate of sufficiency. This aspect, completely unique in the autopoietic modelling of the financial market, will be described, in broad outline, below and will be developed in analytical form in the end of this chapter.

⊳ *Short (Preparatory) Discussion*
Before analytically unfolding the property of autopoieticity in the financial field, some considerations regarding the linkage between the autopoiesis in the (natural) living world and the autopoiesis in the (cultural) non-living world[20] can be of usefulness.

Firstly, the non-living character of the artefacts (in our case, of social or institutional artefacts) is specious, because it can be imaged a genus for different species of living entities—for example, the concept of logically living systems can be such a genus, so containing at least two species: (a) BLS—biologically living systems; (b) SLS—socially living systems or, equivalently, ILS—institutionally living systems. The idea here consists in finding the sufficient predicates which (seems to) define the property of living, no matter it is about the natural or cultural field.

Secondly, both in the case of BLS and in the case of ILS (as the financial market is) the systems involved have internal 'programs' for at least three fundamental functions: (1) knowledge on the environment (no matter if it is a conscious knowledge or not); (2) choosing of the niche (i.e., an area into the environment that allows the fitness maximization), according to the knowledge already acquired; (3) replicating by itself, that is, based on internal principles. It is obvious that the three functions, *mutatis mutandis*, are present at both BLS and ILS. In such a context, it is justified to accept a conceptual, methodological and pragmatical continuity from the autopoieticity in the natural world to the cultural one.

Thirdly, autopoiesis process in the ILSs is a mix between normative framework which regulates the financial market (in an imperative way[21]) and the free will of the human agents who make decision and perform actions. By contrast with the BLSs, where the Darwinism is dominant, in the ILSs case the Lamarckism becomes dominant.

Autopoietic Selection at the Level of the Trading Strategy

This selection refers to the TS adjustment as a result of the adjustment (previous logically and chronologically) of the propensity, regardless of the channel through which this adjustment is 'claimed', according to the typology of the autopoietic mutation presented above. We are therefore dealing with a 'classic' selection, based on a genetic mutation (we remember that the financial genome is the very propensity or belief system—from which emanates the preference, especially the adaptive preference, discussed in FMAB-APH (Dinga et al., 2022)—of the human economic agent). Therefore, this type of selection will have to accept/validate or reject/invalidate the propensity adjustment, through (perfectly analogous in financial theory and biological theory) the inter-action between the phenotype (which manifests itself in the form of individual transaction, as particular hypostasis—occurrence—of the new trading strategy initiated by the propensity adjustment) and environment (mainly cultural geodesic[22]). There is, in this selection mechanism, a 'protection' of the trading strategy, a 'protection' which is achieved by the first line of confronting the phenotype with the environment, namely, by individual transaction (or rather by the set of individual transactions) inferred or inferable from the adjusted trading strategy in question),[23] in a way (which we have previously suggested) similar to the mechanism of functioning of the research programme concept proposed by Imre Lakatos (Lakatos, 1978) in the field of epistemology.[24]

Autopoietic Selection at the Level of Individual Transaction

This selection refers to the adjustment of the individual transaction, that is, the actual manifestation of the trading strategy, without this adjustment being generated by any adjustment of the trading strategy itself which, as we know, occurs only as a result of and after the propensity adjustment. In other words, it is a matter of confronting the 'protection belt' of the trading strategy (to use the terminology of Lakatos, mentioned above) with the environment (i.e., mainly with cultural geodesic) until reaching a threshold of significance that would suggest the agent economic to move to change the propensity itself, that is, to move to the first type (discussed above) of autopoietic selection. Noting that, as in the first case of autopoietic selection, here we make only a conceptual sketch of the problem, while it will be developed, in all relevant aspects, in the end of this chapter. We think the following considerations are useful:

- the autopoietic selection of the individual transaction is a selection based on an epigenetic mutation, as it results from the fact that it does not involve the adjustment of the genome, that is, the propensity;
- being a selection based on epigenetic autopoietic mutation, it will act strictly within what we can call the 'dead zone' (Dinga, 2012) of the trading strategy to which the individual transaction in question is associated, that is, within the variation area of the individual transaction whose variation do not go beyond the basic logic of the master-trading strategy;
- from a qualitative point of view, of course, the 'dead zone' for adjusting the individual transaction can be as extensive—for example, it can refer to both relatively small (though significant) changes in the individual transaction and, in extreme cases, the complete elimination of an individual transaction and (possibly) its replacement with another individual transaction that verifies the logical anchoring to the operational trading strategy in place.

Gradualism and Saltationism in Autopoietic Selection

The issue of gradualism and/or saltationism in the evolutionary selection associated with the symbolic species called the financial market was discussed quite analytically in FMAB-APH (Dinga et al., 2022), when the hypothesis of adaptive preference was examined. Of course, given that, in our opinion, the hypothesis of the autopoietic market is more comprehensive, from the point of view of the referential (denoted), than the hypothesis of adaptive preference, all assertions, claims and arguments presented to the hypothesis of adaptive preference are also valid for the case of the autopoietic market hypothesis, *mutatis mutandis*. However, moving from species to genus, we cannot use the logical argument *a fortiori*,[25] so we need to examine, in a dedicated way, the problem of gradualism versus the problem of saltationism directly in the case of the latter hypothesis. Our considerations in this matter are as follows:

- the evolution of symbolic species (in our case, of the financial market) is not of the gradualist type, but of the saltationist one. This means:
  - any mutation (but especially any epigenetic mutation, as discussed above) must be of a certain level in terms of the amount of mutation,[26] which is to remove it from the 'dead zone' of the trading strategy to which the individual transaction in question is belonging to;
  - as long as the mutation remains in the 'dead zone', it is not selected, that is, does not contribute to the adjustment (neither in the case of the individual transaction nor, even more so, in the level of the trading strategy);
  - if the mutation leaves the 'dead zone' it is immediately and completely taken over in the phenotype (in our case, in the trading strategy);
  - obviously, as shown in the case of the adaptive preference of the financial market, there is a 'dead zone' at the level of the individual transaction and one at the level of the trading strategy;
- the existence of the two 'dead zones' leads us to the concept, which we want to introduce in this point of the discussion, namely, that of *selective inertia*.[27] By selective inertia we mean the property of an evolutionary mechanism to make a discrete selection, somehow a quantified one, that is, a selection that is triggered only when a minimum quantity of change is formed (which can no longer be reduced, in terms of eligibility for selection); this minimum amount could be called—literally, not just metaphorically or by analogy—the *quantum of mutation*. In our opinion, the concept of selective inertia, with its

logical 'product'—the quantum of mutation—could be developed through follow-up research, so as to build a *sui generis* predictor of financial market behaviour.

Autopoiesis and Self-Selection

The main predicate of the sufficiency of the autopoiesis of a system (as it was highlighted by Maturana and Varela) is that of the operational closure, provided that the relational openness of that system is maintained. Naturally, the question arises as to whether autopoiesis entails (i.e., necessarily claims) self-selection. To examine this issue, it is, of course, necessary to define the concept of self-selection and then to verify whether the process of autopoiesis (or, equivalently, the property of autopoieticity) can 'deliver' the characteristics of this definition.

The Concept of Self-Selection

Self-selection differs from the more general concept of selection in that it is operated not by the environment but by the phenotype itself. Of course, this transfer of the operational character of the selection from the environment to the phenotype can be examined either from the perspective of the modality (direct transfer vs. indirect transfer) or from the perspective of the sphere (complete transfer vs. incomplete transfer).

- Modality/the way
  - We have previously shown that in the case of the symbolic species called the financial market, the autopoietic mutation is always performed by the human agent (economic agent), regardless of the channel through which the pressure on that mutation comes and regardless of whether the mutation concerns only the individual transaction (i.e., contextual—space–time—hypostatising of the trading strategy), which represents an epigenetic mutation or directly targets even the trading strategy (i.e., the propensity of the economic agent), which represents a genetic mutation;
  - in this context, it is obvious that, for both the epigenetic and genetic autopoietic mutations, we are in the presence of a decisional autonomy of the economic agent;
  - the new individual transaction, which occurred as a result of the epigenetic mutation, or, as the case may be, the new trading strategy, which occurred as a result of the genetic mutation, is, how-

ever, subject to the environmental verdict—in our case (mainly) the cultural geodesic verdict. The problem is that, unlike the case of selection in the biological evolution, in our opinion, here there must be a ratification, by the economic agent, of the 'decision' of selection or non-selection, made by cultural geodesic, of the mutation in question. In other words, as in the case of a mutation which, in the last resort, is a decision of the economic operator, that is, it is a self-mutation, and in the case of selection, the economic agent must accept (ratify, as we said) the selection made by the environment;

- therefore, from the perspective of the modality/way of selection in the financial market, we can note, following this qualitative analysis, that the selection is an *indirect* one, that is, it is a selection that takes place in two steps: (1) *factual* selection—made by the environment (cultural geodesic, mainly), which is, somehow, a selection ... 'recommended' to the economic agent; (2) *decisional* selection—made by the economic agent, which is, somehow, a ratified selection,[28] having the nature of a ratification of the recommended environmental selection;
- another very important aspect of the indirect character discussed here, namely, that of the transfer of the operational character of autopoietic selection, refers to the recipient of this transfer: thus, in the case of a non-symbolic species (i.e., in the case of a biological, natural species) the transfer in this case, if it were possible—but obviously it is not possible—it would be from the environment to the phenotype, that is, to the adult biological individual, while in the case of the symbolic species called the financial market, this transfer is made from environment (cultural geodesic) not to the phenotype (trading strategy), but to the human support of the phenotype in question (human agent or economic agent);[29]

- Sphere
  - The assessment of the transfer sphere of the operational nature of the autopoietic selection from the environment to the economic operator (and not directly to the phenotype) is dependent on the assessment already made as to how this transfer is to be made (see above);
  - therefore, from the fact that both the selection of the genetic mutation and the selection of the epigenetic mutation are carried out, ultimately, by the economic operator and not the environ-

ment (namely, through the ratification of the environmental 'proposal'), it follows that, from the point of view of the sphere of this transfer, it must be considered as *complete*;
- in other words, the financial market environment (i.e., cultural geodesic, mainly) acts only for the formulation of a 'draft' of the selection, since the actual selection, manifested in the form of ratification of the said draft, is at the discretion of the economic agent.

Nota bene: it is clear that both conclusions were reached (namely, in terms of modality: the indirect nature of the autopoietic selection, based on the pair 'draft–ratification', respectively, in terms of the scope: completeness of the transfer of selection from the environment to the economic agent) are possible and justified exclusively from the perspective of accepting the autopoieticity which, in turn, imposes its predicate of sufficiency called operational closure.

Logical Relationship Autopoiesis – Self-Selection

The logical relationship between autopoiesis and self-selection can be described, in a synoptic way, as shown in Fig. 4.2. The significance of the dynamics of this relationship is as follows: (1) objectification of a hypostasis

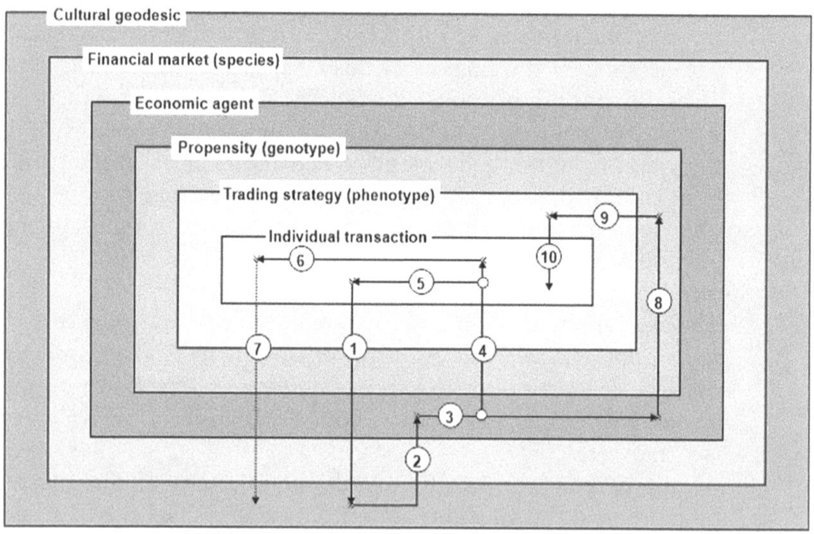

Fig. 4.2 Logical relationship autopoiesis—self-selection. (*Source*: Authors)

of trading strategy (an individual transaction); (2) the reaction of the environment (cultural geodesic) to the action of the individual transaction); (3) assessment of the environmental response in relation to the significance threshold relative to the individual transaction; (4) non-adjustment of the individual transaction (the 'recommended' environmental mutation is below the significance threshold); (5) (indefinite) resumption of the individual transaction; (6) adjusting the individual transaction by selecting the epigenetic mutation; (7) objectification of the adjusted individual transaction; (8) propensity adjustment (genetic selection); (9) selection of the genetic mutation (at the level of the phenotype); (10) designing/adjusting the individual transaction in accordance with the new trading strategy.

Designing of the Autopoietic Model al the Financial Market

General Framework of Research

As mentioned above, our research intends to propose three alternative models to the existing ones regarding the functioning of the financial market. We consider the following five existing models (which were briefly examined in earlier stages of the research): (1) Efficient Market Hypothesis (EMH), (2) Fractal Market Hypothesis (FMH), (3) Cost Matters Hypothesis (CMH), (4) Behavioural Market Hypothesis (BMH) and (5) Adaptive Market Hypothesis (AMH).

In terms of our own proposals, they are three in number: (1) Adaptive Preference Hypothesis (APH), examined in FMAB-APH, (2) Autopoietic Market Hypothesis (APMH), which will be finalized in this chapter, (3) Natural Price Hypothesis (NPH), which will be the subject of further study (possibly a new book of this research).

Therefore, the Autopoietic Market Hypothesis (APMH) is the second proposal made in this research, intended to provide a logical and, as far as possible, quantitative model of the functioning of the financial market. We mention, in short, the main coordinates on which the elaboration of this model is inscribed:

- *evolutionary origin*: the APMH model comes out from under the physicalist-mechanistic constraint of the neoclassical economic theory, that is, from under the methodological umbrella of the *homo œconomicus* model.[30] The evolutionary basis of the APMH model lies in the evolutionary theory which, in certain directions and in certain areas of interest, has already made contributions that can support our approach to modelling of the financial market functioning and the financial field in general;

- *symbolic character*: the object of the APMH model is a symbolic system (or logical one, which is equivalent), called logically living system (*LLS*)—see previous discussions on this concept. This means that, compared to the evolutionary model in biology (applicable to some natural species), this model will contain both elements of similarity and elements of difference from the latter—so, for example, the symbolic species is, like the species natural, a dissipative system (of course, with direct reference to the individuals of that species) but, at the same time, unlike the natural species, this dissipative refers to social entropy (or organizational entropy, as the case may be—*Nota bene*: called by us behavioural entropy), not thermodynamic (or energetic) entropy;[31]
- *autopoietic nature*: the APMH model considers that the symbolic species represented by the financial market, that is, by a logically living system, is a second-order cybernetic system, in which the observer sub-system is included in the observed system;[32]
- *reflexive cognition*: from the autopoietic nature it results that the observer observes himself, which leads to the replacement of the concept of general cognition (proposed by the Santiago school) with a concept of special cognition: reflexive cognition, specific to second-order cybernetic systems;
- *holistic approach*: methodological individualism, typical of the neoclassical approach, is replaced by methodological holism which takes into account, as a cause (formal, especially) the action of the economic agent, and cultural geodesic, as it is generated by the situational framework of society, not only the proference[33] of the human agent;
- *re-anchoring of nominal flows to real support*: the APMH model, which, as shown above, includes the predicate of sustainability, recovers, through this predicate, the fundamental link between nominal flows in the financial market and real support (i.e., flows in the real economy)[34] of them;[35]

- *hybrid evolution*: the APMH model is an evolutionary one but, referring to a symbolic species (financial market), the evolutionary mechanism is hybrid, that is, combines, at the structural level, two complementary mechanisms:[36] (a) a spontaneous, automatic, non-deliberative mechanism; (b) a designed, discretionary, deliberative mechanism.[37]

An image of the 'location' of the APMH model in relation to the other existing models, our already proposed models, and the model our research will still propose later (the NPH model of the financial market), is shown synoptically in Fig. 4.3.

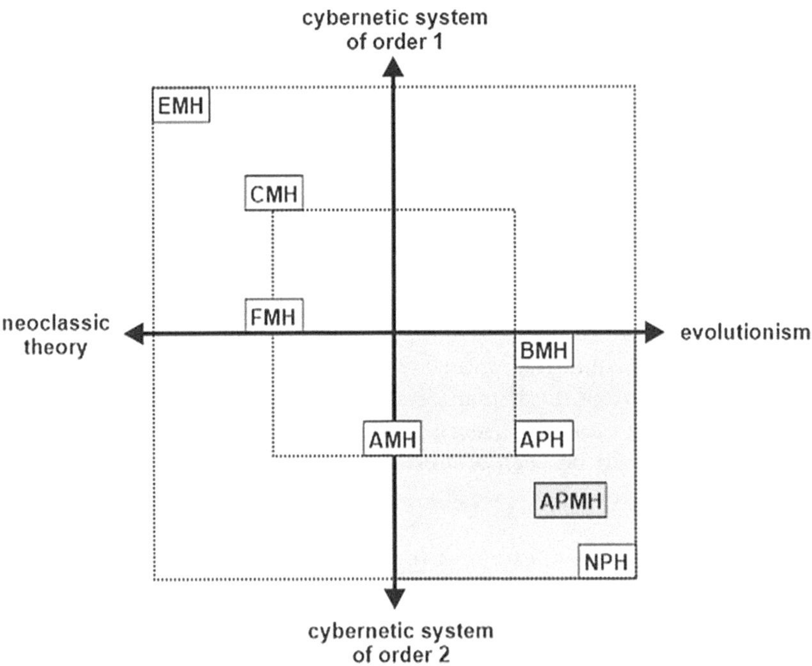

Fig. 4.3 APMH positioning on the 'map' of financial market models/modelling. (*Source*: Authors)

The Concept of Integral Utility

Motivation

The APMH model requires, from the perspective of its paradigmatic analysis (see below), the concept of ***integral utility***.[38] Integral utility combines (or rather integrates, in a synergistic way) the three relevant categories of utility: substantive utility, evidential utility and symbolic utility. Given the theoretical and methodological impact of this concept, we consider it is necessary to dedicate this section to the examination and clarification of the most important issues involved in the concept of integral utility.

Rationality and Intelligibility, Again

Authentic (and, ultimately, relevant) behaviour in society is that of the individual, whether it is considered a representative individual (or, equivalent, average one) or an idiosyncratic[39] individual. The behavioural criterion of the individual has long been identified in the concept of utility.[40] Note that substantive utility requires a rational individual, that is, an individual capable of developing a cost–benefit analysis and optimizing functions–objective subject to given sets of constraints (we have here, again, the well-known and omni-present *homo œconomicus* model, no matter if and how much it was adjusted by various relaxing assumptions—e.g., by Simon's bounded rationality).

However, (a) could the rationality of individual behaviour be replaced by another feature of the human being that could be the basis for modelling (theorizing) economic (more generally, praxiological) action? And if so, (b) what could be such a substitute? We will briefly consider these questions:

(a) rationality is both a feature of the individual and of a representational model of reality, which the individual and, moreover, society, designs and implements, through cultural means, in order to introduce a predictable order into the functioning of society. It is not even certain that such an order exists as such in reality or is, in fact, a projection of the intelligibility of the human being on that reality. Regardless of the case of the mentioned model of representation of reality, especially if it becomes accepted at the level of society, we usually call this representation with the syntagm *model of rationality*. Thus, in an abstract understanding, a model of rationality is a set of assumptions that 'throws' a kind of order on the world. Consequently, what we need to look for now is an alternative to rationality by which order (either economic or social) can be established in the world.[41] In our opinion, rationality is a kind of intelligibility, that is, an intelligibility that is deduced by abduction[42] from reality itself, so it can be said that the model of rationality (*MR*) is an ***abductive intelligibility***. It seems that we cannot get out of intelligibility when we talk about order, but we can get out of rationality instead. Specifically, by naming the a-rational model of intelligibility as a model of ***intuitiveness*** (*MI*)—as opposed to the model of rationality—we can define the model of intuitiveness as a ***deductive intelligibility***;

(b) we now need to develop the concept of deductive intelligibility as a model of intuition 'thrown' over the real world. First, the primary (and incomplete) induction provided by the abduction process is arbitrarily generalized to deductive intelligibility, and second, such a model behaves further like any representational model that is subject to (factual) falsifiability.

The conceptual diagram of the two representational models can be described synoptically as in Fig. 4.4.

Thus, the model of rationality is specific to the natural sciences, when necessity (i.e., complete and perfect predictability[43]) is sovereign. The sovereignty of necessity in the natural sciences is generated by the fact that, in these sciences, the observer/cognitive subject does not interfere with the observed/known object. Instead, contingency is specific to the social

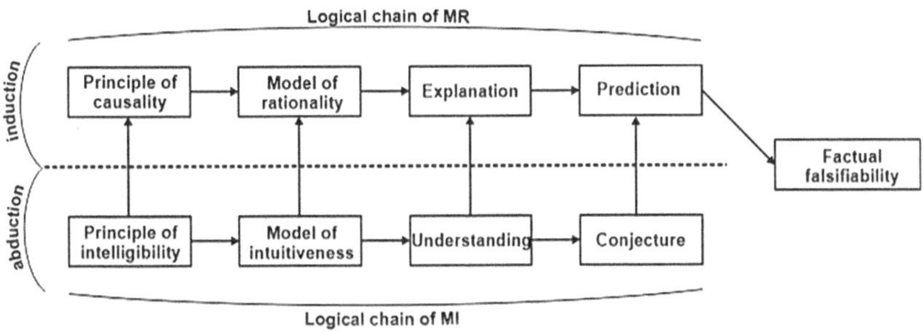

Fig. 4.4 The two representational models. (*Source*: Authors)

sciences (and humanities), when the subject and the object interfere with each other and, so, influence/modify each other.[44]

Of course, we must make a firm distinction between rationality, rational and rationalization. Rationality refers to a model of reasoning (e.g., *homo œconomicus* in economics), rational is any valid logical inference from a model of reasoning or, equivalently, model of rationality, and rationalization is the process of constructing an *ex-post* causal narrative on an event or phenomenon (e.g., any science is essentially a precise narrative about a certain type of causality). This conceptual 'map' allows a useful distinction between rational, irrational and a-rational, namely, the rational, as defined above, is always attributed to a model of rationality, so we have here a kind of theoretical closure (in the sense of Heisenberg), the irrational is an invalid result deduced from a model of rationality (i.e. it is also attributed to that model of rationality, albeit in an 'illegal' way), and the a-rational is a result which cannot be attributed to any model of rationality.[45]

Explanation, Comprehension/Understanding and Complexity

As shown in Fig. 4.4, the explanation is anchored to causality, while the understanding is anchored to intelligibility. In fact, intelligibility can be accepted as a weakened version of rationality.[46] Such a weakening of causality occurs when interference between subject and object occurs, whether the subject is cultural (i.e., capable of generating representations) or a-cultural (i.e., capable of generating only perceptions).[47] Of course, the weakening of rationality against to intelligibility is much stronger in the case of cultural subjects since, in the latter case, we have free will. The presence of free will in the process of understanding leads us to the very concept of *complexity*. So, a system is complex if and only if it contains (cultural) subjects and, consequently, is 'endowed' with free will.[48] Complexity should not be confused with complicatedness—while complicatedness is a historical difficulty, that is, local and temporary, to produce explanations, complexity can be, in fact, extremely simple. The difficulty of explanation and prediction in complex systems[49] are necessary, it will never be overcome as long as the free will of the subjects still remains in the structure of the system, while the difficulty of explanation and prediction in complicated systems are contingent (usually has a historical or contextual character).

Now, we can see that in the economic (broader, social) field, when free-willing cultural subjects interfere with objects (both ontologically and praxiologically), the explanation must be replaced by understanding, and complicatedness must be replaced by complexity.[50] Based on the weakening of rationality on its track towards intelligibility (i.e., the weakening of the explanation on its track towards understanding), there are, in our opinion, the following steps (Fig. 4.5).

As suggested in Fig. 4.5, there is a kinematics of the transition from explanation to understanding. We consider that there are five landmarks in this kinematics:

(1) (pure) *explanation*: a world model based on causal anchoring;
(2) *plausibility*: a world model based on anchoring in intelligibility;
(3) *belief*: a world model based on anchoring in acceptability;

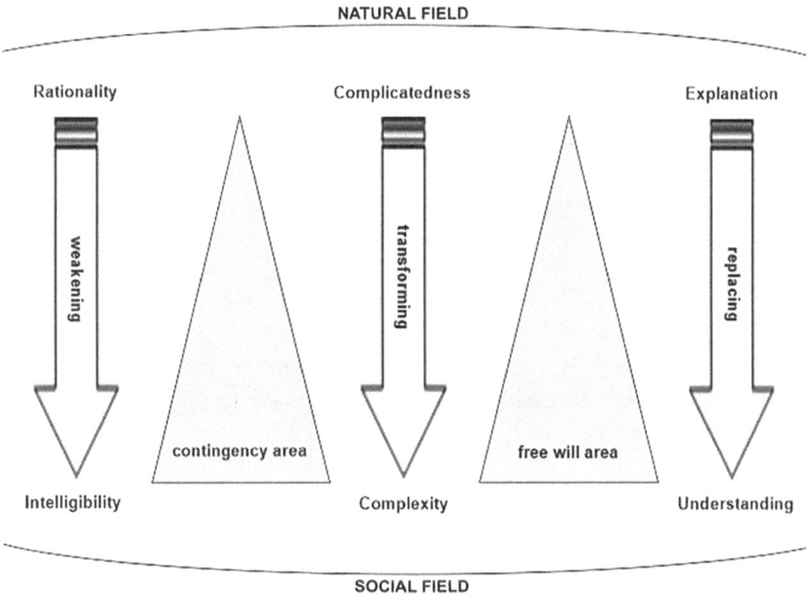

Fig. 4.5 The three entangled processes to pass from the natural field towards the social field. (*Source*: Authors)

(4) *justification*: a world model based on anchoring in preservability/conservability;[51]
(5) *hypothesis*: a world model based on anchoring in belief/faith.[52]

It can be seen that by gradually moving from (1) to (5) the exteriority of the model decreases with increasing interiority, so that the maximum exteriority of the world model is the explanation, and the maximum interiority of the world model is the hypothesis. There is an increasingly insistent assessment in the literature of justification as the basis for any narrative (including scientific narratives) (Haack, 2009; Lo, 2019). This shift from exteriority to interiority is consistent with our assumption, according to which both the contingency area and the free will area increase as rationality weakens towards intelligibility.

Symbolic Utility in Literature

The best-known concept (and, in fact, the only systematic and profound theorizing we know of) about symbolic utility is provided by Robert Nozick's *The Nature of Rationality* (Nozick, 1994). The basis of Nozick's position is closely linked to his conception of principles. This basis can be summarized as follows:

- the principles subsume, as a general integrator, the particularities, by their analogy, thus ensuring a similar justification of similar opinions or beliefs;
- in essence, a principle is a rule that regulates the rules, that is, it is a meta-rule;
- principles have four distinct functions: (a) *interpersonal* functions: the principles we rely on provide others with the best public predictors of our (future) actions, provided the principles are accompanied by a (publicly) announcement and a (publicly assumed) commitment to respect them; (b) *personal* functions: the principles define the identity of the individual who implemented them; (c) *intrapersonal* functions: principles allocate utilities to individual actions (either real or potential); (d) *intellectual* (or epistemological) functions: principles avoid their own preferences in judgements, that is, in deducing conclusions from premises;

- the principles act in the form of *sui generis* causes, because they imply patterns of behaviour of the actors of those principles, which means that the future behaviour of actors concerned will have the same meaning as the present (or past) one;[53] in fact, the existence of a prin ciple increases, for others, the probability (or expectation) that the individual under the aegis of that principle will continue/replicate the same action expecting the same utility;
- the stronger the principle, the more expensive is to violate it;[54] this means that a principle introduces into society a belief that others acquire about a person's behavioural invariance, even if such a belief is only partial (Ramsey, 2013).[55] Of course, a meta principle could be adopted (and publicly announced and assumed in turn) which states that a principle can never be violated. A particularly important logical consequence arises here: a principle (hence, *a fortiori*, a meta-principle) does not seem to be evolutionary, because an adaptation of the principle diminishes the belief of others—for the latter, the adaptation of a principle could mean just a violation of the principle in question.[56]

Starting from the above-mentioned theoretical basis of the concept of principle, the key features of Nozick's understanding of symbolic utility can be summarized as follows:

- by adopting a principle, the utilities falling under that principle are modified accordingly for the one acting on the basis of the principle in question;[57]
- the principle signifies/signals for the others—precisely this signifying constitutes, for Nozick, the very symbolic utility;
- the magnitude of the symbolic utility signalled by one principle is directly proportional to the magnitude of the reaction of others, once that principle was born (through its publicly announcement and publicly commitment to it);[58]
- for Nozick, substantive utility (also called economic utility), as an expected utility, is, in fact, generated or at least dimensioned by such a symbolic utility. Of course, in this interpretation, any rule governing economic or social behaviour is a principle that plays an institutional or conditional role in the formation of substantive utility.

We will conclude with a few remarks on Nozick's position on symbolic utility:

(a) symbolic utility is, in a very deep sense, a 'fruit' of the principles of behaviour, which means that it has no autonomy in its birth and existence; for example, it cannot arise from an action (linguistic, praxiological or practical) of others, independent of a principle (known to the public)—in other words, symbolic utility is *non-autonomous*;
(b) symbolic utility is seen as generated by an individual and directed to others, but not to him/herself—in other words, symbolic utility is *non-reflexive*;
(c) symbolic utility is the form in which the meaning (adequacy, relevance, coercive force and so on) of one's principle is perceived by others and could affect others—in other words, symbolic utility is a *sign*.[59]

In our approach to symbolic utility, the predicates of non-autonomy and non-reflexivity, retained by Nozick, will be rejected, but instead the predicate sign will be retained.

Utility and the Representational Models

The concept of utility is not about a property, but about a relationship. Considering the three entities that make up our world, namely, things, properties, relationships, utility is a relationship between subject and object. More specifically, utility must be seen as a property of the subject generated by the relationship between subject and object.[60]

It seems to us that there are three perspectives on the behaviour of the human being that generate utilities, namely, (a) *rational* perspective—see TEU;[61] (b) *emotional* perspective—see behavioural model; (c) *symbolic* perspective. Rational and emotional perspectives on utility are generally discussed (and empirically tested) in the literature, but the third perspective is much less present. This last perspective will be examined in detail below.

Based on the three perspectives mentioned, three representational models of economic behaviour have been issued (or should be issued, for the third perspective):

- from a *rational* perspective: *homo œconomicus*.[62] Such a representational model generates the *substantive* (economic) type of utility, that is, the most used form of utility in all areas of economic theory—from the most abstract approaches to financial markets approach. Substantive utility is mainly related to non-evolutionary preferences (so-called given preferences[63]) that exist as such rather than are generated or modified;

- from an *emotional* perspective: *homo biologicus*. Such a representational model generates *procedural* utility (or, as it is also called, *evidential* utility). Procedural utility is much less used in economic modelling.[64] However, it is massively present in the theory of social justice, which is developing more and more connections with economic (and social) behaviour. In the economic field, procedural utility has recently been associated with the evolutionary (including institutional) approach to the economic process;
- from a *symbolic* perspective: *homo significans*. Such a representational model generates the symbolic type of utility.

According to the three types of utility,[65] it seems that three representational models (or paradigms) of praxiological action (such as, in fact, the economic process) can be conceptualized:

1. paradigm of *optimality*: a completely rational model of praxiological action (i.e., *homo œconomicus*) that is associated with substantive utility (or, rather, substantive utility is the main utility or the main engine of the optimality paradigm). Today's capitalism operates within such a paradigm. This paradigm is concerned with extremized praxiological solutions (for decisions and/or actions),[66] by targeting individual *satisfaction*;
2. paradigm of *viability*: a combination of rationality and emotion in the behaviour of the human being (i.e., *homo biologicus* or, equally, *homo viabilis*). This combination provides survival solutions rather than extreme ones.[67] The anomalies (both economic and social or moral) that the paradigm of optimality brings (especially through its necessary effect called globalization) put pressure in the direction of building the paradigm of viability. Basically, the viability paradigm is associated with the procedural/evidential utility (or rather, the procedural utility is the main utility or the main engine of the viability paradigm). This paradigm is concerned with survival solutions (or, in other words, viable

solutions) both in terms of decisions and actions, by targeting the *satisficing*[68] of the individual;

3. paradigm of *sustainability*: a combination of rationality, emotion and symbolism in the behaviour of the human being (i.e., *homo significans*). The anomalies of the optimality and viability paradigms are solved by putting the symbolic utility as the main utility (or as the principled engine of this paradigm). This paradigm is concerned with sustainable solutions (or, in other words, symbolic solutions) both in terms of decisions and actions, by targeting the *symboficing* of the individual.[69]

Nota bene: in this study we try to build, in fact, a fourth paradigm (particularized in the financial field, but which can easily be generalized to the whole human action in society), which could be called the paradigm of *autopoieticity*: combination of rationality, emotion, symbolism and self-organization in the behaviour of the human being (i.e., *homo perennis*). In such a paradigm, the integral (global) utility could be called, with full justification, the *mazifficing* of the individual.[70]

The association of symbolic utility with the paradigm of sustainability will be discussed below (because it might seem quite 'un-natural'). The above considerations are all incorporated in Fig. 4.6.

The three representational models are developed on quite different scales. The most elaborate (and most award-winning Nobel!) is the *homo œconomicus* model, with (especially in the financial field) the Efficient Market Hypothesis (EMH). This paradigm (of optimality) came with a solid theory, very grounded mathematically, but far from the real economic and social world. On the 'second place' is the *homo biologicus* model with its evolutionary hypothesis (Adaptive Market Hypothesis—AMH). This paradigm (of viability) has yet to build its own theory, but so far, no solid foundation for such a theory has been built. The least elaborate representational model is the one called *homo significans*. Although the term sustainability is used extensively in many studies (both in articles and in books), a coherent, consistent and complete view of this model does not seem to have been crystallized. To most scientists, this model seems to be a managerial tool rather than a theoretical concept, but we 'prophesy' that things will change. As for the autopoietic model (which we did not include in Fig. 4.6), it will result from the examinations completed in this chapter.

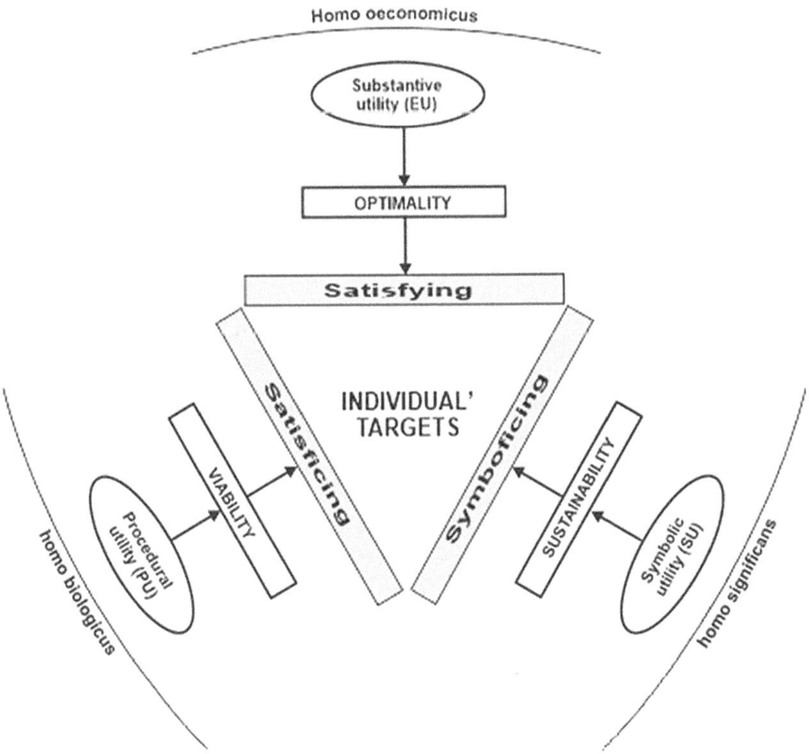

Fig. 4.6 Logical correlation among types of utilities and types of actional paradigms. (*Source*: Authors)

Conceptual Ground of Symbolic Utility

Social Capital

Capital means a real entity that verifies cumulatively two predicates of sufficiency:

- (**K1**) keeps the accumulated low entropy. By low entropy we have to mean a high degree of accessibility of the potential use of a certain entity, regardless of its nature. Thus, we want to reject a *tale quale* import of the concept of entropy in Thermodynamics, which means the amount of energy related to its physical support.[71] According to this predicate, the different elements of capital have different degrees of accumulated low entropy, being, thus, of different qualities;

- (**K2**) is issued as an artefact.[72] Capital must be considered only as a result of human activity of any kind.

There are, in principle, three categories of capital: (a) economic capital, (b) social capital and (c) intellectual capital. Such a typology is based on the three distinctive hypostases that K2 can take, as follows:

(a) the general concept of *economic capital* can be constructed on the basis of the general concept of capital by adding an additional predicate of sufficiency (more precisely, a specification of K2, which becomes, as a result of this specification, E2).

(**E2**) is a *praxiological* artefact. To be of the economic type, a generic capital must be only the result of economic activity. Thus, although a virgin forest or a natural coal deposit may have a (high) degree of low entropy stored, they are not of the nature of capital. The old term used for their name—natural resources—correctly preserves their essence.[73] Apparently, the more human civilization advances, the more natural resources are replaced by economic capital. The economic product is itself the result of the functional (conditioned) combination of capital and labour (no matter how directly or indirectly that combination occurs). Economic capital can be, in principle, of two kinds:

- *material* capital—incorporated in physical (material) support: for example, an excavator;
- *informational* capital—embedded in non-physical (non-material) support: for example, a (software) computer program.[74]

In modern economies, economic capital enters, in a given entity, simultaneously in the form of substantial/substantive capital,[75] respectively informational capital. It should be noted that economic capital is involved in praxiological action—by praxiological action must be understood the relationship between subject and object. Economic action is the prototype of praxiology because it combines labour (the subject) with economic capital (the object).

(b) The general concept of *social capital* can be constructed on the basis of the general concept of capital by adding an additional predicate of sufficiency (more precisely, a specification of K2, which becomes, as a result of this specification, S2):

(**S2**) is a *practical* artefact. To be social, generic capital must be a result of sociality. By sociality we mean the ability and desire of people to issue, implement and use rules (either codified or informal) for individual practical interactions. An individual interaction is of a practical nature if it addresses the relations that concern only the interests of the subjects in social cooperation, that is, the subject–subject relationships. Examples of practical relationships are moral, political, religious and other relationships of the same nature. The social capital is of two categories, according to its purpose:

- social capitalization of *individualization* (i.e., aiming at building the individual through social causation), with three sub-categories:
  - *freedom*: the degree to which individuals can use their own free will;[76]
  - *trust*: the degree to which individuals freely agree to transmit, either to the state (Government) or to other private persons, some of their rights or interests;
  - *symmetry*:[77] the degree to which individuals have equal access to the positive externalities of society (education, justice, health, other public goods or opportunities);
- social capital of *socialization* (i.e., aiming at building society through individual causation), with three sub-categories:
  - *communication*: the degree and quality in which individuals can communicate,[78] live and work freely with other individuals; this type of social capital is, in particular, 'responsible' for the communitization process (building communities such as families, teams, clubs, organizations, countries, integrated regions and all types of social networks);
  - *participation*:[79] the degree and quality in which individuals have the opportunity to participate in public decision-making;[80] this type of social capital is, in particular, 'responsible' for building the political structure[81] of society;[82]

- *mutualisation*: the degree and quality in which common goals and common means can be built on the basis of inter-individual either harmonization or competition; this type of social capital is, in particular, 'responsible' for all contractual associations[83] between individuals (from private to those involving the nation or state).

(c) The general concept of *intellectual capital* can be constructed on the basis of the general concept of capital by adding an additional predicate of sufficiency (more precisely, a specification of K2, which becomes, as a result of this specification, I2):

(**I2**) is a *theoretical* artefact. To be of the intellectual type, a generic capital must be a result of spirituality (or, logically equivalent, of intellectuality). By intellectuality we mean the ability and desire of people to issue, implement and use rules (either codified or informal) for the formation of individuals' knowledge of reality (objective, subjective or objectified). This type of capital does not involve relationships between human individuals but consists in the knowledge of human individuals about objects (which can be, from this point of view, also subjects, obviously). Thus, intellectual capital addresses object-to-object relations. Figure 4.7 shows the structural relationships between the three species/categories of capital.

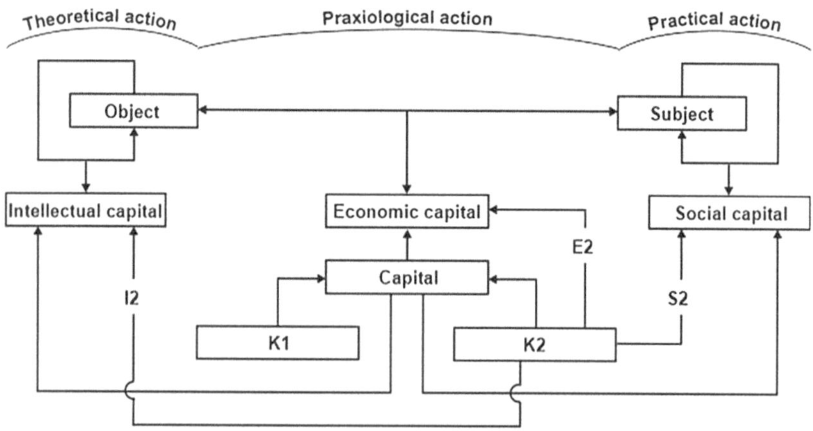

Fig. 4.7 Logical correlation among the three species of capital. (*Source*: Authors)

Symbolic Utility

The first economists to develop, in a systematic way (and, as it seems to us, in a rather fundamentalist way), the concept of utility were the so-called marginalists. Although some of their intuitions and technical abilities cannot be ignored, they have focused, almost entirely, on a substantive species of utility, more precisely, on the utility that verifies the following predicates of sufficiency: (a) it is measurable; (b) the measure is cardinal;[84] (c) its final significance is of an economic nature (either income or wealth, as a rule). In addition to being located on the lower floors of Maslow's pyramid of needs, substantive (or economic) utility seems to have no rational limit—so it can grow to infinity without any asymptotes. Among other things, this concept certainly underlies the current consumerism that capitalism has delivered (and continues to deliver) to human society. The present paragraph aspires to go beyond (or, rather, laterally from) the substantive utility, by introducing into discussion the concept of symbolic utility. We ignore the 'middle' species, introduced above, namely, the procedural (or evidential) utility.[85]

Many scientists and philosophers have defined the human being as ***homo significans***, meaning a being who gives meaning to the world or, equivalently, who sees the world through its meanings. Even in Maslow's pyramid of needs, as we 'climb' into that pyramid, needs gradually shift from basic (with a high degree of necessity from the perspective of survival goal) to symbolic ones. This means that, above a sufficient guarantee of life (survival), the human being aspires more and more to satisfy its symbolic needs. In this context, the symbolic utility could be introduced through the following coordinates (we will use Fig. 4.8 in this regard):

Short Discussion

- Symbolic utility is attributed more to ethical than moral values—the distinction between ethical and moral (as predicates of behaviour) is particularly important here, which is why we will make a few additional considerations:
- ethics is attributed to the idiosyncrasy of the individual, as its own instance (incommunicable and immeasurable) of validation/rejection of a behaviour, regardless of who performs that behaviour, either the individual himself or another individual (Foucault et al., 2005);

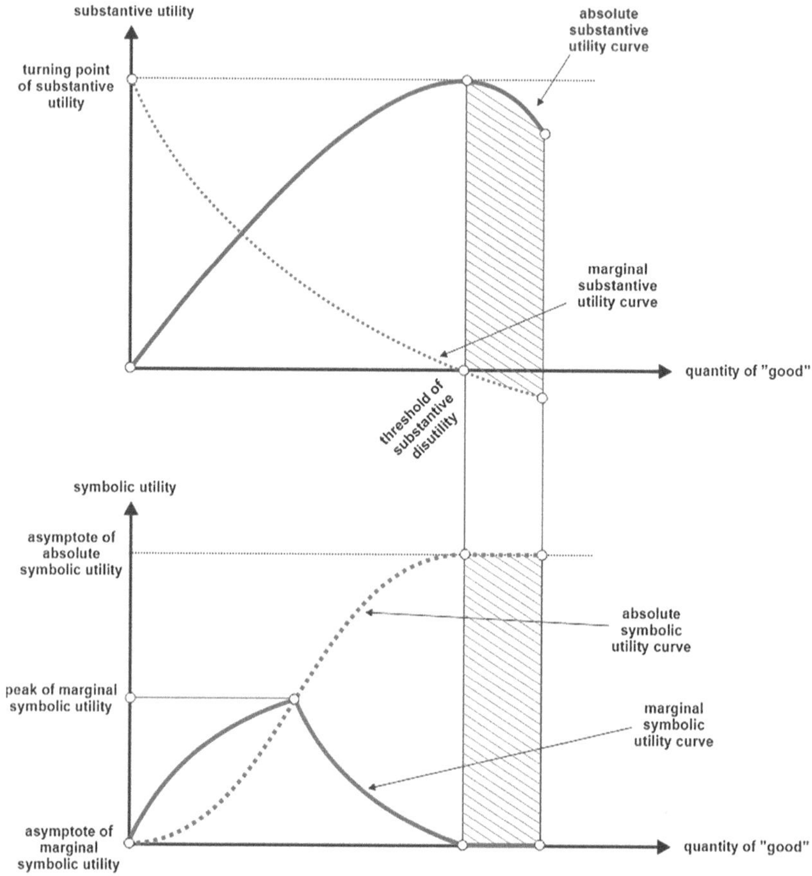

Fig. 4.8 Comparative forms of substantive and symbolic curves (absolute and marginal) of utility. (*Source*: Authors)

- morality is a community agreement of (informal)[86] social norms that regulates (and, consequently, judges) the behaviour of any individual, so it is a communitarian court of validation/rejection of a behaviour;
- ethics and morals do not always coincide, either quantitatively (same rules) or qualitatively (same prescription); it is acceptable, however,

that the most fundamental[87] ethical precepts have entered the common core of moral precepts[88] or are liable to enter into that common core;

- the absolute substantive utility curve is asymptotic and concave increasing one, while the marginal substantive utility curve is non-asymptotic and convex decreasing one;
- there is a quantity of consumption of 'good' beyond which absolute substantive utility becomes decreasing and, accordingly, marginal substantive utility becomes negative (falls below the threshold of substantive disutility);
- the curve of absolute symbolic utility has the shape of an elongated '*S*', which ends its concave side with a horizontal asymptote; with a technical (jargon) term, it is, until it meets the asymptote, a logistic curve;[89]
- the marginal symbolic utility curve increases concavely from the origin to the inflection point of the absolute symbolic utility curve, then decreases convexly to the point where the absolute symbolic utility curve reaches its asymptote;
- symbolic utility is, in principle, immeasurable (as opposed to substantive utility which is measurable); it appears in the mind of an individual through judgement; this means that symbolic utility is, much more than substantive one, a matter of individual belief or conviction;
- there is no area of disutility in terms of symbolic utility, as in the case of substantive utility, which means that its 'value' (if measurable, which is not the case, as stated) is always positive or zero;[90]
- as will be shown below, substantive utility and symbolic utility are not interchangeable;
- substantive and symbolic utility are causally asymmetric—while the variation of substantive utility (may) determine a directly proportional variation of symbolic utility, the inverse causality is false: in fact, the variation of symbolic utility has no impact on the variation of substantive utility;
- however, symbolic utility also retains the rational determination of substantive utility.

Phenomenology of Praxiological Representational Models

Praxiological models or paradigms are the result of the evolution of both human being and his/her environment (anthropic, i.e., society and non-anthropic, i.e., nature). In fact, the human being and his/her environment have co-evolved, based on rules of mutual reaction caused to each other. Consequently, any praxiological paradigm was (is and will be) optimal if it is matched with the (ultimate) goal of survival. From the perspective of the observer, on the historical scale there is a logic that pushes the succession of praxiological paradigms over time.

We can highlight four praxiological paradigms (or representational models) in history:

(a) the *stationarity* paradigm;
(b) the *optimality* paradigm;
(c) the *viability* paradigm;
(d) the *sustainability* paradigm of Bonneuil and Boucekkine (2009) and Heal (2003).

The last three paradigms have already been discussed above, and the stationary paradigm is not of much interest for the present discussion. We will examine, however, the kinematics of the transition from one paradigm to another, highlighting the 'necessary forces' that causally act in such a transition. Table 4.1 summarizes the main ideas in the field (the four paradigms are introduced in the historical chronology). Fetal vulnerability refers to the basic internal contradiction (inconsistency) that builds the effective cause for the transition to the next (logical and chronological) paradigm; the basic impact refers to the specific result of the paradigm in society as a result of the transition to the next paradigm.

An interesting discussion could perhaps be developed on the nature of either the necessary or contingent nature of the linear transition from stationary, throughout the intermediate chain, to sustainability. From an evolutionary perspective, the *statu quo* of such a transition is, of course, necessary, although from a logical perspective (i.e., if the human being had been able to develop society as an intellectual, deliberative project), it seems that stationarity should have been followed directly by sustainability, not optimality. From this last perspective, both optimality and viability appear as historical self-experiments of mankind, of trial-and-error type. Therefore, a general assessment of this issue is presented in Table 4.1.

Optimality Versus Sustainability in Economic Behaviour

In short, as already stated, the optimality of a process (or system, as well) is that property of the process/system to extremize (i.e., maximize or minimize) a function-objective under a given set of constraints[91] (Bonneuil &

Table 4.1 Dynamics (causal kinematics) of the praxiological paradigms in the history

Paradigm	*Stationarity*	*Optimality*	*Viability*	*Sustainability*
Content/Target	Meeting current economic needs, outside any model of rationality	Satisfying the current economic needs, with the optimization of the result (first best)	Meeting current and future economic needs without optimizing the result (second best)—outside of morals	Meeting current and future economic needs without optimizing the result (second best)—inside of morals
Fetal vulnerability	Emergence of resources scarcity	Globalization	Lack of moral anchor	?
Basic impact	The exponential increase in human instrumental effectiveness	Re-assigning of the rationality model to genuine needs of human being	The subordination of instrumental efficacy to moral significance	?
Negative praxiological externality	Non	The threat of depletion of resources	Non-economic and non-moral constraints in models of praxiological rationality	Non-economic and moral constraints in models of praxiological rationality
Negative practical externality	Non	Moral regression (consumerism)	Moral indifference	Non

Source: Authors

Boucekkine, 2009). Optimality is not always possible—for example, when the set of constraints is inconsistent, that is, when at least two of the restrictions are contradictory with each other.[92] In such a case, especially in the economic field, the solution called *first best* is replaced by one called *second best*, that is, with a solution immediately acceptable after the best solution as being inaccessible. Whether you are talking about *first best* or *second best*, you are always talking about optimization. Obviously, optimization is associated with the substantive utility discussed above (for this reason, a kind of measurable utility is needed, as is, in fact, substantive or economic utility).

In contrast, the sustainability of a process (or a system, as well) does not imply any extremization (Bonneuil & Boucekkine, 2009). We call a process as sustainable if it has the structural potential to replicate itself.[93] Regarding the concept of sustainability, two questions seem useful to examine: (a) Why is extremization not compatible with sustainability? (b) Why is the lack of extremization better than its presence?

(a) By leading the reasoning to the last of its logical consequences, the continuous optimization of the process[94] (e.g., the permanent maximization of the function-objective) will lead, rather quickly, to the depletion of the resources involved in that process.[95] But such a result is clearly inconsistent with the concept of sustainability, as it undermines the very replication of the process involved over an indefinite time horizon. Thus, sustainability must reject any optimization. On a global scale, it is not an exaggeration to say that the praxiological paradigm of optimality is simply a Ponzi[96] scheme that works impersonally;
(b) this question is a little more difficult. Essentially, we might be wondering if, by ensuring an indefinite replicability of the process/system, we are not, in fact, providing a kind of optimization of that process/system. The question is not superfluous, as the term 'indefinite' attributed to the time horizon considered connotes something equivalent to the best case, that is, something that could be connected with the concept of the optimality. We believe, however, that there is a crucial difference here: while optimality is completely linked to a measurable quantitative property (the very level of extreme value, in this case), sustainability is rather related to a qualitative property (i.e., immeasurable—in any case, not necessarily quantitatively measurable—or measurable with qualitative, usually ordinal scales[97]). Moreover, while optimality is not a condition of existence for the process/system in question (but only for its excellence), sustainability is exactly the condition for the process/system existence.

Recent developments in economic theory (including, in particular, financial market theory) shift the discussion from the supposed full rationality of the individual to his/her heuristic behaviour, that is not about the optimum, but about survival.

A synoptic picture (Fig. 4.9) provides the general conceptual distinction between optimality and sustainability.[98]

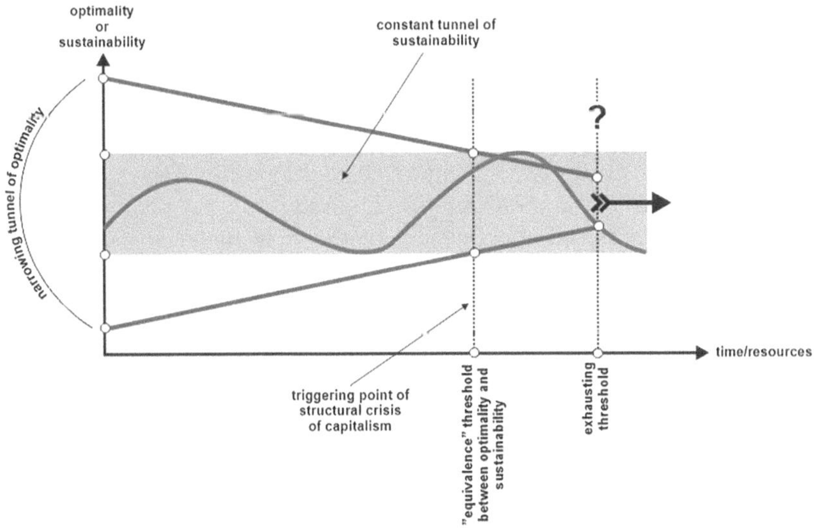

Fig. 4.9 Tunnel of optimality vs. tunnel of sustainability. (*Source*: Authors)

Structure of the Integral Utility
As shown above, symbolic utility is, however, a utility. The symbolic character comes from the fact that, by its variation, it does not change the substantive state (i.e., of the substantive utility) of the individual in question,[99] so neither the integral utility. One may then ask whether the integral utility of the individual will change the symbolic utility. Of course, the concept of the integral utility of an individual must now be introduced. In principle, as mentioned above, there are three types of utility: substantive (or economic), symbolic and procedural/evidential.[100] Since the evidences (which are, especially, behavioural in nature) are of negligible relevance in this discussion, we can assume that integral utility (TU) is the (logical) sum of substantive (EU) utility and symbolic (SU) utility: $TU = EU \oplus SU$, where the logical constant $\oplus$ means 'logical sum'. Thus, the integral utility should change when either component utility changes. At least three questions arise here: (a) How does the change of each type of utility influence the change of the other type of utility? (b) How does the change of each type of utility influence the modification of the integral utility? (c) Is there a curve of indifference between the two types of utilities which compose the integral utility? And if so, what can be said about it?

(a) As stated above, no change in symbolic utility introduces changes in substantive utility. However, the reverse is true: that is, it is possible that a change in substantive utility will cause changes in the symbolic one—for example, an increase in salary leads to the residential relocation of the individual to live outside the city, which is a sign of a higher standard of living and an improved social position or leads to the replacement of a modest car with a more prestigious one, which also sends messages, on the outside, of the new better social position and so on;
(b) continuing with the above idea, it can be said that when there is an increase in substantive utility, it increases both integral utility and symbolic utility, but the latter does not cause any change in substantive utility, and only (namely, directly and autonomously) does this on integral utility;
(c) our answer to this question is affirmative. But, given the asymmetry between substantive and symbolic utility in conveying their impact on integral utility, a comprehensive response needs to be more nuanced. To simplify the clarification, we will use Fig. 4.10.

The mechanism in Fig. 4.10 works as follows:

- when the EU increases from EU_1 to EU_2, if EU and SU are substitutable, SU_1 should decrease, according to the indifference curve TU_1, to SU_2; thus, the integral utility would have remained unchanged on the basis of its indifference to its structural change. But such an impact is forbidden (EU increase also leads to SU increase), so the SU moves (increases) to $\overline{SU}_2$;
- by increasing from SU_1 to $\overline{SU}_2$, that is, to the new value EU_2, a new, higher TU is needed, so that TU_1 increases to the level TU_2;
- in the new state of integral utility, that is, at the value of TU_2, if there is an increase in SU, for example, from $\overline{SU}_2$ to SU_3, there is no impact of SU increase on the variation of EU, so the new 'point' (EU_2, SU_3) needs a new, even larger TU, namely, TU_3.

A Transformation Operator

The very idea of assigning symbolic utility to the sustainability paradigm (especially for the economic field, but in general for any individual behaviour) is based precisely on the structure of integral utility and the

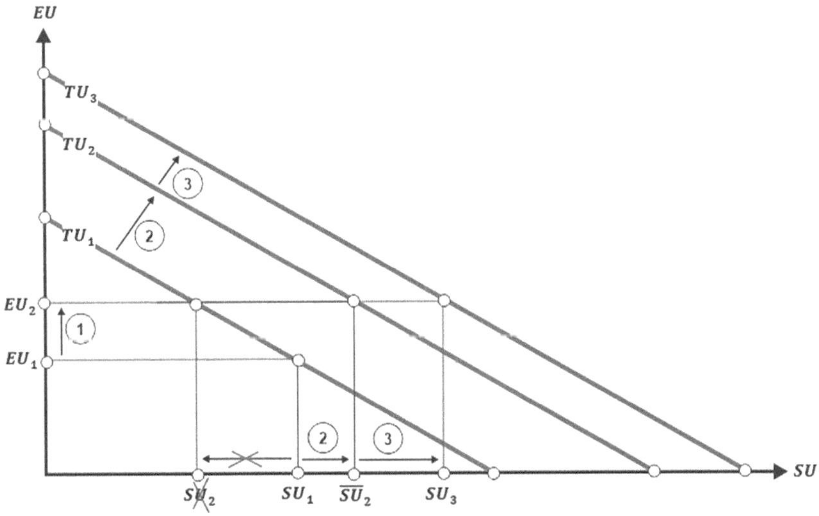

Fig. 4.10 Impact of substantive utility and symbolic utility on integral utility. (*Source*: Authors)

mechanism described in Fig. 4.10. More analytically, the construction of symbolic utility as a logical operator for transforming optimality into sustainability consists, in principle, in the following:

(a) as has been shown, there is an asymmetry in the mutual impact of the *EU* and the *SU*—namely, while changes in the *EU* generate changes in the *SU* as well, *EU* is rigid about *SU* change;
(b) on the basis of that rigidity, if there is a decrease in the *SU*, the *EU* remains, in principle, constant, as the 'shock' of such a decline is only taken up by a decrease in the *TU*;
(c) but preserving the *EU* from *SU* variation means, conceptually, a kind of *EU* sustainability;
(d) for this mechanism to be feasible, the inverse causal relationship must be examined, namely, what happens if the *TU* changes; more precisely, the issue that needs to be clarified here is: assuming that the *TU* increases (regardless of whether it is due to *EU* or *SU* enlargement), then there is some impact of *TU* on *EU* or *SU* or both?

- our hypothesis in this matter is as follows: symbolic utility has three channels of variation: (a) substantive utility (as already shown), (b) the symbolic utility itself (e.g., a gesture of merits recognition of the individual in question, made by society) and (c) integral utility;
- as the operation of the first two channels is beyond doubt, it remains to be seen whether and how the change in integral utility can have an impact on the change in symbolic utility. It seems that a kind of self-catalysis of symbolic utility acts here, namely:
  - as the *TU* grows, the *SU* sees an increase generated by its better framing (or better wrapper). We would like to introduce here the concept of ***contextual symbolic utility*** (*CSU*)—thus, by contextual symbolic utility we must understand that marginal symbolic utility which is caused only by an increase in *TU*: $CSU = \frac{\Delta(SU)}{\Delta(TU)}$
  - thus, an ***effect of self-catalysis*** appears: when the symbolic utility increases, the total utility increases, so the symbolic utility increases and so on;
  - of course, such self-catalysis must logically decrease with increasing *TU*. Such a decrease in the self-catalysis rate of the symbolic utility can be explained as follows:

    marginal symbolic utility is descending when absolute symbolic utility becomes concave (see Fig. 4.8);

    therefore, the impact on the *TU* is decreasing; based on the linear relationship between cause (marginal symbolic utility variation) and effect (integral utility variation), integral utility variation results (which is the next cause of symbolic utility variation), so symbolic utility variation (as effect) decreases relative to integral utility variation and so on;
- what is relevant in identifying the self-catalysis of symbolic utility is that this property is typical of a sustainable process/system, so that symbolic utility is 'qualified' to express sustainability while the substantive is 'qualified' to express optimality.[101]

Figure 4.11 shows a graphical suggestion of the conclusion of this discussion.

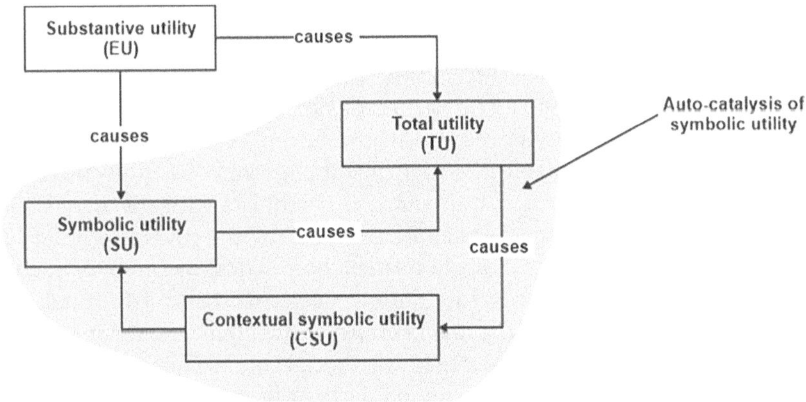

Fig. 4.11 Self-catalysis of the symbolic utility. (*Source*: Authors)

Sustainability, Social Capital and Symbolic Utility

By extending Nozick's concept of symbolic utility, this type of utility not only belongs to behavioural principles (publicly announced and engaged), but also addresses any utility that is not substantive in nature. Social prestige, the (recognized) hierarchy in a social, scientific, artistic, sporting, political, military and other fields, all these give a symbolic utility to the individual who is the object of such a qualification and recognition. If the substantive utility provides the material resources regarding the praxiological paradigm, instead the symbolic one provides the motivational resources for that paradigm. When we talk about social support for an initiative within society, we are addressing both material and symbolic support. In fact, the symbolic resource (which is self-catalytic to a greater degree than the substantive one) is placed at the basis of any sustainable process within society. Such a role of symbolic utility is, as outlined above, transmitted through social capital. We thus have a triad—*symbolic utility*, *social capital*, *sustainability*—that functions at the level of society, as a mechanism of self-support. From an instrumental point of view, we think that it is quite difficult to formalize in an equational way the takeover of symbolic utility in our models of economic (or social) behaviour, because the equations are rather elaborated quantitatively, while symbolic utility is rather a qualitative predicate of an agent. The individual agency[102] is, however, founded and fundamentally driven by symbolic utility—remember concepts such as loyalty or solidarity or, even better, the types of social capital, which stimulate individual action (either as an act or an abstention) more (and more durable) than substantive utility. Perhaps, a new type of formalism, in which symbolic utility could be a good engine of such a formalization, should be invented and sufficiently developed in the future. The integration of the three concepts—sustainability, social capital and symbolic utility—cannot be spontaneously generated by society, this requires a vision, that is, an intellectual/moral project that can be managed by the (most likely) minimal state (Farzin, 2010). We believe that the political ideology of such a state, which has the capacity to combine sustainability, social capital and symbolic utility, should be the *ordoliberalism*. Through ordoliberalism, the (free) economic process is associated with social (moral) justice. This combination of human purposes probably has no better alternative, so it is impossible to overestimate it.

Symbolic Utility and Adaptive Preferences

Being linked to the paradigm of sustainability (both praxiological and practical), the symbolic utility is the main filter through which individual wellbeing is perceived and even evaluated and capitalized. Because wellbeing is strongly and inherently linked to preferences (seen as the primary crystallizations of desires/motivations), one last question that addresses the issue of symbolic utility concerns its relationship to preferences. We will further develop a brief discussion of this important issue.

(a) Preference (in its most general sense, not restricted to the economic one) is a 'choice of choice' that the individual makes regarding his/her goals, means, modalities and action in the social game of cooperation,[103] so, a choice that involves the individual in question. Although behaviour, as it is predominantly treated in the literature, is still subordinate to pure rational models (such as *homo œconomicus* or, in the financial field, the Efficient Market Hypothesis (Fama, 1970)), for (at least) several decades, psychologists (including neurologists) have convincingly demonstrated that real behaviour is an inextricable mixture of rationality (driven by the prefrontal cortex) and emotion (driven by the amygdala). Moreover, it seems that real (i.e., effective) rationality is not possible without emotion (fear, greed, pain, pleasure, etc.) (Lo, 2019);
(b) both rationality and emotion are the result of the evolution of the human being, so they are the result of interactions between the indi-

vidual and his/her environment of all kinds (which obviously includes other individuals);[104]

(c) practically, adaptive preferences are downward adjustments of the well-being benchmark, that is, of the quality of life and, therefore, of the symbolic utility of life (Elster, 2017; Sen, 2000). However, there are other positions in which adaptive preferences are seen not only as reducing the level of wellbeing, that is, implicitly the level of symbolic utility—these positions conceive the adaptive preferences as also having positive (or favourable) consequences (Nussbaum, 2006), which represent upward adjustments to the welfare benchmark;

(d) consequently, preferences have, in fact, been modelled as adaptive preferences. It is difficult, if not impossible, to establish a 'point' in time by which preferences are rigid, given, invariant, that is, not dependent on the environment, and then become adaptive, flexible, non-invariant (*Nota bene*: however, many researchers distinguish between authentic/real[105] and adaptive preferences, without providing a criterion for stopping from the inevitable regression to infinity);

(e) preferences (usually those revealed—which is a conceptual proposition of Samuelson—i.e., manifested or objectified by actual behaviour) act like Nozick's announcement of the principles of behaviour, both for the person who reveals his/her preferences and for the others that are affected in any way by them, that is, they are, in fact, symbolic utilities.[106] We would say, even more, namely, veiled preferences should be considered as genuine preferences (many of them could simply be more or less utopian), and revealed ones should be considered adaptive preferences. The explanation is quite simple: a rational individual (i.e., as noted above, an individual who functionally combines rational and emotional reasoning) will objectify (e.g., by action—whether act or abstinence) only adaptive preference, for to ensure their chances of success;

(f) it follows from the above that any revealed preference is attributable to adaptive symbolic utility. Thus, *homo significans* appears *a priori* in the social game, by (publicly) exposing his/her choices. Of course, a baroque discussion could be initiated here regarding the negative (Sen, Elster) or positive (Nussbaum) connotations of adaptive preferences and, implicitly, of adaptive symbolic utilities, but these developments are far enough from the aims of the research, so it will be postponed for further communication. We just wanted to relate the (adaptive) preference[107] to the symbolic utility;

(g) ultimately, adaptive preferences have the significance of evolution (either biological or cultural). Consequently, their negative connotations, mentioned in particular by Elster and Sen, and balanced (to some extent, at least as a programmatic intention) by Nussbaum, are directly transformed into positive connotations by Lo, for the financial sphere, but also into the economic area of human action (Hodgson, 2004; Nelson & Winter, 1985).

The Logical Model of the Autopoietic Financial Market

The Fundamental Principle

We will remind the fundamental principle of the autopoietic hypothesis of the financial market previously formulated: the ***distribution of the return of the financial market on the trading strategies follows the distribution of the replicability of the fitness of those strategies.*** We will examine the significance of this principle, including in relation to other financial market models.

General Meanings of the Basic Principle

- It targets the return, as the variable (or parameter) of last resort interest for the economic agent, a common aspect with all the other models of the financial market;
- the targeting of the return is done not informationally (as, e.g., in the EMH model), but behaviourally;
- the behaviour, in turn, concerns not the level of return, but its distribution;
- the distribution of the return does not refer to its distribution in time and/or space, but to the distribution by trading strategies (which, of course, also involves a spatial and temporal distribution, respectively, but not as a first instance or distributional criterion);
- the criterion of similarity of the distribution of the return on trading strategies is exactly the replicability of the fitness;[108]
- the replicability of fitness has a potential character, not necessarily actual one: thus, if a trading strategy verifies all the predicates of sufficiency to be replicable (i.e., to reproduce its own identity), then the

return associated with it (which has potential character also, until that trading strategy is operated through an individual transaction inferred from it) follows approximately the distribution of that replicability;

Nota bene: the emphasis on replicability (and not on actual replication) is likely to give predictability in the APMH model, which can be used in empirical testability, because, as in the case of Popperian falsifiability, it implies potentiality, not actuality.

Comparative Meanings of the Fundamental Principle
We organize the comparability of the fundamental principles of the known models of the financial market in Table 4.2, in order to identify the peculiarities of APMH from the perspective of its fundamental principle.

▶ *Short Discussion*

- Direct analogies of APMH can be established with three of the five financial market models:
  - with AMH: both are based on behaviour, not information;
  - with FMH: both work through return distribution;
  - with APH: both involve perpetuation/replication/evolution.
- The APMH model is (net) distinct:
  - both from the perspective of the base and from the point of view of operation: of EMH, respectively by CMH;
  - from the perspective of the base: of FMH, respectively of APH;
  - from the perspective of operation: by AMH.

Table 4.2 Logical positioning of fundamental principles of financial markets models

		Functioning		
		Through level	*Through distribution*	*Through perpetuation*
Base	Informational	EMH	FMH	
	Structural	CMH		APH
	Behavioural	AMH	APMH	

Source: Authors

- APMH model works both from a distribution perspective and from a replicative (identitary perpetuation) perspective being the only model of this type of financial market.

The Paradigmatic Structure

In this paragraph we will provide the paradigmatic analysis of APMH, based on the proposed methodology (already applied on EMH, respectively on AMH), in FMAB-APH. The purpose of this analysis is to determine whether APMH is or can be considered a paradigm.[109] Since the general structure of a paradigm is already presented in FMAB-APH (Dinga et al., 2022), we will take the methodological framework from there and apply it to the APMH model.

Methodological Framework
In general, a paradigm is a model of rationality, regardless of its purpose (cognitive, practical or praxiological). We remind you that a paradigm, in the most abstract way, has a structure based on four components:

- *value* (**V**): the value addresses the foundation of the paradigm. For example, complete rationality (or hyper-rationality) in the *homo œconomicus* model;
- *nucleus* (**N**): the nucleus addresses the prime (primitive, fundamental) principle of the paradigm. For example, selfishness;
- *function* (**F**): the function addresses the purpose of the paradigm (in fact, the purpose of the actors who use that paradigm). For example, minimizing opportunity cost in neoclassical economic theory;
- *logic* (**L**): logic addresses the principles of paradigm rationalization. For example, methodological individualism.

The four structural components of the paradigm must be consistent two by two and convergent in function (**F**). Therefore, for any particular logical model that is analysed, the two 'Cs' (consistency and convergence) must be checked to get a positive answer to the question of whether we are really dealing with a paradigm. There can be three distinct types of paradigms. This typology is based on the distinction between three fundamental types of human activities, as they result from the general relationship between subject and object: (1) *theoretical* activity is given by the 'object–object' relationship (e.g., physics or biology)—it generates *cognitive* paradigms; (2) the *praxiological* activity is given by the 'subject–object' relationship (e.g., economics)—this generates *actional* or praxiological paradigms; (3) *practical* activity is given by the 'subject–subject' relationship (e.g., politics or religion)—this generates *practical* or moral paradigms. Only the praxiological paradigm has all the components mentioned above. As the APMH model of the financial market is of a praxiological type, the praxiological paradigm is applicable (or not, as the case may be) to it.

Assessment
We have previously proposed three criteria/conditions to be verified by a logical model, regardless of its nature, so that that model is qualified as a paradigm: (1) *institutional*/structural criterion (or condition): the model/system in the case must verify the four structural components of a paradigm, as mentioned above (V, N, F, L); (2) *conservative*/homeostatic criterion (or condition): the model/system examined must maintain its identity (i.e., structure) in a sustainable manner under theoretical criticism and/or empirical tests; (3) *regulatory*/homeorhetic criterion (or condition): the model/system in question must have internal principles, devices and/or mechanisms in place to maintain its trajectory, while accepting dynamic adjustments.

Institutional (Structural) Criterion
The verification of the institutional criterion refers to the verification (and establishment of the identity) of the four structural components of the APMH model. Of course, the components in question are examined from the perspective of the economic operator, which in turn generates the (symbolic) financial individual called the trading strategy and, from a population point of view, generates the financial species called the financial market.

(1) **V**—*value*: we consider that the value (the one that primarily bases the finality) of the APMH model is the *adaptive replicativity*.[110] The problem of adaptability has already been discussed in connection with our previous hypothesis on the modelling of the financial market functioning (it is about the adaptive preference hypothesis—APH), but APMH is a model that, as we will show later, integrates APH, logically, structurally and functionally, so we shall make a few more clarifications here:

- adaptability (or plasticity) of a behaviour refers to the variation of that behaviour by overcoming the 'tunnel of variation' that preserves the identity of the system in question.[111] More specifically, as adaptability is manifested by the change in the propensity of the economic agent behind the financial individual, it is a matter of changing that propensity so that the trading strategy, which is the direct effect of the change in propensity, loses its current identity;
- loss of the current identity of the trading strategy, which is a necessary condition for the production of adaptability (plasticity), must be 'done' but to the extent beyond which the replicability of that trading strategy becomes impossible. Therefore, we have, in fact, the following behavioural thresholds, from the perspective of the value (V) (i.e., the foundation of finality) of the APMH model:
  - *plasticity threshold* (*PT*): the threshold of variation (adaptation) of the propensity of the economic agent below which the adaptation of the trading strategy (TS) does not occur—that is, TS is still elastic, but adaptations (i.e., plasticities) of individual transactions (IT) which make up the TS concerned can occur; therefore, the plasticity threshold refers to TS, not IT;
  - *replicability threshold* (*RT*): the threshold of variation (adaptation) of the propensity of the economic agent (established above the plasticity threshold) below which the replication capacity of the TS is not yet compromised, although its adaptation occurs.[112] Beyond the replicability threshold, however, TS cannot longer be replicated;
- the issue of replicative adaptability raises a question that directly refers to the very concept of replicability itself. In connection with this issue, we make the following considerations:
  - in general, replicativity 'requires' the predicate of identity, that is, replication is always considered to be identitary. Of course, identity is a non-point predicate, it is rather an interval predicate—for example, about the thresholds of variation of propensity, mentioned above, below the plasticity threshold, the trading strategy maintains its identity exclusively in terms of its potential to generate individual transactions that are consistent (i.e., non-contradictory) with it, but those individual transactions no longer replicate their identity. Therefore, in the case of the variation of the propensity below the plasticity threshold, the identity replication

of the trading strategy is a replication of the potentiality, not of the actuality. In conclusion, identity replicability (or replication) refers only to a generative identity that, as we said, has a potential character;

- in the area of variation of the propensity between the plasticity threshold and the replicability threshold, the replicability (replication) of the trading strategy is no longer a potential one, but becomes the actual replicability (replication). One of the logical consequences of such a phenomenon is that the new individual transactions generated (causally, especially from the perspective of the formal cause) by the new trading strategy may be (*Nota bene*: usually, they are) inconsistent with the 'old' individual transactions. In fact, we have, here, a kind of paradigmatic incommensurability between the logical content of the two 'generations' of trading strategies;[113]
- therefore, it can be said that adaptive replicability establishes/substantiates a *quasi-identitary* replicability (replication) of the trading strategy; this replicability can occur exclusively in the area between the plasticity threshold and the replicability threshold, beyond which the trading strategy disappears in terms of identity (respectively quasi-identity)—in other words, it is rejected from the perspective of selection applied by the environment (namely, cultural geodesic) to the financial individual called trading strategy.

Figure 4.12 shows a synoptic suggestion of the APMH model value (V).

(2) **N**—*nucleus*: we consider that the fundamental principle[114] of functioning of the APMH model is mazifficing.[115] By mazifficing is meant obtaining the integral utility, as described above. The nucleus of the APMH model has the following features:
   - the satisfaction of the human individual remains, even in the APMH model, its crucial goal, and represents, as in the case of other models of the financial market, the content of the fundamental principle of supporting the decision and the action;
   - mazifficing is also claimed from selfishness,[116] but it is an 'adjusted' selfishness from two perspectives:
     - a perspective of *finality*: the human individual no longer pursues optimization (either rigid, i.e., based on an invariant preference,

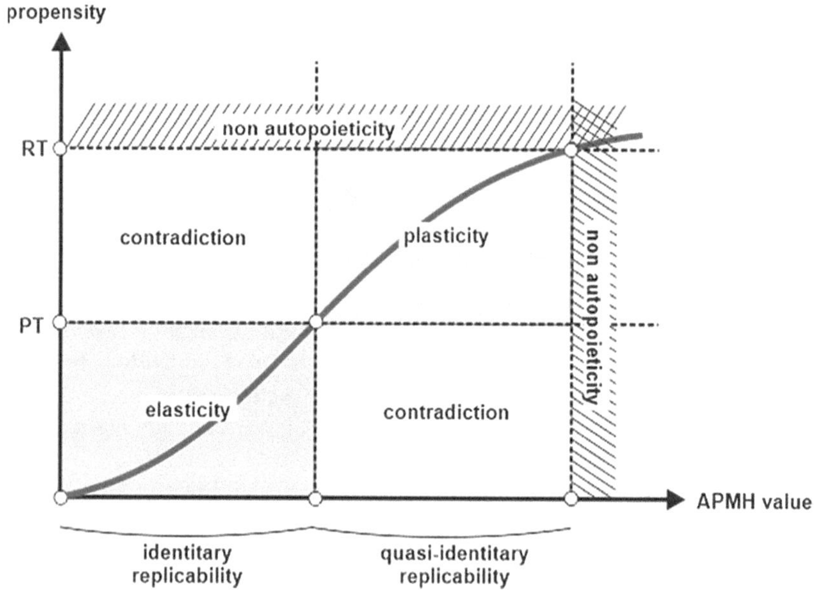

Fig. 4.12 The APMH thresholds of value (V) functioning. (*Source*: Authors)

or plastic, based on adaptive preference), but sufficiency: a utility that is sufficient for the replicability of the human individual (both from a biological perspective and from an economic one)—we find, here too, the idea of a second best solution, to the detriment of the first best solution;

- a perspective *sphere*: the sufficient utility pursued by the human individual (economic agent) is no longer seen exclusively at its substantive level (or nature)—that is, aiming at the utility called economic utility—but at its integral level (or nature): the logical (and synergistic) sum between substantive utility (*EU*) and symbolic utility (*SU*);[117]

Nota bene: although, as we have shown, we ignore, for now the evidential utility in the structure of the integral utility, the nucleus of the APMH model refers to the integral utility which includes the evidential one;

- therefore, the nucleus of the APMH model aims at a second best solution that aims at a combination between the current goal and the future goal—a combination that forms the content of the value called *adaptive replicativity*.

Figure 4.13 illustrates the three versions of nucleus in the EMH, APH and APMH financial market models.

(3) **F**—*function*: based on the value of the APMH model, we consider that its function (i.e., its purpose) is *co-evolution*, with reference to the replication of the financial individual (trading strategy) in tandem with the environment (cultural geodesic). Of course, the function is inferred (and inferable) from the value—that is, from the adaptive replicativity, keeping in mind both specifications: the replicability, respectively the adaptability, which, functionally integrated, lead to the concept of co-evolution.[118] The function of the APMH model therefore ensures the continuity of the financial individual, from the perspective of ensuring sufficient conditions of reproduction, and the latter is, in fact, a simultaneous and inter-conditional reproduction of the trading strategy and

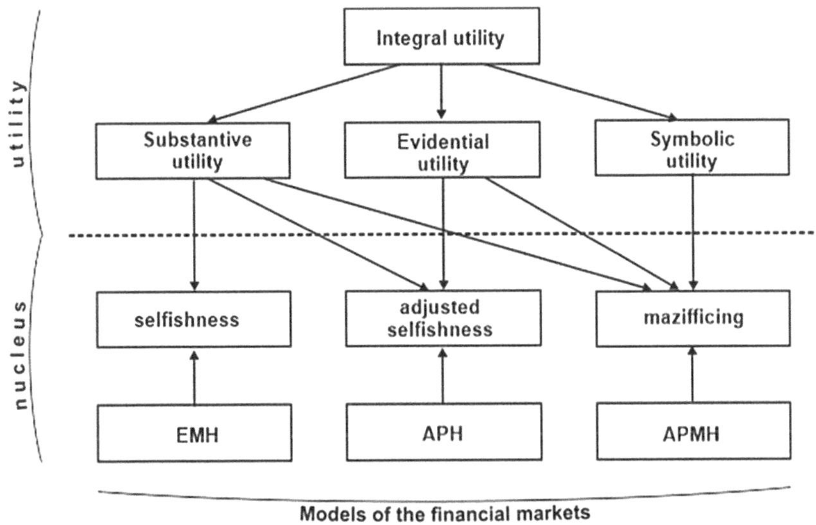

Fig. 4.13 The APMH thresholds of nucleus (N) functioning. (*Source*: Authors)

cultural geodesic.[119] The logically necessary link between autopoiesis and co-evolution can hardly be overestimated, and we consider it a *conditio sine qua non* for treating the APMH model;

(4) L—*logic*: based on what has been said and argued above, we propose that the logic of the APMH model be formulated as *methodological co-evolutionism.* Of course, the concept of methodological co-evolutionism must be related to the other two logics presented above (see FMAB-APH): EMH model logic—*methodological individualism* (a microeconomic statics)—and AMH model logic—*methodological holism* (a macroeconomic statics). Therefore, the logic we propose for the APMH model is of the type of a *microeconomic kinematics*, from which it results that the logic of the APMH model has the following characteristics:
   - considers the package 'system–environment', in our case the package 'trading strategy (with the species that contains it: financial market)–cultural geodesic' or, in abbreviated format, the package 'TS–CG';
   - the number of 'freedoms' that cultural geodesic allows for the trading strategy is neither limited nor invariable,[120] because it is refreshed precisely by the co-evolutionary functioning of the 'TS–CG' package.

We conclude that, from the point of view of the institutional (structural) criterion, the APMH model of the financial market, which we propose in this study, verifies the paradigm statute of the financial market.

Conservative (Homeostatic) Criterion

The conservative or homeostatic criterion must, as its name implies, ensure the preservation of the *state* of the system in question. Applied to our discussion, the conservative criterion must answer the question of whether the financial individual (trading strategy) is replicated (in the sense of ensuring sufficient conditions for replication or replicability).[121] To examine this criterion, that is, to see if it is verified (according to the theoretical assumptions of the Kuhnian concept of paradigm), we will develop some considerations on the testability of predictions developed under the APMH model.

- *First of all*, it must be established whether the fundamental principle of the model allows the issuance of conjectures on the basis of which empirically testable predictive statements can be formulated:

- to resume the formulation of the fundamental principle of the APMH model: ***the distribution of the financial market return on the trading strategies follows the distribution of the fitness replicability of those strategies***;
- a type of conjecture subsumed to the fundamental principle could have the following wording: 'increasing the fitness of a trading strategy implies increasing the return of the financial market related to that trading strategy');[122]
- the type of predictive statements inferred from the type of conjecture mentioned above could have the following wording: 'covariation between the kinematics of fitness of a trading strategy and the kinematics of the return of that trading strategy is positive';
- it is obvious that such a predictive statement is perfectly testable empirically (i.e., it is falsifiable, from the Popperian perspective) because:

  the time series on the return can be built in association with the trading strategies operated in the financial market—these are in limited numbers (the literature often inventories them) and their essence can be easily extracted through qualitative analyses; although it is less obvious how fitness could be identified from the perspective of adaptive replicability, as we propose in this research (both qualitatively and quantitatively, including kinematics, so, based on a cardinal measure or, in the worst case, ordinal one), this problem is not insurmountable, based on the considerations and clarifications made in connection with the concept of social fitness;

- *secondly*, it is necessary to establish the way in which the structural components of the APMH model (those discussed at the institutional criterion) react to anomalies, that is, in other words, to refutations[123] of conjectures if the factual predictive statements are proved, following experiments (artificial or natural), as false:[124]
  - from the perspective of ***value*** (V): as we have shown, the selective impact of the environment on the phenotype (trading strategy) is made at the level (through) the individual transaction which represents (as in the case of biological entities) the operational, manifest, concrete, particular hypostatisation of the phenotype. It follows that, below a certain critical mass (threshold), which was

previously theorized, the trading strategy will be preserved even if certain individual transactions will be rejected, replaced or selected by the environment (cultural geodesic) but with mutations that do not lead to replacing of the trading strategy. Therefore, in the case of falsified factual predictions, there is a possibility that, from the value perspective, the trading strategy maintains its replicability—the adaptability related to this replicability can refer, however, not only to individual transactions, but (below a certain identity threshold) even at the level of the trading strategy. We can consider that, below the two thresholds of variability, the anomalies are ignored or tolerated, exactly in the way that the Kuhnian theoretical paradigmatic model ... predicts, regarding the behaviour of normal science;

– from the perspective of ***nucleus*** (N): the nucleus, which is represented, in the case of the APMH model, by maziffficing, that is, the sufficient satisfaction of the human individual behind the trading strategy at the level of integral utility (*TU*),[125] behaves in relation to environment's refutations, like this:

as long as the integral utility remains on the indifference curve between the substantive utility and the symbolic utility (respecting, of course, the thresholds beyond which the substitutability no longer works), no anomaly is registered from the point of view of falsifying the prediction. Of course, the question here is whether the prediction (predictive statement) should contain (verbal) clarifications about the substitutability thresholds between the two categories of utility. Our answer to this possible question is negative: the predictive statement must refer exclusively to integral utility, only the human individual involved (economic agent) has the latitude and, moreover, competence and interest, to assess whether the current variation of substantive utility is counteracted by variation (in the opposite direction) of the symbolic utility, so that the integral utility is maintained on the indifference curve between the two utilities;[126]

the preference between two types of integral utility has its origin, as well as the preference for the trading strategy or for the individual transaction, in the propensity of the economic agent. In other words, the economic agent has only one preference for integral utility, which contains information about both its components;[127]

as well, in the case of the APMH nucleus, therefore, the rejection of a conjecture, based on the falsification of the inferred prediction from that conjecture, is subject to a certain elasticity (or a certain margin or validation tunnel), so that, analogous to the APMH value case, anomalies can be ignored, under a certain critical mass;[128]

- from the perspective of *function* (F): the co-evolutionary function of the APMH model is related, in the most direct way, to a negative result of the empirical testing of some conjectures. Indeed, a refutation of a conjecture following the falsification of a prediction that it has generated means an impact (with the corresponding thresholds, of course) on the propensity of the economic agent. At the same time, the financial market environment may change as a result of these refutation, either to manage modified trading strategies (or individual transactions) or to create (usually normatively) avenues of movement for trading strategies that have been rejected (negatively selected). We believe that, in this functional framework, there is a certain margin (a certain dead zone) both for the adaptation of the trading strategy (or individual transaction) and for the cultural geodesic, so that the anomalies generated by the empirical refutation can be, at least in a certain measure and for a certain period, introduced 'under the carpet'. In conclusion, the conservative/homeostatic criterion of the APMH model function is operational;
- from the perspective of *logic* (L): methodological co-evolutionism (interpreted as a microeconomic kinematic pattern) has the following characteristics:[129]

  it focuses on the adaptive individual (whether it is the human individual, when the adaptation refers to the change in propensity, which leads to the change or adaptation of the proference, or the financial individual—i.e., the trading strategy), which means it remains at the microeconomic level;

is becomes a theoretical basis for the macroeconomic level, because microeconomic adaptation (respectively adaptability) is a result of environmental pressure (i.e., macroeconomic one);[130]

consequently, is not enough neither a model of (hyper) rationality of the individual nor (correlatively) a holistic model of rigid normativity, but an inter-active micro–macro model or, in other words, individual–environment inter-activity is required, so that the two parts to react to each other and permanently (through fetal reaction rules, as shown above) and necessarily leading to co-evolution;

in the particular case of the financial market, the co-evolutionary pattern of the APMH model ensures what, in the following, will be examined from the perspective of self-(re)organization, that is, it ensures a certain behavioural inertia generated by the need to harmonize co-evolution-specific reaction norms. This means that the anomalies associated with the refutation of the tested conjectures can be attributed, at least in part, to imperfections/ co-evolutionary accommodation delays and, therefore, have the effect of preserving the *statu quo*, both in terms of trading strategies and of individual transactions.

We conclude that, from the point of view of the conservative (homeostatic) criterion, the APMH model of the financial market 'qualifies' itself as a paradigm of the financial market.

Regulative (Homeorhesic) Criterion

The regulative (homeorhesic) criterion aims, from a conceptual point of view (although not exactly as a denotative sphere), to resilience, that is, that property of a system (in our case, property of the APMH model of the financial market) to bring back the real system it 'manages'—the trading strategy and, through populational cumulation, the financial market—on the *trajectory* from which, possibly, disturbances (such as the expected return on financial market operations or reaching a critical mass of anomalies generated by empirical testing) deployed the system concerned. Of course, the regulative criterion governs not only, as mentioned above, the resilience, but also the variation of the target of this resilience. Some additional explanations may be helpful at this point:

- *first of all*, the resilience must not be 'perfect', that is, the return of the disturbed system must not occur, necessarily in a punctual manner, on the previous trajectory of that system but, most often, on a range (basin) that contains that trajectory, a range of acceptable[131] variation of the trajectory in question;[132]
- *secondly*, it should be noted that the regulative procedure is applied not only by cultural geodesic, since, in the case of logically living systems (or, equivalently, symbolic species) there are two types of selection, which interact with each other through processes of reciprocal augmentation or, conversely, reciprocal inhibition, as the case may be:

(a) *formal* selection—applied by cultural geodesic, which is the normative component of the financial market environment;
(b) *effective* selection[133]—applied by the symbolic component of the environment (the other trading strategies, i.e., the other economic agents that are 'behind' those trading strategies).

Let us examine the functioning (or non-functioning) of the regulative criterion in the case of the APMH model of the financial market. Specifically, we will need to determine the impact of the anomalies or, more accurately, the finality of the anomalies in this model. We will use, for our analysis, the synoptic picture presented in Fig. 4.14 (with TS the trading strategy was noted, and with IT the individual transaction was noted).

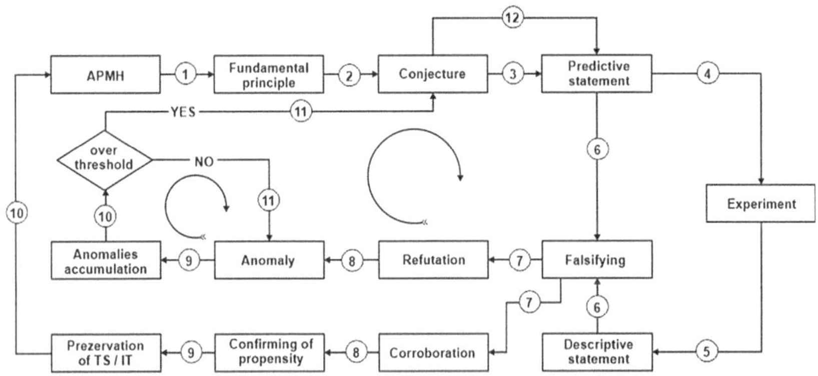

Fig. 4.14 Functioning of the regulative criterion of APMH paradigm. (*Source*: Authors)

Short Discussion

- APMH model generates its fundamental principle (1), on the basis of which conjectures can be issued (2) which, then, form the basis for the formulation of factual predictions (3) in the form of predictive statements (usually verbal or verbalizable);
- starting from the predictive statement, an experiment (either artificial or natural) is conceived (4);
- following the observation of the results of the experiment, a descriptive statement is formulated (5) (usually also in verbal or verbalizable form);
- by comparing the two statements—predictive and descriptive, respectively—the result of the factual test in question is determined (6):
  - corroboration of the conjecture (7) if, semantically, the two statements are equivalent;
  - refutation of the conjecture (7) if, semantically, the two statements are not equivalent (usually if they are contradictory);[134]
- the refutation is an anomaly, from the perspective of the APMH (8), and the corroboration is the 'confirmation' of the propensity (8);[135]
- the anomaly is added to the other anomalies generated by the empirical testing (9), and the confirmation of the propensity leads to the preservation (or increase of the chances of preservation of) TS/IT (9);[136]
- the accumulation of anomalies is verified in terms of exceeding a certain threshold (10), while the TS/IT preservation is 'returned' to the APMH model, to function as a *sui generis* confirmation (10);
- if the anomaly accumulation threshold is not reached, the process continues, including through new anomaly accumulations (11), and if it is reached, the conjecture involved (11) is affected, which could possibly be eliminated or at least adjusted;
- either it is removed (and therefore replaced by another conjecture) or it is adjusted (which also leads to the change of identity of the initial conjecture), a new predictive statement is formulated, based on the new conjecture (12) and the process is resumed from step (4).

Given that all three criteria for evaluating the APMH *qua* paradigm are verified, we conclude that this model can be considered as a financial market paradigm.[137]

Functionality

The functionality of a system refers, as it is known, to the set of relationships among the component elements of that system, that is, to the relationships that take place inside the membrane of the system. Therefore, in order to examine the functionality of the APMH model, it is necessary to establish its structure.

APMH Components

In fact, in this section, we will systematize the disparate elements examined or evoked previously, in order to identify how they relate to each other and support the APMH model. We consider that the list of these components is as follows:

- *fundamental principle* ($\mathcal{FP}$): this principle represents the backbone of the APMH model, on which and starting from which all other structural components will be built. (*Nota bene*: we recall the formulation of the fundamental principle—*the distribution of financial market return on trading strategies follows the distribution of fitness replicability of those strategies*; the fundamental principle is invariant, i.e., it represents the very identity of the APMH model);
- *propensity* of the economic operator ($\mathcal{P}$): refers to the belief (either conscious or subconscious, respectively, either of a rational or irrational type) based on which all evaluations, decisions and actions (either acts or abstentions) of the economic agent in cause are designed and implemented; the propensity is not immutable, but (relatively) flexible/adaptable, although its inertia to change/adjust is very high;[138]
- *trading strategy* ($\mathcal{TS}$): is the financial individual (see the discussion on the AMPH phenotype, above), generated by propensity (either as initiation or as modification/adjustment). The trading strategy verifies the fundamental principle, which means that, at the level of APMH functionality, there is an internal selection of trading strategies, independent of the environment and (both logically and chronologically) prior to the environment. Moreover, it can be said that this selection is an *a priori internal selection* (${}_a^i\mathcal{S}$), because it takes place before any confrontation of the trading strategy with the environment,[139] when the second selection occurs, an *a posteriori external selection* ($\mathcal{S}_a^e$) of the trading strategy. It should be noted that both types of selection are necessary and, moreover, they enter into a *sui*

generis process of co-evolution; obviously, the trading strategy is non-rigid (i.e., it is plastic);[140]

- *individual transaction* ($\mathcal{IT}$): the individual transaction represents an 'application' of the trading strategy in a concrete, particular case, a hypostasis of the strategy in question in a given historical context (time and space). The individual transaction in the APMH model is analogous to the manifestation of the biological individual (phenotype) in concrete, particular cases. We specify that the external *a posteriori* selection, exerted by the environment, applies to the individual transaction which, as shown, takes over the mutation produced either directly at the level of the individual transaction or by inferring from the trading strategy;[141] of course, the individual transaction shows the greatest plasticity ('appetite' for adjustment) of all the components of the APMH model;
- *internal regulator* ($\mathcal{R}^i$): refers to the device, logical and psychological, associated with the economic agent involved, which performs the function (F) of the APMH model, based on the value (V) of the model, as these two criteria were presented and applied above. The internal regulator is, of course, closely related to the propensity through which it acts, so it should not be considered completely rational (so completely predictable) but rather as a mix between the component of rationality and that of irrationality, a mix that works at the level of the human individual (economic agent). This property of the internal regulator (similar to the corresponding propensity property) means that, conceptually, the APMH model can be considered as a *sui generis* integrator of the other models existing in financial theory and concerning the modelling of the financial market: EMH, FMH, CMH, BMH and APH.

APMH Functionality

The relationships between the five structural components of the APMH model of the financial market can be represented as in Fig. 4.15.

Short Discussion

- The fundamental principle is 'isolated' from the rest of the components in terms of bearing influence (except, of course, the abandonment of the APMH model, when it should be replaced by the

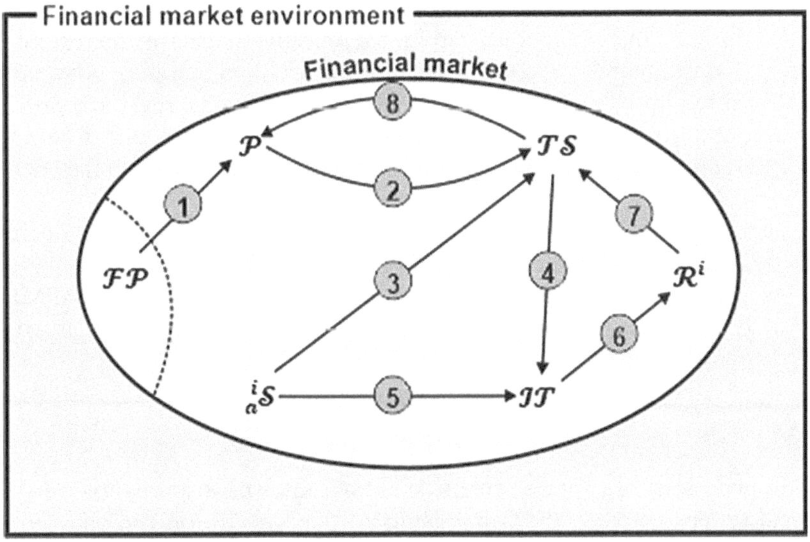

Fig. 4.15 Functionality of APMH paradigm. (*Source*: Authors)

fundamental principle associated with the new financial market model assumed); the fundamental principle has an output (1) that enters, as input, into the propensity of the economic agent which it adjusts both qualitatively and quantitatively (as Bayes' *a priori* probability);

- the propensity directly generates the trading strategy or set of trading strategies (2) which the economic operator operates in the financial market;
- once the trading strategy has been established, the internal *a priori* selection device validates it or not, as the case may be (3); validation or invalidation is performed from the perspective of propensity;
- the validated trading strategy generates (4) the individual transaction (or the set of individual transactions compatible with that trading strategy);
- again, the internal *a priori* selection device verifies the acceptability of the individual transaction (or set of individual transactions) in question (5);

- if the individual transaction is validated, it is operationalized, bearing, through this operationalization, the selective impact of the external environment (which will be discussed below, and therefore not represented in the picture); more specifically, the internal regulator carries out an assessment, for the time being, internal, that is, only from the perspective of the economic operator (e.g., on the return in the financial market) (6);
- subsequently, the internal regulator shall forward the result of this assessment to the relevant trading strategy (7);
- as a result of the assessment by the internal regulator of the APMH model, the trading strategy may change, but only through propensity (8).

Behaviour

The behaviour of a system refers, as is well known, to the whole of the relationships between the components of that system, on the one hand, and the environment of the system in question, on the other hand, that is to say to the relationships which take place through transiting of the system membrane. Therefore, in order to examine the behaviour of the APMH model, it is necessary to determine the composition of its environment.

APMH Environment

It must firstly be said that, in the APMH model, the environment is the second component of the pair 'species–environment', the two components being opposable, structurally and functionally, to each other, although, as shown and will continue to be shown, they are in a co-evolutionary relationship within the APMH model. The financial species is, in this case, the financial market that contains, as individuals (population) the trading strategies, with their concrete ways of manifestation within the environment, called individual transactions.

The components of the environment in the APMH model of the financial market are the following:

- *cultural geodesic* ($\mathcal{CG}$): cultural geodesic is a normative 'attractor' (either with formal/codified norms or informal norms, including values, historical traditions, customs, etc.) that 'curves' any behaviour (i.e., any decision that leads to an action—act or abstention). Cultural geodesic obviously has a strong contextual character (of space, respectively time) and is adjustable, both by its own logic and as a result of its co evolution with the actually influenced behaviours. Cultural geodesic is the main factor in the selection of trading strategy—in terms of *force* of selection;

- the *rest of the financial individuals* ($\mathcal{RTS}$), that is, the other trading strategies within the species: a given trading strategy faces, of course, all the other trading strategies that are operated in the financial market by other economic agents, namely, the trading strategies with which it enters into competition, cooperation or mutual memetic influence. This component of the environment ranks second in importance—related to cultural geodesic—in terms of the force of selection exerted on a given trading strategy;[142]
- *external regulator* ($\mathcal{R}^e$): refers to the device, normative and behavioural, associated with the environment of the species called financial market, which ensures the co-evolutionary dynamics of the environment, in tandem with the financial species. The external regulator is the one that generates the mutation in the two operational components of the environment (cultural geodesic, respectively other financial individuals, of course, closely related to propensity).

From a theoretical point of view, we therefore have the following types of selection that are exerted on a given trading strategy:

- *semetic selection* ($\mathbb{SS}$): selection exerted/operated, directly, by cultural geodesic—that is, $\mathbb{SS} = f(\mathcal{CG})$;
- *memetic selection* ($\mathbb{MS}$): the selection exerted/operated, directly, by the other financial individuals present (contemporary) and active in the financial market—i.e., $\mathbb{MS} = g(\mathcal{RTS})$;
- *mesetic selection* ($\mathbb{MSS}$): the selection exerted by a *sui generis* combination (also of co-evolutionary type) between the semetic selection and the memetic selection, that is, between two functions:[143]
  - either $h_{\mathbb{S}} = f \circ g$
  - either $h_{\mathbb{M}} = g \circ f$

All three categories of the above selection form the external *a posteriori* selection module ($\mathcal{S}_a^e$):

$$\mathcal{S}_a^e == (\mathbb{SS}) \vee (\mathbb{MS}) \vee (\mathbb{MSS}) \vee [(\mathbb{SS}) \wedge (\mathbb{MS})] \vee [(\mathbb{SS}) \wedge (\mathbb{MSS})] \vee [(\mathbb{MS}) \wedge (\mathbb{MSS})] \wedge [(\mathbb{SS}) \wedge (\mathbb{MS}) \wedge (\mathbb{MSS})]$$

In addition to it, operates also the internal *a priori* selection module (${}_a^i\mathcal{S}$).[144]

Therefore, the overall selection under the APMH model is:

$$\left({}_a^i\mathcal{S}\right) \vee \left(\mathcal{S}_a^e\right) \vee \left[\left({}_a^i\mathcal{S}\right) \wedge \left(\mathcal{S}_a^e\right)\right]$$

APMH Behaviour

The relationships among the five structural components of the APMH model and the three structural components of the environment in which this model operates can be represented, in a synoptic way, as in Fig. 4.16.

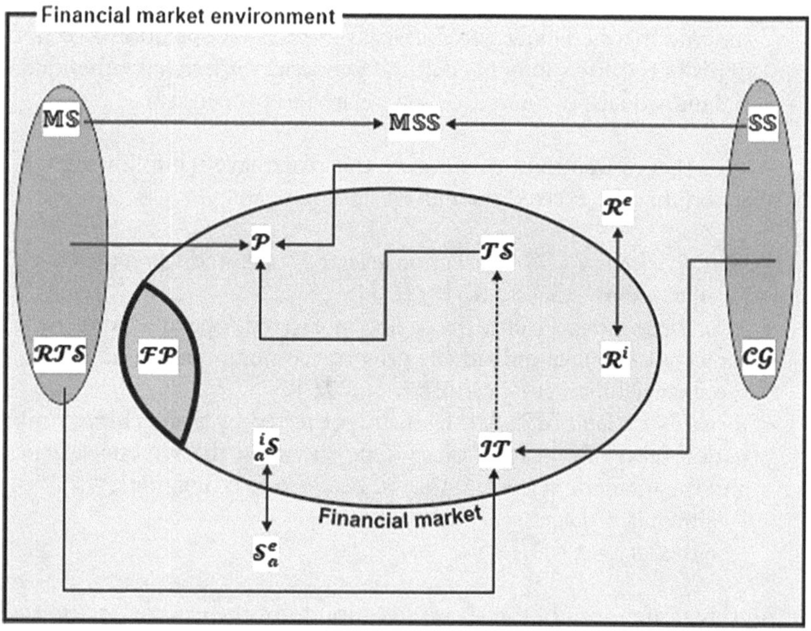

Fig. 4.16 Behaviour of APMH paradigm. (*Source*: Authors)

Short Discussion

- Also, within the behaviour associated with the APMH model, the fundamental principle remains isolated, in the sense that it manifests a total invariance, precisely in order to preserve the model itself;
- propensity (or proference) is affected, on the part of the financial market environment, both by the semetic selection (i.e., through cultural geodesic) and by the memetic selection (i.e., through other trading strategies operated on the market and contemporary with the trading strategy concerned);
- the trading strategy is affected exclusively through the individual transaction which, in turn, is subject to both semetic selection and memetic selection, as soon as the elasticity of the individual transaction is exceeded, as we have already shown in FMAB-APH (Dinga et al., 2022);
- in turn, when the own pressure threshold from the individual transaction is exceeded, the trading strategy can affect the propensity, leading to what we will discuss below regarding the genetic mutation within the APMH model;
- there is an inter-conditioning, often causal, between the two categories of selection (internal and external), on the one hand, and between the internal regulator (of functionality) and the external regulator (of behaviour), on the other hand.

Notes

1. We remind that the individual (phenotype) of this species is the trading strategy, whose praxiological hypostasis is the individual transaction.
2. The hypothesis of financial market autopoieticity is a more general hypothesis than that of adaptive preference (so it encompasses the latter). Specifically, as we will show below, the hypothesis of autopoieticity involves the functioning of both adaptive preference (by adjusting propensity) and constructal law or, more generally, minimal entropic interaction—both discussed very briefly above.
3. Given the sufficiency predicate called relational openness, operational closure can, of course, use flows that come from the system environment (substance, energy, information)—it is important that decisions do not come directly from the environment, as can happen in the case of sustainable systems, where we have operational openness.
4. It is about the trinomial $RE^{(1)}E^{(2)}$ (reason/rationality–experience–emotion), which is the modal filter discussed in FMAB-APH (Dinga et al., 2022).

5. We remind that freedom means the capacity of the human individual to oppose social necessity (in this case, normative necessity). *Nota bene*: of course, not the natural necessity, although some nuances may exist here: for example, self-murderers may choose (based on free will) not to feed—feeding is a natural necessity, generated by the principle of survival.
6. Of course, from a logical point of view, it is a question not of associating the propensity of a *TS* but, but conversely, of associating a *TS* with a propensity, since several *TS*s can be associated with a propensity, while several propensities cannot be associated with a *TS* (obviously related to the same human individual).
7. Although it may also be an inertia that is claimed from the archetype (Gustav Jung's term for the appointment of the collective unconscious—a relatively common unconscious of all human individuals, on which the modelling, logical and, partially, quantitative, of behaviourism is based). The possibility that the archetype is used as a predictor of the emotional behaviour of human individuals is not negligible, despite the approximation it implies (an approximation that is, moreover, much reduced by the 'law' of the tendency to average, also valued by behaviourism–see here, especially Kahneman).
8. As we have shown in detail above, here are a number of significance thresholds that must be exceeded quantitatively for the propensity adjustment (which means the production of the genetic autopoietic mutation) to be achieved.
9. Obviously, the adjustment of adjustment is simply an adjustment of the *statu quo*, so it falls under the first type of propensity inertia.
10. That is why it was so easy for Samuelson to propose the concept of revealed preference—it would have been much harder to propose a measure of (variation of) propensity, that is, a measure to act *ex-ante*.
11. Note that the modal filter $RE^{(1)}E^{(2)}$ is applied in 'reverse' order: $E^{(2)}E^{(1)}R$ (see FMAB-APH (Dinga et al., 2022)).
12. As we have already shown, some normative constraints have to go through the modal filter of the economic agent in order to have an impact on the propensity, but this time it is about external constraints that are imposed without the mediation of the economic agent.
13. But, of course, there may be considerations that do not appeal to the loss–gain binomial: for example, ideological considerations or those related to religious traditions or general cultural value and which have the same result as cost–benefit analyses.
14. Here, of course, we recognize the exercise of free will.
15. These mutations are mainly subject to the threshold effect, so to speak.
16. The fact that we do not have six (3 × 2) distinct types of autopoietic mutations is explained by the fact that, logically, we have two exclusions: fol-

low-up mutations cannot be, at the same time, strategic, respectively induced mutations cannot be operational in nature (given the freedom of the financial market).

17. The model of rationality (i.e., justification), itself, is not acquired, selected, assumed and so on, necessarily, in ways that, in turn, are rational. In fact, most of the time, the model of rationality is a set (system) of beliefs that, as accepted, are (or even must be) a-rational. For example, any propensity (which can 'come' even from the oldest archetypes—in Jung's terminology, here) is such a model of rationality/justification. *Nota bene*: conceptually, the rationalization operation and the justification operation are equivalent, regardless of whether such an operation is performed *ex-ante* or *ex post*.
18. It is simply a belief, in the sense of credence (see also David Lewis, with his concept of *finkish*, discussed in the semantic margin of the concept of propensity).
19. This is, of course, a logical consequence whose inference respects the rules of validity in this case (e.g., the rules of syllogistics).
20. Some scientists think that the institutional artefacts (as, e.g., the financial market) should be considered as non-living entities. Indeed, they are not at all biological entities, that is, they are not biologically living systems (BLSs). However, according to our considerations on the concept of living entity, such artefacts could be, with sufficient entitlement, as logically living systems. As we speak about living systems (no matter as biological or logical ones), it is obvious that the passing from (natural) biologically living world to (cultural) logically living world is a natural passing, from scientific perspective.
21. Here, we have the very concept of social necessity, which is different from the natural necessity.
22. Threshold, accumulability, inertia aspects and so on, which have been discussed in the case of the adaptive preference of the financial market, are valid, *mutatis mutandis*, also in the case of the autopoietic market hypothesis, which we discuss here (*Nota bene*: we believe that we can even talk about a paradigm, but this conjecture will be rigorously examined, based on the methodology proposed by the authors in this matter in FMAB-APH (Dinga et al., 2022)).
23. Of course, at the right time, the quantitative measures (or metrics) needed to rigorously model and (as far as possible) to obtain the predictability of the behaviour involved will be proposed.
24. Lakatos' intention was to 'reconcile' Thomas Kuhn's historical vision (the concept of paradigm, introduced in his work, *The Structure of Scientific Revolutions* (Kuhn, 1970)), with Karl Popper's logical vision (set out in *The Logic of Discovery*) (Popper, 2005) but, in the end, a new conceptual

model of research and testing in science resulted. And yet, the impression of an *ad hoc* hypothesis (in Popper's sense) is difficult to avoid in connection with Lakatos' proposal: saving the hard core as the source of the refuted conjecture does not increase the probability of refuting it (as Popper demands in exchange for accepting *ad hoc* hypotheses) but, obviously, it reduces it, because it sacrifices in the 'first line' (the protection belt) pawns through which it saves the 'king', to make an analogy with the game of chess.

25. This argument has logical validity only when passing from genus to species.
26. We repeat that by the amount of mutation we mean a product between the size of the mutation (or its intensity) and the duration over which the mutation manifests (or, in almost all cases, its repetition). Somehow, it is about exceeding an energetic (more precisely, entropic) significance threshold.
27. Of course, selective inertia also acts in the case of selection specific to biological evolution, if the saltationist hypothesis proposed by Gould is accepted.
28. Obviously, in the case of biological selection, the two steps overlap, that is, the environment of the biological system performs both the factual selection and its ratification (decisional selection).
29. The discussion could be extended (which will not be done here, for obvious reasons), so as to highlight an even more general result than the one stated, namely, that any symbolic species is a quasi-autonomous exosomatic device, and this quasi-autonomy necessarily requires the intermediation of the human agent in the matter of mutation, respectively of evolutionary selection.
30. It can be shown that the APMH model could be operationally named as a *homo socionomicus* model—a *sui generis* combination of the *homo œconomicus* model with the *homo biologicus* model (Dinga, 2017).
31. Sporadic references to this type of entropy, different from the thermodynamic one, have been made before but, in the following, the concept in question will be developed to a sufficient extent to substantiate the autopoietic model of the financial market.
32. The careful reader has noticed, of course, the semantic equivalence between the autopoietic system and the second order cybernetic system.
33. We remind you that the *proference* (concept and term proposed by us) represents the methodological mix (pair) propensity–preference.
34. See, about the distinction between real *economic flows–financial economic flows–nominal economic flows*, also Emil Dinga, *Rebuilding Economics. A Logical, Methodological, and Epistemological Approach* (Dinga, 2012—Chap. 9, Sect. 9.2). An excerpt from this chapter is presented in Annex 6.1.

35. The main impact of this functional restoration is the reduction of the risk of autonomization of nominal flows in relation to real flows—the autonomization in question is the origin of the so-called financial bubbles.
36. To some extent, the two mechanisms are also substitutable, but up to a threshold that will be examined in detail below—above that threshold, substitutability becomes inhibitory.
37. As we will show below, the two mechanisms are contingent, but this contingency contains a certain necessity, which we can call contingency-generated necessity or intra-contingent necessity.
38. This term, respectively the concept it designates, is introduced by the authors of this study.
39. It should be noted that we are, in this respect, on nominalist ontological positions.
40. The concept of *ophelimity* (proposed by Vilfredo Pareto) seems to be more appropriate but, from the perspective of this paper, it will be considered substitutable with that of utility (strictly limited to economic satisfaction). It should be noted that both utility and ophelimity were, in turn, rejected and replaced by Irving Fisher with the concept of *wantability*.
41. Conceptually, a crisis (economic, social, political, cultural, etc.) is a pressure of real events on the established order—this can lead either to an improvement of the current order or to its replacement with another order. An improvement/adjustment of order could be achieved through reform, while its replacement is the result of a revolution (either cognitive, social or political, as the case may be).
42. We remind the reader that an abduction is a *prima facie* explanation, or rather, the most plausible *prima facie* explanation that further enters into a deductive process of reasoning as incomplete primary induction.
43. Where and when this complete and perfect predictability does not take place, the cause for this is our incomplete and imperfect knowledge, that is, it is a temporal or local (historical) accident.
44. Moreover, in this field (especially in practical relationships) there is a certain indiscernibility between subject and object or, in other words, there is a permanent and unpredictable transition of the subject into object and vice versa.
45. Most often tacitly, such an attribution system is used when talking about something rational, irrational or a-rational. So, some results are rational, related to a certain model of rationality, but could be irrational, related to another model of rationality (generally contradictory to the first). Basically, nothing can be absolutely rational or irrational, but only relative to a model of rationality (similarly must be thought about a-rational).
46. The weakening of intelligibility related to causation occurs by replacing the cause (understood as a primary cause or as a cause of last resort) with

the *causal mechanism* or causal device. A causal mechanism/device is a causal chain that does not aspire to obtain the primary cause, but only the proximal one. For example, most economic or social correlations are nothing more than the most plausible proximal cause (*Nota bene*: note the semantic intersection of the concept of the most plausible proximal cause with the concept of abduction).

47. The difference between perception and representation (as suggested by cognitive psychology or phenomenology) is as follows: perception involves the presence *hic et nunc* (i.e., in person) of the perceived entity, while representation can perform perceptions without requiring presence (in person) of the entity concerned (e.g., by memory, fantasy, etc.—*Nota bene*: phenomenology refers to representation as a *presentification*, as opposed to perception which is called *presentation*).
48. Perhaps, free will should be accepted in any subject who is 'endowed' with psychism, without requiring the more restrictive condition of intellectual (or rational) capacity.
49. Logically, the explanation (as a coherent description of causality) and the prediction are equivalent. In other words, the prediction is a previous explanation, while the explanation is a future prediction. It is easy to see that this equivalence is true only in the natural realm (i.e., in the realm where necessity is sovereign).
50. Of course, complexity can characterize both simple and complicated systems. So, in the economic and social field we can have difficulties of understanding (due to complicatedness) like in the natural field, but such cognitive and praxiological difficulties based on complicatedness are not necessary but contingent.
51. A systematic examination of the problem of justification in epistemology (and, more generally, in gnoseology) is provided by the philosopher Susan Haack in her work *Evidence and Inquiry: A Pragmatist Reconstruction of Epistemology* (Haack, 2009).
52. The type of belief, rational or irrational (e.g., faith), is irrelevant.
53. We have here a support for justifying the phenomenological extrapolation of behaviour, which statistical data (in time series, e.g.) cannot do at all (see the risk of too much confirmation of the past, i.e., the risk of too much $R^2$of the time series).
54. Nozick insists on the need to construct a theory of choice of principles analogous to the theory of choice of goods (or, we might add, to the theory of public choice), because it is not clear why a less powerful principle would not be chosen so as to less penalties will be paid if it is violated.
55. Ramsey delimits himself from Keynes's approach to subjective probabilities (also based on beliefs), as he considers that Keynes introduces a circularity in the justification of belief, namely, the circularity between two

logical sentences. Here lies, in fact, the vast problem and the literature of justification.

56. Based on the entire discussion in this research, it follows that propensity cannot be a principle (although it can be a mechanism). We will return to this consequence.
57. The principle acts as a geodesic that 'curves' the behaviour and thus changes the meaning of that behaviour.
58. The suggestion that the symbolic utility (i.e., the usefulness of a principle) depends on the impact that that principle has on others has a special importance that deserves to be theorized, especially from a co-evolutionary perspective. An evolutionary (or co-evolutionary) model of principles could be of the greatest theoretical and, especially, praxiological interest (but, of course, also practical).
59. We strongly insist that the sign not be confused with the symbol—from the name of symbolic utility it does not follow at all that the principle (which is the institutional source of symbolic utility) is itself a symbol. It, the principle, acts, as we have suggested, as a sign.
60. The relationship between subject and object is a praxiological action (or activity). The symbolic utility implies, however, especially subject–subject relations, which constitute practical actions (activities).
61. The theory of expected utility, proposed by John von Neumann and Oskar Morgenstern (*Theory of Games and Economic Behaviour*) (von Neumann & Morgenstern, 2007).
62. With all the adjustments that have been made over time (starting with Simon's bounded rationality) but that keep the model within the axioms of neoclassical economic theory.
63. And, in most cases, considered invariant over the time horizon of the analysis in question.
64. For example, even the research direction associated with behaviourism also uses the substantive utility for the development of individual decision systems.
65. Whether we are talking about a cardinal utility or an ordinal one—both offer measurements or measures, although the former is able to provide direct quantitative comparisons, while the latter is only able to provide hierarchical comparisons.
66. From a technical point of view, this means obtaining an extreme value (either maximum or minimum, as the case may be) of a function-objective that is subject to a set of constraints, usually expressed mathematically/equationally.
67. One of the most ingenious (and already influential) proposals for financial market theory is made exactly from the perspective of survival, not optimi-

zation, that is, similar to the functioning of the biological world—it is about Adaptive Market Hypothesis (Lo, 2019).

68. The term *satisficing* is a terminological invention of Herbert Simon, related to his hypothesis of bounded rationality. From a technical point of view, it is a combination of the terms satisfying and suffice, that is, it means sufficient satisfaction, not optimal.
69. It is obvious that here we are committing a method plagiarism (from Simon, mentioned above) by constructing a hybrid term, *symboficing* from the terms symbolic, and suffice.
70. Similar to those mentioned in the previous note, we construct a hybrid term, *mazifficing*, from the Greek term μαζί, which means together, in one place, integral and suffice, that is, a sufficient satisfaction at the integral level, so which refers to the integral utility felt by an individual—substantive, evidential and symbolic.
71. Perhaps, among the well-known extreme positions on the concept of economic value (on the one hand, the Marxist basis of socially necessary time, and, on the other hand, marginalism) a third could (or should) be examined as a more important anchor of the economic value, namely, the amount of low entropy with which a given entity is endowed. Of course, in such a 'theory', goods and services also constitute capital. By the way, a (considerable) part of the goods and services produced in the economy are intended for intermediate consumption, that is, they are considered conceptually to be capital goods and services.
72. Of course, the question of so-called natural capital arises here: in our opinion, the concept of natural capital is a *contradictio in terminis* if we consider the two predicates of sufficiency mentioned. *Nota bene*: any human intervention on a potential natural resource transforms it into capital (provided that it does not enter into final consumption, but into intermediate consumption) but only with this interventionist condition (e.g., a virgin forest is not of the nature of natural capital, it is only a natural resource).
73. Consequently, the phrase 'human capital' (see, here, the (too) enthusiastic works of Gary Becker) regardless of what is meant by it—physical strength, intellectual education, health and so on—is, at most, a metaphor (failed, we believe).
74. It is obvious that the instruction and education of the individual (including the qualification) cannot be of the nature of capital, because people are not artefacts as a result of economic action, although, in part, it is an artefact as a result of cultural action.
75. Not to confuse the predicate *substantial* (regarding substance, physicality) with the predicate *substantive* (regarding palpable, fungible reward).

76. In short, free will means the possibility, capacity and desire of individuals to oppose or reject external decisions or acts (more precisely, to ignore or reject them directly) of social origin (generally, not of natural source).
77. Perhaps, a more appropriate name for this concept could be *homogeneity*.
78. The concept of communication used here has nothing to do with that of communication used by Niklas Luhmann in his famous theory of autopoietic society—in the present discussion, this concept has its usual meaning, of transmitting information or data between a sender and a receiver. (*Nota bene*: this is exactly what was considered in the theory of information entropy proposed by Claude Shannon.)
79. The notions of commitment or involvement can be considered as equivalent.
80. This includes the formal construction of the institutions themselves, which are to facilitate the participation of individuals.
81. Here the notion of politics has the widest possible meaning.
82. What is called, in the theory of social justice, the basic structure of society.
83. In general, a contract is simply a free will agreement, without the obligation of any means of proof, written or otherwise (e.g., the J.J. Rousseau-ian social contract).
84. What is called ordinal utility (or, more pompously, the ordinal theory of utility) is just a clumsy attempt to order ... the cardinality, which also means a cardinal approach: for example, to say that utility *A* is greater than utility *B* is equivalent to saying that utility *A* is situated, in order of preference, to the left of utility *B*, on an imaginary line oriented from left to right, supra-posed, for example, on the straight line of natural numbers (which, as a set, has, as is well known, dimension 1, so it contains elements with dimension 0, such as the numbers associated with cardinal utilities).
85. This ignoring does not detract from the generality of the discussion, because the evidential utility has a rather different role from both the substantive utility and the symbolic utility.
86. It should be noted that those moral norms that are codified (formalized) leave the moral territory and enter the legal one.
87. Of course, the fundamental character of the issue must be discussed separately.
88. Otherwise, there is a rupture between the individual and society (see, e.g., the historical cases of dissidents), generally for political reasons, but it should be noted that political precepts are, in essence, moral precepts, not legal/positive ones.
89. Most economic phenomena/processes are modelled with logistic function/curves, which means that, at the beginning, those phenomena/processes show an accelerated 'accumulation', then, after a threshold (inflection point from a mathematical point of view) decelerates to a new

threshold that could be of three kinds: (a) a new inflection point, (b) a turning point and (c) an asymptotic point (as in our case). *Nota bene*: the same seems to happen in the case of economic crises (more precisely, financial ones).

90. Unlike the absolute substantive utility which, by decreasing, generates a negative marginal substantive utility, the absolute symbolic utility cannot decrease when the 'consumption of symbolic goods' increases above the asymptotic point, it simply becomes stationary; consequently, the marginal symbolic utility becomes null, but not negative.
91. In essence, maximization/minimization, on the one hand, and optimization, on the other hand, are much different processes: maximization/minimization is not always subject to constraints (e.g., a mathematical function has a maximum/minimum point as a solution of the first derivative, when the second derivative is negative/positive, without any other conditioning outside its own parameters/coefficients), while optimization is possible only within a set of constraints (we have, here, a conditional closure similar to the theoretical closure of Heisenberg).
92. To review, here, the enthusiasm (almost impossible to discourage) with which many quantitative analysts of the economy 'optimize' a function-objective according to two concomitant and … contradictory criteria (the best-known example: maximizing the effect and minimizing the effort).
93. The question whether such a replication should be of the same size as in the previous replication episode, or should be at a larger or smaller size, is not relevant from a theoretical point of view, but only from an empirical (i.e., contingent) point of view. For example, regarding consumerism, as a moral, perhaps replication should occur to a lesser extent than in previous episodes of replication (in general, it seems that sustainability is attributable, from such a perspective, to symbolic utility as well).
94. It should be noted that the permanent replication of optimization is (ironically) a kind of sustainability of optimization, according to the definition provided for the concept of sustainability. Of course, some theoretical (somehow speculative) developments can be started from this point.
95. This is how the phenomenon of globalization came about.
96. A peremptory example here is the relocation of economic activities caused either by lower costs (e.g., moving companies to lower-wage countries) or by easier access to natural resources of raw materials and energy.
97. See the 'indispensable' (though trivial) Likert scale.
98. That is, as suggested above, a shift from rationality to intelligibility.
99. We will ignore, as we have already mentioned, the procedural/evidential utility, because it has justifying functions, not being additive to either the substantive or the symbolic utility, although it can increase the integral utility.

100. The procedural/evidential utility is less obvious (and, moreover, less used in the literature). We recall that it refers to that utility which has (or contains or can mobilize) principles to prove or justify or test either a decision or a behaviour and so on.
101. Some elementary (defining) mathematical features of integral utility (IU) are the following: (1) $IU = EU \oplus SU$; (2) $SU = \alpha \cdot EU$; (3) $CSU = \beta \cdot IU$; (4) $CSU = \frac{\Delta SU}{\Delta IU}$; (5) $\frac{\partial EU}{\partial q} > 0$; (6) $\frac{\partial^2 EU}{\partial q^2} < 0$; (7) $\frac{\partial^3 EU}{\partial q^3} > 0$; (8) $\frac{\partial SU}{\partial q} > 0$; (9) $\frac{\partial^2 SU}{\partial q^2} > 0$; (10) $\frac{\partial^3 SU}{\partial q^3} < 0$, where α and β are structural parameters (more or less empirical) and q is the 'quantity' of good involved.
102. The phrase 'individual agency' has, here, the meaning of individual activism (diligence).
103. Despite the fundamentalist belief of economists, the social game is dominated by cooperation, not competition. Moreover, conceptually, competition is a kind of cooperation.
104. It should be mentioned that it is not only about contemporary individuals, with whom one actually interacts, but also about non-contemporary individuals, from whom one borrows beliefs, ideologies, principles, models, reasonings, arguments, evaluations and so on.
105. It is obvious that by so-called authentic preferences, these authors mean the invariant, given preferences. We do not think that anyone could prove that adaptive preferences are not genuine preferences—in fact, perhaps a solution to this problem would be to consider as genuine preference exactly the preference objectified by decision and action (not limited to what Samuelson calls revealed preference but generated, as we do in this research, by propensity).
106. The idea of the symbolic nature of revealed preferences is one that deserves further development, because these revealed preferences can 'hide' (i.e., contain) principles of behaviour.
107. We recall that the concept of adaptive preference, as a hypothesis of the financial market, was addressed quite analytically in FMAB-APH.
108. It is, of course, about social fitness, previously discussed, customized for the case of the trading strategy in the financial market.
109. We remind the reader that while EMH verified the sufficiency predicates of a paradigm, AMH failed in this verification (see FMAB-APH).
110. At this point, the following problem arises: we remember that, in the case of AMH, the value of that model was the *heuristics*, so we need to operate the semantic distinction between heuristics and adaptive replicativity. Firstly, heuristics do not logically involve either adaptation or replication (in their rigid sense) and, obviously, neither adaptive replicativity (i.e., the two phenomena taken in their synergistic interaction). Heuristics is simply

a value that rejects rationality (and, *a fortiori*, hyper-rationality, as in the case of value in the EMH model) and can, at most, establish replicativity (as a singular property) or replication (as a singular process). In conclusion, the value called adaptive replicativity is a conjunction between replicability/replication and adaptability/adaptation, which, as we will show below, involves both rationality and heuristics—of course, it does not follow that APMH achieves an integration of EMH and AMH, in the mirror with Lo's claim to be integrated EMH and BMH. The question might also be asked: why we do not formulate the value of the APMH model simply as self-replicability, instead as adaptive replicability? Our answer is this: although the property of autopoiesis, essential in the APMH model, has the connotation of self, however replication of the trading strategy (which is the phenotype in this model) is not, in itself, a self-replication, because, as we have shown (and we will insist on this important aspect), the replication of the trading strategy is an effect of the combination of emergence and deliberation, sufficient to reject the wording 'self-replicability'. This 'obstacle' lies in the fact, already mentioned before, but to which we will refer further, that the financial individual is not autonomous—its genotype (propensity) is external to it, being a psychic (structural) property of the human individual.

111. As we have shown before, the variation that is preserved, from a dimensional point of view, inside the 'variation tunnel' is subsumed to the elasticity, not the plasticity of the respective system.
112. It is understood that the variation (adaptation, plasticity) of IT occurs both under PT and between PT and RT.
113. Incommensurability (which we can qualify as inter-strategic) not much different from the inter-paradigmatic incommensurability theorized by Kuhn (Kuhn, 2012).
114. We draw attention to the fact that the *fundamental principle* phrase of the APMH model refers, here, exclusively to the core of the model and there should be no confusion with the fundamental principle phrase used to describe the essence of the APMH model. Perhaps, from the perspective of the APMH core, we could use the phrase *principle of substantiation*, instead of fundamental principle, this being, moreover, the direct meaning of this expression in this use.
115. Regarding the term maziffìcing, see also note 259.
116. We saw, in FMAB-APH, that, in the case of the Adaptive Preference Hypothesis (APH) model, the core is represented by an adjusted selfishness, compared to the Efficient Market Hypothesis (EMH) model where selfishness was seen in its original (non-qualified) denotation.
117. Further developments could introduce into the 'equation' the evidential utility (procedural, behavioural).

118. The value of the APMH model, as formulated here, will be the conceptual link that will allow the APMH model to integrate the APH model (*Nota bene*: and, moreover, the NPH model—natural price hypothesis—which will be addressed in a subsequent study).
119. As we have noted before, many times, there is no evolution (neither in the biological case nor in the logical case), but only (and always) co-evolution. Of course, in order to make a verbal saving, we can talk about evolution, but every time we use this term we will have to understand that it is about co-evolution. Note also that, logically, evolution (understood outside the meaning of co-evolution) is impossible: let us admit that we have a S system that works (e.g., lives) in a E_S environment. Suppose, further, that we accept only the evolution of S, while E_S is considered invariant. Although it is invariant (in relation to the variation of S), however E_S has a number of 'degrees of freedom' (which is rigid in relation to S) within which S can vary so as to ensure, at the same time, its eligibility for positive selection by E_S—we denote the set of these 'freedoms' with $F^{E_S} = \{e_1^S, e_2^S, \ldots, e_{n_e}^S\}$. It follows that, as long as the variation of S does not violate any of the values (quantitative, qualitative, rhythm, etc.) e_i^S (with $i = \overline{1, n_e}$, S) can evolve within E_S. Since n_e is a finite (natural) number, after the exhaustion of all 'freedoms', S can no longer evolve, since E_S no longer produces other 'freedoms' as an effect of the evolution of S, because it is invariant related to S. Obviously, the production of new 'freedom' of E_S is possible if and only if we have co-evolution, that is, if we consider the co-evolutionary pair (S - E_S). Therefore, an environment that does not co-evolve is an environment that does not allow any evolution (or only a finite evolution).
120. The double clarification is needed here, since a number of freedoms may be limited, but freedoms as such may be variable. Variability within the same number of freedoms can increase the scope of eligibility for a positive selection. If, to this plasticity of freedoms is added the variability of the number of freedoms, then we obtain a complete picture of the evolutionary availability of the concept of methodological co-evolutionism.
121. Therefore, the conservative criterion does not refer to the actual aspect (or only to the actual aspect) but mainly (or also concerns) the potential aspect, that is, it does not refer only to replication, but also to replicability.
122. We repeat the crucial difference, which we make in this research, between the usual definition of fitness (including financial one, *mutatis mutandis*), as a degree of adequacy to the environment or to the interaction with the environment, and the definition we make: degree of adaptive replicability. Of course, the biggest and most relevant consequences of this distinction will be highlighted through the formalizations associated with the logical model of APMH.

123. For the moment, we do not discuss the problem of the two objections to the criterion of falsifiability proposed by Popper (but which we can resume later), namely, (a) Duhem-Quine thesis and (b) Lakatos thesis.
124. We still hold within the bivalent epistemic logic (proposed by Aristotle), in which the principle of the excluded third $\left(A \vee \bar{A}\right)$ is valid.
125. In this reasoning we will also ignore the evidential utility component of integral utility.
126. Of course, another problem may arise here: perhaps the discussion should be deepened to the concept of the structure of preference regarding the utility. Thus, an individual might have a greater preference for substantive utility, compared to a preference for symbolic utility, within the same level of integral utility. Even in this case, we consider that such a possible preference regarding the structure of integral utility will be manifested directly in establishing the substitutability thresholds between substantive utility and symbolic utility, so there is no need for separate theoretical or methodological considerations. However, finer analyses of preference and, in particular, adaptive preference, could make interesting contributions to the behaviour of economic actors in the APMH model.
127. From an instrumental point of view, we could conceive the preference generated by propensity (i.e., as we called it in this research, proference) as a vector with two components: one on trading strategy (or a distribution of trading strategies), and another on the structure of integral utility. In this case, the proference could be analysed as a vector of position (or positional vector).
128. The critical mass of anomalies can be viewed from at least four significant perspectives: (a) the number of accumulated anomalies; (b) the gap of the anomalies compared to the 'normal' expectation; (c) frequency of occurrence/reporting of anomalies and (d) the sensitivity of the economic agents to anomalies. The most important perspective is, of course, that of the sensitivity of economic agents: their perception of anomalies can operate relatively independently of the integral utility of financial market operations, so a decision on the choice of trading strategy and its content from the point of view of individual inferable transactions can be, to some extent, in a position contrary to the decision based directly on return.
129. We present these characteristics given that it is a new concept, proposed in this study—by positioning in relation to both methodological individualism, which is specific to neoclassical economic theory (i.e., microeconomic approaches), and methodological holism, which is specific to macroeconomic approaches, but both with a static 'posture'.
130. Of course, with the necessary precautions regarding the transition from microeconomic to macroeconomic, in order to avoid (or sufficiently reduce) the paradox/fallacy of composition.

131. This acceptability is judged (and judgeable), of course, from the perspective of the integral utility that the economic agent involved obtains from the operationalization of a trading strategy (through the set of individual transactions consistent with that trading strategy).
132. From an instrumental point of view, here appears the possibility of topological modelling and analysis, because the concept of neighbourhood intervenes—we can talk about a homeorhetic neighbourhood.
133. We have also mentioned before that the use of the phrase 'efficient cause' is inappropriate, because in the action of that cause no optimization occurs (*Nota bene*: efficiency means either maximizing the effect at a given effort or minimizing the effort at a given effect—i.e., involves optimization). The appropriate name is 'effective cause' or 'efficacy cause', which we use as well.
134. Of course, from a logical point of view, the two statements can be opposite without being contradictory, but we accept that refutation refers to both opposition and contradiction.
135. Here arises a debatable problem: in the theory of factual falsifiability, as conceived by Popper, corroboration is not only considered to be a non-decisive result (*Nota bene*: it can be defined, in fact, as a … yet non-refutation) but, in addition, it is considered as not modifying the credibility (or probability of being true of) the corroborated conjecture. In our opinion, at least in the social field (i.e., in relation to individuals and symbolic/logical species), the corroboration is likely, from a psychological point of view, to increase the propensity regarding the conjecture in question and, if the probability is inferred from conjecture, to increase the likelihood, for the economic operator concerned, of retaining that conjecture or to increase the economic agent's affinity for that conjecture. The inferencing of probability from conjecture consists, as we have shown elsewhere, especially in determining the *a priori* Bayes' probability.
136. Of course, this is a logical (and even psychological) summation, not an algebraic one. Behaviourism correctly observes, for example, that the individual operates rather with a mental accounting (see, in this matter, the work of Richard Thaler, *Misbehaving: The Making of Behavioral Economics* (Thaler, 2016)).
137. The authors have, of course, to show, in accordance with Kuhn's theory of the concept of paradigm, the way (mechanism) by which the AMPH paradigm is constituted and positioned, in an incommensurable way, compared to previous paradigms of the financial market. *Nota bene*: as we mentioned before, FMAB-APH shows that, while EMH is a financial market paradigm, AMH is not such a paradigm. However, here are still to be analysed, from the perspective of their paradigmaticity, the models: FMH, CMH, BMH and APH.

138. According to the fundamental principle, propensity is the next most rigid component of the APMH model of the financial market.
139. The introduction of the *a priori* internal selection of the trading strategy is a necessary result of the proposal of the APMH model of the financial market in this research and represents, as we will see, a crucial element of the mechanism of functioning of that model (*Nota bene*: the mechanism integrates the functionality as well as the behaviour of a system), especially in the form of what is called self-organization (or autopoieticity) of a system.
140. We also referred to this aspect in detail in FMAB-APH, but, where it will be necessary, we will provide additional details in this regard.
141. We remind you that the two thresholds that condition the production of the mutation work here—one referring exclusively to the individual transaction, the other referring to the trading strategy.
142. We recall that this component of the environment of APMH model exerts a double selection which is called, in the literature, intra-specific selection, as opposed to the selection exercised by cultural geodesic, which is of the type of extra-specific selection (consistent with the idea that the relationship between the system and the environment is, in general, a relationship between co-species—the environment being, logically, one of the co-species).
143. Of course, from an algebraic point of view, the conditions regarding the fields of definition, respectively the ranges of values involved in this composition, must be ensured.
144. The two selection modules will be combined in the APMH model mechanism, see below.

References

Bonneuil, N., & Boucekkine, R. (2009). *Sustainability, Optimality, and Viability in the Ramsey Model*. Department of Economics, University of Glasgow, Working Papers.

Dinga, E. (2012). *Rebuilding Economics. Logical, Methodological and Epistemological Approach*. Lambert Academic Publishing.

Dinga, E. (2017). The Homo Socionomicus Model of Rationality. A Logical Analysis. *Economic Growth under Globalization: Models of Sustainable Development, 1*(12), 21–25.

Dinga, E., Oprean-Stan, C., Tănăsescu, C. R., Brătian, V., & Ionescu, G. M. (2022). *Financial Market Analysis and Behaviour: The Adaptive Preference Hypothesis*. Routledge & CRC Press.

Elster, J. (2017). *Sour Grapes: Studies in the Subversion of Rationality*. Cambridge University Press.

Fama, E. F. (1970). Efficient Capital Markets: A Review of Theory and Empirical Work. *The Journal of Finance, 25*(2), 383–417.

Farzin, Y. H. (2010). Sustainability, Optimality, and Development Policy. *Review of Development Economics, 14*(2), 262–281.

Foucault, M., Davidson, A. I., Ewald, F., & Fontana, A. (2005). *The Hermeneutics of the Subject: Lectures at the Collège de France 1981–1982.* Picador.

Haack, S. (2009). *Evidence and Inquiry: A Pragmatist Reconstruction of Epistemology.* Prometheus.

Heal, G. (2003). *Optimality or Sustainability.* American Economic Association Meetings, July 27–30, Montreal, Canada.

Hodgson, G. M. (2004). *The Evolution of Institutional Economics.* Routledge.

Kuhn, T. (1970). *The Structure of Scientific Revolutions.* Chicago, IL: University of Chicago Press.

Kuhn, T. S. (2012). *By Thomas S. Kuhn – The Structure of Scientific Revolutions.* University of Chicago Press.

Lakatos, I. (1978). *The Methodology of Scientific Research Programmes.* Cambridge Core.

Lo, A. (2019). *Adaptive Markets. Financial Evolution at the Speed of Thought.* Princeton University Press.

Nelson, R. R., & Winter, S. G. (1985). *An Evolutionary Theory of Economic Change.* Harvard University Press.

Nozick, R. (1994). *The Nature of Rationality.* Princeton University Press.

Nussbaum, M. C. (2006). *Frontiers of Justice. Disability, Nationality, Species Membership.* The Belknap Press of Harvard University Press.

Popper, K. (2005). *The Logic of Scientific Discovery.* Routledge.

Ramsey, F. P. (2013). *The Foundations of Mathematics and Other Logical Essays* (R. B. Braithwaite, Ed.). Martino Fine Books.

Sen, A. (2000). *Development as Freedom.* Alfred A. Knopf, Inc.

Thaler, R. H. (2016). *Misbehaving: The Making of Behavioral Economics.* W.W. Norton & Compan.

von Neumann, J., & Morgenstern, O. (2007). *Theory of Games and Economic Behavior (60th Anniversary Commemorative Edition).* Princeton Classic Editions.

CHAPTER 5

Autopoietic Market Hypothesis—The Mechanism

Autopoietic Mechanism

The autopoietic evolutionary mechanism represents the logical combination of the functionality and behaviour of a given system. As a result, it is necessary to make specific clarifications in relation to the components of the APMH model, as they were identified (at abstract, class level) above.

Genotype

We considered the genotype of the financial individual (i.e., the trading strategy) to be the *propensity*. There is a possible conceptual vulnerability here, because propensity is a property of the human (biological) individual, more precisely, of the human individual operating in the financial market, that is, the economic agent, while the phenotype is represented by a symbolic/logical individual, belonging to a symbolic/logical species, called financial market. It is useful, therefore, to make some clarifications in this matter:

- as being a symbolic species (financial market), the individuals of this species do not have ontological autonomy, although they can have a (wide) functional autonomy;[1] the non-existence of ontological autonomy refers exactly to the fact that the genome of the symbolic species is outside the symbolic phenotype, unlike the case of the

E. Dinga et al., *Economic and Financial Market Behaviour*, https://doi.org/10.1007/978-3-031-31702-6_5

biological species, in which the genome is located in the very structure of the biological individual in question;

- the lack of ontological autonomy of the symbolic individual is a necessary property, not contingent, namely, it is not an imperfection that could be remedied under certain conditions, that is, it does not have a contextual/historical character, but represents an invariant as such;[2]
- the symbolic individual (and, correlatively, the symbolic species), as artefacts, represent exo-somatic instruments of the human individual;[3]
- the functional autonomy of the financial individual (trading strategy) is obviously relative to propensity (i.e., to genotype) as in the case of any individual (biological or symbolic);
- it should be noted that the financial genotype is essentially of the type of theoretical rationality (i.e., that rationality that is claimed from a belief as a fundamental axiom);
- an important conclusion of this discussion is the following: the biological individual (economic agent) is a causal condition (both formal and effective) for the generation and functioning of the financial phenotype, precisely because the seat of the financial genotype (the propensity) is inalienable in relation with the human individual.[4]

Let us now make some clarifications regarding the particularization of genotype (propensity) in the case of the APMH model of the financial market:

- although the financial genotype has a certain plasticity (otherwise mutations would not be possible), this plasticity must be kept within the 'breaking limits', that is, in the margin of replicability.[5] However, this characterization of the plasticity and replicability[6] of a genotype is common to any type of genotype (including biological genotype[7]). So, what is the particularity that the APMH model of the financial market gives to the financial genotype? We consider that this particularity consists in the following:
  - regarding the repli.cator of the financial genotype, we consider that it must be understood as a *basic belief*[8] of the human individual as an economic agent, that is, a basic belief that is the equivalent of the axiom in the field of knowledge, therefore we can also call it a praxiological axiom;[9]

- in line with Lakatos' suggestions, the financial genotype (propensity) therefore consists of the core belief (as a hard core) and a '*protective belt*' of derived beliefs. The pressure of selection[10] (either internal or external) is firstly exerted on the protective 'belt', among which it can generate changes that do not affect the basic belief or, in any case, affect it only after the changes induced in this 'belt' exceed a certain limit (threshold) that requires reconsideration of the core belief itself;
- in order to make a connection with the trading strategy, on the one hand, and with the individual transaction, on the other hand, we could say, here, that the basic belief is the one that generates the trading strategy and the secondary beliefs, located in the 'protective belt', are those that generate (or rather, customize) the individual transaction inferred from the trading strategy in question;
- therefore, the elasticity of the basic belief is maintained as long as the plasticity of the 'protective belt' is not yet exceeded;

• the financial genotype, that is, of belief type, based on psychism, is much more stable (more precisely, more inertial) than the natural genotype, which is based on biological support. The explanation for this crucial difference lies in the following:
  - modification of the biological genotype (through genetic mutation) changes the structure of the future phenotype (obtained by intergenerational replication), which makes it impossible (or almost impossible) to return to the previous structure—in other words, there is an arrow of biological time, to say so, caused by finality (not purpose!);
  - changing of the financial genotype (also through genetic mutation, of course) does not change the structure of the biological individual (who is the 'depository' of the financial genotype, i.e., propensity), but only changes the configuration of the trading strategy; this change is the result of a free decision, based on the free will of the human individual, even if the pressure for change comes through a cost–benefit calculation. Exactly the decisional determinism coming from the free will (which considers the purpose, not the simple finality, the last being proper to the biological case) ensures, so to speak, the reversibility of the decision regarding the modification of the financial genotype;

- (apparently) paradoxically, based on the above arguments, it appears that the inertia of the financial genotype is accompanied, as an alternative (perhaps even as a companion), by the saltationist variability of the financial genotype.[11] This can also be expressed as follows: the financial genotype can change (usually consciously/programmatically, but we do not exclude an unconscious way of this change or, most often, a mix between the two modes) by the simple choice of the human individual, without this decision having its causal origin outside the respective human individual: thus, the simple idiosyncrasy or a somewhat mechanical memetic alignment to the behaviour of other economic agents can lead to such a change.

Phenotype

The financial phenotype (individual) is, of course, the trading strategy, which is located, unlike the financial genotype, outside the human individual, as being a symbolic/logical individual.[12] The features of the financial phenotype, previously evoked in various places of this research and according to the internal logic of this research, apart from the external one in relation to the human (biological) individual, also has the following characteristics, especially from the perspective of the APMH model of the financial market, of course:

- it is subject to adaptive replicability, as required by the value (V) of the APMH paradigm. This means that the identity mark of the trading strategy is not necessarily punctual, but allows a certain range within which the trading strategy is still assessed as preserved by adaptive replication, as being the *same* trading strategy;
  - like any other symbolic phenotype, the trading strategy is born directly as an adult, more precisely, its new version is obtained directly by operating the mutation (either genetic or epigenetic) on its old version. The consequence is that there is no (not necessarily) required time for the phenotype to develop until it reaches adulthood (as is the case, however, for the biological phenotype/individual);
  - as a result, the variation (adjustment, modification) of a trading strategy can be done at extremely irregular intervals over time—a trading strategy can be used without interruption, and while

maintaining its identity, for several years, as it can be modified by several times, at weekly intervals or, in some cases, even daily;[13]
- there is no deterioration of the functions of the financial phenotype (unlike the case with the biological phenotype) as the phenotype in question functions—more precisely, the financial phenotype verifies one of the logical conditions of any theoretical model (which, *note bene*, is also an artefact, as well as the trading strategy), namely, the preservation of performance in case of repeated use; therefore, the adjustment (including replacement) of the trading strategy is done exclusively for reasons related either to the economic agent's free will (and which are directly related to propensity) or to the cost–benefit calculation performed by the economic operator concerned; the lack of performance or the deterioration of the performance of a trading strategy are directly assessed in relation to the norm of the reaction of the environment to the action/reaction that the trading strategy (through individual transactions operated in the financial market) exerts on the environment (either financial geodesic or the rest of the financial individuals contemporary with the trading strategy concerned);

- the APMH model gives the financial phenotype a self-feeding from the validation perspective. As we have previously suggested, since it is not talking about an epistemic truth, but a praxiological 'truth', the corroboration of the trading strategy increases its credibility from the perspective of the economic agent and, therefore, the *affinity* of the latter for the trading strategy in question. The concept of affinity, which we want to use in the description of this phenomenology, needs some additional clarifications:
  - affinity has a double conditioning: a subjective one, originating in propensity, and an objective one, originating in the cost–benefit calculation performed by the human agent. The subjective component is, in terms of intensity, directly proportional to the initial level (the one in which the trading strategy concerned was chosen) of the propensity and to the duration in which that trading strategy has been continuously corroborated (i.e., yet non-refuted). The objective component is proportional to the intensity of the (net) return[14] provided by the trading strategy and also to the length of time that trading strategy has been continuously corroborated;

- if we denote by $\mathcal{C}$ the affinity,[15] with $\mathcal{C}_a$ an actual affinity, with $\tilde{\mathcal{C}}$ the normalized affinity at the interval $[0,1]$, with $\mathcal{P}$ the propensity, with $I_0^{\mathcal{P}(\mathcal{S})}$ the initial intensity of the propensity related to the trading strategy $\mathcal{S}$, with d the duration of time that the trading strategy $\mathcal{S}$ is corroborated (yet non-refuted)[16] by the environment, without interruptions, with $\mathcal{R}^{\mathcal{S}}$ the (net) return of the trading strategy $\mathcal{S}$, with α the affinity proportionality factor with the subjective component, with β the affinity proportionality factor with the objective component (we assume, for simplification, that α, β are non-negative real numbers verifying the condition $\alpha + \beta = 1$), then we have:

$$\tilde{\mathcal{C}} = \frac{\mathcal{C}_a - \mathcal{C}_{\min}}{\mathcal{C}_{\max} - \mathcal{C}_{\min}}$$

where

$$\mathcal{C}_a^{\mathcal{S}} = d_a^{\mathcal{S}} \cdot \left(\alpha \cdot I_0^{\mathcal{P}(\mathcal{S})} + \beta \cdot \mathcal{R}^{\mathcal{S}}\right)$$

$$\mathcal{C}_{\max}^{\mathcal{S}} = d_{\max}^{\mathcal{S}} \cdot \alpha \cdot I_0^{\mathcal{P}(\mathcal{S})} \quad (\text{for } \beta = 0)$$

$$\mathcal{C}_{\min}^{\mathcal{S}} = d_{\min}^{\mathcal{S}} \cdot \beta \cdot \mathcal{R}^{\mathcal{S}} \quad (\text{for } \alpha = 0)$$

$$\mathcal{C}_{\max}^{\mathcal{S}} - \mathcal{C}_{\min}^{\mathcal{S}} = d_{\max}^{\mathcal{S}} \cdot \alpha \cdot I_0^{\mathcal{P}(\mathcal{S})} - d_{\min}^{\mathcal{S}} \cdot \beta \cdot \mathcal{R}^{\mathcal{S}}$$

$$\begin{aligned} \mathcal{C}_a^{\mathcal{S}} - \mathcal{C}_{\min}^{\mathcal{S}} &= d_a^{\mathcal{S}} \cdot \alpha \cdot I_0^{\mathcal{P}(\mathcal{S})} + d_a^{\mathcal{S}} \cdot \beta \cdot \mathcal{R}^{\mathcal{S}} - d_{\min}^{\mathcal{S}} \cdot \beta \cdot \mathcal{R}^{\mathcal{S}} \\ &= d_a^{\mathcal{S}} \cdot \alpha \cdot I_0^{\mathcal{P}(\mathcal{S})} + \beta \cdot \mathcal{R}^{\mathcal{S}} \cdot \left(d_a^{\mathcal{S}} - d_{\min}^{\mathcal{S}}\right) \end{aligned}$$

so:

$$\tilde{\mathcal{C}}^{\mathcal{S}} = \frac{d_a^{\mathcal{S}} \cdot \alpha \cdot I_0^{\mathcal{P}(\mathcal{S})} + \beta \cdot \mathcal{R}^{\mathcal{S}} \cdot \left(d_a^{\mathcal{S}} - d_{\min}^{\mathcal{S}}\right)}{d_{\max}^{\mathcal{S}} \cdot \alpha \cdot I_0^{\mathcal{P}(\mathcal{S})} - d_{\min}^{\mathcal{S}} \cdot \beta \cdot \mathcal{R}^{\mathcal{S}}}$$

Therefore, we can state the following in connection with the concept of affinity of the economic agent with a given trading strategy:

- given that the frequency of a trading strategy differs greatly depending on the object of the transaction (this frequency can be from the order of seconds to the order of years), we will measure the duration of such a trading strategy by the number of corroborations, without interruptions, which it record;[17]
- the increase of the corroboration duration of a trading strategy directly affects the factor α and inversely proportional the factor β. The justification for this assertion is as follows:
  - the seat of affinity is the psychic world of the economic agent. To some extent, the psychism of the human individual is 'blind' to reality,[18] assuming a certain autonomy from it;
  - much more evidence is needed to defeat a belief than to defeat an objective reality;[19]

Nota bene: we will admit, however, that the maintenance of the sum $\alpha + \beta = 1$ is not done linearly (e.g., by a line with a negative slope), but by a decreasing convex curve;[20]

- then, we can write: $\alpha = f(d)$, with the proposition that f has as equation a logistic one: $f(d) = \frac{A}{1+e^{-d}}$. *Nota bene*: symmetrically with respect to the abscissa axis, we have $\beta = g(d)$, so that $g(d) = 1 - f(d)$, that is, $g(d) = \frac{1-A+e^{-d}}{1+e^{-d}}$. Figure 5.1 provides a graphical picture of these non-empirical assumptions (with $\overline{d}$ a value of the duration of the trading strategy corroboration was noted—i.e., the uninterrupted number of corroborations[21]—where the two factors of affinity proportionality with this duration are equal, $\alpha = \beta = 0.5$, meaning, from a psychological point of view, a maximum of 'comfort' for the economic agent: the belief is confirmed by objective reality and vice versa);[22]
- we are interested, of course, in determining the values of the parameters A, $d^S_{\min}$, respectively $d^S_{\max}$. For this purpose, the equation of the curve $\alpha = f(x)$ could be examined qualitatively, where x was denoted the duration of the corroboration of a given trading strategy.[23] An analytical algebraic development in this problem is, of course, useful (this aspect will be examined, however, elsewhere, because it does not fall within the direct target of this study).

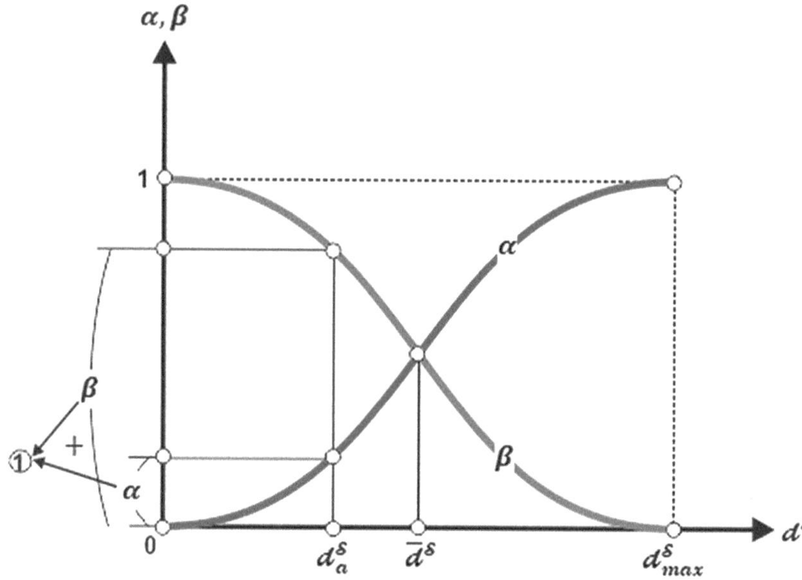

Fig. 5.1 Dynamics of affinity proportionality factors with the duration of phenotype uninterrupted corroboration. (*Source*: Authors)

Mutation

In the APMH model, too, the mutation is of two types: genetic mutation, respectively epigenetic mutation.

Genetic Mutation

Genetic mutation occurs at the level of propensity, which is the genotype in this model. Considering what has already been said in this matter, here we will make only a synthesis of the problem, particularizing it, however, to the structural, functional, behavioural and evolutionary characteristics of the APMH model.

- From the perspective of genetic mutation, the core of the model (in the sense of Lakatos) is represented by the trading strategy (or set of trading strategies) operated by the economic agent, while the protection belt is represented by individual transactions inferred from and associated with each such trading strategy;

- environmental pressure (either as cultural geodesic or as other contemporary trading strategies operated in the financial market) is exerted directly on the individual transaction, which is the contextual (spatial–temporal particular) hypostasis of the trading strategy (i.e., the phenotype);
- the protection belt ensures a dead zone (and by force of circumstances) a dead duration from the perspective of the core: as long as the amount[24] of changing pressure from the environment remains inside the dead zone, the genetic mutation is prevented (*Nota bene*: variation of individual transaction does not represent a genetic mutation, because the phenotype—the trading strategy maintains its identity although there are small variations in its manifestation);
- when the dead zone is overcome, obviously, the selection pressure shifts to the trading strategy and, thus, to the propensity. In other words, at this point, the genetic mutation occurs. We would like to highlight, at this point in the discussion, an extremely important aspect, which is a fundamental difference in relation to the phenomenology of genetic mutation in biological species. We will describe this aspect in the following:
  - in the case of the biological species, the genetic mutation occurs randomly, at the level of DNA (biological genotype);
  - the genetic mutation, through the transmission of altered DNA in the sexual reproduction of the biological individual, is transmitted to the next generation;
  - in the case of the symbolic species, the genetic mutation does not appear directly to the genotype[25] but, paradoxically, it appears to the phenotype, following that from the phenotype it is transferred to the genotype (i.e., to change the propensity);
  - this phenomenology is possible because the trading strategy is a logical inference from propensity (in part, metaphorically, it can be said that propensity is the model of rationality, from which, by valid inference, the trading strategy is projected as a theorem);
  - being a logical inference from propensity, the trading strategy can only be adjusted if the propensity is adjusted (*Nota bene*: here we are dealing with similar processes in the biological case and in the symbolic case) but the propensity is adjusted only if the trading strategy is adjusted—and the adjustment of the trading strategy is done … without this adjustment being 'ordered' by the prior adjustment of the propensity;

- it is obvious that this process (reversed from the biological case) is one of the main reasons, along with free will (i.e., deliberation, which is specific to artefacts) for which, in the case of symbolic species, Lamarckism works rather than Darwinism (or, in any case, there is a relevant dominance of Lamarckism over Darwinism).[26]

This causal difference is, of course, consistent with everything we have seen throughout the research (including FMAB-APH), regarding the essential difference between the biological species and the symbolic/logical species and with all the signals that we made them, at various points in the discussion, to avoid a *tale quale* import, comfortable or even, sometimes, spectacular, from biology to economics. Given the particular theoretical and methodological significance of this difference in terms of genetic mutation between biological and symbolical, we describe the difference in question, synoptically, in Fig. 5.2 (by the notation '(p)' we wanted to express the fact that it is about a predominance, not about an exclusivity, of a certain phenotype selection mechanism).

Nota bene 1: the impact of free will on the trading strategy is also done through propensity (see Fig. 5.2) but without this impact being caused either by the action/reaction of the environment on the trading strategy or by pre-existing procedures at the level of the economic agent.

Nota bene 2: random factors affecting propensity in Fig. 5.2 are partly generated memetically and partly constitute prediction errors that the economic agent makes regarding the functioning of the financial market—the fact that these prediction errors are considered random factors, and not deliberative factors (although the prediction is a deliberative event), is explained by the fact that we are talking about competent economic agents, which, when they behave sub-rationally (or even irrationally), exactly become the unsophisticated economic agents from Fama's theory, that is, the creators of noise in the financial market.

Epigenetic Mutation

In the case of epigenetic mutation, the phenotype (trading strategy) changes without the propensity undergoing any change. This is possible only through what we propose to call a *memetic* mutation. The memetic mutation is a contagion-type mutation and has a value, from the perspective of the economic agent, purely functional. For example, the economic operator observes the operationalization, in the financial market, of some trading strategies[27] and, on an intuitive basis or, sometimes, out of an

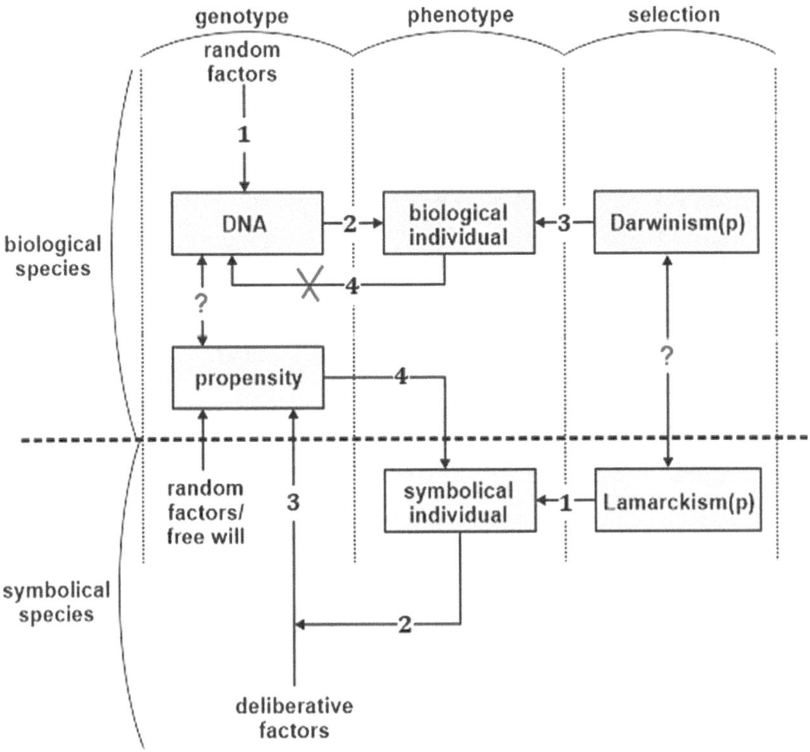

Fig. 5.2 The logical difference of the mutation between the biological and the symbolic species. (*Source*: Authors)

analytical laziness (or incapacity), imitates those strategies—more precisely, s/he imitates the observed individual transactions.[28] Either as a result of the success of individual transactions imitated, or as a result of a large 'quantity' of such imitations, eventually its own trading strategy may change or, in extreme (rare) cases, be completely replaced. Therefore, we have a variation of the phenotype, without this being a logical/generative/causal effect of the variation of the propensity,[29] which indicates exactly the content of the concept of epigenetic mutation. The way in which the epigenetic mutation is combined with the genetic mutation, at the level of changing the weights of the two factors of the economic agent's affinity in relation to a given trading strategy, can be shown as in

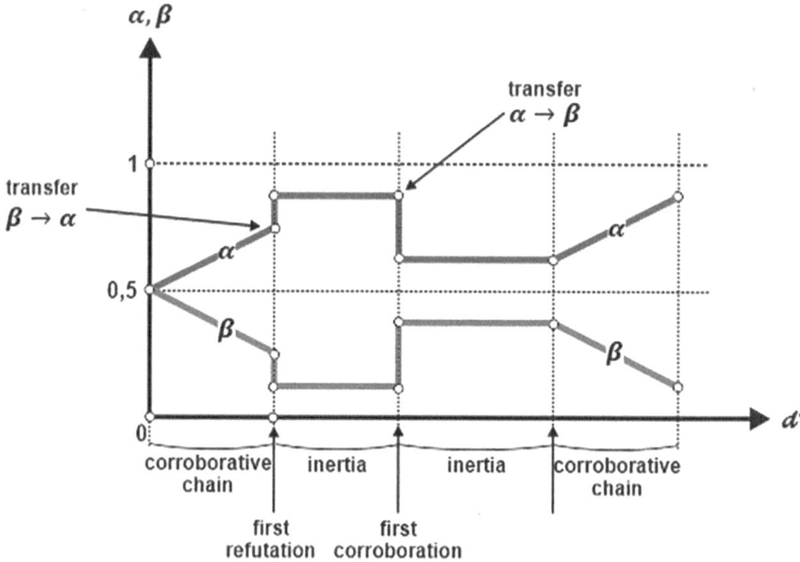

Fig. 5.3 The reciprocal relationship of the affinity proportionality factors with the duration of the phenotype corroboration. (*Source*: Authors)

Fig. 5.3 (*Nota bene*: to simplify the representation and increase the suggestiveness logistics in Fig. 5.1 with a linear function, which does not change the essence of the demonstration).

Therefore, the genetic and epigenetic mutation form, within the APMH model of the financial market, a *sui-generis* mix that ensures the autopoietic property of this model. Moreover, through the structure and kinematics of the affinity in relation to a given trading strategy, the self-organization that we will discuss below is ensured.

Fitness

As established previously, the APMH model has its own two classes of financial fitness: (i) class 6—financial fitness regardless of average; (ii) class 7—competitive financial fitness. To refresh the memory, we resume the description of the two classes of financial fitness:

- (class *F6*): financial fitness regardless of average—that financial fitness which, from the perspective of the *SPm*[30] criterion, is at the level of the market average:
  - (subclass $F6^+$): financial fitness regardless of average, *positively oriented*—that financial fitness regardless of average that tends to move to right compared to the financial market average;
  - (subclass $F6^-$): financial fitness regardless of average, *negatively oriented*—that financial fitness regardless of average that tends to move to left compared to the average financial market;
  - (subclass $F6^0$): financial fitness regardless of average, *non-oriented*—that financial fitness regardless of average that is stationary (inertial) in the position indifferent to the occupied average;
- (class *F7*): *competitive* financial fitness—that financial fitness that is placed with a performative depth above the market average and, of course, below the value associated with the market champion;
  - (subclass $F7^+$): competitive financial fitness, *positively oriented*—that competitive financial fitness that tends to move to right from the position occupied;
  - (subclass $F7^-$): competitive financial fitness, *negatively oriented*—that competitive financial fitness that tends to move to left from the position occupied;
  - (subclass $F7^0$): competitive financial fitness, *non-oriented*—that competitive financial fitness that is stationary (inertial) in the occupied competitive position;

We will first make some considerations that indicate the adequacy of these two categories of fitness[31] to the APMH model of the financial market:

- class *F6* of financial fitness has the highest compatibility with APMH, since this model has as paradigmatic value (V) the *adaptive replicability*. Replicability requires behaviour that does not exhaust the reserves on which this replicability itself is based (as opposed to what happens, e.g., in the case of optimizing models). In this sense, obviously, the financial fitness pursued will be, especially, of the type $F6^+$—which is the representative autopoietic variant of financial fitness in class *F6*;
- with regard to financial fitness class *F7*, its adequacy with the APMH model requires some specific clarifications:

- although it is above market level, this fitness is also not of the optimizing type (e.g., it is not maximizing in terms of return, respectively it is not minimizing in terms of the cost of the operation)—thus, it should be noted that it is below the 'possible' level, which is represented by the fitness of the financial market champion;[32]
- unlike the *F6* financial fitness class, the *F7* class operates with all three kinematically possible versions. The updating of one or the other of the three versions is done from the perspective of ensuring the autopoietic functioning of the related trading strategy, that is, still under the requirement of verifying the paradigmatic value called *adaptive replicability*.

Selection

The selection of the phenotype in the APMH model is a tripartite[33] one: (a) an *autonomous* selection, whose effective cause is exclusively the free will of the economic agent; (b) a *normative* selection (i.e., that made at the level of the species), whose effective cause is within the cultural geodesic of society; (c) a *performative* selection, the effective cause of which is the nomenclature of contemporary trading strategies with the considered phenotype.[34]

Autonomous Selection

Autonomous selection is one that depends directly on the free will of the economic agent, his/her personality, his/her idiosyncrasy, the level of instruction/education, in a word, the habitus[35] of the human individual behind the financial phenotype. The autonomous selection has, in our opinion, the following characteristics:

- autonomous selection is unpredictable, in the sense that there is no predictor that, through its variation (variation which, in turn, may or may not be predictable[36]) to provide indices/signals regarding the economic agent's intentions in relation to a given trading strategy; it can be said, therefore, that the affinity of the economic agent in relation to a given trading strategy is, in the case of autonomous selection, random;
- autonomous selection does not need any objective argument, it is the result of a completely subjective decision; in this context, the

question of the rationality of this selection arises, in connection with which we make the following considerations:

- the type of rationality involved is, obviously, the theoretical one;[37] as a result, any cost–benefit analysis is missing from the substantiation of the selection, regardless of whether this analysis refers to aspects of (economic) performance, survival, social prestige and so on;
- although it is a predominantly subjective decision, a memetic influence cannot be ruled out (as we will see below, when we examine the selector mix formed by the three types of selection in the APMH model), but this memetism is external to any calculation cost–benefit, as mentioned above;

- autonomous selection is, in terms of occurring frequency, of the '*rarest*' type, because the pressure of return associated with a trading strategy is high enough that other selection considerations, apart from return, are sent on two or three 'positions' of relevance;
- autonomous selection is the ***most persistent***[38] selection over time (the most sustainable) of all three types of selection, because, once operated, as being the effect of free will, there are almost no empirical falsifiers for it—autonomous selection can be changed only by another … autonomous selection;
- the most important feature of autonomous selection is, however, that it somehow establishes a selector that is not part of the environment and does not represent an internalization,[39] at the decision-making level, of the environment, as happens with the other two types of selection in the field of symbolic species;
- it should be added that the autonomous selection does not operate directly on the fitness of the trading strategy concerned. In our opinion, the autonomous selection does not refer, in fact, to the level (or quality) of the fitness of the trading strategy, but to a certain eligibility of it from a non-performing perspective. However, the fitness is directly related, from a conceptual point of view, to the performance of the trading strategy, of course, through its hypostasis in the form of individual transactions (similarly to the case of biological species);

Normative Selection

Normative selection is that type of selection that is found only in the case of symbolic species. In this sense, one of the components of the environment of the financial species called financial market is a decisive formal cause in the social selection of this species—as we proposed earlier, we call this component selectors as the ***cultural geodesic***. The main characteristics of this type of selection can be systematized as follows:

- normative selection has the highest degree of predictability among all three types of selection, primarily because the selector filters that cultural geodesic contains are known (exist) before the design and/ or implementation of any trading strategy;
- it can even be said that the normative selection is, in fact, a pre-selection, in the sense that the informed economic agent (therefore, informationally competent one) designs his/her trading strategy in such a way that it verifies the normative filters implied;[40] in other words, normative selection acts, in principle, *ex-ante*. The question here is whether a so-called *ex-ante* selection is, in fact, a very selection. Our opinion in this regard is as follows:
  - it is true that the selection is seen (primarily, as a result of its old pattern in the case of biological species) as a feedback that the environment of a species exerts on that species from the perspective of fitness. Specifically, if the individuals of the species exhibit insufficient fitness in relation to the environment,[41] then that individual will be rejected by the environment (namely, negative selection or adverse selection[42]);
  - note, however, that *ex-post* selection is not independent (or completely independent) of a so-called *ex-ante* selection (possible, we repeat, only in the case of symbolic/logical species[43]): indeed, many negative selections can be (and actually are) avoided by a design of the trading strategy that already takes into account the requirements of the normative filter generated by cultural geodesic;
  - somehow, based on the above, we can say that, in the case of symbolic species (such as the financial market) the design of the phenotype uses feed-forward to avoid many of the possible penalizing feedback exerted, *ex-post*, by cultural geodesic;
  - somehow, the following conclusion may follow, as well, from the above: the deliberative nature of the symbolic species has both an objective component (cultural geodesic, which anticipates the common goals of society regarding the functioning of the financial market) and a subjective component (the interest of the economic agent to reduce the likelihood of refuting its trading strategy for formal reasons);

- in conclusion, we consider that, despite (or perhaps by virtue of) its mixed character, *ex-ante* and *ex-post* normative selection retains its quality of being a genuine selection in the case of the symbolic species called the financial market;

Nota bene: normative selection is therefore applied by the artefact component of the financial market environment, because cultural geodesic is, obviously, an artefact (perhaps, the most representative for the mankind).

Performative Selection
Performative selection is that type of selection applied, also in an inter-conditional way, by the environment component constituted by the other contemporary trading strategies (from the point of view of operating in the financial market) with the trading strategy concerned. It must be said that the return of a trading strategy that verifies the subjective conditions (related to propensity, respectively free will[44]), on the one hand, and the objective conditions related to cultural geodesic, on the other hand, depends directly (functionally, one could say) of the economic game in which the whole set of contemporary trading strategies operated in the financial market is included. From a technical point of view, once the other two types of selections have corroborated the trading strategy, the final verdict of the selection process comes, which is given by the performative selection. It is, at the same time, obvious that performative selection is also dependent, in the positive selection of fitness, on the degree of eligibility of the trading strategy from the perspective of the other two types of selection—the probability of positive selection of fitness through performative selection is directly proportional with this degree of eligibility, not only with the nominal eligibility itself.

A positional image of the three types of selection in the APMH model is provided in Fig. 5.4, in the form of a Karnaugh-type diagram.

The mechanism of trading strategy selection is, of course, a mixed one, which always combines all three distinct types of selection. A synoptic picture of the selection process within APMH is shown in Fig. 5.5.

Short Discussion

- The pre-existent propensity of any manifestation of the economic agent in the financial market, so, step (1), means designing a trading strategy inferred from that propensity—we call this step as *basic choice*;

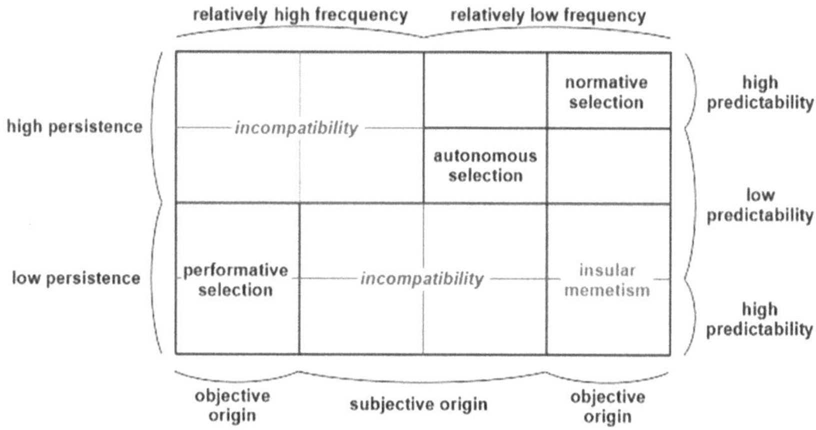

Fig. 5.4 Qualitative/logical positioning of the three types of selection in the APMH model. (*Source*: Authors)

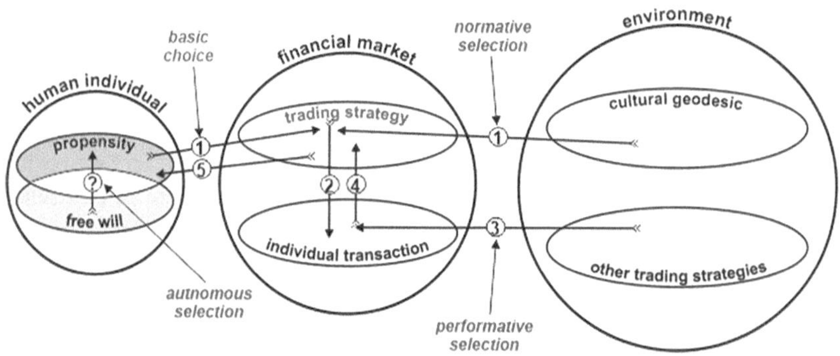

Fig. 5.5 The mechanism of selection in APMH model. (*Source*: Authors)

- the design of the trading strategy is done simultaneously from the perspective of cultural geodesic (one of the two components of the financial market environment), in an attempt to avoid the costs of violating the rules of conduct in the operation of financial transactions—so, the step (1) too; this step is what we have called above *normative selection* which acts, in particular, as a pre-selection or as an *ex-ante* selection;

- based on the trading strategy, individual transactions are designed by logical inference (step 2);
- individual transactions are operated in the financial market and are, thus, exposed to *performative selection*, which is, in a way, the 'true' selection of trading strategy (step 3);[45]
- once the selection pressure threshold is exceeded at the level of the individual transaction, the selection pressure moves to the hard core (trading strategy) (step 4);
- exceeding the selection pressure threshold exerted on the trading strategy leads to changes in propensity (step 5) and the process described above is resumed from the new propensity configuration;
- the *autonomous selection* (originated in the free will of the economic agent) acts at unpredictable moments of time and without a necessary causal link with the other phenomena described in chain (1)–(5).

Transcription and Translation

Dealing with the issue of transcription and translation of mutation (both genetic and epigenetic) after examining selection is, of course, unusual, since the 'standard' being that these issues be analysed immediately after studying the concept of mutation and before studying selection. Our justification is that, without taking into account the selection process, both as a typology and in terms of the implementation mechanism, neither the transcription nor the translation of the mutation can be properly addressed in the case of symbolic species called financial market.[46] Therefore, the selection process was first examined.

Transcription

Transcription Process

We recall that, in the case of biological species, the genetic mutation occurs at the DNA level and is then transcribed into messenger RNA (m-RNA). In the case of symbolic species, the mutation occurs at the level of propensity (which is the genotype of the financial individual called trading strategy). The content of the transcription of the genetic mutation occurred in propensity refers to the modification of the trading strategy according to this genetic mutation (e.g., if the financial market environment negatively selects individual short-term transactions originating in a trading strategy with long-term risk aversion, then after reaching the appropriate selection pressure threshold, the trading strategy will need to acquire a logic of deriving individual transactions that will generate—perhaps, entirely, as the case may be—individual transactions mainly for the long term).[47]

Transcription Errors

Transcription errors are, of course, as important in the case of symbolic species as in the case of biological species. There is, however, an important difference between the two 'species' of transcription: thus, while transcription errors in the biological case are generated by 'mechanical'[48] causes, in the symbolic case these errors are generated by cultural causes. We will develop a brief argument in support of asserting this distinction:

- although the change in propensity (i.e., the change in genotype) is a mixed phenomenon (it depends on both the unconscious[49] and the free will), however, the (re)designing of the trading strategy based on this change is a cultural phenomenon (it is an artefact);
- more precisely, the transcription of the variation of the propensity into the variation of the trading strategy requires an interpretation of the variation of the propensity. This interpretation has the role of extracting the denotations (and connotations[50]) of the variation of propensity, or, equivalently, of the variation of belief (which is, of course, partly rational, partly irrational), so that these meanings to be encapsulated in the updated trading strategy;
- therefore, between the variation of the propensity and the variation of the trading strategy, a hermeneutics is interposed. This hermeneutics is, in fact, the cultural device that transcribes the genetic mutation in the case of symbolic species. It is problematic enough to require a few brief comments:
- *first of all*, it should be established what is the relationship which this hermeneutics has, on the one hand, with the propensity and, on the other hand, with the trading strategy. In our opinion, the hermeneutics associated with transcription in the case discussed here must have a relative independence from the propensity itself, as well as from the trading strategy that is the subject of the transcription. We argue as follows:
  - a human individual has a nomenclature of activities, within society, much wider than those of the type of economic activity or, even more restricted, of the type of financial transactions;

- consequently, the total habitus of the human individual is much more populated with values, principles, goals, objectives, feelings, attitudes and evaluations, than the habitus associated with the action in the financial market;
- this means that, in fact, financial hermeneutics (so to speak) represents only a part of the general hermeneutics that forms, from a cultural point of view, the human individual;
- based on the above, the general hermeneutics is relatively independent of the propensity that generates the trading strategy;

- *secondly*, given this financial hermeneutics,[51] on the basis of which the genetic mutation is transcribed, we must ask ourselves: how do we know that a transcription error has been committed and, more precisely, what would it mean that a transcription error has been committed? We comments as follows:
  - in fact, it seems that there is no benchmark against which a transcription error can be judged, since any financial hermeneutics would have an economic agent, it is a … good hermeneutics. This conclusion is based both on the idiosyncrasy of the economic agent and on his/her freedom of decision (or, equivalently, of choice);
  - in this sense, we propose to build such a benchmark that works on principles analogous to the functioning of Popper's factual falsifiability: namely, that the sign (in the semiotic sense) of a transcription error is the very failure of the trading strategy just updated using financial hermeneutics;
  - therefore, if a trading strategy required, based on the variation of the propensity, a reconfiguration, and the reconfigured strategy was rejected by the financial market environment (especially through performative selection, as shown above), then we can infer from this an error transcription, based on the (reasonable) premise that the first rejection of the trading strategy was not, in turn, erroneous.[52]

Translation

Translation Process

If the transcription refers to the causal relationship from the variation of the propensity to the variation of the trading strategy, the translation, in the APMH model, refers to the causal relationship from the variation of the trading strategy to the variation of the individual transaction.[53] Given that the financial individual always manifests itself in the form of the individual transaction,[54] the economic operator will have to infer, from the updated trading strategy, the updated individual transaction.[55]

Translation Errors

Translation errors should be treated similarly to the ones in which the transcription errors were treated. However, this time there is no need for specialized hermeneutics, as was the case for the transcription, since the pattern of the individual transaction is logically inferred (based on a *sui generis* rationality model) directly from the trading strategy. We mention that a model of rationality, once adopted/assumed, the valid inferences made on its basis are necessary, not being able to be the object of choice and, therefore, even less of interpretation.

The general scheme of transcription and translation within the APMH model is shown in Fig. 5.6.

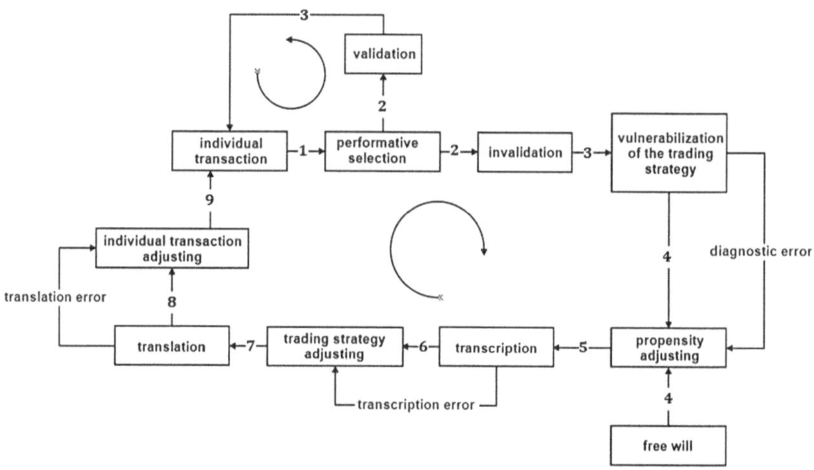

Fig. 5.6 The mechanism of transcription and translation of genetic mutation in the APMH model. (*Source*: Authors)

Evolution—General Framework

Evolution is a process that concerns the species—in our case, the financial market. Therefore, based on the above in relation to genotype, phenotype, mutation, fitness, selection, transcription and translation, we will propose, in this paragraph, a logical model of the financial market evolution,[56] from the perspective of APMH.

First of all, we specify the fact that, even within the symbolic species called financial market, the evolution refers to the *populational* aspect. This means that the evolution is identified by the existence, at the time of assessment, of a dominance of the number of adult individuals (trading strategies) in the total population of individuals of the species in question. Here we need two clarifications:

- the adjustment suffered by an individual, as a result of the total mutation,[57] must be discernible from an environmental perspective, which means that this adjustment must exceed a certain significance threshold in terms of fitness. For example, at the level of the set of individual transactions related to a trading strategy, certain behavioural functions may occur that increase the fitness of the trading strategy in question at a purely functional level, not at a structural one. And even if there is a certain structural variation of the trading strategy, this variation must be above that threshold of significance (or discernibility);
- the variation of the share of individuals (trading strategies) that have undergone positive variations[58] of fitness must also have a dimension that exceeds its own threshold of significance. Such a threshold is perhaps an empirical issue rather than a theoretical one, but it must be considered in order to 'decree' the occurring of an evolution in that species.

Secondly, we remind that, in the field of symbolic/logical species, there is a co-existence of Darwinism and Lamarckism in the process of evolution, and even there is a predominance of Lamarckism in relation to Darwinism.[59] From a conceptual (very general) point of view, between Darwinism and Lamarckism there are two major differences: (a) in Darwinism, the structure/organ generates the function, while in Lamarckism, the function generates the structure/organ; (b) in Darwinism, mutations (either genetic or epigenetic) are transmitted exclusively inter-generationally, while in Lamarckism, mutations can be transmitted both inter-generationally and intra-generationally.[60]

Thirdly, the evolution of symbolic species is characterized by more than the simple directionality indicated by the adequacy of fitness (as it happens in biological evolution), this time appearing a teleological aspect: the goal. In fact, we will have to accept (as we mentioned earlier, during the research) that there is a mix between the impersonal character of an end directed by the adequacy of fitness at the level of effectiveness and the teleological character of a fitness directed at the level of deliberativeness.[61]

Fourthly, and much more obvious than in the case of biological species, in the case of symbolic species (as in the case of the financial market), the evolution is reversible.[62] In addition to biological species, evolutionary reversibility occurs not only in the co-evolutionary context with the environment, but also autonomously, generated by the free will of the economic agent—for example, for reasons that exceed its action to operate in the financial market, an economic operator may suddenly give up an entire trading strategy (or may return to a trading strategy s/he had previously given up), which changes the populational structure of the financial market.

Fifthly, the evolution of symbolic species is, with very rare exceptions, of the saltationist type. The saltationist nature of evolution should not be confused with the existence of points (thresholds) for the accumulation of change tensions. The difference in this matter is fundamental: the existence of accumulation thresholds is generated by the need for the existence of significance thresholds (such significance thresholds do not exist in biological evolution—*Nota bene*: however, they somehow exist, but only from the researcher's perspective, not from that of the phenotypes actually involved), while, in the case of symbolic/logical species, no decision is taken until after reaching a certain significance threshold. Therefore, until the significance threshold is reached, nothing is selected (so nothing is selected gradually), and when this threshold is reached, the selection is sudden and total.

Sixthly, in the case of symbolic/logical species, the epigenetic mutation is much more present than the genetic mutation—it can even be said that the epigenetic mutation is predominant in the whole mutational phenomenon. The explanation consists, of course, both in the dominance of Lamarckism in relation to Darwinism and in the dominance of deliberation in relation to emergence, in the evolutionary process of symbolic species.

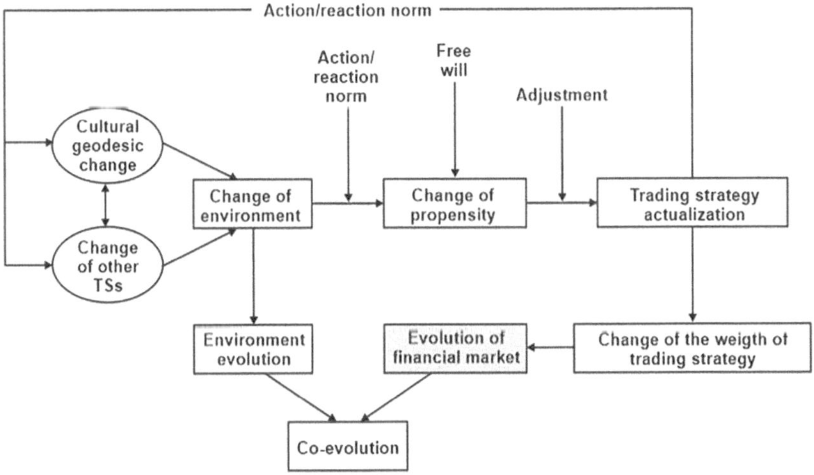

Fig. 5.7 General scheme of the financial market evolution within APMH model. (*Source*: Authors)

Seventhly, mutations (either genetic or epigenetic) are transmitted not only vertically (e.g., by creating the chreode of the trading strategy concerned), but also horizontally, that is, to other individuals (contemporary trading strategies) or obliquely, that is, inter-species,[63] but it cannot be denied that such a feature is not properly a feature, as it seems to be found also in biological evolution.

The general scheme of the financial market evolution within the APMH model is presented in Fig. 5.7 (with TS was noted the trading strategy).

Evolution—Autopoietic Individuation and Speciation

Evolution is, from a dynamic point of view, a bilateral process: the individual creates the species, and the species, in turn, generates the individual. Of course, this bilateral process takes place in inter-action (more precisely, as we have shown, in co-evolution) with the environment.

The creation of the species through individuals is called *speciation*, while the generation of the individual through the species is called *individuation*. In the case of the symbolic species, both processes are relevant.[64]

Autopoietic Individuation

The individuation will be examined by its customization to the APMH model of the financial market. In this context, we make the following considerations:

- individuation is a singular and complete event, based on the fact that the financial phenotype—the trading strategy—appears fully developed, that is, it appears directly in the adult stage, able to function (including to reproduce) as soon as it is 'born';
- as shown above (namely, in the section on transcription and translation of mutation), the variation of the financial phenotype occurs through the transcription of the variation of propensity (i.e., financial genotype) in the structure and logic of the trading strategy;
- therefore, financial individuation is a purely deliberative phenomenon, including in its epigenetic aspect (as, e.g., the case of memetism associated with other contemporary trading strategies on the market);
- the very mechanism of individuation has the following basic components:
  - *proximity analyser* of the variation of the propensity under the impact of the environment (more precisely, of the selective pressure of the environment). The proximity analyser signals to the economic agent that the preservation threshold of the targeted trading strategy is about to be reached. Here there is obviously a suggestion of gradualism, but it is a gradualism of perception (which involves evaluation), so a predominantly subjective aspect; it is not necessary to change our position by which we claimed that selection, in the case of symbolic species, is saltationist. The signal of the proximity analyser triggers, it is true, in a cumulative manner, the preoccupation (attention) of the economic agent for the redesign of the trading strategy. Full awareness of the need to redesign the trading strategy results in a change into propensity, that is, genetic mutation occurs;[65]
  - *inference device* of the trading strategy (or its redesign, as the case may be). It is about the procedure—fully aware and rational[66]—of extracting the structure, logic and operational configuration of the trading strategy as a result of the variation of the propensity. Of course, the fact that such an inference is (or must be) considered fully aware seems more acceptable than stating that it must also be fully rational. Although idiosyncrasy should not be com-

pletely eliminated here, nevertheless, in our opinion, the complete rationality of inferring the variation of the trading strategy from the variation of the propensity cannot be eliminated;

- the autopoietic component or ingredient of the individuation consists of the following:
  - the economic operator already has an affinity for the trading strategy 'in functioning', based on both the α factor and the β factor (see the discussion on affinity);
  - the corroboration of the trading strategy increases the weight of the α factor of the affinity and decreases, correlatively and implicitly, the weight of the β factor;[67] the refutation of the trading strategy increases, again, the weight of the factor α;
  - therefore, the α-factor kinematics of the economic agent's affinity to the trading strategy ensures, to a very large extent, the stabilization of that trading strategy (of course, the mechanism is not infallible, since exceeding the environmental pressure threshold will lead to a non-identitary adjustment of that strategy or, in extreme cases, to its replacement);[68]
  - most of the time (e.g., for menu cost[69] reasons or simply due to the α factor[70]), the economic operator ignores (until the last moment) the decision to adjust (including replace) the trading strategy targeted by the selective pressure;
  - from the last remark it seems that two categories of individuation can result in the APMH model: (a) an individuation of the *reluctance* type—generated by *alpha-affinity* or *alpha-attachment*—which is an individuation by preserving or postponing the change;[71] (b) an *appetite*-type individuation—generated by (as we might say) *beta-affinity* or *beta-attachment*—which is an individuation by innovation, by taking into account the cost–benefit calculation indicated by the selective pressure of the environment.

Autopoietic Speciation

Autopoietic speciation is a speciation that is characterized by the pursuit of autopoieticity, that is, self-organization in order to what is the paradigmatic value (V) of the APMH model—*adaptive replicability*.

We will examine, from the perspective of APMH, the two categories of speciation (i.e., creation/generation of the financial market—the symbolic species of the mentioned model), which are common, moreover, to biological speciation: (a) *sympatric* speciation and (b) *allopatric* speciation. In addition, we will examine a category of speciation that is specific to symbolic species and which we can call (c) an ***induced*** speciation. As we will show, induced speciation is the result of the deliberate creation, from 'zero', of a new species (i.e., a new private financial market) that did not exist before and which could possibly originate in a radical financial innovation. (*Nota bene*: we should not confuse ***mechanism-type*** financial innovation—e.g., the digitization of financial transactions—with ***product-type*** financial innovation—e.g., a new financial instrument as an object of financial transactions.) The fact that the introduction of a new transactional financial instrument may be accompanied by the introduction of a particular trading mechanism is irrelevant and does not justify in any way the possible confusion on which we have just drawn attention. *Nota bene*: we are talking here about financial innovation of the product type.

Sympatric Speciation
The sympatric species is due to the differences that appear regarding the behaviours of the individuals of a species, individuals that function (or live—either biologically or logically) on the same area (either natural, artefactual or, several times, mixed one). It is therefore a matter of differences in the behaviour of different contemporary trading strategies on the same financial market (i.e., within the same species). The main ways in which such inter-individual differences may occur are the following:

- the free will of the economic agents, which can modify, autonomously (as previously shown), the propensity, which can generate variations of the trading strategy so that it presents great differences compared to the 'average' of the contemporary other trading strategies on that market. (*Nota bene*: an important conceptual point must be borne in mind at this point, namely that, as in the case of the markets for goods and services, the financial market is always the market for a particular financial instrument traded on that market.) Therefore, when the variation of the trading strategy is large enough to either propose another financial instrument[72] or modify an existing financial instrument in such a way, then a new financial species appears, that is, what we have called sympatric speciation occurs;
- of course, not only the change of propensity under the impact of free will can lead to sympatric speciation, but also the 'standard' change of propensity, under the selective pressure of the environment (either cultural geodesic or other contemporary trading strategies oper-

ated). In this way, of the selective pressure, the sympatric speciation mechanism passes through the intermediate channel of the individual transaction, because the first 'experimentation' of a behavioural differentiation of the trading strategy (e.g., in case of innovation of a new financial transaction instrument) is done at an individual 'rebellious'[73] transaction, which, most likely through memetism (i.e., through our concept of implicit information), acts through proselytism in the direction of sympatric speciation;

- sympatric speciation is the dominant mechanism in the financial field, so the kinematics of particular financial markets (related to a certain type of financial transaction instrument) is, in most cases, determined by this mechanism. From a conceptual point of view, we must therefore make the following clarifications:
  - the financial market (in this generic formulation, similar to the term 'market for goods and services') is, in some way, the area of manifestation of particular financial markets (i.e., assigned, each of the latter, to a product/instrument of financial transaction). However, from a nominalist perspective, the (integrated) financial market does not exist, it is a verbal (ideal) construct, since real, ontological existence has only particular financial markets;
  - when the term 'financial market' is used, with the meaning of financial species (as we have used it throughout the research) it is understood that we refer to a particular financial market, even if, depending on the generality of the discussion, it is not always (not indispensable) to specify the product/trading financial instrument related to that particular financial market;

Allopatric Speciation

Instead, allopatric speciation refers to the emergence of new species (in our case, new private financial markets) as a result not of the interaction between individuals of the same species on a common area, but between individuals of the same species which, however, are separated (to one degree or another, greater or lesser, in one way or another) from each other in the process of functioning/living, which means that this separation of areas (which may also be physical, although this is not, generally, the case here) must be, firstly, identified.

The cases of areal separation, so to speak, between individuals of the same financial species (i.e., between the trading strategies of the same particular financial market) can be mainly the following:[74]

- *institutional separation*: areas of a given financial market may be located in national economic systems (or in economically integrated systems at a certain level horizontally, as is the case, e.g., in the European Union) which are subject to different cultural geodesics. As a result, trading strategies concerning the same financial product are differently designed (we refer to the normative pre-selection), applied and, finally, selected. Also, within the institutional separation must be included the cases in which certain products/financial instruments have a specific treatment, temporary or under other criteria of exemption from the general rules;
- *cultural separation*: the cultural separation of financial market areas is not superfluous in relation to institutional separation, for at least two reasons: (a) there are, within large national systems,[75] areas, regions, where there is a specific, either normative or, more often, informal (based on different traditions or even different religions) way of trading strategies functioning of a certain product/financial instrument; (b) there are, in particular in integrative economic systems (as in the case of the European Union, but also in other cases of association), preferential treatments—including 'most favoured' trade clauses, situations in which, in relation to financial markets of third parties, certain particular features are applicable (e.g., on taxation or other facilities);
- *physical separation*: in some cases, the same particular financial market may be separated into financial sub-markets from the perspective of physical obstacles—mountains, large watercourses or (in the case of island-type territories) seas and oceans. Physical separation,[76] in a manner similar to biological selection and evolution, generates allopatric speciation.

In all these cases of areal separation of a particular financial market, kinematics of trading strategies may differ from area to area, so that at some point (analogous to the way things happen in the biological case) allopatric speciation occurs. *Nota bene*: as a rule, this speciation, at least in the case of symbolic/logical species, stops at the level of so-called (or possibly to be called) sub-species, not even new species, but, of course, this issue has, more, an empirical significance.

Induced Speciation
Induced speciation is closest to what is usually called financial innovation (we repeat, at the level of product/financial instrument, not trading mechanism). Financial innovation has not only a positive but also a negative significance—thus, unsophisticated economic agents (as they are called in the EMH model of the financial market) can generate, through their decisions and/or actions, the so-called noise in the financial markets; this noise is of the nature of a financial innovation, with a pejorative meaning this time because, in principle, it can produce, in terms of the 'rationality' of the functioning of the financial market, effects similar to the positive financial innovation. Taking into account only positive financial innovation, a speciation can be induced simply by introducing a completely new marketable financial product/instrument, which, of course, creates a new particular financial market.

If we were to order, from the perspective of the frequency with which one of the three categories of speciation can appear, we consider that the highest frequency has the sympatric speciation, then the induced speciation and, with the lowest frequency of production, the allopatric speciation.[77]

Self-Organization

Adaptive replicability—the paradigmatic value (V) of the APMH model of the financial market—is objectified through the self-organization of this model.

The Concept of Financial Self-organization
Self-organization is a concept that has emerged in relation to living systems/entities, that is, in relation to biological individuals and species. In this sense, it is usually related to the dissipative property. In this paragraph, we will examine the two concepts, by customizing them to the APMH model.

Financial Self-organization
In general, the self-organization of an entity is the property of that entity to have sufficient (usually minimal) internal principles for its own replicability.[78] We note that the property of self-organization is fully inherent, especially in the APMH model, although we also encountered elements of self-organization in the hypothesis of adaptive preference (APH, see

FMAB-APH).[79] We present, in the following, the basic elements of financial self-organization.

- On the financial individual[80] (trading strategy):
  - the replicability of the trading strategy is ensured, from the perspective of the selection pressure coming from the environment (i.e., through the individual transaction) by the fact that the variability (in many cases, even volatility) of the individual transaction configuration is allowed within the same configuration of a given trading strategy. The higher number of degrees of freedom of the individual transaction to a degree of freedom of the trading strategy is a sufficient condition for the self-organization of the financial individual (*Nota bene*: simple replication, including in the form of preservation, of the trading strategy means that this self-organization works). In other words, the self-organization at the level of the financial individual consists exactly in the inertia with which the trading strategy resists the pressure coming through the selection pressure exerted on the individual transaction;
  - a symmetrical inertia must be accepted, for the trading strategy, also towards the pressure of change coming from the variation of the propensity—this refers to the fact that the affinity of the economic agent towards its own propensity is even (and much) greater than its affinity for the trading strategy;[81]
  - the two inertias (which have the effect of preserving the trading strategy as long as possible, sometimes to some extent, even beyond the *breakeven point*) ensure the phenomenon of self-organization at the level of the financial individual in the case of the APMH model of the financial market;
- on the financial species (financial market)
  - self-organization at the level of the financial species (which is the financial market) is manifested on the whole population of this species, that is, taking into account the multitude of contemporary trading strategies operated on the market at a given time or, more relevantly, over a certain period;
  - the self-organization of the species also refers to adaptive replicability but, this time, what needs to be replicated is the financial market as such;[82]

- to (adaptively) replicate the financial market admits (not of a necessary nature, but of a contingent one) failures of the various trading strategies to adaptively replicate (i.e., in fact, their disappearance) provided that the trading of the product/financial instrument in cause to continue, supported by the working trading strategies—either among existing ones that have managed to replicate or new trading strategies generated by the selective pressure of the environment or the free will of the economic agent;
- there is, therefore, a ventilation (either competitive or cooperative) of trading strategies (including, of course, the individual transactions associated with each trading strategy), so that, at the level of the financial market, the trading activity of the particular financial product/instrument in the case is 'shifted' from a trading strategy that is rejected by selection to one that is corroborated by that selection, thus maintaining the adaptive replicativity of the species;

Financial Dissipativity

The concept of financial dissipativity must, of course, be discussed in association with the concept of financial entropy. We have previously shown that, in our view, the financial market should not be considered an informational entropy (as, e.g., EMH does) but a behavioural entropy. Behavioural entropy is a property of the financial market that 'moves' inversely proportional to the behavioural efficiency (as, in turn, opposed to informational efficiency, on which EMH is based). The behavioural efficiency is that state (or property) of the financial market in which its strategic heterogeneity or, in other words, the heterogeneity of contemporary trading strategies (compared to each other) in that market is high enough, so the return of the financial market not to be generally reduced to the average.[83]

In this conceptual context, dissipativity must acquire a particular expression in relation to what is allowed from the perspective of Thermodynamics, and this can be done by replacing the homogeneity of temperature in the natural domain with the homogeneity of behaviours in the economic/financial environment. We briefly develop this idea in the following:

- behavioural efficiency in the financial market means the existence of diversified possibilities (avoiding homogenization, e.g., through memetism) of designing and operating trading strategies. Therefore, the higher the nomenclature of feasible trading strategies (namely, it includes more individuals), the higher the behavioural efficiency[84] of the financial market concerned, respectively, in the mirror, the lower the behavioural entropy on the market;[85]

- therefore, analogous to the case of thermodynamic (or energy) dissipativity, in the financial case, the system—in this case, the APMH model of the financial market—tries to maintain a low behavioural entropy by extracting it from the environment (in principle, from cultural geodesic and, of course, from the set of other contemporary trading strategies[86] as well) of low behavioural entropy and by 'outflowing' of high behavioural entropy into the environment. Of course, further clarification is useful here:
  - extracting low behavioural entropy means to identify in the environment (with its two components), those trading strategies that move away, as much as possible, from the average (in terms of net return) of the contemporary working trading strategies. This can be done either by more subtle exploitation of the normative framework (i.e., cultural geodesic) or by designing new trading strategies starting from the observation and analysis of other contemporary working trading strategies;
  - to introduce high behavioural entropy into the environment means that, precisely by identifying, designing and operationalizing new trading strategy(s) that deviates from the average of contemporary trading strategies, the potential to identify new such trading strategies is reduced. In other words, any reduction in behavioural entropy in the system (the APMH model) has the effect of increasing (even faster[87]) the behavioural entropy in the environment.[88]

Self-organization and dissipativity within the APMH model are, of course, interdependent. Moreover, one is actually achieved through the other, forming a functional pair. Therefore, in describing the mechanism of financial self-organization, the two phenomena will be connected in a logical way.

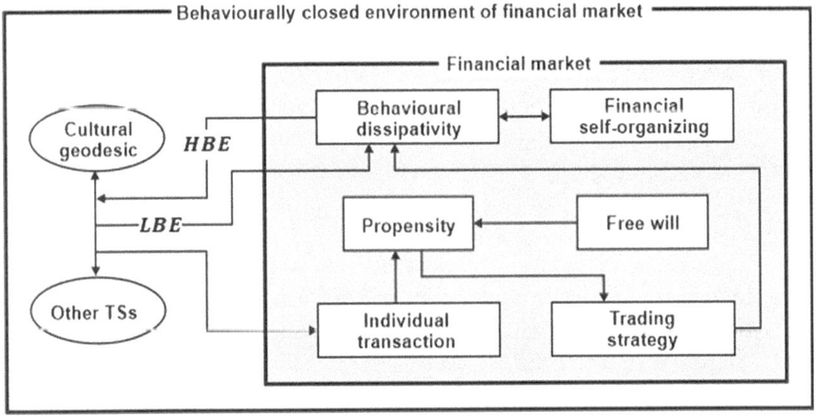

Fig. 5.8 The mechanism of financial self-organization within APMH model. (*Source*: Authors)

The Mechanism of Financial Self-organization

We will describe the mechanism of financial self-organization within the APMH model of the financial market through the synoptic representation in Fig. 5.8 (with *LBE* the flow of low or neg-behavioural entropy was noted, and with *HBE* the flow of high behavioural entropy was noted).

Antifragility

The concept of antifragility is well known (Taleb, 2014), so here we will make brief considerations only regarding financial antifragility, as it occurs (or can occur) within the APMH model of the financial market. We are therefore interested in whether and how it is possible to gain from the perturbations in the autopoietic functioning of the financial market.

Financial Perturbations/Disturbances

Perturbation/disturbance generally means a deviation of a phenomenon or process (or, more generally, of a system), following a shock, either internal or external, from its state or from its trajectory. Of course, the idea of a significance threshold of this process also arises in this matter—from what size or speed of the deviation it is considered that we are dealing with a perturbation.[89] In this context, we consider that there are two main classes of potential financial disturbances: (a) *state* disturbances (static disturbances) and (b) *process* disturbances (kinematic disturbances). State disturbances refer to the deviation of the financial market from its structure and configuration above an accepted significance threshold, and process disturbances refer to the deviation of the functioning of the financial market from the trajectory on which it is inscribed at a given time. Each of the two classes of disturbances can have one of the following two concrete hypostases:

- increasing of the predictability of the financial market beyond the threshold at which the establishment of maximum behavioural efficiency of the financial market[90] is irreversible;[91] this (first) 'red line' blocks the functioning of the financial market from the perspective of behavioural efficiency in the same way that another 'red line' (this time related to informational efficiency—see EMH model) blocks the functioning of the financial market from the perspective of informationally beating the market;
- decreasing of the predictability of the financial market below the significance threshold at which the establishment of the behavioural efficiency of the financial individual (trading strategy) is irreversible; this second 'red line' refers to the fact that, symmetrically with the irreversible increase of the predictability of the financial market, its irreversible decrease is also undesirable because, in the latter case, the economic behaviour would become purely random, not allowing the development of performance involved in adapting (or rather, adaptive replicability) the trading strategies, respectively the individual transactions.

The following question can be raised here: disturbances can, of course, be either systemic (when a disturbing cause has a high 'energy' potential to produce deviations, either from the state or from the trajectory) or local (when a disruptive cause affects a relatively small sphere—either spatially, temporally[92] or qualitatively). The question is whether they are institutive disturbances or corrective ones. By institutive disturbances we mean those disturbances which initiate the deviations previously spoken of, while corrective disturbances are those disturbances which act as negations (cancellations) of the institutive disturbances. In our opinion, in both situations it is about disturbances, the distinction between them consisting obviously in their deliberative or non-deliberative character—thus, the institutive disturbances are of non-deliberative type, while the corrective disturbances are of deliberative type.

Nota bene: an important problem concerns the non-achievement of the objective set for the operation of a trading strategy (more precisely, by the operation of the set of individual transactions associated, by inference, with that trading strategy). Is this a disturbance? The question is not superfluous, since the non-realization of the financial objective (e.g., not obtaining a certain net return) represents, from a logical point of view, a deviation of the trajectory of that trading strategy from the anticipated (or expected, as the case may be) trajectory. Our position in this matter is as follows:

- the non-achievement of the expected objective from a trading strategy is not of the nature of disturbance, because it represents, simply, the result of the selection process carried out by the environment. The main role in this selection process is, as we have shown, the component called 'other trading strategies', which acts either cooperatively or competitively, on the trading strategy concerned, so we are not in the presence of a perturbation/disturbance that would possibly change the 'decision' of the selection;
- the change (more precisely, reversal) of the selective 'decision' as a result of a disturbance is, of course, possible, but this time the impact of the disturbance can be identified and assessed, so we still have a disturbance, which is distinct from the selection process.

Autopoietic Financial Antifragility

Financial antifragility means the possibility (and degree) in which, under the APMH model, the impact of the disruptions mentioned above is turned into advantage.[93] The concept of advantage, in the context of this discussion, can be characterized as follows:

- from the perspective of the structure and functioning of the APMH model (paradigm), an advantage of perturbations should be such as to verify its paradigmatic value: *adaptive replicability*. Therefore, if a certain disturbance leads to an increase in the probability of this adaptive replicability (at the level of the financial individual, i.e., of the trading strategy), then it can be said that the system in question has manifested the antifragility property;

- the following conclusion is immediately drawn: the gain from disruptions, ensured by the antifragility properties of the APMH model, has nothing to do with the financial (possibly monetary) gain associated with the operation of a certain trading strategy (or individual transactions),[94] that is, the gain (net return) obtained by the economic agent from operating that trading strategy; the gain/advantage obtained (or obtainable) from disruptions refers exclusively to the adaptive replicability of the trading strategy.

Of course, the question arises here: does the gain from perturbations refer only to the trading strategy involved (i.e., affected by that perturbations) or does it target the financial market as a financial species? In other words, the question is: How can the antifragility property be 'transferred' from the level of the trading strategy to that of the financial market?[95] We recall that we discussed such an issue of aggregation (or synergy/emergency) in connection with sustainable systems, respectively with autopoietic systems. Antifragility properties can obviously be found in both sustainable and autopoietic systems. Here we are interested in examining the link between individual/particular antifragility (associated with a trading strategy) and aggregate or induced antifragility that could characterize the system of particular financial markets, that is, what we call the financial market, without adding the predicate 'particular'. In this regard, we make the following two brief considerations:

- consideration 1: *an aggregate financial market that contains (at least) a particular antifragile financial market is antifragile*
  - argument: there is no question of a disturbance directly (and, possibly, exclusively) targeting a particular private financial market, since antifragility is not a distributed[96] property, but a general one. This means that it is sufficient for a disturbance to be 'adjudicated', in terms of capitalization (in the form of a gain or advantage) of a particular financial market, for the aggregate financial market, in which that particular financial market is contained, to benefit from this gain/advantage. So, if there is (at least) a particular antifragile financial market, so able to capitalize the disruption (more precisely, its impact), then, at the level of the aggregate system, antifragility works;[97]

- consideration 2: *autopoieticity does not imply antifragility nor vice versa—the two properties are simply logically, structurally and functionally additive*
  argument: autopoieticity requires *adaptive replicability* (or actual replication), while antifragility requires the capitalization (of the impact) of the disturbance in the 'interest' of the disturbed system. It is obvious that we can have autopoietic systems that are not antifragile and vice versa, namely, to have antifragile systems that are not autopoietic. At the same time, the two properties are not incompatible with each other—they are not contradictory to each other and, moreover, they are not in adversarial relations with each other, hence their logical additivity mentioned above. Therefore, systems that are both autopoietic and antifragile are not 'prohibited'.

Financial Autopoietic Chreode

The term chreode was introduced by biologist Conrad Hal Waddington (Waddington, 1957), to describe the concept of the necessary pathway on which a biological cell develops.[98] Of course, the term (and also the concept) in question are now taken over and used from other perspectives, including in the general sense of the concept in question.

From the perspective of this study (i.e., with reference to the functioning of the autopoietic financial market), we are interested in the relationship between the concept of chreode and the concept of autopoieticity, with the connecting element between them, which is fitness (in our case, financial fitness, as previously examined). In this context, we will define the financial autopoietic chreode (*FAPC*) in the following way: *the quasi-necessary trajectory on which the financial fitness of the trading strategy from an autopoietic perspective is inscribed.* In this sense of the concept of the chreode, it is, of course, typical of the APMH model of the financial market.[99] We develop, below, this proposal for the concept of financial autopoietic chreode.

Some Conceptual Precautions

- the predicate of necessity from the *FAPC* wording does not have the meaning of the same predicate considered from a natural perspective, but it must be understood from a cultural perspective: it is a logical necessity, most often rational or rationalizable;[100]

- the additional diminution (compared to the replacement of the natural necessity with the cultural one, generated by the presence of deliberation) of the degree of necessity from the *FAPC* formulation by using the qualifying prefix 'quasi' is justified by the presence (and action) of free will in modifying the trading strategy, as previously shown;
- the concept of trajectory is the one as generally used, that is, a chronological succession of the state vectors involved.[101] In the case here discussed, the state vector refers to the trading strategy and, of course, through the aggregation effect of the trading strategies (i.e., of the particular financial markets), to the financial market as a whole;

The Financial Autopoietic Chreodic Process

The financial autopoietic chreodic process involves the examination of three issues: (1) the need for the financial chreode, (2) autopoietic causality/causation in the financial chreode and (3) the overall mechanism of the financial autopoietic chreodic process.

The Need for Financial Chreode

The (cultural) necessity of the financial chreode consists in the following:

- the propensity of the economic agent is the fundamental and permanent 'provider' of logical schemes of behaviour in the financial market (more precisely, of configurations of trading strategies). But propensity is a persistent psychological property (it has a great deal of inertia and, consequently, an extremely high degree of kinematic self-similarity);[102]
- this persistent identity of propensity is the main source of need for the financial chreode, as it aims at the effective causal aspect;[103]
- it can be said, therefore, that the source of the need for the financial chreode is in the implicit rationality (i.e., more or less aware) of propensity, the latter can be considered a model of 'hard' rationality, that is, established in the material structure of the economic agent;
- given that propensity is the very genotype of the financial individual, it can be said that the need for the financial chreode simply lies in its pre-programming (*Nota bene*: here appears, in fact, the formal aspect we discussed above) in genotype.

Autopoietic Causality/Causation in the Financial Chreode

Although, in part, the aspect of causality in the financial chreode has already been mentioned above, it is useful to make some additional clarifications, especially from the perspective of the autopoietic character of this causality. In this regard, we make the following considerations:

- all four Aristotelian causes can be invoked in the formation and functioning of the financial autopoietic chreode: (i) the *formal* cause—exerted, in particular, by the passive component of the financial market environment, that is, cultural geodesic selection or an *ex-ante* selection of the trading strategy, respectively of the individual transaction, (ii) the *efficacy* cause or, with a usual term, although inappropriate, the efficient cause—exerted, in particular, by the propensity of the economic agent; (iii) the *material* cause—exerted, in particular, from the active component of the financial market environment (i.e., all other contemporary trading strategies operating on the market), (iv) the *teleological* or final cause—exerted, in our opinion, mainly by free will;[104]
- the way in which the four causes are integrated in the general phenomenology of construction of the autopoietic financial chreode is represented synoptically in Fig. 5.9.

The Mechanism of the Chreodic Autopoietic Financial Process

In this paragraph we will describe the mechanism (from a logical perspective, especially) of generating the financial autopoietic chreode within the APMH model of the financial market.

General Aspects

- the autopoietic financial chreode is generated and maintained by devices of robustness, resilience (either homeostatic or homeorhetic) and antifragility—we will note from now on this triplet with *RRA*;
- the *RRA* device acts by means of automatic stabilizers;[105]
- however, automatic stabilizers achieve stability (at most sustainability) and anti-fragility. According to consideration no. 2, antifragility does not logically imply autopoieticity.[106] Therefore, the possibility and operation of new devices, which we propose to call *adaptive*

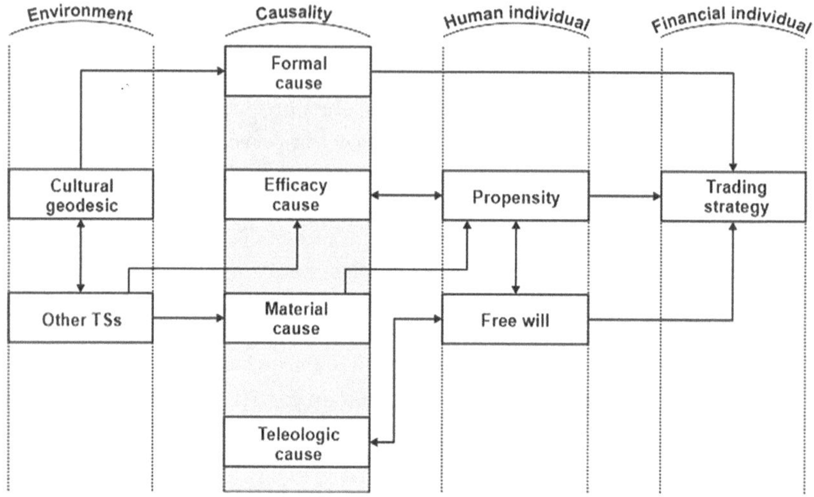

Fig. 5.9 The causal device in the financial autopoietic chreode of APMH model. (*Source*: Authors)

replication devices (hereinafter, noted with *ARD*), must be examined. *Nota bene*: note that while the *RRA* is a static device or, at most kinematic, the *ARD* device is a dynamic one;[107]

- therefore, similar to the automatic stabilizers that work within *RRA* device, automatic adapters (or automatic adaptive replicators—henceforth, noted *AAR*) are needed to ensure autopoieticity. An *AAR* must be characterized by the following two properties:
  - (*PI*) *propensity inertia*: this property has already been discussed—we consider it a psychological feature inalienable to the economic agent (human individual), having the nature, so to speak, of a self-fed belief;[108]

    impact: the propensity behaves saltationistly—only when a sufficiently high selection pressure from the environment accumulates, there will be variations in propensity, and these variations will occur suddenly, non-gradually;

- (*PB*) *protection belt* around the trading strategy (i.e., the set of individual transactions, endowed with a large number of degrees of freedom or adaptability, compared to the case of the trading strategy);

  impact: the selection pressure from the environment occurs, in the first instance, on the individual transaction/transactions, until their degrees of freedom are exhausted and only then is it exerted on the trading strategy which, in turn, is exerted on the propensity to receive, from the latter, the new configuration (structure and functions). It should be noted that the trading strategy also has a certain number of degrees of freedom (much lower, of course, than that of individual transactions), so that the pressure of the trading strategy on propensity will occur only after exhausting the degrees of freedom of the trading strategy concerned,[109] also in a saltationist way.

Structural/Functional Aspects

We consider that the following three structural components of the mechanism that function in the financial autopoietic chreodic process must be taken into account:

- (*AL*) *attitudinal leverage* (or *propensity analyser*):[110] it is, as we already know, the 'energy' factor that triggers the behaviour of the economic agent in the financial market. Without this attitude originated in the belief, no financial behaviour can occur;
  - role: initiating the decision to carry out transactional acts in the financial market. This initiation is a nominal one, without any particularization of mode, degree and the like—all these last configurations of financial behaviour come only after the awareness of this attitude. *Nota bene*: this is the subjective factor of generating financial behaviour, a persistent factor, only partially subject to rational questioning;
- (*PL*) *positional leverage* (or *net return analyser*): even if APMH is an evolutionary and autopoietic model of the financial market, the objective component (which ensures the determination of the position of the economic agent, ensured by the given trading strategy, on the particular financial market where the economic agent concerned

operates) is still the 'old' cost–benefit calculation. Of course, habitus, idiosyncrasies and contextual conditions may establish different decision points at the same result of cost–benefit calculation, but calculation as such remains an important structural component of the financial autopoietic chreodic mechanism;

  - role: this leverage pilots the attitudinal leverage (which, in turn, has, of course, a certain sensitivity of reaction to the impulses received from the positional leverage). In essence, the positional leverage decides only within the attitudinal decision, being, therefore, a regulatory decision-maker, while the attitudinal lever is an institutive (or constitutive) decision-maker;

- (*SR*) *secondary* (or operational) *replicator*:[111] this may be the individual transaction (as long as it has not yet exhausted its degrees of freedom, i.e., it has not yet exhausted the versions it can objectify below the accumulation threshold of the selection pressure—this represents what we previously called the dead zone or area of elasticity) or the trading strategy, with the same specifications regarding its viable versions;
  - role: this component of the chreodic mechanism represents its factual operation (the two leverages mentioned above represent non-factual operations), that is, the objective way in which the financial autopoietic chreode is constructed (and reconstructed) within APMH.

Figure 5.10 shows a 'map' of the placement of the different structural components of the financial autopoietic chreodic mechanism, from the simultaneous perspective of the frequency of change (or, equivalently, volatility) and the number of degrees of freedom, and Fig. 5.11 shows a simplified scheme of phenomenology the financial autopoietic chreode of the APMH model (with *TS* the trading strategy was noted, with *IT* the individual transaction was noted, with *E* the environment was noted and with *P* the propensity was noted).

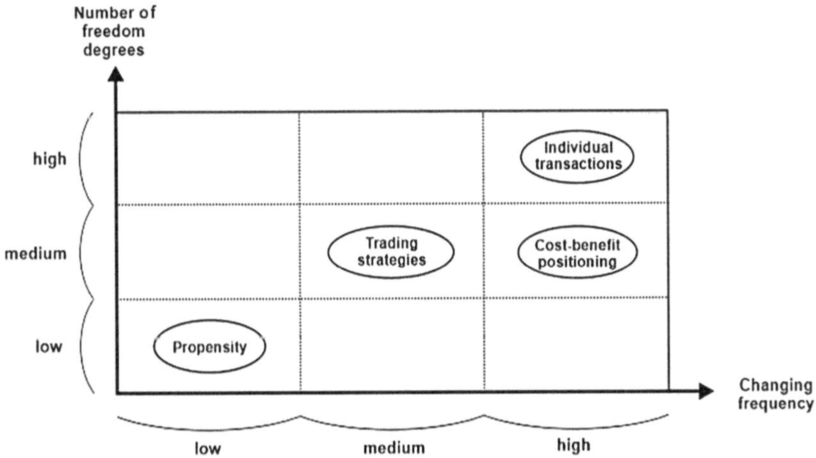

Fig. 5.10 Reciprocal positioning of the structural components of the chreodic mechanism. (*Source*: Authors)

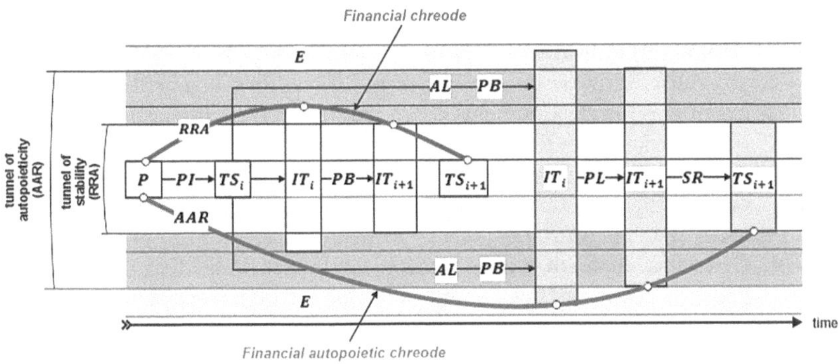

Fig. 5.11 Phenomenology of the financial autopoietic chreode in APMH model. (*Source*: Authors)

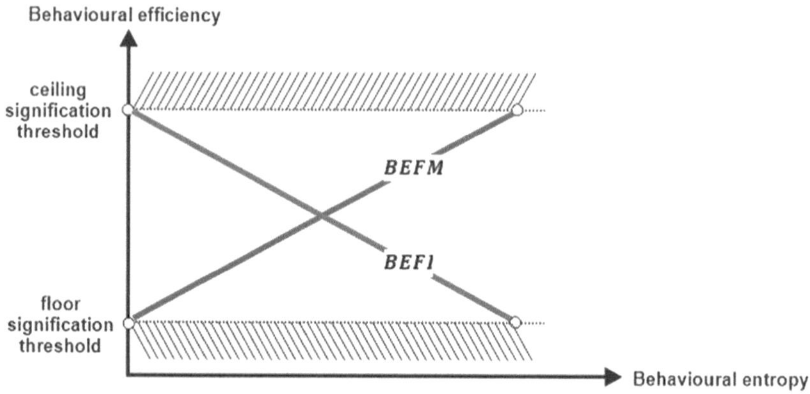

Fig. 5.12 The two meanings of the behaviour efficiency. (*Source*: Authors)

Notes

1. The phrase 'invisible hand', for example, expresses a very broad impersonality of the functioning of the economic system as a whole, although at the origin of the changes in this impersonal functioning is the human (biological) individual.
2. Of course, artificial intelligence (especially in its fundamentalist version) can offer opposite arguments about the necessary nature of the symbolic/logical lack of ontological autonomy of the species.
3. From a theoretical point of view, the APMH model (like all social sciences or institutions) is an exo-somatic tool of the biological individual. Society itself, as an institution, is such an instrument, as well.
4. Of course, it is not mandatory for any human individual to 'secrete' a financial genotype, but any financial phenotype is necessarily located in the human individual. This does not exclude more sophisticated cases (see, here, artificial intelligence—*AI*) in which the genotype of the symbolic individual is transplanted into the symbolic individual in question (e.g., the so-called phenomenon of self-learning) but, as we have argued in other places in the present research, even in this case, the 'pips' of last resort of that genotype are also in the biological individual.
5. Recall that in the case of the APMH paradigm, the component called the value of this paradigm is the adaptive replicability, which means the operation of the channel of adaptability (or adaptation, adjustment) but only by maintaining the replicability (replicability means identitary preservation) of the system in question.

6. The genotype contains, in essence, the replicator, which, in the case of the biological genotype, is DNA.
7. The financial genotype also shares with the biological genotype the irreversibility although, in fact, in the biological case, we have an absolute irreversibility (i.e., a principled impossibility of reversibility), while in the financial case, the irreversibility is relative (i.e., it is a 'vulnerable' impossibility, as it is, to a large extent, contingent).
8. Basic belief should not be equated with *belief* or *faith*, but rather with David Lewis' *credence* (as he himself does when discussing the concept of propensity).
9. Of course, there may be a set of basic praxiological axioms but, in principle, it is likely that in any such system of axioms, one will be able to stand out as master—that is, it may represent the axiom of last resort (possibly the most representative or most general) of all the axioms in that set.
10. In our opinion, this model, with two 'floors', of the financial genotype, is not applicable to the biological genotype, in which we have a single 'floor'.
11. This possibility has been mentioned before, in several places, and is peculiar to symbolic species, as is the case of the financial market.
12. We remind you that the exteriority of the symbolic individual is also accepted by Niklas Luhmann, the creator of the theory of autopoietic society, who proposes *communication* as a phenotype (adult individual) of this social model.
13. But, obviously, the frequency of adjustments is much higher in the case of individual transactions that are associated or could be associated with a given trading strategy.
14. Here is shown the correctness of the position supported by CMH, in relation to EMH.
15. The notation has its origin in one of the English terms for the concept of affinity, namely, *congeniality*. The meaning of the concept of affinity is the following: acceptance, support, attachment, mutual adequacy, sympathy and diffuse (vague) preference.
16. From a 'technical' point of view, the corroboration/confirmation of a trading strategy means that trading strategy is selected by its environment (cultural geodesic plus the other contemporary trading strategies).
17. Thus, for someone with analytical skills in the field of fractals, an opportunity could arise for the development of formalizations of equivalence between the frequencies of operating the trading strategies and their uninterrupted corroboration durations.
18. Both research in psychology (either cognitive or behavioural) and economic behaviourism have shown, implicitly or explicitly, that there is an

innate inclination of the human individual to 'see' and consider only (or preponderantly) confirmations of existing belief and to ignore evidences that would invalidate that belief. No matter how small this asymmetry of 'good faith' of the human individual, we consider it sufficient to support our assertion.

19. This assertion is immediate given that the assessment of objective reality is always made in the light of an already existing belief.
20. The explanation for this graphical form is that, depending on the dominance of one or the other of the two factors at a given time, the marginal substitution rate may differ as the ratio of factor weights changes.
21. A separate direction of research, at this point, could be that which would study (including from a formal-quantitative point of view) the moments regarding the corroboration of a trading strategy, in a similar way to the one in which the moments regarding prices or returns (yields) are now studied. For example, time series could be built with these moments of corroboration or even refutation and so on.
22. The concept of mental comfort, as a criterion of sub-optimal behaviour (i.e., specific to the APMH model), seems to be a productive direction for further research, especially from a theoretical perspective but also in terms of quantitative formalizations and, consequently, of the formulation of predictive statements.
23. One can examine, of course, a corroboration duration at the level of a set of trading strategies (if an economic agent has such a thing), which would thus be an average corroboration duration not at the level of the trading strategy, but at the level of the economic agent. However, the duration of the corroboration has, from another perspective, the significance of a life of the trading strategy (respectively, if one considers a set of trading strategies of an economic agent, we are speaking of an economic life of that economic agent). Perhaps, a similar lifespan could be determined for the financial species as a whole, that is, for the financial market (either particular or 'general').
24. Recall that by quantity of pressure (Q^p) we mean the product between the intensity of pressure (k^p) and the duration (t^p) (measured in clock time) of exerting pressure: $Q^p = k^p \cdot t^p$, with the associated indifference curve, obviously, which allows the substitutability, respectively the complementarity between the two multiplicative factors for keeping the quantity of pressure as invariant.
25. In fact, there is a problem that needs to be clarified: free will can change also directly the phenotype, but here it is an epigenetic mutation, so there is no question that free will counts as the impact of genotype on the phenotype, that is, similar to the case of biological species.

26. Therefore, so many articles that strive (how else but by the irresistible econometric method?) to prove that there are genes of … economic behaviours are just as many clogged roads (although, of course, cannot be eliminated any link between natural Darwinism and social Lamarckism—*Nota bene*: many, however, imported Darwinism from nature directly into society and generated the mule called social Darwinism. Perhaps Edward Wilson himself was a little too enthusiastic in this matter).
27. It is worth noting, here, a very important aspect, which is related to the structure of information in the financial market: the economic agent never observes a … trading strategy, but only individual transactions (i.e., as we said, contextual hypostases of a trading strategy). It is the role of the economic agent that, based on its own observational and resolutive competence (Dinga et al., 2022), generates what we call implicit information, to infer from this implicit information the trading strategy that is likely to stay behind the hypostasis in question. As can be seen from the reference mentioned in this note, in the financial market we have a dominance of behaviour over information, one of the deep reasons why EMH is a simple (and simplistic) intellectual game.
28. The question of whether the memetic mutation affects only the individual transaction (i.e., whether the economic agent who observes an individual transaction of other financial market participants directly imitates that individual transaction or strives—the famous conative test in praxiology—to find, by *modus ponens*, the grounding trading strategy is not superfluous. We are therefore of the opinion that only a part (how big this part is seems to be an empirical rather than a theoretical problem) of the individual transactions observed by the economic agent leads to the modification of its own trading strategy (such a modification may involve, at the limit, even its replacement), otherwise a contagion occurs exclusively at the level of the protection belt. In any case, the epigenetic mutation cannot exist outside the variation of the phenotype (of the trading strategy).
29. Obviously, the production of an epigenetic mutation, as shown in this discussion, cannot remain without consequences on propensity, especially after a time when the epigenetically modified trading strategy is accompanied by success in terms of return. It is about the fact that the weight of the β factor of the affinity with respect to the trading strategy increases significantly so that this increase will be reflected in the increase of the weight of the factor α, with the corresponding 'fall', following this transfer of 'affinity' of the weight of the factor β (*Nota bene*: it seems that we can accept, from a theoretical point of view, a cyclical evolution of the ratio between the weights of the two affinity factors).

30. We remind that *SPm* represents the sub-criterion of positioning compared to the market average, within the static positioning of the performative depth of fitness (*SP* criterion).
31. It is, obviously, about social fitness categories customized to the case of the financial market (i.e., the financial species). As we have shown before, in the case of symbolic/logical species, we speak exclusively of social fitness, that is, not in the sense (dominant, unfortunately, in the dedicated literature) in which the social predicate is used with the meaning that the fitness in question is a phenomenon that occurs in social worlds (either human or non-human), but in the sense that it is simply not about natural fitness, as is the case with biological fitness.
32. We specify that this 'possible' is a relative and not an absolute one: depending on the set of trading strategies operated on the market, the 'possible'—which is, of course, contingent—varies, although accidentally, so it can reach the maximum under the given conditions, that is, it can reach an extreme value.
33. It should be noted that the selection in the APMH model follows the pattern of any selection regarding a symbolic/logical species, namely, it always occurs through the human individual who operates the individuals of that symbolic species.
34. It is, as we mentioned before, about the selection known, in the literature, as intra-species selection.
35. Here, in the broad sense of this term, accredited by Pierre Bourdieu (see his work, *Language and Symbolic Power* (Bourdieu, 1993)).
36. Predictability of the predictor is a concept that can lead to an interesting discussion (both theoretically and methodologically) about what we might call the *predictive chain*.
37. We recall that theoretical rationality is claimed exclusively by belief, while practical rationality has to do with the decision-making process within a given theoretical rationality (see, in this issue, Alfred R. Mele & Piers Rawling, *The Oxford Handbook of Rationality* (2004), especially Chapter 2 (*Theoretical Rationality: Its Sources, Structure, and Scope*, by Robert Audi) and Chapter 3 (*Practical Aspects of Theoretic Reasoning*, by Gilbert Harman)).
38. It is about what could be called (as a psychological property of the human subject) the *inertia of own choice*.
39. As we have shown in several places, unlike the case of biological species (natural, non-symbolic), in the case of symbolic/logical/artefactual species the selection operated by the environment is an internalized one, that is, it occurs through the human individual, which means that the selection in the field of symbolic species is a mediated one, as it may undergo alterations between the 'proposed' version by the environment and the

version actually operated by the human individual. Here is, moreover, the problem of transcription, respectively of translation in the mutation and selection of symbolic species. This is also where, obviously, free will intervenes, which can distort the 'suggestion' made by the environment.

40. A trading strategy can violate cultural geodesic in two cases: (a) it is erroneously designed, due to the incompetence of the economic agent in question; (b) is deliberately designed against the norms contained in cultural geodesic, precisely in order to exploit this normative violation to obtain an additional return. In both cases, the normative selection will act *ex-post* but, as we said, usually, the normative selection acts *ex-ante*.
41. The environment of a species (whether it is a biological species or a symbolic/logical one) has four components that, of course, inter-act: (a) the non-anthropic natural environment; (b) the anthropic environment (artefacts); (c) the other natural species; (d) the individuals of the species in question (*Nota bene*: as shown, in the latter case we have an intra-species selection).
42. The concept of adverse selection, introduced here as another term/phrase for negative selection has the known significance of the economic theory of informational asymmetry (see, in particular, the works of Joseph Stiglitz in this matter).
43. Genetic engineering, respectively transhumanism, has as a potential result, in our opinion, a certain synthesis between the biological species (or the biological individual) and the symbolic species (or the symbolic individual). This phenomenon has, of course, its relevance in a broader discussion (a discussion that, however, will not be developed in this research).
44. The careful reader has already noted that free will is credited by us with a certain autonomy in relation to the economic agent's own propensity, which means that s/he can change it without any 'reason'.
45. Of course, here are applicable what discussed above about the hard core and the protection belt in the 'factual falsification' of the trading strategy.
46. A justification for this methodological reversal is given, in graphical form, in Figure 2.31.
47. We do not examine separately the epigenetic mutation (that mutation 'indicated' by the memetic contagion exerted on the economic agent, which does not affect the propensity, but directly the phenotype—the trading strategy), since it does not pose specific problems to transcription.
48. Here, the meaning of the term *mechanical* refers to the fact that the subjectivity (e.g., psychism) of the biological species is not involved in this transcription.

49. Perhaps even the collective unconscious (i.e., the archetype, as Jung would say), since the individual's habitus emerges from the entire (historical) psychic dowry of his/her ancestors.
50. In an approximate formulation, from a semiotic point of view, meaning refers to denotation, and sense refers to connotation.
51. We specify that the existence of such a hermeneutics is a necessary fact, that is, it is impossible for an economic agent not to have the hermeneutics in question (of course, the degree of sophistication of that hermeneutics is irrelevant).
52. This clarification is not superfluous at all, since the change in propensity is at the discretion of the economic agent (human individual) who can be wrong. An important theoretical conclusion follows from this commentary on clarification: in addition to transcription errors (and, as we shall see immediately, also translation errors), there may be a third category of error: the error of propensity change, which we would like to call a diagnostic error, that is, an error that leads to an inappropriate change in propensity under the selection pressure.
53. The analogy with translation in the case of the evolution of biological species is, again, obvious: in the biological case, translation means the conversion of m-RNA into proteins, that is, in the 'bricks' of the future biological individual.
54. In a firmer formulation, we can say that nominalism is also valid here, in the sense that only the individual transaction has symbolic reality, while the trading strategy is only a family name for the set of individual transactions related to the trading strategy. Note that, in fact, here we have a pair of nominalism—realism not from an ontological point of view, but from a gnoseological one, since both the individual transaction and the trading strategy are ideal entities but, even so, only individuals exist … gnoseologically.
55. A theoretical observation here: we think that the volatility of the individual transaction is higher than the volatility of the trading strategy associated, so we can calculate a *sui generis* multiplier of volatility in the evolutionary process of the APMH model (but we will not further develop this analytical suggestion). We are not just referring to the well-known phenomenon of error accumulation (although it can also be studied), but rather to the fact that a small variation in the trading strategy can result in a much larger variation in the individual transaction (something analogous to the sensitivity to the initial conditions considered in the case of modelling non-linear dynamical systems—chaos theory).
56. We remember that, in the case of symbolic species, the phenotype appears directly in the adult stage, without undergoing growth processes.

57. By total mutation we mean the logical sum (including the synergy effect) between the genetic mutation (produced at the level of propensity) and the epigenetic mutation (produced at the level of the trading strategy by 'bypassing' the propensity).
58. We remind the reader that, in evolution, the variation of fitness can never be qualified as being, in itself, a phenomenon such as increase/decrease and improvement/worsening, but only as a better fit or a weaker fit in relation to given environment (*Nota bene*: to observe an interesting parallelism between the character of rationality, which is relative exclusively to a model of rationality, respectively the character of adequacy, which is relative to an environment of adequacy).
59. The emergent–deliberative relationship should not be confused with the Darwinism–Lamarckism relationship: while in the case of the first relationship, it is the relationship of dominance between finality and purpose (emergence favours finality, while deliberativity favours purpose), in the case of the second rapport, it is about the relationship of dominance between structure and function (Darwinism favours the dominant role of structure over function, while Lamarckism favours the dominant role of function over structure).
60. For example, a variation of a trading strategy can lead, through memetic contagion, to mutations in contemporary trading strategies.
61. We mention here our concept of *randoberativity*, introduced in FMAB-APH.
62. Of course, we are referring to reversibility over time (which, however, is not very relevant), because genuine reversibility must be judged in relation to the environment. But in relation to the environment, any evolution is reversible (including biological) precisely for the reason that any evolution is a co-evolution. Once again, it is clear that evolution has no axiological significance, such as the idea of progress or the like.
63. In our research, we assumed the hypothesis (or axiom) that, in financial matters, there is only one financial species—the financial market, composed of adult individuals called trading strategies (each trading strategy, or a group of such strategies, being assigned to an economic agent, or a group of economic agents).
64. For the case of biological species, where there is no deliberation in the selection stage, the individuation does not have the same relevance as the speciation.
65. We specify that, as previously shown, the change in propensity can take place in a direct way, that is, based on the autonomous action of free will, so unrelated to the selective pressure of the environment.
66. In the case discussed here, the rationality model that allows inferring of the variation of the trading strategy from the variation of the propensity

is the APMH itself. In fact, the same model of rationality—APMH—is the basis for inferring (as a secondary inference) the individual transaction (or set of individual transactions) from the trading strategy.

67. This kinematics is, to some extent, counter-intuitive, so we will make the following reasoning in this matter. Corroboration means the 'confirmation' (of course, as in the case of the falsification of factual predictions, it is a question of a provisional 'confirmation' or, more precisely, of a delayed refutation, this being the exact meaning of the corroboration concept) of the trading strategy. It seems that in this case, since the corroboration comes from the environment, the share of factor β, not factor α, should increase. However, the fact that the corroboration is always just provisional (since it does not provide the certainty of its repetition), it increases, in fact, the belief that the trading strategy in question is adequate, that is, increases the share of the factor α. Conversely, at the first refutation of the trading strategy (in the whole process related to the protection belt provided by the set of individual transactions), instead of decreasing the weight of the β factor, as it seemed *prima facie* (since the refutation also comes from the environment), in fact the economic agent's confidence in its own propensity decreases, that is, the share of the α factor decreases. Rightly, one may ask why two more affinity factors are needed, because it seems that one alone would be enough, since only this one changes its weight, both in the case of corroboration and in the case of refutation? The answer contains two parts: (a) in fact, when α changes it changes, implicitly, β (by the difference from 1); (b) β has a very important role (most importantly, in fact) at the level of the individual transaction, while α has the main role at the level of the trading strategy.
68. Logically, the non-identitary adjustment, that is, the adjustment that does not preserve the identity (*Nota bene*: the identity is given by the structure and the logic related to that structure) is equivalent to the replacement.
69. Menu cost means the cost of a change (usually institutional, but not only of this type) in the set of conditions that accompany a certain behaviour. Changing these conditions may only have a tangential link to that behaviour, but it still generates costs—for example, if you change the name of an organization, you have to change the header, stamp, maybe the labels on the office doors and so on.
70. This possible *alpha-attachment* (or *alpha-affinity*) of the economic agent to the trading strategy in operation can be a very eloquent element of testability in well-designed experiments.
71. Following David Lewis' line of argument, this category of individuation is based on (is anchored in) the *credence* component of propensity. Perhaps we should accept a bipolar structure of propensity: (a) the com-

ponent of rational belief and (b) the component of the a-rational belief (credence). The fact that, from this proposal, it results, implicitly, that trust (effect of the component called credence) has an a-rational nature is, of course, fully assumed by the authors.

72. As was the case, for example, with the introduction of financial derivatives or the introduction of the index of financial assets or funds—each of these financial innovations has generated a specific financial market, that is, a new kind of financial market.
73. We remind the reader that, even in the field of biological evolution, sympatric speciation also begins with the 'rebellion' of an individual of an existing species (*Nota bene*: there is no case of developments, at this point in the discussion, in this matter, but we, however, mention the fact that, even in the Kuhn-nian paradigm, anomalies are part of a rebellious behaviour of facts tested on the basis of predictions allowed by the 'normal component' of that paradigm, for example, that of dissidents in relation to the *statu quo*, and let us not forget that in the religious field (such as Christianity), Protestantism was initiated following a rebellion or a dissidence of Martin Luther.
74. Please note that the expression 'financial market', which refers to a particular traded or tradable product or financial instrument, does not refer only to a national market, nor even to a regional market, but denotes the global market of that product or trading instrument (especially in the current conditions of globalization of economic flows, including financial, labour and capital flows).
75. For example, China, USA, India and Russia, but also in some federal or confederal states, which have a certain autonomy in the internal states of the federal/confederal state.
76. There have been cases in recent history where an institutional separation has been accompanied (in fact, generated) by an institutional separation—for example, the case of the Berlin Wall.
77. This clarification has, however, almost no theoretical, methodological or instrumental value, in exactly the same way that the typology of market informational efficiency (in the EMH model) has no such value: strong, semi-strong and weak efficiency.
78. Recall that, for example, sustainability, as opposed to autopoieticity, also requires external principles/resources to ensure replicability.
79. In fact, APMH includes (even in the sense of set theory) APH or, logically, APMH is a generalization of APH.
80. As it has already turned out, by force of circumstances, that is, given that we are dealing with symbolic/logical species, which are artefacts, the financial individual cannot be 'broken' from the human individual—let us remember that propensity (i.e., financial genotype) is, from a structural

point of view, inside the entity of the human individual and not (analogously with the case of the biological individual) in the entity of the financial individual. In this context, often when we talk about the financial individual, we refer, in fact, to the package financial individual—human individual (a kind of a *finhuman*).

81. Perhaps even an affinity (or part of affinity) should be accepted as irrational, more precisely, of an emotional type, which the economic agent manifests towards his/her own propensity, while his/her affinity for the trading strategy has a more pronounced character of rationality. This irrational (emotional) affinity for propensity is common, moreover, to any type of belief of *faith* nature.
82. Obviously, as we said before, when we say financial market for an operational purpose, we always mean a particular financial market, that is, associated with a fixed financial product/instrument.
83. The phenomenon of reduction to the average, which we invoke here, is analogous to that discussed by Kahneman and Tversky in their works of behavioural psychology, with the difference that the authors mentioned refer to a behaviour induced by human psychism (probably with reference to universal features or, anyway—in the Jung key—generated by the archetype), while we are talking about a quasi-objective behaviour (more precisely, about a behaviour of a symbolic or logical individual, which has a nature of objectified inter-subjectivity rather than an objective nature—the *finuman* evoked above).
84. We resume the specification that the phrase *behavioural efficiency* (like the phrase informational efficiency) is counter-intuitive: thus, in the case of market informational efficiency, the market is all the more efficient as it can earn less than its average, while in the case of behavioural efficiency of the market, the market is all the more efficient as there are fewer trading strategies distinct from all other contemporary trading strategies in that market.
85. As with thermodynamic entropy (and as with many economic phenomena, such as the underground economy), behavioural entropy cannot be measured in terms of level, but only in terms of change. Thus, there can never be a maximum behavioural efficiency, nor a minimum one (respectively, there can never be a minimum behavioural entropy, nor a maximum one). Recall that in the case of EMH, maximum informational efficiency of the financial market is accepted (when no price can be predicted). The Grossman–Stiglitz critique of EMH can also be applied, *mutatis mutandis*, to behavioural efficiency, in the sense that it prohibits maximum behavioural efficiency (or, equivalently, minimum behavioural entropy).
86. Through implicit information (see FMAB-APH).

87. Demonstrating that reducing behavioural entropy within the system (APMH) has the (necessary) effect of increasing the behavioural entropy faster in the APMH environment (cultural geodesic, respectively other contemporary trading strategies) remains a goal that this research sets for a subsequent intervention and communication. As it is known, such a demonstration exists, however, for the case of thermodynamic/energetic entropy.
88. For obvious logical reasons, it will have to be considered that the financial market is, from a behavioural point of view, closed, a property that is, moreover, quite intuitive, because financial transactions cannot exist outside the financial market. To accept an environment of … the financial market would mean to accept the idea that a financial entity can exist outside the financial realm (it is as if we would say that the environment of the Universe is … a larger Universe). We remind the reader that the same problem was encountered by Niklas Luhmann, when he built the autopoietic model of society and when, trying to find the environment of the social system he could not identify it in a larger social system, and had to decree that it is, in fact, an environment of a psychological nature, separate from the social environment itself (*Nota bene*: the fact that human psychism is, at least in part, of social origin did not in any way disturb the remarkable sociologist).
89. The problem of the significance threshold is important in two respects: (a) not every deviation is something negative—all balances in the economy and society are dynamic, that is, it supports small oscillations (periodical or not) that ensure this balance (which is also called, by the way, dynamic equilibrium); (b) the significance threshold does not always coincide with the threshold of 'breaking' the dynamic balance (although, it may coincide, of course), since the meaning differs from individual to individual (because individual idiosyncrasy) or from group to group. The issue of the significance threshold in the phenomenology of the financial market has been discussed, quite analytically, previously, so it will not be resumed here.
90. We need to make an important clarification here: the expression behavioural efficiency within the APMH (analogous to the expression informational efficiency within the EMH) has two opposite meanings: (a) when it refers to the financial market, that is, when we talk about the behavioural efficiency of the financial market, it means the impossibility of finding a trading strategy that returns above the market average (analogous to the way in which the informational efficiency of the financial market generates the impossibility of finding a price that brings a return above the market average); b) when it refers to the behavioural efficiency of the economic agent (or of the trading strategy, which is equivalent), it means

the existence of the possibility to find trading strategies (or individual transactions, as the case may be) that bring back above the financial market average. The first meaning makes the kinematics of behavioural efficiency directly proportional to the dynamics of behavioural entropy, while the second meaning makes the kinematics of behavioural efficiency inversely proportional to the dynamics of behavioural entropy. In a linear and symmetrical manner, the two meanings can be represented as in Figure 5.12 (*BEFM* noted the behavioural efficiency of the financial market and *BEFI* noted the behavioural efficiency of the financial individual, associated with the human individual or the corresponding economic agent).

91. Using a paraphrase of a syntagm used in the field of cosmology, but which fits, semantically (of meaning) also in the problem discussed here, we could call this threshold (or this limit) as *horizon of predictability* (*Nota bene*: syntagm 'plagiarized' is the *horizon of events*, or the Schwarzschild boundary, in relation to the distance from which no real entity can escape the attraction of a black hole). However, this irreversibility is 'opposable' only to a particular financial market, in which, therefore, the same product/financial instrument is traded. Financial innovation can, however, lead to the emergence of another particular financial markets. On the other hand, it is clear that increase of the predictability of the financial market has the effect of bringing the functioning of the financial market closer to the threshold of its maximum behavioural efficiency, because this predictability, acting relatively homogeneously for all economic agents (*Nota bene*: observational access to trading strategies operated in the financial market is not discriminated either normatively or objectively) allows precisely the homogenization of trading strategies, thus increasing the behavioural efficiency of the financial market.
92. As is the case with the two (non-economic) disruptions that are still ongoing (overlapping, to a large extent) at the time of this research: (1) the COVID-19 pandemic and (2) the war initiated by Russia against Ukraine. Previously, the financial (and, in part, economic) crisis that erupted in 2007 in the USA and in Europe in 2008 also acted as a systemic disruption.
93. It should be noted that we are not talking neither about robustness (resistance to disturbances, of course, below the significance threshold of the amount of disturbing action) nor about resilience—the return of the system to the state from which it was disturbed (return by homeostasis property) or the trajectory from which it was disturbed (return by the homeorhesis property), but about 'accepting' the disturbance (Mr. Taleb even speaks of a deliberate non-avoidance or, at the limit, deliberate

search for the disturbance) and acquiring a gain, an advantage from the disturbance in question.

94. For example, in financial practice, there are cases known as 'financial cannons', which refer to obtaining a large gain at the level of the economic agent, including the cost of compromising (or functional exhaustion) of the trading strategy used to obtain that gain (as a rule, it is a gain that can even exceed the return of the champion of that financial market). It turns out that such practices are incompatible, logically and operationally, with the APMH model, because they make vulnerable/undermine exactly its paradigmatic value: adaptive replicability.
95. This time, it is clear that, given that each trading strategy targets a particular financial market (because it targets a particular financial product/instrument), we need to discuss how an 'antifragile' aggregate financial market can be 'built' from particular antifragile financial markets.
96. A distributed antifragility would mean that there are distinct antifragility devices on various categories or classes of disturbances (or on concrete, particular disturbances). However, the concept of antifragility refers to a general property (i.e., non-distributed) to obtain gains/benefits from disturbances.
97. Obviously, real disturbances have very rarely (and this, especially in the case of systemic disturbances) a nature of generality, i.e., the property of targeting, simultaneously, several particular financial markets or, at the limit, all particular financial markets and, thus, the aggregate financial market. But even in this case, of 'diffuse' disturbances, a single particularly antifragile financial market ensures the antifragility of the integrated system of particular financial markets.
98. We specify that the term chreode was introduced in the 'package' with the term (and the concept) of homeorhesis, mentioned by us before.
99. Moreover, in an implicit way (since the concept and term autopoiesis were introduced only in 1980, by Chilean biologists Maturana and Varela), autopoieticity was also considered by Waddington, at least at the concept level, when asserted the necessary character of the chreode.
100. We specify that any model of rationality introduces a logical necessity: for example, any inference (such as a hypothesis or a conjecture) from a model of rationality is completely devoid of any degree of freedom, it cannot be realized (validly) than in one way, pre-determined, that is, it can only be made necessarily—for example, the decision taken on the basis of the rationality model called cost-benefit analysis has a necessary character, devoid of any freedom of choice.
101. It is a *sui generis* time series, that is, exactly the time series of the mentioned state vectors. For operational reasons, the state vector can be replaced by a single representative variable and then the time series in

question is analogous to any time series that records the kinematics of a given variable.

102. The kinematic self-similarity of propensity refers to the tendency (natural, but also cultural—e.g., the conscious association of behavioural principles in the deep structure of propensity, which of course refers to the concept of symbolic utility discussed above, gives the propensity a strong tendency to replicate, a 'basic conservatism') of propensity to self-replicate, including through resistance (known as robustness) to the pressures of change coming from the financial market environment in the process of selection of trading strategy, respectively of individual transactions. Not to make the simplistic transition from this property of self-similarity to self-similarity specific to fractal behaviours—there is no fractal behaviour related to propensity although, as we have shown, the fundamental principle of the APMH model of the financial market makes a pretty transparent reference to fractality but, obviously, from another perspective.
103. In part, we also have a formal causality here (although, to some extent, it is an almost completely subconscious formal cause), but we will not further develop this aspect in the present discussion.
104. We recall that freedom is defined as the absence of private external constraints on the choice of individual goals (i.e., the choice, made by the individual, about their own goals).
105. There has been talk of automatic stabilizers before.
106. The same can be said about robustness or resilience.
107. We mention, here, the fundamental distinction between kinematics and dynamics: kinematics aims at the change (of any kind) in time, without taking into account causality (equivalently, it can be said that the passage of time is, in the case of kinematics, the 'cause' of change), while the dynamic aims at the change in time taking into account the causality of that change.
108. Obviously, any authentic belief is self-sufficient, whether we are talking about a rational belief, an irrational belief (faith) or an a-rational belief (credence). This second-order belief (belief in one's own belief) is of the utmost importance in the analysis, design and prediction of economic behaviour in the financial market, and it acts as an *inertia of the statu quo.*
109. We can introduce, here, something similar to a coefficient of friction in mechanics: therefore, the selective pressure on the trading strategy, exerted by the environment, after this strategy exhausts its degrees of freedom (i.e., after reconfiguring within the same propensity) is transferred to propensity. The propensity will change according to the pressure coming from the trading strategy and, after reaching its new state (i.e., after the economic agent's basic belief is reset), this new state will lead to a redesign of the trading strategy (*Note bene*: being about the same trad-

ing strategy, it results that we consider the maintenance of the product/financial instrument traded through that strategy). We notice, therefore, that we have two channels of impulse transmission: once from the trading strategy to propensity and, the second time, from the new propensity to the new trading strategy. Like any transmission channel, the two mentioned can generate disturbances (or 'rubs') of the message, both in one direction and in another. Appropriate analytical developments will be able to take these observations into account, including from the perspective of Shannon informational entropy.

110. It seems that, from an abstract point of view, the behaviour in the financial market has two basic benchmarks: (a) an *attitudinal* benchmark—generated, in an overwhelming degree, by propensity and free will (*Nota bene*: the measure and the way in which propensity and free will inter-conditioning is an issue that should still be considered more closely), and which has a relatively high stability/inertia, and representing the subjective factor of behaviour; (b) a *positional* benchmark—generated, in an overwhelming degree, by the cost–benefit calculation, which represents the objective factor of the behaviour. We must note that what we call the model of rationality as a result of the inextricable combination (this relative indeterminacy must be clarified by cognitive psychology and behavioural psychology) between the two benchmarks—in our opinion, the model of rationality emerges in a quasi-rational way, only its functioning (i.e., the potential set of inferences that it necessarily allows, without right of appeal) is completely rational.

111. We call it so as not to be confused with the primary (or institutional) replicator which is the propensity, that is, the 'DNA' of the financial individual.

References

Bourdieu, P. (1993). *Language and Symbolic Power.* Harvard University Press.

Dinga, E., Oprean-Stan, C., Tănăsescu, C.-R., Brătian, V., & Ionescu, G.-M. (2022). *Financial Market Analysis and Behaviour. The Adaptive Preference Hypothesis.* Routledge, Francis & Taylor Group.

Taleb, N. N. (2014). *Antifragile: Things That Gain from Disorder.* Random House Trade Paperbacks.

Waddington, C. H. (1957). *The Strategy of the Genes.* Routledge.

Index[1]

[1] Note: Page numbers followed by 'n' refer to notes.

E. Dinga et al., *Economic and Financial Market Behaviour*,
https://doi.org/10.1007/978-3-031-31702-6

Q

R

FSC
www.fsc.org
MIX
Papier | Fördert gute Waldnutzung
FSC® C083411

Kolibri 360 GmbH
Ferdinand-Jühlke-Straße 7
99095 Erfurt, Deutschland
produktsicherheit@kolibri360.de